APRIL 1915

Haig Tahta

To Anthony,
With all my best wishes.
Haig

Taderon Press
London and Reading

Published by Taderon Press, PO Box 2735, Reading RG4 8GF.

Printed in association with the Gomidas Institute.

2006 5 4 3 2 1

ISBN 1-903656-54-0

DISTRIBUTED WORLDWIDE:
Garod Books Ltd.
42 Blythe Rd.
London, W14 0HA
Email: *info@garodbooks.com*

For my first granddaughter - Pia - in the hope that at some future date it may give her some idea of how she came to be what and where she is.

Acknowledgements

In researching and writing this novel I owe a debt to my wife Sonia who for forty years urged me to make the effort to dramatise history. I would also like to acknowledge my brother Dickran who patiently and vitally corrected all those punctuation and stylistic errors which are mine alone, my friend Bill who spent hours in discussion with me about 'identity' and the 'nation-state' at the core of the novel, and finally Dan Jacobson whose book 'Heshel's Kingdom' inspired me to write in the first place, and whose gentle criticism persuaded me to tear up my first effort and led me to a better understanding of what writing is all about

Chapter Headings

MAPS

APRIL 1915

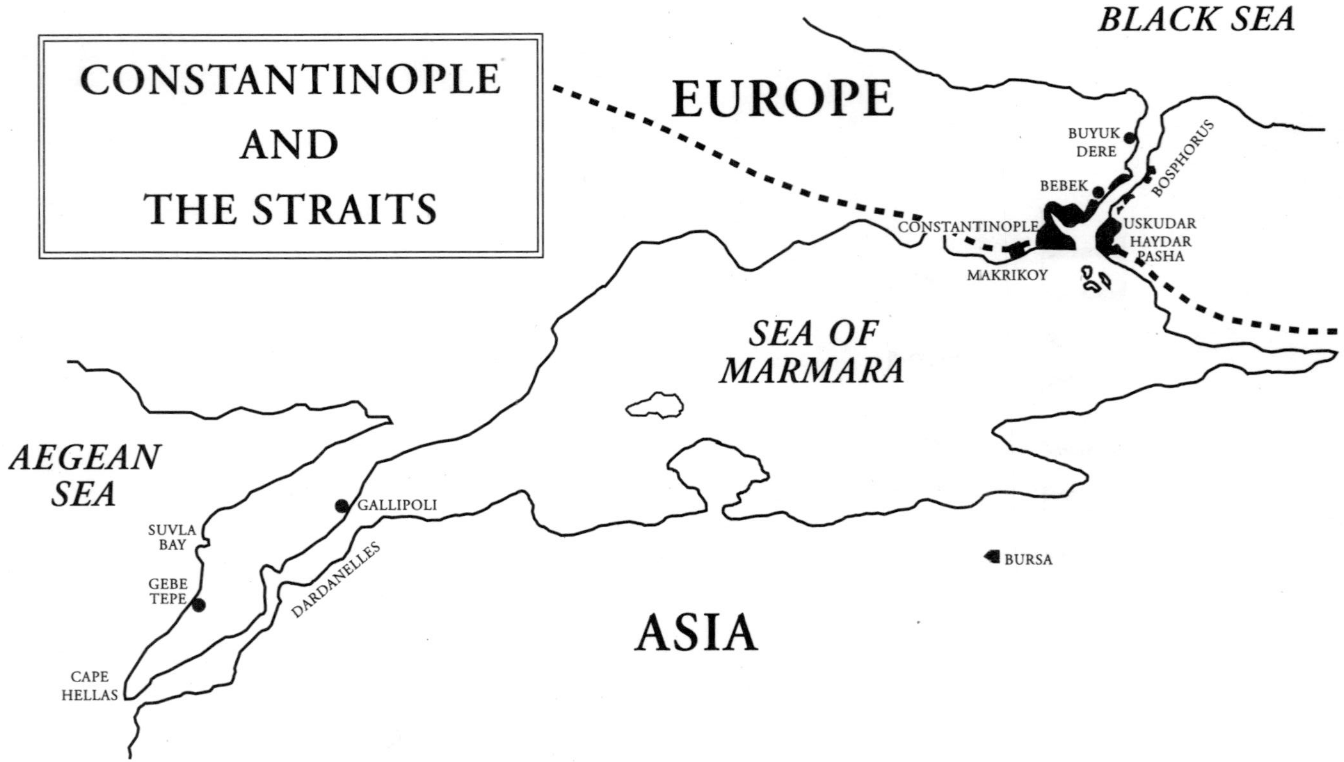
CONSTANTINOPLE
AND
THE STRAITS
BLACK SEA
EUROPE
BUYUK DERE
BOSPHORUS
BEBEK
CONSTANTINOPLE
USKUDAR
HAYDAR PASHA
MAKRIKOY
SEA OF MARMARA
AEGEAN SEA
GALLIPOLI
SUVLA BAY
GEBE TEPE
DARDANELLES
CAPE HELLAS
BURSA
ASIA

Prologue

1915—the world was still living in the twilight years of the era known as the 'long' nineteenth century. The slaughter of the first few months of the Great War had still not triggered the enormous changes which were soon to come.

1915—the Ottoman Empire, the so-called 'sick man of Europe', was not really as sick as the vultures surrounding it liked to make out. In this year, the reputedly moribund Empire was to inflict on the proud British navy a major defeat for the first time in over one hundred years. The world would never be the same again.

1915—the Austrian Empire, in some ways even more suited to be considered the sick man of Europe, with its equally diverse and fascinating collection of peoples, cultures, and ways of life, would scarcely ever manage to win a single major campaign in the Great War, except perhaps against the unfortunate Italians, who only just made it as a major power anyway.

But were either of these two generally tolerant, inefficient and perhaps muddled, multiracial and multicultural organisations, the real 'sick men' at all? Hard and virulent unicultural nationalism was the growing creed in the world, and neither of these old and anachronistic empires sat comfortably with the seething tribal passions of the sovereign territorial nation-state. But who in truth were the really sick men? What after all actually happened in the twentieth century, which established the assertion that the Hapsburgs or the Ottomans were so hopelessly 'sick', when compared with their powerful neighbours?

Russia gave way to a materialistic Revolution, which within not much more than ten years resulted in the massacre, death and misery of millions upon millions of uncomprehending peasants. The German Empire—so much more efficient, monocultural and monoracial than the Austrian Empire—gave way to a tribal nation-state in arms, whose hysterical demand for uniformity and racial 'purity' resulted in one of the greatest crimes in history. The other petty nation-states that sprang up on the ruins of the two, so-called 'sick', Empires consistently had a history throughout the century of tyranny, pogroms, and in the end 'ethnic cleansing', far outweighing the evils of the bureaucratic inequalities and random cruelties of the old empires.

After the Ittihad revolution of 1908 in the Ottoman Empire, the Young Turks, acting through their Committee of Union and Progress, impatiently thrust aside the multi-national and tolerant legacy of the old Ottoman Sultans, substituting for it the narrow and prejudiced exclusiveness of the tribal nation-state. This then resulted in the first of the great massacres leading to ethnic cleansing, of which this so-called enlightened century has been so full.

In August 1914, Europe entered into the destructive, purely European, war, which was known then, and for its first few months, as 'the Third Balkan War'. It was the entry of the Ottoman Empire into this war, in November 1914, which turned it into the First 'World' War.

1915—In the Ottoman world, people referred to their loved ones by many differing endearments, which went far beyond 'my dear' or 'darling.' These endearments, when translated literally into English, may appear somewhat stilted and artificial. Armenians, for example, used the word 'hokis,' when addressing their children, or spouse. This translates as 'my soul', and has been preferred here throughout, as has 'my lovely father' or 'my little father' rather than always just 'dad.'

1915—Finally. The Dardanelles campaign, fought within actual sight of that very first epic war of Western tradition—the Trojan War—was one of the great 'what-ifs' of history. It was also one of the greatest disasters suffered by the British Army until the fall of Singapore, twenty-five years or so later. Both defeats, ironically, were at the hands not of any recognised traditional European rival, but of a despised oriental foe. The world was changing, and here was the pivot.

Constantinople—Stamboul—Bolis. . . The City.

Introduction.

A recent conversation.

"But, Dad, it's all very well telling me all these stories about your mother and her parents—half the time I don't know what you're talking about. There isn't even any town called Constantinople nowadays."

"Look, Garen, son, it's worth making a bit of an effort. Just take it from me that whilst your background doesn't interest you at all now—after all, at fifteen what do you care where your grandparents came from or who they were—believe me—just trust me on this—after everyone has died, you'll be sorry that you didn't find out more whilst they were alive."

"OK, Dad, but you know you confuse me! I'm doing history at school and we've been learning a lot about the Great War and how awful it was—and how we are still living today with its results—but when you tell me what life was like in those days where Grandma came from, you sometimes say Constantinople, sometimes Stamboul, sometimes Bolis or something like that, and for God's sake it's now none of these but is called Istanbul."

"Garen, don't swear, it's quite unnecessary."

"Sorry, but Dad, I do know about the Ottoman Empire. We learnt all about it at school, the sick man of Europe, or so they used to say. We are learning about the Great War, and I've seen some super tapes that our teacher shows us about trench warfare and how awful it was and how many young men died. Then we saw some film about the landings at Gallipoli—wasn't that near where Grandma came from."

"Yes it was, and it was there, in that city, that your grandmother met your grandfather."

"Well, Dad, I do know that much, but I still find it a bit confusing. Can we at least get the name of the town where she was born right?"

"Garen, to be honest, we can't. The different names came naturally to the people who lived there. The whole city with all its additions and suburbs, both north and south of the Golden Horn—ok, don't glare at me like that, that's the inlet that sticks into the coast giving the town its natural harbour—and the towns and villages on the Asian side was called Constantinople. The Greeks, Armenians and Jews referred to it as Polis or Bolis, which simply means City. The Turks referred to the original old Byzantine city behind the great Walls as Stamboul."

"For Christ's sake, Dad! Oh, I'm sorry, I'm sorry. . . but look, you're confusing me all over again!"

"Well, just look at a map then. Anyway, I've had enough. Time for you to get down to your homework. Your Mum will kill me if, when you go back to her after school tomorrow, she finds that you didn't do it all whilst staying the night with me."

"OK Dad, but one last question before I go up. Why, when you report conversations you had with your mother before she died, do you use words like "my soul," or "my loved one" which sound so silly."

"Garen, *my soul. . .* There! I got you, didn't I? Don't wince like that, there were none of your snooty school friends around to hear me. Look, in that part of the world, even now, people use much more varied terms of endearment than we are used to here in England. So, for instance, Armenians use the word 'hokis' when addressing their children, spouse or very close friends. This translates as 'my soul'. Even if it sounds a bit stilted in English, it's better than saying 'my dear' or 'darling' all the time. Don't you like it?"

"Frankly Dad, no! I certainly wouldn't want you to say it in front of my school mates."

"Well, I promise I won't, but the fact is that in those days you didn't just say 'Dad' all the time, you used all sorts of endearments in which the word for father appeared."

"Well, if there were so many, how did you choose."

"Oh Garen, honestly—that's enough, go up and start your work. We'll go into all this further one day."

Chapter 1

Makrikoy. Breakfast at the Avakians.

"I simply don't agree with you, Nerissa," said Sima, the tall and statuesque eldest daughter of the Avakian family, haughtily addressing her younger sister. Sima, dressed in flowing white summer frocks, sat bolt upright at the breakfast table with a stiff straight back in the required fashion, and continued, "I see no reason at all why we ever came into this war in the first place; so why ever should the British, or the French for that matter, bother to attack us? Their real enemies surely are the Germans. What have we ever done to harm them?"

"But Sima, my darling," replied Nerissa, as she sipped her tea, "don't you see that all that bombardment by the British navy in the straits last month must surely be the preliminary of something. . . another attack. . . or, I don't know. . . something?"

"For heaven's sake, can't you two talk about something more interesting?" said Olga, the family's second daughter. "I'm getting thoroughly bored with all this talk of war, which is all happening so far away from us anyway. All that we have actually seen is that there are no longer any decent clothes to buy in the shops"

Dressed rather simply in a college uniform, nevertheless, Olga managed to present an elegance in the simple lines of her green skirt, which Sima in her expensive white muslins failed to achieve. Quite outstandingly pretty, Olga had a stunning flashing smile, which coupled to her large inquisitive brown eyes, she would use without shame on all whom she wanted to impress. However, such artificial charm was used without avail on her two sisters, who ignored her comment and continued their discussion as if she hadn't spoken.

"Haik, will you please eat something instead of incessantly chatting about nothing. For heaven's sake, a piece of toast and honey isn't so difficult to swallow," snapped Armineh, as she pushed his neglected plate back at him. She knew perfectly well that continually nagging at her thin and wiry twelve-year old son about his hopeless incapacity to eat anything at meal times was a totally pointless exercise. However, she couldn't help herself.

She was beginning, at last, to look older than the thirty-eight years that she was prepared to acknowledge publicly, and her noisy family was trying her patience more and more often in these difficult days. Her figure had always been round and short, but the birth of five children had already caused her to get increasingly dumpy. Armineh drew a deep breath, firmly trying to put out of her mind all irritation at the sight of her son toying with his food, and surveyed the rest of her family at the breakfast table.

Karekin, her husband, had not yet come down, and she glanced up at the stairs that led from the centre of the large hall where most of the family's activities took place. Here, in the centre of the house, immediately beyond the main entrance door, were the table and chairs for all the family meals. On one side of the great room were the kitchens, and on the other side the formal sitting rooms. Dotted about the marble floor were settees and comfortable sofas and some large slightly faded but still beautiful Persian carpets.

Marie, a large and comfortably buxom figure, the family's long-time nanny, was bustling round the table, going from the table into the kitchen and back, pouring the tea and helping Seta, the eight-year old youngest of the family. It was never entirely clear whether the lively Seta was eating or talking, sitting still or just getting ready to get up and run off, as she was in a state of constant motion of one kind or another.

Breakfast at the Avakians was never silent, but on this beautiful spring morning on the 1st day of April 1915 it was particularly noisy.

Everyone was talking at once, when Karekin appeared at the top of the stairs.

It would be an exaggeration to suggest that there followed any sort of respectful silence as he walked purposefully down the stairs. There was, perhaps, a tiny imperceptible drop in the decibel level, but the animated conversation carried cheerfully on. Only Nerissa looked down at her plate and stopped talking. Sima smiled up at her father, whilst Olga turned round, jumped up and gave her father a great kiss and a hug as he arrived at the bottom of the stairs.

Karekin was a tall and upright figure, almost always dressed very formally in a grey suit of English cut. He was never seen in public, and indeed rarely even outside his bedroom, without an impeccably knotted tie. Every inch of his tall frame, with his long prematurely bald head, was held stiff and dignified. He walked ramrod tall with his hands often held clasped behind his back. However, underneath all this formality was an ultra-liberal with outstanding ideas about education for girls. His wife—Armineh—was not at all so sure and regularly complained to Karekin that formal education for the girls was an expensive irrelevance.

It was unusual for a daughter of an Armenian merchant family, as opposed to any son, to be sent for her education to one of the Western schools in the City of Constantinople and in this respect Karekin had always been considered a little eccentric by his business friends and neighbours.

Armineh herself, more traditional in her outlook, had not been so happy about all this book learning, and was relieved that Sima had left school and was no longer being exposed to temptation by her daily trips into the city during the school terms. The fact was also, that by being at home, Sima could always help Armineh in dealing with the hyper-sensitive Haik and the lively Seta. Marie, the family's old nurse, could no longer cope alone, and servants were getting more difficult to find.

That very morning, in the privacy of their bedroom before coming down to breakfast, Karekin and Armineh had had one of their discussions about the girls.

"Karekin, this war has dulled your senses as to what needs to be dealt with in the family."

"Oh, my soul, are we going to have all this again? You worry too much, and in any case. . ."

"Karekin, you must look at the situation here in your own home and stop spending your time with those political friends of yours—and those. . ."

"Armineh, my love, . . ."

"No, listen. We have three problems. First, you have to consider that Sima is nineteen and you must start thinking about her marriage prospects. It really is time you were reflecting a bit about this. Times haven't changed so much that you can shirk this duty—war or no war. Then there is Haik. He's twelve Karekin, and he is peculiarly innocent. I happen to know that he's well into puberty—oh Karekin pay attention—you know perfectly well what I'm talking about. He still runs about in the garden naked sometimes. You have to talk to him and guide him and find out what he knows and what he doesn't."

"What you mean is that you want me to have him start feeling guilty about his body," replied Karekin, rather absently, as he stretched his neck to knot his tie.

"Karekin, don't be obtuse—we're not talking high philosophy here—we're talking about your son, and what he should be made aware of."

"Armineh—that's enough—I agree with you, and I'll think about it, I promise. And now, my dear, what is your third problem?"

"Oh, Karekin, I just don't know. Olga is up to something—I know—I just know in my bones that she is hiding something from us, but what it is I have no idea."

"Come on Armineh, my soul, this is you panicking as usual—a vague anxiety about everyone in your brood. Relax! There's nothing wrong with her. Look, Haik is my problem, I do accept that—but you deal with whatever is worrying you where Olga's concerned. She's getting a good education, and she knows wrong from right—which is more than can be said for most of the seventeen-year old young girls round here. As for Sima, we'll deal with her position during the next month, so long as the British leave us alone."

"Karekin, honestly, you always. . .

"Armineh, my sweet, don't stamp your foot in vexation. I'll be down to breakfast shortly, and that's an end to it."

Karekin, on arriving at breakfast, sat at the top end of the table, and was immediately served with his usual light Russian tea and a slice of lemon by Marie. This was invariably followed by olives and white cheese, and usually ended with him taking a slice of toast and the family's own honey.

"Baba, Nerissa and I were talking about the possibility of a Western Allied attack on us here at Bolis—what do you think? Do you really think it likely? I myself can't believe that there's any reason why the British should attack us here. They and the French have always been supporters of the Ottomans haven't they?" said Sima, as she passed the toast to her father.

"Sima, my soul—Marie some more tea please—I think Nerissa is right actually. Now that the British have failed to drive their battleships through the Dardanelles, they're surely going to try something else, don't ask me what."

"But, Baba, the French and the British have always been friendly to the Ottomans and. . ."

"Yes, but they aren't now, and as they can't seem to get at the Germans, they're going to come at us. I'm afraid, girls, we are going to be facing some sort of attack somewhere near here sooner or later. Hello Olga, where are you off to in such a hurry?"

"Oh father," Olga said as she arose from the table and went round giving everybody a quick kiss, "you know that I have to get an earlier train than you. Come, Haik, why don't you keep me company on the walk down to the station? Then you can go on to school after the train goes."

Haik shook his head, whilst Armineh looked at Karekin meaningfully, as if to suggest that all this continual hurry and pressure to get away showed that she had some good reason after all for believing that Olga was acting oddly. Karekin merely waved his hand at her, making it clear that he was in no way in agreement with her, and clearly dismissing the whole subject. Meanwhile Olga, grabbing her bag, flashed her smile at everyone, and hurried out to catch her train to the city.

Nerissa, usually quieter than the rest of the family, didn't say much, especially as her father was around. However, when Karekin rose to take his hat and stick, she came and kissed him as always before he went out to go to work. As he began walking out of the main door, Haik finally pushed his plate away, grinning at his exasperated mother, and said, "Baba, is there actually going to be any fighting here? Are we going to see the British battleships firing their guns. . . I mean at us even. . . can their shells actually reach us here?"

Karekin turned and looked at his eager son and said as he reached the front door, "No, my son, that's pretty unlikely. In any case, things are never quite so exciting as they might seem when they are actually happening. Look, my boy, I am proposing to take you with me to the office one day during the next holidays, so that you can see how it all works. You might then be able to give me a hand sometime."

"Oh, Baba, that's marvellous—when—when. . . ?"

"We'll see, my boy."

Karekin, having already received his kiss from everyone, straightened up even more, if that was possible, and walked out of the front door.

Chapter 2

Makrikoy. Karekin.

Karekin would now usually catch the 8.15 a.m. local train from Makrikoy to the city.

Before the outbreak of this interminable war, he used to make a point of getting the later train so that he could stand on the platform and watch the slow passage of the magnificent train from Paris—the Simplon-Orient Express—with its long line of mysterious dark blue Wagon-Lits sleeping coaches, often with the blinds still down in the windows, although the city was by then only fifteen minutes away.

Trains and ships were often late or delayed in the Ottoman world, but it was rare for the Simplon-Orient not to be dead on time every day. Some of the smart, dark-coated conductors would, even as early as here at Makrikoy, already be pulling down the windows of their carriage door, preparatory to leaning out ready to open the door as the train would pull into the European terminus at Sirkedji Station. The sight of the great train as it passed never ceased to give Karekin a frisson of simple childish delight as the coaches slowly passed by the little station, some from Paris, some from Rome and other great cities, and even one each day all the way from London.

Karekin, whose main business activity was the importation of fine muslins largely from Lancashire in England, had once travelled to Manchester before the war with his eldest daughter, Sima, with a view to creating a direct personal contact with his main supplier. He knew no English apart from the necessary mercantile words required in the whole world of shipping and commerce, where English was the lingua franca for all the great trading houses of Europe. Sima, herself, had attended the English High School for Girls in the City, and had gone on that same trip with her father so that she could translate for him. He recalled that his journey to the West had been on this same inter-continental service, and on that same once-a-day sleeper coach that would be shunted across Paris, eased onto the train ferry across the Channel, finally arriving at Victoria Station in London three days after setting out from the City.

But now, in April 1915, there were no more trains coming from Europe, with the exception of the occasional German freight train routed through neutral Rumania and the wavering Bulgaria. So he had taken to catching the earlier train to town in order to get back to his family in the early afternoon while it was still light.

Karekin had had no hesitation in placing Sima in the prestigious English High School for Girls. However, Constantinople was a city in which the influence of the European Great Powers waxed and waned throughout these years. Wealthy Greek and Armenian families tended to put their sons into the schools of the dominant and most highly regarded European Power of the day. The influence of France and England had been slipping, as they both got ever closer to Russia in their anti-German alliance. Russia, of course, was always the permanent, age-old enemy of the Ottomans. The corollary of all this was a rise in influence and prestige in Constantinople of Imperial Germany, and the popularity of new German schools. Karekin, who was not overfond of Prussian militarism and values, had as a result decided to place Olga, his flirtatious and sprightly second daughter, in the American School—Robert College—where she was still flourishing.

The long walk to the station was Karekin's main daily exercise and he strode on occasionally raising his hat to neighbours and acquaintances, but with nothing more than a muttered morning greeting. His large house, with its walled garden and orchards, lay just south of the new district of Osman Aga. He never took the short direct road alongside the Valli Effendi racecourse, but took the longer road which took him above the little town, past a spot from which he could stand and look down on the little town of Makrikoy—the ancient Hebdomen of the Eastern Roman Empire—seven miles out of the city.

Here Karekin would sit on an old wooden bench for a few moments and muse in the warm morning sunshine. It was not that he didn't discuss matters with his wife, Armineh; he did, and he often took her into his confidence. However, he was much older than her, and they had married in the old arranged style when she was barely sixteen. Sharp, intelligent and formidably strong-willed, nevertheless her upbringing in the Armenian heartlands of Erzerum in Anatolia had been traditional, and she had had little formal education. Within his household on the other hand, he had encouraged his four lively daughters to chat away and give their views volubly, with spirit and without fear. He had as a result paid the inevitable price of being the head of a fairly noisy and not entirely peaceful home.

Here, however, sitting on the old bench staring at the old Ottoman town houses crumbling away among the ruins of the ancient Hebdomen palaces, he could let his thoughts wander in some peace. Whilst musing, he could pick out the old Palace of Magnaurus and see the old granite column which had carried the statue of the Emperor Theodosius, and which stood, now empty, right by the shore. All along the coast lay the ruins of more decrepit cisterns, ivy-creepered walls and the old Imperial Byzantine jetty, now almost entirely collapsed into the water.

Karekin, was in no way romantically dominated by the past. The old ruins were there—they were an absolute part of the accepted background to his life and those of his friends—whether childhood memories that lay deep in the Caucasian Highlands, or in the streets of Constantinople, or on the shores of Trebizond. In the end, however, he thought little about them. He had his life to lead, his family to raise, and the fact that he was doing it in one of the oldest and most historically significant cities in the world was coincidental.

So, he sat on the old bench and stared out at the little town and the ruined palaces without registering all these ruins in any significant way. No, what he mused on was his two elder daughters, Sima and Olga. The question of the marriage of Sima was looming and Armineh had been quite right to draw his attention to it this morning. Already two or three of his business colleagues had referred fairly openly to eligible sons already in business with their fathers and looking for another good merchant house with which to join forces. Yes—it was time that the proud Sima was introduced to some young men.

The position with Olga was quite different. Vivacious and full of a rather shallow determination, Olga, he felt, was already meeting far too many young men at the American Girls College, attached to Robert College. She had a wide circle of girl friends who, he understood, went to tea with each other, in the more fashionable tea-shops of the city.

Karekin sighed. He had no real fears at all in his own mind that any of his daughters would go too far. Under all the froth, even Olga, he was sure, had a clear understanding of what was right or wrong. However, as he had already seen this morning, Armineh could not see it that way at all, and regularly panicked when Olga returned home on a later train than usual, having stayed on for tea at a friend's house in the city.

The War of course was changing everything. This was for the first time a war which was not just being fought by the traditional patient Turkish Anatolian peasant led by an odd Pasha or two, but one in which all classes of Ottoman society—even the wealthy cosmopolitan society of Constantinople, were being sucked in.

Karekin rose. Even in early April, the sun was coming up fast and he had little time left to get to the station of Chobancheshme, the local station for this end of Makrikoy, to catch his train. He strode down putting aside all thoughts of Olga and Sima, with his mind beginning to turn to the business needs of the day. He crossed the line and walked into the little station and onto the platform. There, standing with others waiting for the next local train, he saw his old friend Doctor Manuelian.

"Parev Doctor," he greeted, pleased as always whenever he met his friend Aram, with whom he regularly played backgammon every Sunday morning after Church. They stood together waiting for the train.

"What news, Aram" said Karekin.

"Well, you know that concert of local culture that was held in Galata in the city. Both Talaat Bey and Djavid Pasha were there. The enthusiasm for the performance of our own Father Komitas was enormous, Karekin."

"No, I've already heard about that. I meant whether you had any news about the War."

"Oh, it's the same old stuff, Karekin, large numbers of young men dying just to gain a few more yards one side or the other. Let them get on with it, its not going to affect us here in our backwater. Ever since the failure of Enver's Caucasian campaign last year, even he, I'm sure, is now sorry that we joined in the War. No, no, my dear friend, all we need to do is to sit tight and let them all exhaust themselves. Don't worry man—you'll soon be getting your precious Lancashire cotton again."

At this point the local train pulled in. Nodding to each other, Dr. Aram Manuelian clambered into his first-class carriage, whilst Karekin walked down and got into a second-class compartment.

"Stubborn old bachelor," thought Karekin, "why won't he ever change his habits of a lifetime and join me on this short trip to town."

"What a ridiculously rigid fellow Karekin is," thought the Doctor at the same time, "he could easily afford to come with me and forget his liberal and egalitarian principles for once."

Stopping at every small station along the way, trundling along beside the Sea of Marmara, the train shortly passed through the gap cut into the ancient great Theodosian Walls of the City, and skirting round the Topkapi Palace, found its way into the European terminus of the railway—Sirkedji Station.

Chapter 3

Constantinople. Vahan and his father.

On that same first day of April in 1915, Vahan bounced, rather than walked, down the road to the Galata Bridge, on his way to his classes at the University. Ever since he had won his scholarship to the Music and Drama Department of the university, from his provincial home in Caesaria in Central Anatolia, and his arrival in this wonderful city, he had been in a state of high excitement. The world belonged to him, and to whoever was currently his best friend.

The Galata Bridge connected old Stamboul—the original city of Constantinople—to Pera and Galata, the original European trading suburbs. The bridge was as usual teeming with life. Turkish porters almost running along with a thong around their foreheads attached to huge loads on their backs, calling out to the passers-by to make way for them. Gentlemen with Panama hats and walking sticks, striding along dressed in Western fashion, who could be Greeks or Turks or one of the many other races of the Empire. One or two old-fashioned Ottoman gentlemen still dressed in the Stambuliya long coat, with a high collar and reaching down to the knees.

Then, there were the one-horse or two-horse carriages, waiting beside the pavement to pick up passengers coming up the steps from the quayside under the bridge. The ferries themselves, hooting and jostling each other as they drew up, trying to nudge into a spot to come up against the quay, to discharge all their fares coming in from further up the Bosporus, or from the Asian side or from the Marmara coast and the islands. The ubiquitous red fez everywhere, on Muslim and Christian head alike. Old and new, European and Asian, Christian and Muslim, Jew and Gentile, all thronging together in a noisy and jubilant mass. The only human group under-represented, at this time in the morning, being the women.

Vahan was a rather stocky young man, not tall but rather square. He had silky light brown hair and soft brown eyes with a permanently questioning look in them. He was currently dressed in the uniform of the Harbiye military academy. Vahan stood leaning against the iron railings, looking down at the ferries and the crowds tumbling up the steps. Staring across the waters not quite so full of ships as usual now that Turkey was at war, he could just make out the looming, grey shapes of the two German battleships, sitting out in the roadsteads, towering over all the other ships around, with their long heavy guns, pointing straight ahead. He gave a skip of sheer joy and grinned at a couple of urchins, pushing at each other over some trivial argument.

Vahan recalled how eight months ago, at the height of the summer of 1914, he had heard that he had won a scholarship to the Music Department of the university of Constantinople. His mother, Mariam, hiding her tears, had immediately started work on all the little things that he was going to need when he left home. His father Garabed, bursting with pride, had taken him to the bazaar—ostensibly to buy necessities for the journey, but really to show off to all his business friends and associates. Vahan himself had been totally unaware of his mother's patient and secret tears, but he had felt, and in a secret spot within himself had revelled in his father's pride.

Vahan, then just turned eighteen, had never travelled beyond the province. Garabed, his father, used to travel regularly on horseback into the Eastern highlands to visit the many village families, from whom he commissioned wonderful and intricate carpets, worked entirely by hand and made with the bright traditional vegetable-dyed wool. Garabed would sometimes take his second son, Raffi, with him on these trips, but the eldest son Vahan would be left behind.

Vahan, still staring out at the bustle around him, recalled the last occasion, when he was seventeen, that this had occurred, and the sharp words that had been exchanged between himself and his father, as they had stood facing each other in the dark entrance hall of their house. The actual words sprung to his mind.

"Baba, it's not right—you took Raffi with you last time. It's my turn to go with you and meet all these families with whom you do business. Look, I can take my violin with me, and I can play at night—they'll love it."

"My son, I need you to stay at home to look after your mother and sister in case anything happens to me on the trip. Vahan, also consider, life is hard in the highlands, these people have no time for music."

"Oh, father, believe me that that at least is not right. Even the most deprived people appreciate and have time for folk music and melodies, and can get relief from tension and worries with the benefit of music, even after a hard day's work. In any case, both mother and grandma are far more capable than me of managing the house."

"Vahan, you may be right about music, but you don't understand the real issue," said Garabed, and Vahan recalled the mounting anger in his father's eyes at being contradicted.

"We live in a Muslim society. However competent your mother may be, a male head of the family is vital. Officials, or indeed anybody coming to this house are trained to ignore the women—sometimes even to look away from them if they are in the same room. A male is essential, even if he is totally manipulated by the women behind the arras. Enough, Vahan, I will not listen to any more of this thoughtless and childish nonsense. You will do as you are told"

Garabed Asadourian, like many of his generation in Central Anatolia, had missed out on the great renaissance of Armenian culture and education of the late nineteenth century. He could speak only Turkish and whilst of course he attended Church and was an active member of the Armenian community, he had not been overwhelmed by the nationalist fervour rampant not only in the Ottoman Empire but throughout Europe. This late nineteenth century movement was led by teachers and academics from the great cities, who flocked into the local schools, teaching the language, the culture, the poetry and the history of their people to their young pupils. Amongst the Armenians, this fervour was further underlined by the over-enthusiastic American missionaries who, finding it too difficult to convert the Turkish peasants, turned to converting the Christian Armenian local populace from their age-old orthodoxy to an alien Protestantism.

This strident ethnic nationalism appeared and flourished throughout the old, nineteenth-century empires. Suddenly all over Europe there was found something unique about a 'German' forest, or a 'Czech' river. A Bulgarian poem became superior in some indefinable way to a Rumanian one. A Welsh song had a special quality which other songs—particularly English—did not possess. But where did that leave the old multi-lingual and multi-cultural Empires of old Europe.

Garabed, with only a basic education, had sensed it as a problem, even though he was not aware of it intellectually. He had had his children educated by these new enthusiastic teachers, and his children, even his daughters, all now spoke Armenian well. He was very proud of them, and he was proud in a rather casual and unstructured way of the architecture and poetry of his people. Naturally, he deplored the brutalities and excesses of the more vicious side of the Ottoman power. However, he was equally aware that, below the surface, nationalistic and ethnic passions could easily be aroused on both sides by all these well-meaning and enthusiastic academics, and that Armenian nationalism could easily arouse a backlash to a much more dangerous Turkish nationalism. In a shifting and increasingly unstable world, there was a lot to be said for the easy-going tolerance and stability of the old multi-ethnic Empires, and the Ottomans in particular.

Vahan, still musing away on the Galata Bridge recalled that his father had had no problem in acting as a 'Mukhtar'—a local headman—in the town and cooperating as well as he could with the Ottoman authorities. Like most educated Ottoman citizens, Garabed deplored the vicious character of the odious Sultan Abdul Hamid II. However, this did not prevent him from trying to work the system, or cooperating with those of his Turkish Muslim neighbours with whom he had fairly good relations. Relations, which admittedly did not extend to much family contact, but which certainly included having coffee and smoking a pipe together in the local street-café.

Vahan remembered that his father had welcomed the great revolution of 1908, which had eventually resulted in the deposition of the paranoid Sultan, and that he had been prepared to see

Vahan—then only twelve—joining with the other boys dancing together in the streets in celebration. He had not objected or made any comment when Vahan had joined with more of his school friends later—both Turkish and Armenian—who had collected coins on street corners to help pay for the two great new Dreadnought-type battleships ordered by the government from the shipyards of Great Britain.

Vahan realised with a feeling of guilt that Garabed had, of course, known perfectly well, that Vahan's move to the University at Constantinople might estrange him eventually from his eldest son. The difference between life in the great cosmopolitan centre of the Empire and out in the remote provinces was enormous. But Vahan reflected with love that this had been a price his father had been prepared to pay for the inestimable benefits likely to arise for his first-born.

Vahan had left Caesaria early in September with 30 gold coins sewn by his mother into a belt he was to wear under his clothes. Vahan recalled how he had travelled on his own horse with a servant, an old Turkish retainer alongside on another horse, to the nearest railhead, which was some five days' ride away. He had taken some books, his basic clothes, a bible which his mother insisted on his taking but at which he had never glanced, some ready money, and his rolled up bedding.

At nights, he and the old Turkish retainer would stay at a Khan, the traditional resting points for travellers, hardly changed since medieval times. These were almost always large square courtyards, usually with a well in the middle, where the animals would be tethered. These courtyards were surrounded by low buildings, on the first storey of which would be a connected balcony with rooms leading off, with windows and doors only looking out on to the courtyard. There would of course be no women of any kind. Washing and other facilities scarcely existed and the smells were strong and pungent—but the food served was usually surprisingly good and warming. The atmosphere in these khans was nearly always hostile, aggressive, and in a way sexually charged. As a young lad,

Vahan was well aware that he had to be very careful, eye contact being always a particular danger.

On his arrival at Eregli, the railhead, he had handed his bedding and his horse to old Mahmud who had then ridden back to Caesaria. Vahan recollected with some self-disparagement that he had never seen a railway or a steam engine before, and that when he had eventually arrived, after two days on the train, at Haydar Pasha station on the Asian side of Constantinople, the ferry ride across the Bosporus had also been his first sight of the sea. He had slipped onto the ferry with his suitcase and with only the haziest idea of where his Uncle's house in old Stamboul lay, but too excited to care. He remembered looking out at the straits for the first time—full of other ferries chugging back and forth between Europe and Asia—and also filled with all the shipping of the world passing into and out of the Black Sea.

Then, as he had passed Leander's Tower and hit the magnificent panorama of the Constantinople skyline with its wonderful domes, minarets and palaces, he had first seen the two great German battle cruisers—riding at anchor—grey and sleek in the water and both with the Ottoman flag flying from their mastheads. As the ferry passed nearby, Vahan saw the German sailors, all wearing the red fez, but otherwise dressed in smart, white German uniforms. He had noted the impressive 16 inch guns pointing unmistakably at the Byzantine shoreline and the Sultan's palaces. Both ships dwarfed everything else on the waters. Even in his excitement at everything around him, Vahan recalled how he had wondered at that moment how it had come about that these two magnificent ships had appeared in Constantinople—the capital of the Empire.

Vahan, thinking back, reflected that the Ottomans were not then at war, when he had first arrived. All enlightened opinion in the Empire had been quite clear that Turkey must avoid another war at all costs. However, even Vahan, whose vague and scarcely yet properly formed political opinions were bound to be in favour of the western allies and Russia, had felt a frisson of delight that these two great ships had been 'sold' by the German government to Turkey. This supposed sale had ironically immediately replaced the two completed dreadnoughts lying in the British shipyards, which had been fully paid for by the pennies of the whole population. They had been about to be handed over to Turkish crews, when they had been commandeered by the British government on the outbreak of the war.

Vahan, only just eighteen on his arrival, could not of course have been aware of the menace implied in the guns of these two ships—but other more sophisticated observers certainly could.

Within a month of Vahan's arrival in Constantinople, he had managed to find himself a room in the home of a Greek family where he could take lodgings and be independent. But also within three months, the *Goeben* and the *Breslau*, these two great German battle cruisers,—now renamed the *Sultan Selim* and the *Medilli*—sailing under the Ottoman flag but still commanded by the German Admiral Souchon, had sallied out into the Black Sea and had bombarded the Crimean coastline. They had demonstrated their power by arrogantly sailing outside Sevastopol itself, daring the weaker old pre-dreadnought Russian battleships to come out. Partly as a result of this, Turkey had been dragged into the war against Russia and the West. The entry of the Ottoman Empire into the Great War had transformed a basically European war into the first World War.

Vahan finally gave up his musing, and ran to jump on a tram taking him to the University building to which he was heading. This was not the Music and Drama Department, but the military academy attached to the university to which he was now seconded. As a student in the university he had automatically become an officer in the Ottoman Army, and had to spend two mornings a week, learning about the theory of warfare, and the esoteric art of drilling. It was all a lot of fun, and far removed from the stories of what appeared to be happening in Europe in the trenches of France. If he found it a bit odd that he was a citizen of an Empire that was fighting a war with countries he had always admired, he certainly did not let it worry him—that was life and he was prepared to fight if necessary, like everyone else. Did he but know it, it was a feeling that applied to millions of young men throughout Europe on all sides in that year of 1914-1915.

He was unaware, even now, of the effect that the two battle cruisers standing high and proud in the waters of the Bosporus had already had on his life and those of countless others.

Chapter 4

Constantinople. The family of Dr. Nazim Kemal.

By 8 o'clock on this early April morning, the Galata district, on the north side of Halic—the Golden Horn—was already teeming with the hustle and bustle of crowds walking up the hill from the Galata Bridge. Business men and merchants of all kinds walked briskly to their offices after coming off the hooting ferries as they jostled their way up to the quays under the bridge, on which Vahan had been standing musing and watching the world go by.

Doctor Nazim Kemal lived in a modern flat at the top of the road up from the bridge leading to the Grande Rue de Pera, and eventually to Taksim Square. A sparse, thin man with a sharp, well-groomed moustache, he worked in the German Hospital at Siraselviler in Beyoglu, not far from Taksim and well within walking distance to his flat. He was this morning, as always, carefully and slowly shaving himself.

Nazim considered himself to be at the forefront of the modernising influences at work in the Empire. Like almost everyone else in the city—Turk, Jew, Greek or Armenian—he had welcomed the Ittihad Revolution of 1908, when the more exuberant of the citizens had gathered in the streets and danced together, regardless of their racial background. Nazim himself would not have deemed it at all proper to join in such exhibitionist behaviour, but he had not objected when his eldest son—then thirteen years old—had asked to be allowed to join in with the happy crowds in the streets.

Things had of course gone badly wrong since that early fresh confident start. The odious Abdul Hamid had indeed eventually been forced to abdicate, but not until there had been several coups and counter-coups. The loss of yet more of the Christian provinces during the two Balkan wars, had then resulted in an ugly and confused mood amongst the normally tolerant Ottoman elite.

Nazim was a dry and outwardly unemotional man, for whom duty and honourable living took precedence over any personal feelings. His appreciation of the words of all the great Turkish poets, however, and his love of music of all kinds, gave him emotional release from his somewhat tightly controlled inner life.

A month earlier, Nazim, with a group of like-minded friends in a literary circle, loosely referred to as the Liberal Book Club, had decided to organise an evening of music and poetry. Nazim, had a deep loyalty to the basic ideals of tolerance of the old Ottoman Empire and had persuaded his friends that this recital should not only include the great Turkish poets and singers, but should also be representative of the other minorities in the Empire—the Greeks and Armenians on the one hand, and even the Arabs on the other.

The Club had contacted figures in the new government, who had all expressed enthusiasm. However, the new rulers had thought of it as a way of promoting specifically Turkish nationalism and identity, as opposed to the cosmopolitan and international aspect of the old Ottoman Empire—a multi-ethnicism which the new government were in fact planning to repudiate. Accordingly they were not so happy with the suggestion that there might be some Greek or Armenian input into the concert. There was therefore, right from the start, a contradiction between the ideals of Nazim and his associates on the one hand, and the new Young Turk government on the other, of which neither side was aware.

The Ittihad leaders accepted, that as far as the international profile of what they thought of as the new Turkey was concerned, a concert and recital of this sort would be seen as a good example of the fresh modern outlook being fostered by the new government. Ironically, Nazim and his friends, who also thought of themselves as so modern, were in fact much closer in spirit to the great Ottoman Sultans of the past. These Sultans had been ready to accept and imbibe Christian and other cultural influences as well as Muslim, when the Empire was formed.

Nazim had worked hard on the details of this celebration of the diverse cultures of the empire. At the opening of the concert he had stood at the entrance of the hall as the guests had arrived, welcoming the many dignitaries of the Ittihad party currently running the government, including Talaat Bey himself, in addition to two elderly Ottoman princes and numerous writers, poets and Muslim dignitaries. The Greeks were largely absent, but dotted around the hall were several Armenians, including the four current Members of Parliament, together of course with the Ambassadors of the Allied powers of Germany and Austria.

Nazim's hand uncharacteristically slipped a little, and he winced as his razor cut into his chin too deeply and a small scar appeared. He tut-tutted impatiently—he hated any blemish on his person—but continued shaving and musing.

One of the minority performers, whom it had been Nazim's task to persuade to attend was the Armenian priest—Father Komitas—who was currently working at the Armenian Church in Galata, where he was re-organising and improving the choir. Nazim knew that Komitas had for many years been working on the collation and transcription of Armenian folk songs collected from all over the highlands of Eastern Anatolia. He had also worked on the core of Armenian medieval church music, rewriting a lot of the old musical liturgy into modern notation.

Nazim himself had come to know of him through a colleague at the German Hospital. Komitas had only just returned from a trip to Berlin. There he had attended, almost daily, performances of Wagner's music at the Opera House. He had met and made friends with Nazim's German colleague, with whom he had found a common interest in Wagner's music. Komitas was unable to talk freely with other Armenians about such a secular preference as this love of Wagner. Already the Armenian National Church Assembly had published a biting criticism of the mild and gentle Komitas in a Constantinople journal, with the following words amongst many other adverse comments, "Father Komitas has in addition commercialised and popularised sacred songs and dirges of the Holy

Armenian Church, and we ask the leader of the Church to reprimand him severely for this disgraceful behaviour."

Nazim, who like any other intellectual in Constantinople was well aware of all this ferment in the Armenian Press, had found this all faintly amusing, and rather distasteful. Nazim prided himself on his own calm and secular attitudes. His own faith, imbibed through his parents, was mild. However, he was not an atheist, and he certainly admired and even loved the simple virtues of Islam, even though he could not bring himself to the fever-pitch of his humbler compatriots.

For Nazim, the tolerant nature of the old Ottoman Empire, multi-cultural and open to all talents within the Empire, was the ideal to which he would have liked the new state to aspire. He despised both the passions aroused by religion on the one hand, and the nationalistic fervour of the teachers and rabble-rousers on the other. His weakness was his failure to understand the power that these feelings had on other—perhaps less-educated—people.

The cultural evening had gone well. Nazim's friend and colleague—Hamidullah Bey—had been a brilliant Maitre de Ceremonies throughout. His introduction of the pale and sad-looking Komitas had been a masterpiece of modern liberal Turkish sentiment. He had referred to the Armenians as a people who had always been on the frontier of Turkish cultural life, and he had ended with the words, "These are the people with and amongst whom we have lived for centuries."

Komitas had then sat at the piano and sang and played his mainly melancholy songs. Nazim recalled that the Hall had reverberated with ovations and applause. The old Turkish phrase—"May Allah save him from all evil eyes!" rang out from all sides.

Nazim grinned to himself at the recollection. Many of his Christian acquaintances had come up to congratulate him on the part he had played in arranging the evening. How could these people, he thought, spend so much time and energy, and even violence, on their interminable discussions about the nature of their prophet—Jesus Christ. Nazim may have been a liberal intellectual, but he still found it difficult to comprehend what he thought of as a typically Greek attitude to life and philosophy. His mind contrasted all this subtle Greek concept of 'three-in-one' godhead with the simple pure tenets of his own father's faith. To think that the Armenians and Greeks—to him simply infidels together—were insuperably separated by an argument stretching back centuries, as to whether the nature of the Son was 'similar to' or 'the same as' the Father. The whole argument seemed to him to be utterly ludicrous.

Nazim still shaving on this bright April morning laughed out loud at his thoughts. He was then disconcerted, as his son Selim, now a young man of twenty, poked his head round the door.

"What's funny baba"

"Nothing, nothing my son—just a recollection. Are you ready?"

"Yes father—I'm just going. I will be home late this evening, as I am doing some extra study with a friend. I've told Mama. Good bye."

Nazim nodded. His decision not to send Selim to the old Sultan Abdul Mecit University in Bayazit, but to the American College—Robert College—in the north of the city seemed to him to have been a success. Selim was growing up with modern, liberal ideas, but did not appear to have rejected any of the old values which Nazim in his heart felt were important. The small German school, newly opened, did not have the same prestige, whilst Nazim had a faint distaste for the English and had rejected any idea of the English High School at Nishantash.

Nazim finished all his morning rituals and went down to join his wife Halideh for breakfast.

"Husband, come, your tea is ready. Selim has already left. I sent him upstairs to say goodbye to you."

Nazim grunted and began on his usual breakfast of thin Stambouli bread, olives and cheese and weak tea. He eyed Halideh, who was clearly anxious to tell him something important, though not wanting to disturb his first mouthfuls. He showed her sympathetically that he was ready to listen.

"Husband of mine, I am worried about Selim. I do believe, as you know, that your decision to send him to that infidel College was a great gamble. Who knows what immoral ideas he will pick up there. Listen, yesterday he told me that he and a group of his friends had sat and had a little picnic in the College grounds with some of the young girl students. Nazim, it seems that they talked together for about two hours. Nazim, my lord, what self-respecting girl would stoop to such a thing."

Nazim said nothing, continuing to eat his breakfast, and extending his glass for another tea. However, he was listening carefully. Halideh took a breath and continued.

"I understand that they all spoke together, seven or eight boys and about six girls. Can you believe it? He tells me that they spoke about the war, and how badly Enver Pasha's offensives in the Caucasus had been managed. Nazim, listen, they actually openly criticized our government! I suppose I don't mind that so much, though it could be dangerous—but above all what sort of girls are they to talk so freely with young men?"

"Halideh, my beloved one, once I made the decision to send Selim to this western style College, I accepted that that decision must necessarily include everything in which he might get involved. I, myself, as you well know, believe that Enver and the others in the Ittihad party are driving this country fatally into the wrong political and moral direction, so I really have no concern if this turns out to be the view also of Selim and his friends. However, my beloved, I agree that he should be more careful about publicly voicing his criticisms, and I will certainly warn him about this tonight."

"But Nazim, you have said nothing of this disgraceful mixing of the sexes—it's a terrible, infidel thing."

"Halideh, please understand that I probably agree with you on that point. It cannot be right that there should be such unsupervised contact between impressionable young men and women. I agree with you that it could be dangerous. However, it is not our daughters who are involved, and I have every faith in the good sense and honour of our son. He will not be tempted into any wrong-doing, of that I am quite certain. Meanwhile, my beloved, please do not be anxious about our own young girl. I have no intention whatsoever of sending her to any of these smart modern Western schools, and on this point I will surely follow your preferences, if I can."

Rising from his seat, Nazim saluted his wife, and went out.

Shaking his head, but basically unworried, Nazim, went down to the front door, buttoning up his coat, and stepped out into the busy street heading for the Hospital. He could see the two great German battle cruisers, sitting in the harbour. They had, however, since their sudden dramatic arrival in August 1914 at the start of the War, become a part of the spectacular background of his city, so he no longer noticed them The four tall funnels of the *Goeben*, and those of the smaller *Breslau* could be seen at the bottom end of almost every steep street leading down to the Bosporus in that part of the city. He stepped out briskly in the direction of the German Hospital.

Chapter 5

Constantinople. Selim and his father.

Selim Kemal had been attending Robert College since September of the previous year. He was not entirely sure what he wanted to do with his life—but for the moment he didn't care. It was enough for him that he lived in the most exciting city in the world, that he had a close family all of whom loved him and whom he loved in return, that he was young, full of life, and open to everything around him.

Selim was a tall young man of twenty, with broad shoulders and powerful rather long arms. He had black curly hair which he let grow long. He was dark and swarthy and had difficulty controlling stubble on his chin, often shaving twice during the day. He had black deep-set eyes, which usually looked out rather sleepily from under thick eyebrows. Like all the other students he sported the usual Enver-style moustache. He never wore a fez or a hat, and accordingly whilst his father Nazim was one of the few men in Stamboul who was always clean-shaven, his son Selim was one of the few who always went around without any head covering.

Selim was peripherally aware of the enormous political issues facing the Empire in which he lived. Like any educated Turk, he resented the humiliations imposed on the Ottomans by the war against the greedy Italians, and the recent, more desperate, Balkan Wars. However, it hadn't really affected him or his friends directly. These had been wars still fought by the patient long-suffering Anatolian peasants, led by inefficient and effete Stambouli officers. What could you expect?

It was only the day before that Selim and his father had had one of their long discussions at the family breakfast table as to where the Turkish state was currently heading.

"Father, you must admit now that all our Empire in Europe has been lost, probably for ever, there are no longer as many Christians as Turks in the Empire. Don't you think, therefore, that the state should now concentrate on its Turkish identity, rather than continuing to try to be all things to all men, by retaining its multinational character."

"My son, what you say sounds logical, but what about all the Greeks and Armenians still left in Anatolia, and who have been there as long as we have? What about all the Arabs who have lived under Ottoman rule, benign or otherwise for centuries? At least they haven't spent their time murdering each other during the time that the Ottomans have been the dominant power."

"Oh, Baba—forget about the Arabs—they're no problem, they're irrelevant as far as we're concerned. I often think that it would be a good idea if we abolished the Caliphate. It's an anomaly in this modern world. It's an old-fashioned Arab concept that hinders rather than helps us. We are a vibrant Turkish people—what need have we for this ancient Arab institution?"

"My dear boy, even if you are right about removing the title of Caliph from our Sultan, be careful of what you may find taking its place. By having a Caliph—old-fashioned concept though it may be—our faith did at least contrive to respect a single head. Even if sometimes it has proved a broken reed, it has had the effect of being a restraining force on extremists, fundamentalists and crackpots setting themselves up all over the place, claiming to have some sort of divine revelation for whatever happens to be their current brand of murderous faith."

"Well father, let the crackpots get on with it. What we want here is a Turkish state which happens to be mainly Muslim, rather than a Muslim state that happens to be mainly Turkish."

"Well put, my boy, well put. But the original Ottomans were not like either of those. What we had, until the odious Abdul Hamid ruined it all, was a universal empire based on geography and economic convenience, which tried to accommodate many different people, many different customs and many different religions. It may have been somewhat inefficient, but it did at least prevent people trying to eliminate each other in the name of some religious or national unity."

"Father, I know that you disapprove of the current direction that the Ittihad rulers are taking—I know you don't like their exclusive nationalism—but, baba, the Empire is dying, and we must start thinking of putting something new in its place. A state should be based on a 'people'—in this case Turkish."

"Beware, my son, of the passions of the 'people' when they are aroused as a tribal force. However, my loved one, you give me much to ponder over, and your points are well put and clear."

Like any thoughtful father, Nazim broke off the discussion, leaving his eager son the full honours of the argument. He disagreed with Selim much more fundamentally than he had admitted, but he recognised the factor of his own slightly world-weary conservatism, and above all he had no desire to squash his son's enthusiasms in any way.

As a young lad, Selim had gathered enthusiastically with his friends in the streets persuading passers-by to donate their paras and odd coins to the collection for the purchase of the two Dreadnoughts which were intended to recreate Ottoman sea power in the Eastern Mediterranean. But whether he was collecting for the glory of the multi-ethnic Ottoman Empire, of which he was a citizen, or for a new Turkish nation state which seemed to be emerging from the Ittihad party line, he could not have said.

The people of the Ottoman Empire had raised the money by popular subscription to build these two ships in British shipyards. Agents had gone from house to house painfully collecting small sums of money. There had been entertainments and fairs all over the country, and women had sold their hair for the benefit of the common fund. These two ships therefore represented an outburst of popular feeling, affecting all the races, that was unusual in the Empire.

The Ottoman Empire was not Turkish in the way that France was French or Germany German. The Ottoman ruling class, all born and bred in Stamboul, were Turkish only in that they knew and spoke Ottoman Turkish—itself a literary and upper-class language somewhat different to the common Turkish spoken on the Anatolian farms. The very word 'turk' was often used pejoratively by these well-born pashas, to refer to the simple Anatolian peasants of the interior, the cannon-fodder of the old Ottoman armies.

Yet in these proudly collected pennies, like everything in those last few years of Ottomanism, there was a fatal paradox. For whom did all these eager people think that these two great ships were being built—the Muslim Caliphate—a Nationalistic new Turkish state—or the old Ottoman Empire?

An immense anger had swept over Selim and his friends during August 1914, when they heard that the British government, far away on the other side of Europe, had impounded the two battleships. This confiscation had been carried out by a hard-pressed British government at the very moment that they had been fully paid for with the hard-earned pennies of ordinary people throughout the empire, and at the very moment when Turkish crews had already arrived in England to take over the completed ships. In the long run, it had been a terrible mistake. The British fleet was already immeasurably superior to the German, and two more dreadnoughts, more or less, could not have made any great difference. Yet, as always when war loomed, alleged military concerns took precedence over what was obviously to become a likely diplomatic disaster.

Unlike the masses throughout Western Europe, the young men of the Ottoman Empire were not bellicose or interested in getting into the 'excitement' of a war. Turkey had been at war, on and off, for two or three years already. Since the revolution of 1908, Ottoman youths were much more aware of the dreadful side of modern warfare than their French, English or German counterparts, the country having been almost continuously at war of one kind or another.

On the 10th August 1914, just before Selim was about to start at Robert College, the two great German battleships, the *Goeben* and the *Breslau,* had passed through the Dardanelles and anchored in the Bosporus opposite the Dolmabahce Palace. Selim had never realized for a moment how these two ships were going to have such a profound effect on him and his contemporaries. Above all, when he heard that in order to maintain their neutrality the two ships had been "sold" by the German government to the Sultan, and had been renamed the *Sultan Selim*, and the *Medilli*, complete with their full crews, he fell about with all his friends in exuberant joy, enjoying the embarrassed discomfiture and objections of the British Ambassador, all of which had been fully reported in the Press.

Actually for once, it did not matter whether you were a youthful Turkish student, or a young Greek or Armenian one. The 'one in the eye' delivered by the government to the arrogant British Empire gave everyone an immense satisfaction. This seemed to be the first time for years that Constantinople had dared to stand up to the Westerners. However, the fact that Turkey had virtually tied itself to an alternative Western power, Germany, was not considered.

On the day of the announcement of the 'sale', the students flocked to the road along the waterfront and saw the German sailors parading, each with a fez on their heads, and with the Sultan's emblem at the masthead. They cheered and cheered, but with no idea as to how or why the ships had got there in the first place, nor what it would mean to them in the long run.

Selim knew that his father belonged to the school of thought which believed strongly that the Empire should stay out of the war. "Let them get on with killing each other—why should we care if one 'giavour' beats up another 'giavour'" was his continual refrain. Nazim's feelings were of course more complex than that, but it was what he said to his son, and Selim and his friends basically agreed. Meanwhile, the heavy guns of the two battle cruisers, so easily trained on the city shoreline, clearly represented naked power.

In November 1914, whilst Selim was enjoying every moment of his new life at the College, these two ships sailed out of the Bosporus, and into the Black Sea, where they totally dominated the old-fashioned Russian fleet which had no ship which could even match the *Breslau*, never mind the superb *Goeben*. The Crimean coast was bombarded, and the Ottoman Empire found itself at war with Russia and the Western Powers, and in alliance with Germany and Austria. The ability of a few German sailors, the failure of the British and their much-vaunted fleet, and the amateurish arrogance of the Young Turk leaders, had succeeded in pushing the empire into a lethal death-struggle, which the wisdom of traditional Ottoman statesmen had always managed to avert for over a hundred years. The unthinkable had at last happened. The one fatal error that generations of old Pashas and Viziers—Greek, Albanian and Turkish—had studiously avoided, namely a simultaneous war with Russia and the western maritime powers, had come to pass.

But it had hardly yet affected Selim at all. The ambitious, dapper Enver Pasha had gone off to the Caucasus, with an army largely still composed of Anatolian recruits and officered by the old Regular Army officers. Everyone, the old Sultan, the German attaché and most of the Ottoman elite, had advised strongly against a winter campaign in that terrible terrain. But the arrogant Enver had overridden them all, as he had at each critical step throughout the year, and had led the army to a major disaster. Meanwhile Selim's call-up was deferred, though like most University students he was registered at the Harbiye—the military academy for the training of officers.

However, his mind was on none of these matters as he ran down the street, having just left his father shaving. All he could think of was the meeting he had arranged with a girl from the American Girl's College whom he had met during a recent picnic. He simply could not get her out of his mind. He had been shy at meeting all these girls, several of whom were clearly not Muslims. But this girl—he only knew then that her name was Olga—had looked at him with her huge dark eyes, and had smiled so naturally and warmly that his heart had turned over, and he had almost cried out with a feeling of tenderness.

He had discovered after they had all separated, that her name was Olga Avakian, which meant that she must be an Armenian—but what was that to him? Once away from the necessity to conform within his peer group, his natural strength of character reasserted itself and he strove to find out more about her as discreetly as possible. Through another student at the College—an Austrian medical student—he had met her fleetingly again, inevitably in yet another large group, and they had actually exchanged a few words, painful in their banality.

However, today on this glorious first day of April, he was going to ask her to meet him again at some future date at Tokatlian for tea, after the end of the usual college day—he, at any rate, proposing to be for the first time on his own. The butterflies in his stomach at the thought of this proposed approach were worse than before any previous anticipated childhood punishment or academic test. He didn't know how he was going to get through the rest of the day.

Chapter 6

London. Harry and his father.

The whole question of the arrival in Constantinople of the two German battle cruisers at the start of the War was, at this moment and on this same day, in the forefront of Lieutenant Harry Bridgeman's mind. He was currently stationed at the Admiralty, and was in the process of analysing in depth the reasons for the failures of the Navy on that occasion, for use in the coming court-martial of the commanders ostensibly responsible. He was working both on his own recollections, having been present at the very first contact with the two ships, and on a series of further documents surrounding the incident.

It was an equally bright spring morning in London, when Harry Bridgeman left his parents' house in Chelsea and strode off to his work at the Admiralty. Harry, a product of Eton, Oxford and the confident English upper middle classes had originally been marked out for one of the Guards' regiments. However, his sharp mathematical brain, and his own inclinations, led him instead to prefer the Navy. He had tentatively put his views to his alarming father—Colonel William Bridgeman—to be greeted by considerable opposition and pressure. However, in his own more diffident way, Harry was as obstinate as his father, and stood up to him, dispute after dispute.

Harry was an only son. The Colonel had harrumphed and blustered, and the discussions had gone on between them, usually at the breakfast table in their small suburban house in West London, and almost always raised by the Colonel. He would get red and start shouting out somewhat sharply something to the effect that the Bridgemans had always gone into the Guards. He would emphatically remark that he could get Harry into any regiment he might choose—but it had to be the army.

Harry would inevitably reply that he was not cut out to be a Guards' officer. He would claim always that he was more of a technician, and that his interests were more scientific. Above all, he was sure that he would be no good in the cut and thrust of army life, or the direct leadership of men."

And so it would go on, over and over and round in circles with the Colonel calling on generations of Bridgeman tradition, and Harry stubbornly and more and more quietly resisting. In the end, the Colonel had referred his problem to a member of his club, a respected acquaintance.

"Look, Smithson, I am at my wit's end about my son Harry. What the blazes are children coming to these days? I wouldn't have dreamt of contradicting my father on a matter of such importance. You know that we Bridgemans have been in the army for generations—now the little idiot wants to go into the Navy—the Navy damn it—I've no influence there at all, and it goes against one hundred years of tradition."

"My dear Sir" had replied the urbane Smithson "You should consider yourself lucky. Harry might easily have ended up wanting to be a poet or something. Could you have coped with that? Look man, he does at least want to go into one of the services. God, he might have wanted to go into the teaching profession. Think of the horror of that! Let him do as he wants, and be thankful."

William Bridgeman was an alarmingly certain man without any doubts, but he was not unintelligent. He immediately saw the strength of his friend's point. However he wasn't going to give in too easily, and he made Harry repeat his arguments and defiance for a little longer, until he finally, and grumpily, conceded.

Harry was by now twenty-four years old, tall and somewhat angular with rather dreamy vague blue eyes which belied his sharp brain when he felt like using it. His softish eyes tended to sharpen and seem to focus when he became interested in any matter. He was indeed not a natural leader of men and he knew it, even if his father did not. Furthermore, whilst he respected the Colonel, he also feared him, and got most of the love he needed from his gentle and somewhat careworn mother. Harry had no sister, and like so many of his class and time, he had had almost as little contact in his life so far with the opposite sex, as a young man of his age would have had in the Muslim East.

Harry was outwardly a very conformist and archetypal character. He had excelled at sports at his minor public school and had been fairly popular with his peers. He had often been invited to the large house parties of the period, and had had little difficulty in mixing in in these situations. However he himself never invited any of these friends back to his parents' own modest house. He knew perfectly well how to behave towards others in the way they expected and always with impeccable good manners. All of this was not in any way hypocritical or a pretence. Although he found the rituals and clubbability of his peers pointless and trivial, he had no difficulty in keeping up his 'good chap' appearance, even when to their surprise he started quoting poetry. In a sense he simply didn't have the confidence to act in any other way.

So far everything he had done at school or at university, everything he had tried to be in his 'public' life, was because he wanted his father's approval. He was not entirely aware of this consciously. He would lie awake at nights wondering why neither his mother's unstinting love nor the fact that he had a good set of friends, all of whom in their way loved and respected him, was ever quite enough.

Harry was in awe of his father, and had had to pluck up courage, as he grew older, to contradict him. He was totally unaware that he might be craving something more from his father than William Bridgeman was capable of giving. Without realising it consciously, Harry kept having to be sure in his mind that his father approved of everything he did and was proud of him—and yes, for God's sake, 'loved' him. Somehow, he was never ever quite sure.

William Bridgeman, on the other hand, believed that bringing up a son required that the boy should have respect for his father and should learn to be self-sufficient, and that a father should show no weakness of any kind, particularly to an eldest son. He had scarcely ever in his whole life said to anyone—not even his own mother, nor his wife-to-be—the words "I love you." It would for him have been a sign of weakness—a betrayal in a way of his independent honour. Only his gentle wife knew that secretly, and only on rare occasions—

when Harry was a young lad below the age of ten—William Bridgeman would steal upstairs, stare down at his sleeping son, and give him a light kiss on the forehead—tip-toeing away, fearful that Harry might awake, catching him in this moment of weakness.

Harry's step on this bright spring day, was brisk and his ardour was undimmed by the depressing news of the stalemate on the Western Front. He avoided the Underground, preferring to walk all the way to work. On this morning—the first day of sunshine since the end of the winter—he recalled the crowds on this very route on that gloriously sunny day in August 1914 when war was finally declared. The crowds had surged up and down in an ecstasy of patriotic fervour and delight. The war would be over in a few months. Meanwhile what a joy it was for all these eager young men at the thought that they would be going on the greatest adventure of the century—leaving behind the drudgery of their boring daily lives.

For once the ordinary people—the so-called man in the street and his wife—were well ahead of their leaders in the cry for battle. This was not a matter of old men frivolously putting the lives of the young in jeopardy, a myth to be fostered in a later and more cynical age, but of young men and women impatiently urging their elders on. It was all very well for Sir Edward Grey to stare bleakly out of the windows of the Foreign Office, and mutter about 'lamps going out all over Europe', but Harry and his friends had been laughing with high spirits on the streets outside at the thought of flexing their muscles in a stirring camaraderie of danger and honour.

Harry grinned to himself—what was it that that young poet Rupert Brooke had written. He considered and then recited to himself as he walked on:

> "Now, God be thanked who has matched us with His hour,
> And caught our youth, and wakened us from sleeping,
> With hand made sure, clear eye, and sharpened power,
> To turn, as swimmers into cleanness leaping,
> Glad from a world grown old and cold and weary,
> Leave the sick hearts that honour could not move,
> And half-men, and their dirty songs and dreary,
> And all the little emptiness of love."

Harry was only three years younger than Brooke, and had himself met the young poet, having several friends who were mutual acquaintances. He had found Brooke to be not only an extraordinarily handsome young man, but also intensely witty and lively. Brooke had marked left-wing sympathies, and this had disconcerted Harry's circle. However, his youthful and exuberant patriotism had endeared him to all sections of the social class to which they all belonged.

Harry did not have to be at his office before 9.30, even though there was a war on. He decided to sit for a few moments in St. James' Park and watch the ducks whilst he reflected on the report that he had been instructed to compile on the unfortunate event that had occurred in the first few days of the War in the Mediterranean—a failure of the Royal Navy that was destined to become one of the few really decisive moments of the Great War. His task was to put the events on a personal basis from the perspective of his own involvement and that of the central office of the Admiralty, for submission to the forthcoming Court Martial.

He was understandably nervous about this task, as he had been coming to the conclusion that his superiors at the Admiralty were themselves partly to blame for the predicament which had been so badly handled by the men on the spot. He was reflecting, of course, on the escape of the two German battle cruisers—the *Goeben* and the *Breslau*—and the failure of the Navy to catch them before they finally arrived in Constantinople and changed the course of the war.

On his arrival at the office, Henry found waiting for him on his desk a copy of a memorandum—marked Top Secret—clearly written some time ago by Sir Thomas Hankey, the Secretary to the War Cabinet, and addressed to the War Council. It read:

"The remarkable deadlock which has occurred in the Western Theatre of War invites consideration of the question whether some other outlet can be found for the employment of our forces. In the Western Front any advance must be costly and slow. Days are required to capture a single line of trenches—the losses are heavy, and as often as not the enemy recaptures his lost ground on the next day. Any gains are negligible, moreover the advance is so slow that the enemy has time to prepare fresh lines of defence in his rear. Germany can surely be struck most effectively and with the most lasting results on the peace of the world through her allies, and particularly through Turkey. We could, without in any way endangering our position in France, devote three Army Corps to a campaign in Turkey. This should surely be sufficient to capture Constantinople. The capture of this city would force Turkey out of the war, and in addition we would then be in a position to supply Russia directly with all the goods and exchange she so desperately needs, and which is causing such unrest and hardship there."

Attached to this was a note scribbled by Harry's immediate superior in rather poor handwriting, "Harry! Jack Fisher has asked me to pass this highly confidential memorandum on to you, as he thinks that you ought to bear it in mind when preparing your own report on the *Goeben* and the *Breslau.* The court martial proceedings are not of course interested in the far reaching results of Troubridge's failure, but Jack thought you ought to be aware of the way current official circles are thinking, so far as this area of the war is concerned.

Incidentally, Harry, Jack has also indicated that he has had enough formal reports from many people in respect of this matter, and he would therefore like your comments to be entirely informal and a pure reflection of your own personal experience. Attach any other documents separately."

Harry cleared his desk—completed once more his monthly request to be posted back to an active station—then sat down to write out his final draft of his report on the decisive events of the previous August.

THE MEDITERRANEAN

THE ESCAPE OF THE *GOEBEN* AND THE *BRESLAU*

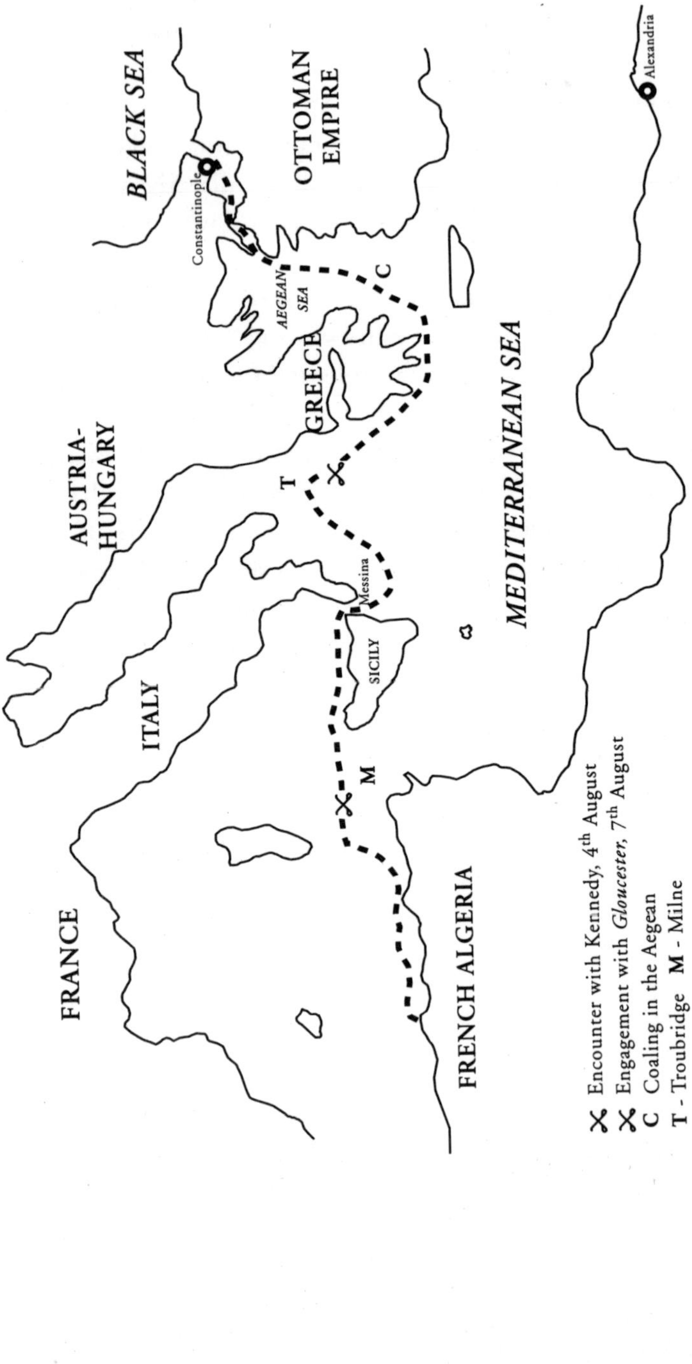

Chapter 7A

London. Harry's Report.

A. The personal account of Lieutenant Harry Bridgeman.

At the time of the events on which I have been asked to give a personal report, I was stationed on HMS *Indefatigable*, a cruiser commanded by Captain Kennedy. We were all aware on the ship of the growing tensions in Europe arising from the assassination of the Archduke Franz Ferdinand at Sarajevo at the end of July.

- It was not however clear to us, even though we were in touch with the admiralty through the radio, exactly what our priorities were in the Mediterranean area. Indeed, on that first critical day of the 4th August 1914 we were not even sure with whom we were actually at war, if anyone at all.

What we did know was that the powerful German 'dreadnought' type battle cruiser, the *Goeben*, accompanied by its sister ship, the *Breslau,* was cruising in the Mediterranean, commanded by the experienced Admiral Souchon. Captain Kennedy said to me on the previous evening of the 3rd August, when we heard that an ultimatum had been sent to Germany:

"You know, Harry, the *Goeben* is undoubtedly the most powerful ship at present in the Med. It outguns and is faster than any current ship in the whole French fleet. Should it join up with their allies—the Austrian Navy, we are going to have a devil of a job containing them."

"Can we take them on sir," I replied.

"Well, perhaps not alone, but if we can get most of the fleet concentrated on them, we could surely prevail. Anyway, whatever happens, they won't be able to get at the slow French convoys from Algeria, so long as we are around harassing them."

On the morning of that 4th August we heard that the *Goeben* and *Breslau* had indeed appeared outside the ports of Phillipeville and Bone in Algeria. Both these harbours were embarkation ports for the French army stationed in Algeria, an army which was destined to be slotted into the Western front for the vital first two months of the War. We all believed that those first few weeks of the war would be decisive, and the Admiralty had conveyed to Sir Berkely Milne—the admiral commanding the whole Mediterranean fleet—that his priority must be to give help, if required, to the French Fleet covering the vital convoys of troops from Algeria to France.

So, that evening, commanded by Captain Kennedy, and with the *Indomitable* alongside, we were sailing fast due west, with orders to help cover the French convoys, and later to block the straits of Gibraltar to prevent the *Goeben* and *Breslau* from escaping into the Atlantic. As we sailed west to the setting sun, we suddenly sighted the two German ships themselves sailing straight toward us due east. I was on the bridge standing next to Captain Kennedy as the four ships moved inexorably towards each other.

"Sir! My God, they are the *Goeben* and the *Breslau,*" I called out as I studied the approaching ships through the binoculars.

"Action Stations" was commanded, and the Gun crews swung into position below us as the Alarm bells rang out all over the ship. The rest of the crew also moved briskly into the locations they were required to take up in the event of hostilities. The whole ship went into a heightened state of tension as all became aware that this might well be the first shots of the coming war.

Captain Kennedy waited calmly, once the ship was fully ready for action, and we watched carefully as the two ships got closer. We knew we were now within range of the *Goeben*'s guns, whereas it would still be a minute or so before our guns would be able to take any effect. Neither flotilla changed direction in any way, and we were therefore due to pass each other about half a mile apart.

"Sir, what are we proposing to do—shall I ready the Gunnery Master?" I said to the Captain

"Look, Harry, we have to be very careful. This could be a decisive moment. We cannot take any action which might jeopardise any moves by our government. The ultimatum delivered by the Foreign Secretary to Germany is not due to expire until eleven o'clock this evening—and whether that is London time or Berlin time makes no difference, there are still some hours to go. We cannot fire the first shot. Make sure, however, that everyone is on top alert."

The four ships passed each other at speed, but all that immense fire power gathered on each ship stayed ominously quiet. My binoculars were trained on the opposing bridge, and through them I clearly saw the little German Admiral—Admiral Souchon—staring straight ahead, and next to him, a lieutenant, my counterpart, who was staring through his binoculars at me, as I was looking at him.

The moment after we passed by each other, with both sets of crews standing on the decks staring at the opposing ships, Kennedy immediately gave the orders to turn around. Our ships swung round slewing over heavily at speed and we set off to shadow the Germans. Captain Kennedy ordered me to go down to the boiler room and inform the stokers of the crisis. But when I got below, into the hot sweaty inferno of the boiler rooms, I saw that the news had already reached below, and that the stokers were already frantically trying to raise the additional steam to increase our speed.

On paper we should have been able to keep up with the *Goeben*—our respective top speeds, when fully manned, were the same. But it was then that I discovered for the first time that we were short of 90 stokers. I was not sure if Kennedy was aware of this, and hurried back up to the bridge to report on the position. I could already see that the two German ships—smoke pouring from their funnels—were very slowly but surely pulling away from us.

"Sir, we are short of 90 stokers down below, and even working flat out those available won't be able to increase the present speed," I said.

"Well, they've just got to do their best," replied Kennedy gloomily.

At this, one of the other officers gathered on the bridge, staring through his binoculars, said:

"Sir, if we deputise some of the gunners to go down and add to the stokers, we will be able to keep up. Our boilers are in fairly good trim, and surely it's vital to keep them in sight."

"But what if they should suddenly stop and turn a broadside on us. If a shooting match was to start, and ninety of our gunners were down below shovelling, we are going to be caught with our pants down for god's sake. I can't possibly risk it. Anyway the priority issued by the Admiralty was that the crossing of the French troops from Algeria is to be protected at all costs. Now, the one thing that is absolutely certain about the present situation is that the bloody *Goeben* is currently going in the completely opposite direction."

It was certainly totally unclear to all of us standing on that bridge where Admiral Souchon was aiming for. Neither Kennedy himself, nor the rest of us gathered there, were aware of exactly who was going to be at war with whom. Our training had all been on the basis that Italy and Austria would be allied with Germany, and that our Mediterranean fleet would have to face the two navies, stiffened by the two German battle cruisers. Even if Italy stayed neutral, a possibility which the Admiralty had already intimated to the captain on the radio, it seemed important not to allow Souchon to join up with the Austrian fleet.

All sorts of conjectures went back and forth between us all on the bridge. But, meanwhile, all the time, in the dying light of this summer day we watched helplessly as the two German ships passed over the horizon until at last we could not even see the distant plumes of smoke. Our radio officer had of course already signalled the news to the Admiralty, but by 11.00 at night, we had to report that whilst we could be absolutely certain that the German ships were heading due east and thus away from the vital French crossings, nevertheless we had lost sight of them.

B. My comments on the next evidence attached.

I am adding to this personal account evidence obtained as to what was happening on the *Goeben* itself during these critical few days. This comes from a Polish officer, Lieutenant Andre Tarkowski, who was born in Miastiko in the German province of Posen. He came from a family which had lived in this part of Prussia for centuries, and to whom speaking German came as naturally as speaking Polish.

Tarkowski, who is the same age as I, was interviewed by our military attaché in Constantinople about four weeks after the arrival there of the *Goeben*. The Ottoman Empire was then still neutral, and our embassy was functioning normally.

Tarkowski appeared, dressed as a civilian out of nowhere, and asked for an interview. He claimed that he was a radio officer on the *Goeben*, that he was currently on a week's official leave, and that he was proposing to desert as he had suffered discrimination due to his Polish background. Furthermore, he claimed that he was acting on his convictions as a Polish patriot.

In return for British travel documents, for himself and a certain young lady, he was prepared to give a series of interviews to our naval attaché giving as much information as he could as to the *Goeben*, its systems, and armaments. The ambassador agreed, on condition that the interviews did not take place at the embassy, and that he officially had nothing to do with it.

Our naval attaché accordingly interviewed Tarkowski in the private house of a Greek family living in Beyoglu. He obtained some information, most of which has been passed on to our technical department here in London. I have extracted from this long statement those parts specific to this enquiry.

May I add that I agree entirely with our attaché in Constantinople that Tarkowski's motivation had nothing to do with 'discrimination' amongst the other officers of the *Goeben*. I am convinced that they were all far too professional for such nonsense. Indeed, Tarkowski's own statement contradicts this suggestion. Furthermore, coming from a family who had lived happily and fruitfully in Prussian occupied Poland for many years, it seems unlikely that Tarkowski was in fact influenced by Polish nationalism either.

We both believe that his motivation was private and personal and that he put those feelings above all honourable considerations of duty and career. I add that the travel documents and passports were duly issued in his name and that of one Elena Patakis for travel to Egypt. I have no idea what happened to them or whether they ever got away. I do know that Tarkowski was posted as missing, and was being sought by the Turkish police as early as November 1914.

There follows here his account of the events on the *Goeben* in those days of early August 1914, as relayed to our Constantinople Intelligence officer.

C. The evidence of Lieutenant Tarkowski.

My family come from Miastko, a small town in the German province of Posen near the Baltic Sea.

As I saw it, when I was younger, my basic allegiance undoubtedly lay with the Imperial German government. As my family had always been associated with the sea, I had no hesitation in joining the Imperial German Navy. It seemed to me, as a German speaking Pole, that in the last resort a German dominated Poland had a better future than a Russian dominated one, though I wasn't sure of anything.

My Polish revolutionary hero was Pilsudski, but despite my thrill at his exploits against the Russian state, I felt that an important part of my identity was German as well as Polish, and when it came to ordinary everyday life, I saw my own future as a sailor in the Kaiser's new and growing navy. I felt that the sense of camaraderie amongst naval officers on a ship was entirely sufficient to overlay any feelings of racial animosity or superiority that may have existed elsewhere in Prussian-dominated political circles, and which I am told certainly made for tensions in the Imperial Army.

I was fascinated in the new technique of radio, and it was as a radio officer that I found myself on the *Goeben* at the beginning of August 1914, when war broke out with Russia and France. The commander of our little flotilla operating in the Mediterranean, consisting of my ship, the *Goeben*, and a smaller less powerful sister ship, the *Breslau*, was Admiral Souchon. Souchon is a man of French Huguenot descent. He is a short dapper and clean-cut sailor to whom his men were devoted. I myself saw and spoke to him frequently, as he would often come to the radio room to check up as quickly as possible on the latest messages particularly from the Kriegsmarine headquarters at Kiel. He is a very sharply alert and energetic man, who, whilst strict, had a flair dealing with ordinary seamen.

On the declaration of war with France and Russia, we were cruising in the western Mediterranean, and were immediately ordered to approach the French Algerian coastline with a view to disrupting the preparations for the convoy of French troops to mainland France, before the French fleet could arrive from Toulon. Whilst the *Goeben* was more than a match for any single ship in the whole French fleet, nevertheless, the French were numerous enough in total, particularly if they were reinforced by any British ships, to be able to take us on with some probability of success.

We bombarded the ports of Phillipeville and Bone, but eventually sailed away. Our engines were in poor repair. Furthermore, we were already running out of coal.

Souchon informed a gathering of his officers that he was intending to make for Italy to take on more coal.

"Gentlemen, we will head for the port of Messina in Sicily, but I must warn you that I have no idea—nor yet has the Kriegsmarine—where Italy will be standing in this conflict. Above all we must avoid any enemy patrols at this stage till we can refuel."

In the early afternoon of the 4th August as we slipped away towards Sicily, coming towards us in the opposite direction we encountered two British cruisers—the *Indefatigable*, and I believe the *Intrepid*. I came out of the radio room and stood and watched as the two sleek grey warships passed us steaming westwards at top speed, less than half a mile away. The tension amongst us all was electric. The order to man the guns had already been given by the time I came out, but the whole ship seemed enveloped in a deep silence. I could see Souchon standing stiffly on the bridge, eyes firmly ahead, almost as if he was afraid to make eye contact with any British officer, though at that distance that was a ridiculous proposition.

An uneasy quiet floated all around me. Clearly however I must be exaggerating, as all ships ploughing through any kind of seas always generate much background noise—but the tension of all around me created a strange feeling of stillness. It was not fear—it was the tension of uncertainty.

Nothing happened. Each ship held to its course without any of the usual courtesies exchanged by passing ships, but also without any guns booming. However within seconds of the ships passing, we saw the British cruisers swinging round without slackening speed, and clearly starting to follow us.

"Full steam ahead!" was ordered from thc bridge, as an Engineering officer came racing down to go the boiler rooms to press for more steam.

The ship seemed to shudder, though this was more psychological than real, as they strained to reach their top speed of 27 knots. But I heard later that we never got above 24 knots, and that, as we raced forward, as the light began to fade, three of our engines failed one by one and our speed dropped even further.

Stokers began to fall unconscious in their enormous effort to raise enough steam, in a climate already heavy with midsummer heat. We were informed later that four stokers had died during this chase. We knew that the two British battle cruisers were perfectly capable of reaching 22 to 24 knots, but to our great surprise we saw that we were slowly pulling away, mile by mile, until we had got away from them completely.

On the 5th August we steamed into Messina. Here Admiral Souchon went ashore to seek out the situation. Although we had heard rumours of the pending Italian declaration of neutrality, nobody on board was at all clear of the situation. I believe that Souchon himself had been warned of the Italian withdrawal from our alliance even whilst we were bombarding Bone, but he had not passed this on to us, nor did we have any idea of what the British position was going to be.

Coaling was already taking place when Souchon returned and informed his officers in some irritation, that in accordance with the rules of neutrality, the Italian authorities had granted us only 24 hours in which to refuel, after which we had to leave. This was clearly not enough time to refill our bunkers. The combination of our leaking unrepaired boilers, and the burst of very high speed which we had raised to get free from the two British capital ships, had depleted our coal beyond normal consumption.

I must say that neither I nor any of my junior colleagues had any idea what Souchon was now going to do. However, we all assumed that we were going to make a dash for the Adriatic in order to join the Austrian fleet, where we could complete our repairs at leisure and refill our coal bunkers. The alternative of another dash to the Algerian coast to try and cause havoc to the French troop movements seemed impossible without sufficient coal. Indeed, I did send several radio messages to Admiral Haus of the Austrian Kriegsmarine, requesting the assistance of the Austrian navy to enable us to escape into the Adriatic.

Souchon was informed by the Admiralstab that the Austrian Foreign Ministry, in a vain attempt to try and avoid war with Great Britain if possible, had given orders that the *Goeben* and *Breslau* were only to be supported once they were actually under the protection of the Austrian fleet by being physically in Austrian territorial waters. However Admiral Haus himself, the Austrian naval commander, indicated in a personal reply to us that despite foreign ministry wishes he was prepared to sail as far south as Brindisi, and would await Souchon there. We later heard that he did in fact sail out on the morning of the 7th, but by then we were miles away.

We sailed out of Messina harbour on the evening of the 6th, and I for one had no idea at all as to where we were going. However, on the evidence of the radio messages going to the Austrians, I assumed we were still heading for the Adriatic. As we pulled away from Italian territorial waters we did indeed seem to be heading for the Adriatic, but fairly soon we changed course decisively and began heading south towards Greece.

None of us had the slightest idea where we were going.

Chapter 7B

Documents attached to Harry's report.

D. Letter from Mrs. Maurice Wertheim to her father Henry Morgenthau, the American Ambassador in Constantinople.

Dear Father,

We all went aboard the *Sicilia*, as scheduled, at Venice on our way to come and see you. We had the most beautiful summer days as we sailed down the Adriatic. The company aboard was aware that the European powers were in some sort of crisis, but most of the passengers happened to be compatriot Americans, and we were all in cheerful mood. Keeping our three little daughters cheerful and amused took up most of my time, and I had no time to notice what was happening around us, and you had in any case assured us that Turkey would keep out of any European War.

We were lunching on deck somewhere between the coasts of Greece and Italy on the 6th or 7th August when I saw two strange looking vessels on the horizon. I ran for the glasses and made out two large battleships. We watched and saw another ship coming up behind them fast. She came nearer and nearer and then we heard guns booming. Pillars of water sprang up in the air and there were many little puffs of white smoke. It took me some time to realise what it was all about, and then it burst upon me that we were actually witnessing a naval engagement.

The ships continually shifted their position but went on and on. The two big ones turned and rushed furiously for the little one, and then apparently they changed their minds and turned away again. Then eventually the little one turned around and calmly steamed in our direction. At first I was somewhat alarmed at this, but nothing happened. She circled round us with her tars excited and grinning and somewhat grimy. They signalled and exchanged converse with our captain, then turned and finally disappeared. The Captain told us that the two big ships were Germans which had been caught in the Mediterranean, and which were trying to escape from the British.

E. The final evidence of Lieutenant Tarkowski, following a second interview.

Shortly after we made the dramatic change of course to the south away from the Adriatic, we were spotted by a small British light cruiser, which I now understand was the HMS *Gloucester*. I was tapping away at my radio when I heard the sound of firing coming from the *Breslau*. I could not immediately leave my desk, but after a few moments, I was able to go on deck and saw that the *Breslau* was in a furious engagement with the little *Gloucester*, which kept darting in and out but which eventually turned away. However, it was clear that our change of course had been spotted and we assumed that the British would shortly be upon us.

Whilst we all knew by that time that the French fleet had finally arrived on the Algerian coast, and that it was now busy covering the crossing of the French troops, we were also painfully aware that the British had several powerful cruisers in the vicinity. It was therefore with a sense of mounting surprise and joy that in the next few days we found ourselves in a calm and quiet sea sailing unmolested round the tip of Greece, without the sight of any other ship of any nationality on the whole horizon.

That day or the next—I begin to forget the actual sequence of days—we sailed up the Aegean and made a rendezvous with a German coaling ship which met us at the little island of Denusa near Naxos. I must say that I and my fellow officers felt proud of our fierce little commander. Souchon had obviously arranged the rendezvous whilst he had been ashore in Messina, and the entire might of the British Navy had been unable to prevent it. We spent almost three days coaling, with the three ships, our *Goeben* and *Breslau*, and the stocky little coaling ship alongside each other in the beautiful blue waters of the Aegean. Here, like everywhere else in Europe in that fateful month of August

1914, the sun shone from a clear blue sky every day. Looking over the side, we could see the little Greek island with its white villages and its timeless quality. Those of us not on coaling duty even had the time to swim. The war seemed far away and at no time did any enemy ship appear.

We set off on the evening of the 9th, and to my surprise our course was northwards. I was on duty when we arrived at the start of the narrow straits of the Dardanelles on the morning of the 10th. I was aware of an enormous amount of coming and going—the arrival of Turkish officials ferried from the shore on small white boats, and eventually the arrival of two clearly high-ranking Turkish naval officers who were closeted with Souchon for hours. I myself spent the morning watching through my binoculars the shoreline on both sides. The Gallipoli peninsula—with its high cliffs on the European side, and the site of ancient Troy on the flatter Asian side.

To the north lay the historic waterway of the Dardanelles—the waters up which Jason sailed with the Argonaut—the water barrier which Xerxes crossed with his bridge of boats to invade Europe—perhaps the most significant stretch of water in history, at present bristling with modern fortifications and guns on all sides. It lay just beyond the tip of the bows of our two great ships waiting, and we were all aware that behind us the British fleet must surely be closing up fast. The Ottoman Empire was neutral, and we knew that by long-standing treaties, during any time of war, the state was not allowed to agree to any war vessels passing through these narrow waters. So where were we to go?

F. Admiralty report on the movements of Captain Kelly and Admiral Troubridge.

By the afternoon of the 5th August, even after the two German battle cruisers had been lost by Captain Kennedy's force the evening before, Admiral Milne, commanding the whole British Mediterranean fleet, had a pretty good idea of the probable whereabouts of the two German capital ships in Sicily. However he had no idea of their intentions.

Aware of the declaration of Italian neutrality, he considered, and it seems to this analyst a fair decision, that after leaving Sicily, Souchon would probably turn west again and resume trying to disrupt the French convoys carrying valuable troops to Marseille. However, he was also aware of the other possibility—namely that Souchon might try to join the Austrian fleet in the Adriatic. Accordingly, he deployed his heavy battle-cruisers capable of taking on the *Goeben*, west of Sicily in order to prevent Souchon doubling back to attack the French convoys. At the same time, to prevent Souchon escaping into the Adriatic, Rear-Admiral Troubridge, with four armoured cruisers, would steam to the east, just off the island of Corfu, in case Souchon came out that way and turned north to the Adriatic.

Just before the outbreak of the war, Churchill, the First Lord of the Admiralty, had signalled that Troubridge, in particular, was not to attack a 'superior force'. By this, the Admiralty had meant the combined fleets of Austria and Italy. At the same time, the Admiralty had made it clear nevertheless, that the *Goeben* was to be Milne's principal objective. Troubridge, however, commanding armoured cruisers not fully capable of standing up to the *Goeben*, misunderstood, and assumed that the 'superior force' referred to by the Admiralty was the *Goeben*, particularly as he was now aware that the Italians were neutral.

So, as the *Goeben* and *Breslau* steamed out from Messina the British fleets were positioned as follows:

–Milne with the main Mediterranean fleet was west of Sicily covering the route to the Algerian coast;

–Troubridge with his four armoured cruisers lay waiting near Corfu at the entrance to the Adriatic;

–Several light cruisers, including the *Gloucester* commanded by Captain Kelly were patrolling between Malta and Corfu

The two Germans were spotted by one of the light cruisers— HMS *Gloucester*. Kelly immediately set off in pursuit, though keeping out of range of the *Goeben*'s big 11 inch guns. By the time that night began to fall on the evening of the 6th it had become clear that Souchon was not heading for the Adriatic at all, but had turned south. This news was duly radioed back to Milne sitting north and west of Sicily, and to Troubridge sitting to the east.

The gallant Captain Kelly could see that if he could delay the two German ships, Troubridge's squadron of four cruisers could sail down and join in intercepting them. Although enormously inferior in armament, though not in speed, Kelly engaged the *Breslau*, and undoubtedly this was the engagement witnessed by Mrs. Wertheim on the *Sicilia*. Like a gnat irritating a great beast, the *Gloucester* darted in and out, causing no damage in view of its relatively tiny guns, but all the time holding back the Germans who twice turned back on him.

But Troubridge did not follow suit.

Worried by the Admiralty's slightly ambiguous instructions not to attack a superior force, he allowed prudence to override the Nelsonian tradition—always to close with the enemy. Instead at 3:47 on the morning of the 7th he took the decision to turn away, and he signalled to Admiral Milne immediately that he had abandoned the chase. It was said by one of his officers that he was in tears when these orders were given—and well he might be—as the consequences of his decision could be said to have had the most far-reaching strategic consequences of almost any tactical naval decision made in any war.

The responsibility for stopping the *Goeben* now passed to Admiral Milne. He, however, continued to believe that the great danger was the possibility of Souchon doubling back towards the Algerian coast and the vital French troopships. But by the same night of the 6th and 7th he was informed by the Admiralty that the French Navy were now at last sufficiently organized to be able to counter such a threat, and he was free therefore single-mindedly to pursue the *Goeben*. He too, however, did not follow the Nelson touch. All his battle cruisers were fully coaled, and he could have set them off in hot pursuit of the Germans without any difficulty, but once again the Admiralty intervened, warning that hostilities had now begun against the

Austrians, so again Milne delayed, and once again the two ships were saved by fortuitous coincidence to make their decisive impact on history.

With the fairly recent advent of radio, the desk-men at Whitehall were suddenly finding that they could influence the fleet in a way that had never been possible before. As can be seen, this was not always with happy results. In the event, whatever the cause, Admiral Milne hung about at the entrance to the Adriatic, and Souchon accordingly enjoyed about three whole days quietly coaling in the Aegean. As British activity finally resumed and Milne began moving to the East, Souchon sailed for the Dardanelles. He had nowhere else to go, but nevertheless he was taking a fairly major risk as he had no idea at that point what attitude the neutral Turks were going to take.

Admiral Milne was of course aware of the Treaty arrangements involving any navigation by belligerents in the Straits, and he knew that the Dardanelles was heavily mined and barred to all warships. He might well have thought that Treaty arrangements would be honoured, and that all he needed to do was to bring up into the Aegean his own three battle cruisers, which added to Troubridge's four armoured cruisers, would be certain to catch and destroy the *Goeben*. So he did not hurry!

Thus it was that in the afternoon of the 10th August the two great German ships, still completely untouched by the British, anchored at the entrance to the Dardanelles. The British Navy with seven large ships was at last moving up fast behind them, whilst ahead of them was a barred and mined passage.

G. Uncensored letter from an unknown German sailor to a girlfriend in Basel intercepted by agents.

On that morning of the 10th I was on duty on the deck of my ship—the *Breslau*—and I could see a hive of activity of small boats going backwards and forwards between the shore and the *Goeben*. I and my mates had no idea what our pipsqueak Admiral was up to, but we all had great faith in the little bugger.

We could see the big guns of the Turkish fortifications on the Asian shore. We also knew that the Brits could not be far behind. Just after midday, the *Goeben* began to steam slowly up the twisting Dardanelles, and I could see the Turkish pilots and naval officers on their bridge—and by now on our's as well. We moved ever so slowly right behind. These were narrow waters which we all knew were heavily mined, and to begin with we were all fairly tense.

We got through all right. We then sailed up to Constantinople. Believe me, our arrival there in the late afternoon, and our dropping anchor at the entrance to the Golden Horde, just before the wedding cake seaside Palace —I don't know its name—with the sun beginning to set in the West behind the domes and minarets of old Stamboul, was a sight and experience I will never forget.

H. The American Ambassador's Diary entries for the events of the 10th to 16th August.

10th August.

I went to visit Baron von Wangenheim at the German embassy on official business. However his animated manner, and nervousness and excitement showed me that he had no interest in our routine discussion. Eventually I got up to go saying:

"Look, something is distracting you, I'll go and come back some other time."

"No, no my dear Morgenthau," he shouted "You stay right where you are. This will be a great day for Germany! I believe I will be able to give you a great piece of news that will have the utmost bearing upon Turkey's relation to the war."

Then he rushed out, and came back a few moments later waving a wireless message form with all the enthusiasm of a college boy whose football team has just won a victory.

"We've got them, we've got them! The *Goeben* and the *Breslau* have just passed through the Dardanelles!"

I immediately understood his excitement. The voyage of these two ships was very much his personal triumph: for it was he who had arranged with the Turkish cabinet for their passage through the Straits. By safely getting the *Goeben* and *Breslau* into Constantinople, he had all but clinched Turkey's eventual entry into the war as a German ally.

But however much I admired today Wangenheim's work as a professional diplomat in getting the two ships into Constantinople, I remain amazed that the large British fleet, dominating as it did the eastern Mediterranean, had failed to prevent this result.

16th August.

The Ottoman government, that had earlier announced that it had 'purchased' the two ships, today hosted a formal ceremony in which both ships hoisted the Turkish flag with great pomp. The sailors, all immaculately dressed in white, wore brand new red fezes, and some German officers were in full Turkish naval uniform. The Turks announced that the ships were substitutes for the two dreadnoughts seized by the British government some twelve days earlier. With the addition of these two capital ships, the Turkish navy became at a stroke stronger than the Russian Black Sea fleet, and the ultimate entry of the Ottoman Empire into war became almost inevitable. I myself doubt if any two individual ships have exercised a greater influence upon history than these two German cruisers.

20th August.

Today I heard that Djavid Bey—the finance minister—met the Belgian military attaché in the street, and stopping him had said:

"I have terrible news for you. The Germans have captured Brussels!"

The Belgian, a large figure more than six feet tall, put his arm soothingly on the shoulder of the little Turk.

"I have even more terrible news for you," he said pointing out to the stream where the *Goeben* and *Breslau* lay anchored. "The Germans have captured Turkey."

Chapter 8

Makrikoy. Olga.

It was still early in April, on a bright afternoon, when Olga returned home to Makrikoy sooner than usual from the city. She and Selim Kemal had had several further chance meetings and general conversations together at the College, though always in the company of others in their same group. On the day that Selim had finally caught her alone and raised the courage to ask her to come out to tea with him one afternoon after college, she had finally, to her own astonishment and Selim's excitement, agreed to meet him at the fashionable Tokatlian Café.

Olga was much the most beautiful of the four Avakian girls, with a delicate thin nose, fine sensitive features, huge eyes, and a smile, which when turned on naturally was devastating. She was also socially serene and confident. However, in this growing relationship she was not entirely sure of her real feelings. Selim was certainly a good looking, darkly handsome, young man and without any trace of the usual young Turkish male's flamboyant arrogance. But where she was usually so clear and direct in her dealings with the world and with nervous young men in particular, she was in this instance somewhat confused. What were her real feelings towards the young man himself? How much of her thoughts only reflected the excitement of doing something that she knew perfectly well to be completely forbidden? She understood perfectly well that what she was proposing to do was not just a matter of ignoring inevitable parental disapproval, but that it was going deeply against centuries-old tribal and religious taboos. Olga was playing with fire and she knew it.

Her sexuality was aroused, but that had happened with her often enough before, and she had always known how to control and manipulate it. But she was having difficulty this time in differentiating between the excitement of the sexual attraction and the excitement of the danger element in the blossoming relationship. However, on one thing she was absolutely sure: there was no way that she was going to go to the proposed rendezvous alone. But if not alone, then with whom? Who could she possibly ask to accompany her? If she went with any of her friends, it would be round the school in a flash and that was something she could not face. Clearly it would have to be one of her sisters.

As she sat in the train on the way home she thought of her elder sister Sima, but immediately dismissed the possibility.

"Oh no, for heaven's sake, she's far too bossy, and over-emotional as well. Afterwards, she'll talk about it the whole time. She'll get excited and sentimental, and above all she will take it all far too seriously. Oh dear, on top of that, she is likely to take over and dominate the whole thing, even at the tea table. On the other hand, little Seta is only ten and obviously she is far too young. Anyway, she is bound to blurt something out to mother—even if she manages not to shout it out from the roof tops."

"That leaves Nerissa—poor Nerissa—but yes, hang on, she will do fine. All she does all day is read English novels curled up in the corner. She hardly says a word to anyone, and she will leave me free to deal with the boy, without trying to butt in and take over like Sima. But will she come—she's far too shy with strangers—how am I going to persuade her?"

When the train arrived at the Chobancheshme station, Olga alighted and hailed Abdul, the sleepy old man, head nodding, sitting in his one-horse droshky waiting for fares. Not for Olga any hot dusty walk home like her Dad, it had to be the 'arrabiya.' Her thoughts on the problem of a chaperone ran on as she clambered into the warm, horsey-smelling, springy carriage, asking Abdul to pull back and open the hood.

When she walked in at the front door and into the marbled hall, she found herself in the middle of a typical Avakian crisis. Her mother Armineh was standing in the middle of the hall holding a largish bottle of what looked like yellow liquid. She had on her outdoor clothes but was not yet wearing a hat, and she was looking rather vexed.

Olga immediately recalled that earlier in the week, there had been a slight possibility that Armineh had again become pregnant. In order to make quite sure that there was nothing wrong, her doctor had asked her to provide a urine sample for him to analyse. For several days now, therefore, the whole household had been thrown into the most delicious turmoil by this entire procedure much to Olga's delight. It had, throughout the week, caused a great deal of fuss in the household, with much shrieking and expostulations. Anyway, at last all was ready—the urine bottle had been filled, a stopper had been fitted, and the indomitable Armineh was holding it in her hand outside the sitting room waiting to put on her hat ready to sally out into the street and face the world.

At this point, however, it appeared that Armineh had suddenly thought that she really could not be seen walking down the street with a bottle of urine in her hand. So, she had arranged to wrap the bottle in a newspaper which on Olga's arrival had just been accomplished. Then there had arisen the question of which of the four girls should accompany her and carry the bottle. There they all were, still standing in the hall—with Armineh holding the wrapped-up bottle, waiting to hand it over, to allow her to put on her coat and hat, when Olga walked in.

Seta was grinning all over and hopping about with excitement, assuring her mother that she would be more than happy to take the bottle and accompany her on this small, but significant, expedition. Of course Sima was far too grand to carry any urine bottle down the street. Olga was clearly not about to volunteer for such an undignified role either, and immediately claimed that she was far too tired, having just got back. Nerissa—well, she was sitting curled up in the corner reading one of her interminable books, and did not appear to have heard or even to be aware of what was going on. So there Seta was—eager and willing to take on this task—indeed jumping up and down in anticipation, whilst Armineh sought a solution.

"Oh mother," said Olga, "for heaven's sake, get Maria to take it down—or even Abdul can take it. He's still outside with the carriage if we are quick about it."

"Never, you silly girl! You don't know what you are saying—it has taken me days to collect all this—I am going to see it safely into the hands of the Doctor or the Nurse at least. Haideh, come on Olga, do something useful for once and walk down with me."

But even as she asked, she knew that she did not need to await a reply, well aware that Olga would be most unlikely to help. "Nerissa . . ." she then called out. However, Sima standing at the kitchen door interrupted as Armineh turned to call Nerissa again, "Oh Mother, leave Nerissa be! Olga why don't you help Mother for a change?"

"Well, what about you—you've been sitting at home all day," snapped back Olga.

At this juncture, Armineh checked what was about to be her next caustic comment, and making up her mind, took control. She certainly was not going to trust any servant, and she was not going to walk down the street holding a bottle of urine herself. Finally, she also suddenly realised that it might after all be equally undignified to have one of her elder daughters do it for her in full public view.

"Well, well," she sighed, "Seta, you'll have to come with me after all," and still grumbling to herself, she handed the bottle to Seta and went to put on her hat.

All except Nerissa were now in the tiled hall. The irrepressible Seta, holding with desperate tightness the bottle wrapped in its discreet cover, stood excitedly by the door waiting for her mother finally to get herself ready for the outside world. As she stood there clutching the newspaper with her little hands, to her horror she suddenly felt thc bottle slipping. The harder she clutched at the paper the more the bottle slipped further and further through, in an inevitable downward movement, until eventually it fell right out of the wrapped-up newspaper and crashed onto the floor. All that carefully collected liquid poured out over the hall. Armineh took one look—plonked herself down on the seat in the hall and wailed, "Oh my God, my God! Even in my peepee, I'm not lucky."

Marie came bustling out of the kitchen into the hall to clear up the mess. Nerissa, who had finally deigned to leave her book, came out of the sitting room to see what was going on. Olga, laughing with sheer joy at the chaos behind her, grabbed Nerissa, and pulled her upstairs into her room.

"Nerissa, my love, I have arranged to meet a friend for tea at Tokatlian next week on the day the schools shut early. Will you come to town and join us? It'll be fun for you."

"Why me, Olga, who is your friend, do I know her?"

"Oh, my dear, just come and have a nice afternoon. We can go to the Bedestan together before, and look at what's in the shops."

"Olga, you're up to something, I can tell. You know that I'd love to come, but you must tell me what it's all about."

Olga sat on her bed and thought a little. Although Nerissa was just sixteen, Olga knew she was young for her age and sometimes rather shy. She read voraciously, mainly English novels of the previous century, and had romantic notions. But Olga did not think that she had any real idea of what it was like to feel a thrill for a young man, at least not like herself. She had certainly never had any really serious chats with Nerissa, and so at this moment she had no idea how Nerissa would react to the truth.

"Look, I'll tell you, but my darling, you must keep it to yourself. I've arranged to have tea with a student friend, a young man."

Nerissa's already large brown eyes opened wide as she looked steadily at her sister.

"You mean, without anyone else there, just you and, er, him?"

"No, silly, that's why I want you to come along too. We'll just have tea, listen to the music a bit, and come home."

"Olga, you can't—do Father and Mother know?"

"Certainly not! Don't be a ninny, Nerissa, it'll be an adventure. I'll tell mother that I am taking you shopping, and that we will stay out for tea together. She'll be well pleased that you're going out for a change—and with me. Come on Nerissa, there's nothing wrong about it. It's exciting. There'll be lots of army officers there."

Nerissa knew that her mother would be happy to let her go out for an afternoon with Olga. She had had a bad attack of rheumatic fever when she was eleven, and had had to stay at home for long months. As a result she got tired easily, and rarely went out, whilst her shyness sometimes left her somewhat isolated, even at the occasional dinner parties to which she went with the rest of the family. In her heart she felt that her mother worried little about her. Indeed, she had been well looked after during her illness, and she always had the sure knowledge of her parents' love for her, like all the Avakian children. Nevertheless, she felt that with so much excitement and exuberance emanating from all her sisters, her mother in a sense neglected her. It was clear that she would be pleased to be told that one of the two elder sisters was proposing to take her out.

Younger than Nerissa came the only boy in the family—Haik—now twelve, and after him, the bouncy ten year old Seta. It was natural that attention would focus on Haik, the only son in the family, and then after him on Seta, the charming and easy-going baby of the family. This left the rather solemn Nerissa with no one on either side, and this accentuated the introverted side of her character. However, she was very sensitive and knew perfectly well that there was more in this matter than she was being told.

"Olga, have I met this young man? Does he come to our church here, or does he go to one in town?"

Olga, suddenly thoughtful, looked at Nerissa steadily. Here in Nerissa's simple, unthinking words, was the first time that she was being confronted with the real issue. A little cold shiver ran through her, but it lasted only a few seconds. Then with a toss of the head and a smile, she dismissed the thoughts from her head, leant forward, and planted a big kiss on the astonished Nerissa.

"All right, Olga, but you must sort it all out with Mother."

"I'll look after everything—you'll have a lovely day!" Olga sang out, as she bounced out of the room, dragging Nerissa by the hand behind her.

Chapter 9

Constantinople. Vahan and Andre.

On the first day of his arrival in the city eight months ago, Vahan had of course eventually found his uncles. However it had become apparent to him after only a few days that he simply could not stay with either of them. Family relationships and obligations were of course, always, absolutely paramount in Armenian culture, and neither uncle would have ever considered asking Vahan to stay anywhere else. However, they had their own lives and families to think about, and the relatively unknown Vahan would have been bound to be a strain. Finance was no real problem. His father's contacts with the two or three carpet merchants of the city with whom he had business arrangements, ensured that Vahan could collect the allowance arranged by Garabed regularly and without difficulty.

Accordingly, within a month of his arrival, Vahan had found lodgings on the Stamboul side of the city with a Greek family which appeared to have fallen on difficult times and who were looking for a lodger. The family owned a small but delightful old Ottoman house set in a quiet cul-de-sac close to the Blue Mosque. This house overlooked the railway line running round the old sea walls, which eventually led round below the Topkapi Palace and into Sirkedji station. It was not possible from even the top storey of the house to see the Sea of Marmara, but it could be heard on quiet evenings.

Vahan, having avoided all the Armenian families to which he had been sent at his uncles' suggestions, moved in with this Greek family after much wandering and searching about the city. All this was taking place during the crucial month of August 1914. Vahan was intelligent, well-educated, and fully aware of what was going on in Europe; however it was all far away, and none of it appeared to him to be half as important as the vital and absorbing matter of finding himself a suitable place to live.

The Patakis family consisted only of females. The family comprised of two daughters, Elena and Maria, a heavy and overdressed mother Christina, and a formidable and sharp-tongued old grandmother. Christina's husband, the father of the two girls, had died recently, and it was his recent death and the subsequent collapse of his retail business selling 'lokum' (Turkish delight) and other sweets that had resulted in the family having to take in a lodger.

Vahan had been brought up in a large, extended family with several sisters. Nevertheless, the somewhat puritanical atmosphere of provincial Armenian life in the country had left him with no experience at all of dealing with girls of his own age. Maria Patakis was only fifteen, but she was a bright and lively girl, aware of everything going on around her. Elena, almost five years older, was quite different. She was a heavy woman with thick, sensual lips, hooded languorous eyes, and large well-developed breasts. She was dark, slow and ponderous, and highly sexed. She was clearly immediately challenged by the arrival in the house of this young, shy, and reserved Armenian boy from the provinces.

Vahan had arranged that he would take breakfast and the evening meal with the family, but that he would be out most of the day at the university. He was always punctilious in letting Christina know when he would not be at home for the evening meal. Father Komitas was reciting and lecturing on Armenian liturgical music in the city during those months in the evenings, and Vahan, a student of music, often attended these recitals.

Now, in April 1915, some eight months after his first arrival, Vahan raced downstairs, late for breakfast as usual. Christina and the old grandmother were still at table, but the young Maria had already left for school. Vahan did not have to be at the university for a couple of hours and relished having a quiet lengthy breakfast if he was allowed. Vahan sat to a long relaxed breakfast and recalled the chat that would take place round the Patakis dinner table in those weeks before the outbreak of the war and the arrival in the household of the disruptive Andre Tarkowski. Maria, always bubbling away with questions about the momentous events taking place around them; Elena, who couldn't say anything at all without some sort of sexual innuendo; Christina, who appeared to have her own agenda where the young Vahan was concerned; and the usually silent, but occasionally vituperative, old grandmother, always dressed in black, sitting toothlessly at the far end of the table.

It was nearly always Maria who would start up a discussion about something she had heard that day at school. Vahan recalled the very last dinner they had had some weeks after the war in Europe had started, the day immediately before the arrival of Andre. Maria had started the conversation as usual, once the family were all seated.

"Listen everybody—did you hear that the *Goeben* raised anchor this morning, sailed up the Bosporus, and then stopped opposite the Russian Ambassador's new house? You know, the one that used to be used as a summer house for the Khedive of Egypt. Well, it seems the ship turned round, broadside on to the road alongside. All the sailors stood in a line facing the house, took off their red fezzes, put on their German sailors' caps, and then sang 'Deutchland uber Alles' at the top of their voices. We heard that the Russian ambassador was furious and put in an official complaint to the old Grand Vizier. Isn't it all absolutely priceless?"

"Oh dear! What could the poor old man do about it anyway?" said Christina. "Enver and Talaat decide everything that goes on nowadays, and they aren't going to raise a finger."

"What do you think, Vahan?" said Maria, ignoring her mother, "Will we go to war with Russia?"

"I don't know, Maria, it certainly is getting to look more and more like it, but surely it would be a terrible mistake if we did. For over a hundred years we've balanced Russia on the one hand, against France and Great Britain on the other. Surely our present leaders wouldn't make the basic error of antagonising all three at the same time. No, no, surely not even our little Napoleon, Enver, would make that mistake, although heaven knows he has made just about every other possible mistake he could—the little jerk!"

"Vahan," interjected Christina, "you really must be more careful how you speak about our current leaders, you can get into trouble."

"But, Vahan, although we won't have the French or English helping us this time, Germany will be with us, and they can deal with Russia far better than the others. There's always those two ships with those great guns sitting in the harbour. No stupid Russki is going to get past them," said Maria.

"But, Maria, for heaven's sake, consider! Why should Turkey go to war? What can we possibly gain?"

"Oh well, everyone else is tripping off gaily to war so why not us. The silly old Russians think that after this war, if they win, they're going to grab Constantinople. So, wouldn't it be better to get the Germans to stop them?"

"Vahan, by the way, what do you say?" Elena, clearly bored had interrupted, "Will you come with me to Church on Sunday? Afterwards, we can walk to the Square and have a sherbet or something."

"Maria, just think about it," said Vahan hastily trying to ignore Elena's remark, "the Russians would only be able to grab the City, as you put it, if we made the mistake of abandoning our neutrality."

"Vahan, you never answered! Are you going to come with me on Sunday or not? You know you haven't even been to your own church once since you've been here—so why don't you accompany me?"

"Er!" Vahan had mumbled looking down at his plate, as Elena grumbled on at him, trying to catch his troubled brown eyes, "I'm not much of a church-goer," he continued lamely, not having the courage to say firmly that he had fast been losing the simple faith of his kindly mother each day that he remained in this town, the centre of so many different faiths.

Christina was well aware of Elena's interest in Vahan, and was happy to ensnare this young man with her daughter, despite her being at least two years older than him. With Elena now dowry-less, and getting on, she worried about her future. Here was a young man who clearly had a good allowance from his provincial parents, and who in any case was registered at the prestigious University. She pulled at his slender arm to get his attention and fixing her black eyes on him said, "Yes, Vahan, I would be most grateful if you could accompany Elena to church on Sunday, as I have to take Maria to meet her aunt, and clearly Elena must have an escort."

Vahan mused on the fact that he had started mumbling again, but he had known when he was beaten. He had realised that he really could not get out of it. He recalled that he had nodded, and then turning to Maria had burst out some political views which had been simmering in him for some time, somehow finding himself giving in to youthful enthusiasm in front of a group of people who really could not have cared less for his passionate but perhaps confused views.

"I don't think that the Russians will ever have Constantinople, whatever the English and French may be saying at the moment, Maria. Why should they? Apart from occasional visitors, there isn't a Russian in the town. This is a Greek city with an Ottoman overlay.

If Turkey joins this war and loses, the city could in the end become part of a tin-pot Greek nation-state, in which case maybe all the Turks and others may have to leave. If on the other hand the new xenophobic state being created by Enver and Talaat takes hold and wins, it could then become part of a vicious Turkish nation-state, in which case this time all the Greeks and everyone else will eventually have to leave. Either way, it will be the end of the glorious days of the old City. Perhaps, after all, we should all give our support to trying to make the old Ottoman Empire work, however flawed it may be."

Vahan recalled how they had all looked at him, surprised at his vehemence, as if he had been giving a lecture. He recalled feeling embarrassed. He was aware of his feelings of inadequacy at having failed to deal with the manipulation by Elena and her mother, to which he had so tamely submitted, and which may have triggered the outburst. At this point the old grandmother had got up and turning to Vahan as she went out had said, "And that, my dear young man, is the comment of a person who belongs to a people who have no hope of ever achieving a nation-state in the first place. Sour grapes, my lad—sour grapes! It's the sort of talk the Jews here in this city indulge in."

Vahan watched the retreating back of the spiteful old lady and said half to himself, "Well, you never know, even the Jews might create a nation-state for themselves one day—the question then will only be whether or not it will end up the same as all the others, with the same intolerance and exclusivity."

The old lady, always capable of hearing even the quietest words when she wanted to, turned and snapped back at the increasingly anxious and confused Vahan, who was not used to speaking like this to his elders, "That comment, little one, would apply equally to any tin-pot state your lot might one day manage to create." And she sailed out.

The next day, Christina having previously announced that the other attic room opposite Vahan's had now been let, Andre Tarkowski arrived at the house.

Andre turned out to be a Pole from Germany. He was a slim handsome young man, five years older than Vahan, with fair hair and grey eyes, and a slight military manner. Vahan never really discovered what he was doing or where he came from. Andre never denied that he was a German citizen, and it therefore appeared to Vahan from fairly early on, that he must either be in some sort of government employ, or be some sort of deserter or conscientious objector. He had turned up with two cheap suitcases, one of which remained locked and unopened under his bed. There was in addition an unusual tin case, also left locked under the bed.

Vahan, still sitting drinking his tea, chuckled to himself, as he recalled how Elena had almost immediately transferred her attentions from the shy Armenian boy to the confident Polish man. Right from the start this had let him off the hook. Even though he was presumably a Catholic, Andre had duly accompanied Elena that first Sunday to the Church, instead of Vahan. He had been escorting her on and off on a similar basis for the next few weeks.

Andre had exuded sexuality in every movement of his eyes and body. He and Elena, without any great objections from the complaisant Christina, often stayed out late, and as this was before Turkey joined the war, there was no curfew. Their heavy flirtation took over the household, leaving Maria confused and silent. For his part Vahan was fascinated and overawed by Andre. He was the first Catholic and Westerner that Vahan had ever come to know at all intimately. Andre used to come wandering into Vahan's room across the corridor in the evenings after getting back from being out with Elena. He would talk about general subjects, never politics or his own past. In particular, he would chat about girls and life in the great European cities, to all of which Vahan would listen with wide-open eyes.

One evening, arriving late from a Komitas recital, Vahan surprised Elena and Andre in the little space between the two rooms at the top of the staircase. They were passionately embracing, and Andre's hand was hidden somewhere around what Vahan could not help but see was Elena's dishevelled skirt.

Both of them turned and stared at him as he came up the narrow stairs. Vahan had had no idea where to look or what to say. His somewhat puritanical nature made him deeply embarrassed. They, on the other hand, did not appear to be the slightest bit put out and made no effort to hide the circumstances in which they had been found. Vahan had mumbled 'good night' and slipped past them and into his room.

That night, as he was undressing, Andre had come barging into Vahan's room—his eyes alight with sexual mischief and violence. "You're a virgin, aren't you, Vahan," he said, "You've never been with any kind of woman, have you? Good Heavens, I do believe that you haven't even yet kissed a girl." Andre laughed out loud, whilst the half-naked Vahan shuffled and stared and could say nothing.

"Oh, for heaven's sake don't look so solemn! Laugh, man, laugh! You're a good kid and I like you. You'll be alright one day. Look, have a look at this."

He pulled out two passports, both of which had clearly recently been issued by the British Embassy. Vahan, still unsure of what was going on, had seen that one appeared to be in the name of Andre Tarkowski, and the other in the name of Elena Patakis. Vahan remembered the shock he had felt, and his sheer incapacity to understand what was going on.

"Elena and I are leaving very early this morning from Haydar Pasha station for Jerusalem, from where we are going to go on to Egypt."

Vahan recalled that he had just stood and stared at him—shivering slightly as he was without shirt or vest. Andre, eyes glittering with sly malice and a hint of sadistic pleasure, had suddenly grabbed hold of him and drawing him close up to his body had kissed him fully, passionately and violently, on his lips, holding the astonished Vahan tight for several seconds. Then with a laugh he had pushed him back onto the bed, and strode out.

Vahan reflected that he had never seen either him or Elena again.

That morning, after a night in which Vahan had not slept, Christina, looking like an old woman, with her dark eyes red from weeping, had come up and cleared the room opposite, saying not a word to Vahan. She had broken open the cheap suitcase under the bed, and dragged it down, but the tin case had disappeared. Vahan had silently offered to help, but had been waved away. As he had glanced at the half-open case as she dragged it down, he had noticed that it seemed to contain some sort of uniform.

Three weeks later the *Goeben* and the *Breslau* had sailed into the Black Sea and Turkey had entered the War. Vahan finished his tea, yawned, called out 'goodbye' to the now always subdued Christina, and left for the university.

Chapter 10

Caesaria. Garabed Asadurian.

Garabed Asadurian was in every way a big man, both physically and morally. His marriage to his gentle wife, Mariam, had softened some of the sharper corners of his character, but he remained a forceful man with a strong temper and a certainty of his moral position in most circumstances.

Garabed had set his hand to many different trades and businesses, but it was as an entrepreneur in the carpet trade that he was best known. Armenian and Persian carpets at the turn of the century were made by hand with pure vegetable dyes in the mountain villages of the Armenian and Persian highlands, and often took families more than a year to make. Indeed, the really large ones, eventually to grace public rooms in London or Paris, could take several years to complete.

The loom would be set up for the carpet according to the size required. The loom itself was built by the father or some other male relative in a traditional form for the area, and according to the type of wood available. The basic design of the carpet would be drawn out and left alongside the loom. It was often just a piece of paper tucked into a crack in the wood. Then the slow painstaking task would be carried out, usually by the women and children after work in the fields, or in the winter throughout the whole day, whilst there was light.

Meanwhile, of course there was the question of where the money was coming from, both for the living expenses of the family and for the costs of preparing the cloth and dyes. It was in many cases affected by an arrangement between the family and their preferred entrepreneur-merchant with whom they often built up a close and mutually respectful relationship. The merchant would commission a carpet according to his own idea of the market currently available, he would agree a price with the family and then pay sums on account as the work progressed until the carpet was finished. He rarely discussed or questioned the design or colours, unless there was a specific request from a client for whom he was specifically commissioning the work.

The relationship was often a very close one with the effendi or bey from the city, when he visited, being asked for his advice on many matters—such as how to write a letter, or how to deal with some Ottoman official or other. Problems with the growing children in the family were discussed between the effendi and the two parents in the evening. This, of course, was one of the differences between the Christian families on the one hand, and the local Kurds and Turks on the other. For the Muslim families the women would not be involved at all in such matters, even though they may well have had the last word, once alone with their husbands.

"Effendim—please remain and accept my poor hospitality," would be the phrase which would signal the close of the purely business aspect of the meeting. Garabed, and latterly with his younger son Raffi alongside him, would then sit cross-legged on the villager's own faded carpet in their one big main room. Bowls of hot water would be brought in and hands and faces would be washed. The children would be introduced and led up to shake hands—it being known that Garabed was opposed to the older, more servile, hand-kissing.

Once the evening food was prepared and brought in, the women would join them—but unlike women in the city they would remain mainly silent. The night would be rounded off with the men smoking a communal 'narghile', tobacco smoked through bubbling rose water. Raffi would manfully try to join in, but never really managed, and would splutter and cough and only pretend to inhale. The guests would remain with their own bedding in the main room to sleep, and leave early the next morning with any completed carpets piled on the back of the donkeys.

The carpets, when finished and taken back to Caesaria, would then be sold at a fair profit to traders from Constantinople, who often would deal almost exclusively with their own favourite middle-man whom they might well have met at some stage. They would then market them to Western Europe with huge mark-ups. Needless to say, once the goods left the Empire, the biggest mark-ups of all would then be made in the smart carpet houses in Paris and London.

One of Garabed's more carefully cultivated families was that of Sarkis, son of Shahan. Sarkis farmed land in the mountains near the town of Malatya, about a hundred miles away from Caesaria. He had a large family, large even by local standards, with two boys aged eight and eleven, two older girls of fourteen and twelve, and two more girls all under seven. The nimble fingers of his children, and the native artistic intuition of his wife—Adrineh—meant that the carpets commissioned from this family were of a very high standard, and Garabed paid accordingly.

The cash generated had put Sarkis in a favourable position as far as his land-holding was concerned. He had accumulated the necessary capital to be able to purchase many of the tools and animals that his neighbours could not afford.

On the last occasion that Garabed had made one of these expeditions, just before the outbreak of the war, he had stayed the night with Sarkis, who had now registered a surname—Shahanian. In the evening, after the other children had left, Adrineh had indicated to her eldest daughter—Anna—that she could remain with the adults. Despite having borne eight children, Adrineh herself was still an attractive if somewhat buxom woman. Anna, thrilled at being able to stay, nestled up to her mother and listened as Sarkis raised one of his concerns with Garabed.

"Garabed, agha, whilst our relations with the local Turks whom I have known all my life remain perfectly amicable as always, we are having more and more difficulty with the officials from the town. My neighbour Mustapha Mahmud and his family have lived next to us all my life, and we work together at harvest time, and have never had difficulties between us. However, he told me that last month, when an Ittihad party official came on a tax assessment visit to our village, he had said to Mustapha and some others that we were not to be trusted, and that one day he hoped we would no longer be here. What does it all mean, Garabed agha? Both my family and Mustapha's have been here living alongside each other for generations."

"What does Mustapha himself say?" asked Garabed

"Oh! he just laughed and told me not to concern myself about what the educated city slickers said. They know nothing about the real way of life of we farmers, and the way the rhythm of the seasons and nature shaped our lives. He said we should all ignore all this shit about races."

"Well, he must be a wise man, this Mustapha. Keep him to your heart, Aram. What about the Kurds here?"

"Ah, well, sir, they are a different matter, I'm afraid. Many of them are landless, and are easily persuaded to go about in groups harassing the settled populations. I try to keep away from them. You know how it is. They shout 'giavour,' 'giavour' mindlessly and get excited and violent."

Garabed became a fairly influential man in Caesaria. During the violence which occurred in 1896, the mob, having been incited with official sanction during the Friday prayers in the main mosque of the town, rampaged through the town for two days killing as many Armenians as they could lay their hands on. Many local Armenians gathered in Garabed's house for safety. Garabed was the local 'mukhtar' (headman for the district). His house had walls 2 feet thick, with only a few windows looking onto the street—and those had iron bars across them. Most of the windows and rooms, like so many of the houses in the town, looked into the inner courtyard, which was totally private and used very much like a sitting room during the summer. The courtyard had a deep well situated in the middle, always providing clear fresh water.

This general massacre, unquestionably ordered and arranged from the office of the odious Sultan, Abdul Hamid, lasted only three days, during which time Garabed's house remained full of women and children, together with a few young men well-armed with many kinds of firearms. The three larger churches in Caesaria were also all filled with people who had locked themselves in. These churches were solidly built, almost like castles, with large high walls all round and which could be entered only by one or two heavy iron-clad doors. The mobs attacked all three, but armed with only axes and sticks and stones were unsuccessful. Nevertheless, many people numbering in the thousands were killed in Caesaria, and many more in other cities in Anatolia during these three days.

On the third day, the town crier began to go round the Armenian quarter shouting out, "All slaughter and pillage must end, this is on the direct order of the Sultan, our great Padishah, Abdul Hamid."

Then within about an hour Turkish soldiers and gendarmes began for the first time to appear on the streets. By then, however, the crowds had already begun to melt away, and the orders of the great and 'glorious' Padishah were being obeyed.

Garabed had two sons, Vahan and Raffi, neither of whom were alive at the time of these 1896 massacres. Each boy later recalled a different aspect of the story as to what had happened to Garabed at that time. The recollection of each, reflected their own character. Thus even a mere twenty years later the events had already achieved the status of a family myth, with the truth hidden for ever.

Vahan, in one of his many evening chats with his Polish acquaintance, Andre told him about these events and said, "My father spent the afternoon of the first day of those terrible three days going round warning his business friends of the rumours he had heard from Turkish associates of the coming storm. Hurrying home, as the officially sanctioned rioting started, he had to pass through a narrow lane with high walls on each side. Most of the old quarters of Caesaria were like this—the houses showing bare walls to the outside world, whilst the windows all opened out to the private inner courtyards. Standing at the end of the lane he saw some Turks, including the local seller of meat, who were all obviously hate-filled and bloodthirsty, looking for 'giavours' (Christian infidels—but in this case specifically Armenians) to murder. However, on recognizing my Dad, who already was the 'mukhtar' of the district, the butcher called out to the others who were clearly not locals, "Let him pass, let him pass," and shouted at Garabed, "Go through man, go through, and for God's sake keep your head down."

According to Raffi, however, on his way home on that day his father indeed had to pass through this narrow lane. However, here at the end of the lane, he saw the local grocer, a mean and vindictive character, standing alone. According to Raffi, this man, standing there with a large knife, clearly bloodcrazed, but alone, knew very well that Garabed was a brave man likely to put up a fight. Raffi, now he was sixteen, would then tell his listeners proudly, "So even with a big crazy knife in his hand, instead of risking his own life in a fight with father, he turned and faced the wall and called out, "Go away man, pass through."

As Garabed himself no longer spoke of these events, it was clearly impossible ever to distinguish between these two stories. Probably in all that excitement and anxiety Garabed returned home to his panicky family and blurted out what had just happened to him. In turn—probably ten years later—the story was repeated by mother or one of their sisters to the two boys. Then, as they began to grow up, the story grew in their minds in two different ways, reflecting their own separate characters, and their view of their own father. Both boys end up giving their father great credit but in different ways. Vahan, by suggesting that it was respect towards his father's character and position which made the local butcher turn away—Raffi, by suggesting that it was fear of his father which made the local grocer turn away. In the end it gives an insight into the respective character of the two boys, rather than saying anything about Garabed.

Garabed, as well as having two sons—Vahan and Raffi—had several daughters, who however much he loved them, simply did not count. He already had had three daughters before the birth of Vahan, and on the day that this, his fourth child, was to be born, he had gone off to work as usual, leaving instructions with the servants that if his wife gave birth to a baby boy they must send for him at once. If, however, it was to be another daughter, it would be all right for him to hear about it when he got home that evening.

That morning, in all the excitement of the birth of the first boy in the family, everyone forgot to send any message to Garabed. Accordingly, as he returned home that evening through the narrow streets, he was thinking that once again he had another girl to add to all the others.

Life in Caesaria revolved strictly round the seasons. The summers were very hot, and without much possibility of any relief. The winters, on the other hand, were bitterly cold, and indeed in the

Armenian highlands to the east it could stay at minus 40 degrees for long periods. There would be three months of heavy snow in Caesaria, and Garabed would often return home on winter evenings with threads of icicles hanging from his moustaches.

During the depth of the winter, Vahan and Raffi would fill the large well, which was about twenty-five feet deep, in the middle of the central courtyard, with snow. They would then put on their boots and jump about, and stamp down the snow until the well again became half empty—at which they would call for a ladder which would be let down to them and they would clamber out. The next day, they would again refill the well with fresh snow, and again yell and stamp it down, like pressing grapes, till once again they were below the level of the lip of the well. This would go on for several days until the well was full of hard packed ice and they could stamp it down no further. The well would then be covered up.

During the hot months of the following summer it would provide the household for a long time with ice and cold sweet water. When Garabed took the family off to the country house that he would rent on the slopes of Mt. Erciyas during those boiling two months, he would instruct the servants who remained to allow any of the neighbours in the little street in which the house stood to come in and take as much ice as they wanted.

Those long summer months were wonderful times for Garabed's boys. The country villa was about two hours ride away from the town centre. Garabed would go in to work two or three days a week, and would often take either Vahan, or later Raffi, with him riding on the back of the horse, holding Garabed tightly round his waist. There they would help—Vahan in the office with the books—Raffi, when it was his turn, in the cloth mill. The cloth was woven on fairly primitive wooden machines run entirely by hand, and worked by about a dozen men and boys—all Turkish. Raffi would join them on the days it was his turn to accompany his father, and work away with all the other young men who became his friends.

The relationship between Greeks and Armenians on the one hand, and the Turks on the other, was quite different to that in the sophisticated city of Constantinople. On the one hand in this provincial town, the Christian minority comprised almost exclusively the middle class of the town—both the professionals and the businessmen. As against this, again unlike in the capital city, the governors and the political leaders of the town were exclusively Turkish, without any minority representation, whether Christian or Jewish. The Turkish leaders here had a particular aversion to the Armenians, who were by far the largest of the minorities, whom they oppressed in minor irritating ways, ways to which the beys and pashas of Constantinople used to a more multi-cultural view would not have stooped. There was of course an irony in this, in that they often had more in common with the Greek merchants and Armenian bankers of the town than with the patient Turkish under class—often peasants, newly become townspeople.

On this early April day, still cold and wet in Central Anatolia, Garabed was becoming anxious and worried by the political situation that appeared to be developing. He was, however, certainly not more worried than would in any case be natural for any Armenian living in the midst of a volatile Turkish community in these clearly dangerous times. Unease was in the air. The Russians, enthusiastically supported by their own Armenian population were moving towards Van. There was an uncertainty about the loyalty of the Ottoman Armenian population. Could the Ottomans continue to think of their Armenian subjects as loyal citizens of the empire—particularly in view of the regular failures of the Hamidian regime to accept them as such—and to give them the ordinary rights of physical protection? Garabed continued to believe, against increasing evidence to the contrary, that the old Ottoman multinational view would prevail.

In the summer of 1914, Vahan had got his place at the University of Constantinople to study Music and Drama, and had left for the city. He never returned. Meanwhile, the rest of the family proposed to continue life as before—going to the summer house on the slopes of Mt. Erciyas at the height of the summer, and battening down the hatches for the bitter winters, without any thought for how those two shots in Sarajevo were going to change their lives for ever.

Chapter 11

Constantinople. Breakfast at the Avakians.

Once again, as this particularly clear and sunny April advanced, the Avakians were gathering, as they did every morning, for the family breakfast in the great family room in the centre of the house. Life for Nerissa, the third and most reflective of Karekin's four clever daughters, was usually fairly tranquil. She listened to her noisy family, putting in the odd pertinent comment every so often. She helped her mother with the younger children and she chatted to the servants.

There was a small Armenian school in the town which she still attended during the mornings. She was a voracious reader, particularly of English literature—Shakespeare and the Victorian romantic novelists. She had an excellent command of the language itself, a fact not been missed by Karekin. Karekin had accordingly already enrolled her in the sixth-form classes at the English High School for Girls in the city, where she would be starting in the Summer. Armineh was not so easily impressed. In her opinion, Nerissa wasted far too much time already, reading books and dreaming about impossibly romantic, and to Armineh's mind rather feeble, young male heroes.

Nerissa, like all her sisters adored and hero-worshipped her father, though not without in her case a small tinge of fear. However, she was clear-minded enough to see that it was Armineh who had to face the daily problems of plain ordinary living—all the silly pains and stresses of her children, their emotional crises, the running of the house—all of which Karekin took for so granted. Armineh's own feelings were that it was all very well for girls to have a liberal education, but what about husbands—and families!

Nerissa had just reached the age of sixteen. Still rather young for her age, she had a special affection for her twelve year old younger brother Haik, with whom she played and chatted in the large garden and walled orchard at the rear of their house. Olga and Sima were far too old and sophisticated for her. They did not often talk seriously to her, and this had thrown her back on the unaffected love and simple affection of her young brother.

Haik, himself, was a lively lad, as quick and as responsive as his clever sisters. He was however somewhat delicate physically, and although now twelve, he had retained childish, somewhat pretty and delicate features, with huge brown eyes, a clear pale skin and a thin, peaky long nose. He had only ever known unbounded love and adoration from a household of sensitive and comforting women, and consequently he trusted everyone, almost to the point of naivete.

Nerissa, for her part, despite the fact that in this bright chatty household she was the quietest and most introverted of the children, had a complex character. She was not conventionally pretty, having inherited her mother's rather dumpy figure. Her nose was that little touch too large, her lips too full. She was however undoubtedly the cleverest of all the children. She was highly critical of what she saw as the heavy ambition of Sima, her eldest sister, and also what she viewed as the shallow flirtatiousness of Olga, whom she saw as a complete lightweight. She was quite unjustified in both cases—and this only reflected the intellectual arrogance of a sharp sixteen year old. She was filled with the romantic ideals of the great English novelists of the previous century, but somehow these ideas did not attach themselves at this stage in her mind to any specific male figure. She desperately wanted her ideal of a Romeo to get his Juliet, but it was all vague and dreamlike, rather than practical.

Nerissa was used to Olga's on-again, off-again ways, and accordingly never really expected to be taken up on the arrangements to which she had tentatively agreed. It was therefore with real surprise that she heard from Olga on this very morning as they all came down to the table in the great central hall of the house. It appeared that they were to go that afternoon to tea at Tokatlian as agreed.

"Nerissa, my love, there is no need for you to walk home from school this afternoon—I'm going to pick you up, and we're going to go to tea at Tokatlian."

"Olga—what do you mean—it's going to be this afternoon! What shall I wear?" wailed Nerissa.

"My dear—you'll be coming from school—just take a scarf or a shawl or something with you—for heaven's sake we're only going to have some tea and cakes and a chat."

Nerissa looked at her mother Armineh who was as usual fussing around the spare and delicate Haik, trying to get him to do more than just peck at his food.

"Mother, did you know that Olga has invited me to go to tea with a friend of her's at Tokatlian this afternoon, after school?"

"My girl," replied Armineh somewhat distractedly, "Olga has already told me—do go if you want to, it'll be a change for you. Now, Olga, mind you make sure that you are both back before six o'clock, and don't walk up from the station, wait for Abdul or Mustafa, even if they are not there when you get off the train."

Nerissa was half hoping that her mother would object. She had been careful not to tell a lie, but she was aware that there was an element of deception in what Olga was planning, and it made her uncomfortable.

Karekin, as always already fully dressed for the outside world, came down and sat at the end of the table in front of his plate of home-made bread, cheese and olives, and a little honey. Maria poured out his tea into his usual glass with a slice of lemon already in it. This was a beautiful engraved example of an old Ottoman tea-glass, used only by him.

"Haik, my boy, don't give your mother such a hard time, just eat up. Armineh, stop fussing over him, he's not going to waste away."

"Father," piped up Haik, "when are you going to take me to the office as you promised one day?"

"I told you, you'll have to wait until the summer holidays. In any case, with this dreadful war there is precious little to do. Armineh, did I tell you that I've had to let Leon and Berge go? There's just not enough work. In any case the government is tightening up on young men with deferment, and the army is certainly going to have them soon in any case."

"Is there any news in the papers of what is happening in Van and Erzerum?" asked Armineh.

"It's serious, my dear, that I can certainly tell you. I'm going to go down to the Patriarchate this morning to find out if there is any more hard news—but the regime is extremely jumpy, the general atmosphere is tense, and I don't like the signs at all. I think for the next few days, Sima, you must go with Haik when he goes to school, and either you or one of the servants must go in the afternoon to pick him up. There was an anti-Armenian demonstration yesterday outside the Bazaar. It was broken up by the police eventually—but only half-heartedly, and only after several shop windows had been smashed."

He turned to Olga. "Now Olga, listen, I must say that. . ."

"Oh father, I'm sorry I've simply got to dash. You know I've got to catch the earlier train than you."

Olga jumped up before Karekin could finish, and ran out grabbing her coat and bags in the hall. She called back to Nerissa, "Remember Nerissa, I will be at your school to pick you up at about two o'clock in the afternoon."

Karekin looked vexed, and was again about to make a comment before Olga had vanished, when Sima forestalled him with a hint of anxiety, rising from her seat.

"Come on, Haiky—finish up! Let's go."

"Aw, Baba, I'm twelve, and I don't need to be taken to school by anyone any more. The other boys will all laugh at me," wailed Haik, looking stubborn.

Karekin rose from his seat. He was clearly angry and at the end of his patience. His face darkened. Even though he was a fair man he felt a deep anger rising in him. He was totally unaware that his anger was rooted in the vague disquiet he was feeling about Olga, a disquiet he could not quite pinpoint. This was coupled to the perpetual nagging worries about the worsening political situation that was threatening not only his family circumstances, but even their very lives, and that now lay at the pit of his stomach every day.

Karekin never raised a hand to any of his children, but when roused he exerted authority absolutely and automatically, and he tended to be very much harder on his only son than on his four clever girls. Nerissa, sensitive as always to atmosphere, opened her eyes wide, fearful of the coming explosion. But Armineh and Sima were quicker and a good deal more practical than Nerissa. Armineh, pretending that Karekin had risen to prepare for his departure, quickly handed him a list of things she had already prepared and which she wished him to fetch on his return from the market, whilst Sima jumped up, tweaked Haik's ears and ushered him out of the room, whilst he complained vociferously.

"Come on, little man, let's get you ready. Don't worry Haik, my mouse, I'll leave you well before the school gates."

Haik, of course had no idea that he had narrowly avoided a very uncomfortable five minutes, due to the efforts of his mother and elder sister.

Karekin, aware in his own heart that some sort of manipulation had taken place, quietly took his hat and coat from Armineh, who looked straight into his eyes, and gave him a kiss—to his surprise right on his lips, even in front of everyone. The tide of anger that had come over him and which he had been about to unleash on Haik, had had nothing really to do with the boy at all. There were worries and anxieties all over the place, and he did not know on which one to concentrate. The news from the Caucasian front during January and February had been bad enough, but that coming from Van was devastating if it was true. He determined to check the latest position at the Patriarchate that very morning. Karekin hurried out and walked straight to the station—no sitting on benches and musing these days.

Once he arrived at the city, ignoring as best he could the tense atmosphere now rampant in the streets of Stamboul every day, as if the town was waiting for a storm to burst, Karekin hurried to the quiet calm of the Patriarchate buildings. Crossing the courtyard, he knocked at the door of Father Haroutioun, one of the secretaries to the Patriarch and a personal friend. He walked into the little room, where his friend was seated at a small desk in front of an old typewriter and several bundles of paper

"Enough rumours, Haroutioun. Hard news—hard news! What is actually happening in Van and the Armenian vilayets?"

The little priest looked up. His eyes were red, and he was shaking and his voice quavered, "My dear friend, I don't know for sure as the news from Van is clearly being censored—but there is obviously some sort of insurrection or trouble there. The army is certainly involved in some way. But it is not only Van. I do believe that something really terrible is about to happen in the interior, even if it has not already started. If the reports are true, nothing like it has ever been seen before. Believe me, Karekin, we're going to look back on Abdul Hamid and his whimsical and random barbarities with nostalgia, when faced with what may be the beginning of a deliberate calm policy of getting rid of a whole population! The more I read of the decrees and proposals emanating from Talaat's office, the more I fear for what may be planned for the future."

"For heaven's sakes man, pull yourself together. All you clerics are the same. You just can't help yourselves making grand moral judgements. Just give me the facts—I'll decide what we have to fear, if anything. For God's sake, Turks have been killing Armenians for centuries, and probably for all I know the other way round as well, so what's different now?"

Haroutioun hung his head in his hands.

"I don't know, Karekin, there's no word for it at the moment. Perhaps the world will make up a word if it ever happens again to someone else, but believe me something evil is about to happen right now in the villages and little towns of the interior. Here, I have prepared a precis of the reports we have been receiving from the interior, from our priests, and from German and American missionaries. Here, take it, read it and let me know what you think."

Karekin always balked at the word 'evil'. A good well-educated liberal did not believe in evil as such.

"Father, everyone is jumpy and nervous. With the failure of the British fleet to break through the Dardanelles a few weeks ago, we all know that they are going to try again with their army soon. So, of course we're all treading delicately on eggs. But, Father, we don't need to talk about 'evil', and start thinking about 'terror' or 'apocalyptic visions'. We're at war and this sort of panic and rumour happens in such circumstances. One of the prices of living in and being part of a multi-national empire like ours is the danger of racial tensions arising like this at moments of crisis. However, we have a duty to try and minimize it. Talking about evil can have the effect of making it happen."

"Karekin, I do hope you're right and I fervently pray that I am wrong. I know I'm a timid and fearful man, but I do sense something different about our new masters, something totally alien to the old Ottoman ruling class under whom we have muddled along for so long."

Karekin straightened up. He looked down at the little man and picked up the bundle of papers. Then, on instinct, he bent down and planted a strong and heartfelt kiss on the man's forehead, and walked out, ignoring the sign of the cross tentatively raised towards his retreating back by the nervous priest.

Chapter 12

Van. The uncontested historical background.

The much vaunted winter offensive by the Turkish Third Army into the Caucasus had been a complete catastrophe. Against the advice, not only of the weary but canny old Ottoman generals, but also of most of the members of the German military mission, including General Liman von Sanders himself, the dapper and supremely self-confident Enver Pasha had overridden all opposition, and marched a badly supplied and totally unmotivated army into some of the most difficult terrain in the world. It had been a devastating experience for the Third Army, which had lost all its artillery and about 75,000 men, leaving only a small force of about 30,000 demoralised men to cover the whole Erzerum region.

Enver Pasha himself had returned to Constantinople towards the end of January. His arrogance and Napoleonic pretensions had not been the slightest bit dented. On his return he made every effort to conceal the truth and to represent the catastrophe as nothing more than a local setback. He was totally indifferent to the dreadful suffering of the ordinary soldiers, huge numbers of whom died of frostbite. On the matter of the possible political fall-out, however, he was very sensitive, and he immediately began searching for some scapegoat to take the blame for his own ineptitude.

In London, the Russian victory had strengthened the position of those who favoured an attack on Turkey. At first, the Russians had asked London to mount a diversion by some naval or military demonstration anywhere, so as to divert some Turkish forces away from the Caucasus front. However, within days of receiving this request early in the winter of 1915, it soon became apparent to the British government that the Russian Caucasian army was no longer in need of any assistance.

Instead, the scale of the disaster to Enver's Third Army seemed to make the proposal for a direct attack on Constantinople more attractive in London. The whole course of the currently stalemated war could be changed. The fall of their capital would undoubtedly throw Turkey out of the war, whilst the opening of the Straits to Allied shipping would give enormous help to the ever-weakening Russia and stave off any possible internal unrest. Certainly, by February the British government was ready to take up some offensive option against Constantinople. New approaches were accordingly made to the Russians as to whether some sort of diversionary operation could not now be mounted by them—perhaps towards the Bosporus, the northern approach to the great city.

The Russians were fairly ready to comply, but as always Admiral Eberhardt—the Russian naval commander in the Black Sea—remained cowed by the presence of the *Goeben* and the *Breslau* in the Straits. The Russians were in a total dilemma. On the one hand there was the old Russian obsession with Constantinople, the centre of their own Orthodox faith, the controller of the vital narrows which led to the only Russian outlet to an ice-free warm sea and the great sea-lanes of the world. On the other hand this had to be balanced against the power of these two great battleships to cripple the Russian fleet, and to disperse with enormous loss of life any expeditionary force the Russians might contemplate to aid any British initiative.

In the end the Admiral prevailed in the Russian deliberations. The continuation of a 'fleet in being' seemed to be more important than any help to the British. After all, from the Russian point of view, a successful capture by the British of the great city was almost as bad as a dramatic failure, and accordingly no diversionary or supporting plan was ever made.

Once again the two battleships had decisively affected history by simply being there.

Meanwhile, back on the Caucasian front, as the harsh winter gave way to a fairly mild April, the Russians began a tentative advance towards the city of Erzerum, in an effort to take advantage of the much depleted Ottoman forces. This was wild and inhospitable country, farmed mainly by a patient and tenacious Armenian peasantry settled there for centuries, with the main towns fairly evenly split between Turks and Armenians, with majorities of one or the other in each. Interspersed with these, roamed fairly lawless nomadic Kurdish tribesmen. As the Russians advanced they naturally tried to exploit these age-old differences to obtain as much support as possible.

The Armenian situation in the high plateau heart lands of the Caucasus and Eastern Anatolia was very difficult. Nowhere, except in one or two of the great cities, were they in a clear majority. It was all very well for sophisticated liberal merchants living in Constantinople to remain loyal to the greater Ottoman ideal of a tolerant and multi-cultural empire. The situation for the peasantry of the wild and mountainous areas of Eastern Anatolia was quite different. Here the mixture of races and religions, coupled to the poor soil and the harsh conditions, had led to the opposite result of intolerance and hate. Here petty officials could and did stoop to trivial tyrannies and irritations against a generally peaceful minority. Here, with a part of the same people living just across the border in Imperial Russia, loyalties, impossibly strained by the terrible Hamidian pogroms of the 1890's, were much more complicated.

As always, the majority of the population were passive, tilling the soil, weaving their carpets, and celebrating age-old traditions at Easter and Christmas and the other great festivals, without too much regard to the troubles around them. But if trouble was to come, it would inevitably fall on this patient uncommitted majority, the family men and their wives and children, who just wanted to get on with their lives. It would not fall on the revolutionaries or activists seeking change.

Early in April, the Turkish High Command, well-aware of the worst-kept secret of the whole war—namely the likelihood of an Anglo-French landing somewhere in or near Constantinople—realised that they needed to shore up the Caucasian front. Here, the remnants of the Turkish Third Army were now being led by an irascible old Ottoman general—Halil Bey—not a member of the Ittihad, but connected to Enver by marriage. He led a scratch force of several battalions of regulars, some bits of artillery, and a great mob of Kurds. He had already complained that there was one major lack for all the forces in the area, and that was proper medical services.

General Yudenich, on the Russian side, gave the greatest attention, like all good commanders, to the welfare of his troops. Supplies and sanitary and medical services were, in the context of Imperial Russia, mainly excellent. This had not been the case with Enver Pasha. The Young Turks as a group were full of high philosophical ideas—Pan-Turanism, nationalist fervour, Western style modernisation, lots of grand Napoleonic visions—but this was allied to a reliance on the dumb patient endurance of the Turkish peasant, for whose welfare they were not in the slightest degree concerned. Whatever the faults of the old regime—and they were many—the old Ottoman Pashas did have some realisation that armies were on the whole more efficient if they were properly supplied and medically cared for.

In the area of Lake Van and the valley of the upper Euphrates, a mob of irregular Kurdish tribesmen, ostensibly part of Halil's force, had put the whole country into a state of tense anarchy. No one—villagers, townsmen, tenant farmers, Armenians or even Turks—felt safe, although of course it was the Christians who were the principle sufferers.

Meanwhile in the city of Van itself, a particularly vicious Ittihad Governor, Djevdet Bey, who had recently taken over from the previous enlightened Ottoman Pasha, had been deliberately goading the Armenian majority by acts of petty tyranny and worse. At last the exasperated and increasingly desperate population of the city of Van, driven to extremity by the tyrannies of the Ittihad Governor and the lawlessness in the countryside around, rose in what appeared to be a revolt. Exploding out of the narrow streets of their quarter, and after fierce fighting between armed young Armenian men on the one hand, and the demoralised garrison and gendarmerie on the other, the Armenians took possession of this ancient city by the lake at the end of the second week in April.

This revolt had nothing to do with Enver's retreat earlier in the year. It remained the spontaneous rising of a population driven to despair. The elements in it were as diverse as revolts tend to be everywhere, although of course the professional nationalists and revolutionaries inevitably soon took over. General Yudenich, well informed of the situation, decided to take immediate advantage of it and ordered infantry units of his advancing Fourth Caucasian Army group to switch their advance towards the beautiful town on the lake. At the same time he mounted a large Cossack cavalry raid through the increasingly lawless Kurdish tribal areas with a view to making an impressive show of force and clearing some of the brigandage rife in the area.

Halil Bey, hearing of the revolt, moved his regulars up to take back control of the city, before the Russians could arrive. Thus it was that the siege of Van, which was to last for weeks, commenced. By the time Halil's regulars moved up to take over the siege from the Governor's scratch forces, his large mob of Kurds attached to the force had deserted, abandoning him and his Turkish regulars. These Kurdish tribesmen were prepared to harry defenceless peasant settlers—a favourite pastime of nomadic people through the ages—but were in no way prepared to act as docile cannon fodder for the Turkish government. Accordingly they had disappeared to join and profit from the general anarchy as soon as they could.

Chapter 13

Van. Dr. Nazim Kemal and the Turkish view.

Back in the capital, Doctor Nazim had been continuing his work at the German hospital. The closure of the French hospital had added to the workload, and he was continually in demand. His criticisms of the Ittihad in general, and Enver and Talaat in particular, had not changed. However, he did modify his comments in public, as he felt that as the Empire was obviously in difficulties, the government should be supported as far as possible. However in private and over the breakfast table he was more outspoken.

"Nazim," said Halideh one morning early in April, "I heard in the ħammam yesterday that Enver is saying that nothing particularly important happened in the Caucasus a couple of months ago during the winter."

"Well, my dear, that is clearly not true, as many of our soldiers died. The number of our men suffering and dying from frostbite was enormous, and I have had this confirmed by several of my colleagues in the medical service, quite apart from the fact of the enormous number of men still in pretty bad conditions at the military hospital at Scutari."

"Nazim, I also heard that he is claiming that a lot of help had been given to the Russians by Armenian irregulars operating in the area, even some who were of Ottoman nationality. Furthermore, that appears to be the reason for the defeats."

"Oh, mother," said Selim, "that sounds like pure propaganda, and even downright lies. In any case, isn't he saying that there were no defeats anyway?"

"Yes, that could be so," said Nazim, who suddenly had the fleeting thought that Selim seemed to be always on the defensive these days whenever Armenians were mentioned.

"Frankly, I am quite sure that Enver made a real mess of the whole offensive. I think that General Yudenich, or whatever his name is, out-manoeuvred him from the start. He is now clearly looking for a scapegoat on whom to blame for his own shortcomings. However, my opinion is that the Armenians themselves are making it easier for him by their ambivalence towards this war. My son, I believe that it was a fatal, terrible error to get into this war at all—but now we are in it we must all rally round the only government we have. They are our soldiers—they must be supported. And that reminds me, son, what we say together between us can be as outspoken as we may wish—but outside!—Look, son, you must learn to keep your opinions to yourself a bit more. We live in difficult and dangerous times. Abdul Hamid's secret police might have been disbanded, but instead we have a mindless mob, listening out for treasonable defeatism."

"Oh, baba, you know I'm all in favour of the Ittihad ideas in principle. I don't even think it was all that wrong to get into this war. We've been pushed around enough by those arrogant Westerners already. No, it's those jerks, Enver and Talaat!"

It was some days after this conversation that Nazim heard that he was to be drafted into the Army as a Major, as his medical and administrative services were going to be required on the Caucasian front. It appeared that the upright but irascible Halil Bey—a Muslim gentleman of the old school—had insisted on an increase in the medical services for his small force situated near Lake Van.

There had been little time for Nazim to deal with all his affairs. He had been continually out of the flat, since receiving his commission, gathering together a scratch medical team to come with him as a supplied and out-fitted army medical unit. On that last day when he had at last left, he had pressed Halideh to him hard as they parted in the little hall of their flat in Galata. She, herself had run to the window as the front door closed. She looked down into the street, as he emerged down below from the entrance of the building. Nazim, in his clean new uniform was carrying his own personal medical bag of surgical instruments. Selim stood alongside his father, carrying his bags.

Selim hailed a passing gharry, and stepped in, taking the bags with him. Nazim turned and looked up for about ten seconds at the window, behind which he knew that Halideh would be staring down. He made no grand gesture, save ever so slightly to raise the palm of his right hand in a discreet salute. He then stepped into the carriage to sit next to Selim.

"The ferry station for Haydar pasha station, driver!" he called out.

Selim and his father were silent as they drove down the hill to the Galata Bridge. They remained largely silent as the ferry chugged its way across the straits and pulled alongside the ferry landing stage for the Haydar Pasha terminus of the Asian railway system.

As they got off and slowly began walking up to the station, Nazim said, "My son, when we get to the station I will be distracted and busy as I am after all in charge of several men who will be waiting there for me. There are a couple of doctors and several staff who will all need to be sorted out. We will not be able to talk. My boy, in case anything happens—you know what I mean—your first duty remember must be to your mother and sister. That done, your next duty is to fulfil yourself. Don't my son hurry to give up your deferment. Make sure you complete your education before rushing off to war, if you have the chance that is."

Selim shuffled. His heart welled up, and he felt a little sick as he looked at his dapper smart well-shaven father.

"Baba, are we fighting a religious war . . . our enemies, Russians or . . . whatever . . . are Christians aren't they. I mean . . .

"No, my son, not at all. This is a totally secular war and nothing to do with religion. The Ittihad may have made a bad mistake in joining in, but there's no doubt that the Empire is beset by predators all round, and we simply have to defend our way of life."

"Father, are we obliged to hate as well I mean, suppose I knew a Russian lady who was a friend, would it be . . . . I mean . . . I don't know, wrong to be friendly with an enemy of the state."

"Don't be silly son, there's nothing wrong with friendship at any level with anyone, so long as it goes no further than that. Life is changing, I accept that, and there's no reason why you can't converse with girls of your own age and class, and make friends. For god's sake don't repeat this to your mother, by the way! I know Selim that you will always be honourable and just in your dealings, and that is all that matters."

"Yes, Father, that's all very well, but what . . .

"Major Kemal," said a soldier, coming forward and saluting, as they stood in front of the station which they had now reached. "Your unit is awaiting on Platform 2. The medical supplies are currently being loaded at the freight depot, and it is felt, Sir, that you are needed to supervise the loading."

Nazim turned to Selim, smiled, clasped his shoulder, and then without another word turned and strode into the station followed by the young soldier now carrying the bag, reluctantly relinquished by an emotional Selim, who stood fighting tears as his father walked away.

The train had slowly made its way to the east, where Nazim had been ordered to join Halil Bey, whom he believed was involved in trying to hold back the Russians moving towards the towns of Erzerum and Van.

On his arrival, Nazim reported directly to Halil Bey, whose HQ was in Bitlis, some miles away from Van.

"Your Excellency, I have the honour to present myself, Major Nazim Kemal, Doctor and Surgeon, with a small medical team raised in Stamboul about a week ago."

"Sit down, Major, sit down. I'm sure you would like to have a coffee." Halil called out to his orderly "Khave! Shekerli?"

Nazim nodded and sat down.

"I am not sure, Major, how much you know of the situation here. I doubt if the government has been at all open in its reporting in the capital of the position here. In fact I know the news has been carefully censored. The Governor here is an arrogant bastard by the name of Djevdet Bey—the new Ittihad breed you understand—who has made a mess of his relations with the infidel Armenians, who incidentally happen to be a majority in this town. Can't stand the fellow myself, but of course this is no excuse for the cursed infidels to revolt. Infamous traitors the lot of them, when you think that the Russian army is close by and moving forward daily."

"What forces do we have available, Sir" asked Nazim.

"Well, I have a military gendarme division, together with four battalions of regulars. Until a few days ago I also commanded, if that's not too strong a word, a mob of Kurdish irregulars, undisciplined and frankly pretty useless except to terrify women and children. Honestly, what a shower! For better or worse they have all melted away and are over in the east pillaging everything they can lay their hands on, which at least gives the pesky Russkis and the Armenians something to think about. Look, this leaves me with about six thousand men, of which over half are now manning the siege lines we have drawn round the city."

"Well sir, I'm amazed. I have some Armenian acquaintances in Stamboul, and I had always supposed them to be fairly loyal to the state, despite their awful experiences under the regime of Abdul Hamid. However, a revolt like this in the face of an invading enemy army is totally inexcusable whatever the provocation. I'm appalled. What numbers and strength are we talking about."

"I don't know, Major. They certainly can't have much ammunition, and they must be using boys and old men. So far as my intelligence officers have been able to gather, the actual numbers facing us with weapons are not much more than about a thousand. Frankly, Major, once we get fully organised we will have them totally dealt with in a couple of days. For the moment they are simply being contained, and that ridiculous strutting idiot the Governor is still in charge. I want you to move your detachment up to the lines as soon as possible, after which I am going to open up a proper military offensive, with eventually a final push to eliminate the bastards. You may dismiss, Major, but please report any problems direct to me."

The next day, when Nazim arrived at the lake-side behind the Turkish siege lines, he looked down at the town, with its walled old city dominated by a castle on a rock, sitting perched by the beautiful deep blue lake, bordered by magnificent mountains still lightly covered with snow. He pinpointed the spot where he would set up his headquarters and went to work.

In his customary cool and efficient way he busied himself with seeing to the setting up of his main tent as a military hospital, and spent the following day inspecting the Turkish front lines drawn around the Armenian quarter of the town. He made many recommendations as to the primitive sanitary arrangements, and slowly, by dint of persuasion rather than confrontation he managed to improve the conditions for the rank and file soldiers in many small but significant ways. The Turkish artillery, meanwhile, both the rather light and old-fashioned pieces in the lines, and the cumbersome cannon on the Rock, poured shell after shell into the old town below.

Nazim worked tirelessly, day and night, tending the wounds and disfigurements of the Turkish soldiers coming back day after day from the continuous gunfire around the old city. Unlike the Ittihad leaders, he slowly came to learn a new respect, which he had never felt before, for the illiterate and inarticulate Anatolian soldiers, who bore their pains so uncomplainingly. Night after night the talk would turn on the question of when the city would fall, and how or why the rebels were still holding on, when by now, surely, their ammunition must be exhausted.

Nazim, himself, punctilious as ever, shaved carefully every day. He spent his spare time writing letters home to Selim and his wife. He never complained in these letters of anything except about the days of boredom, which so often interspersed with the days of violent action. He did however sadly report to his son that the rebellion of the inhabitants of Van, right in front of the Ottoman's historic enemy, had soured his attitude to the Armenians for ever. It was totally clear to him that there could be no excuse at all, regardless of any provocation, for raising a revolt right in front of an advancing enemy army, when your country was in mortal danger.

Chapter 14

Van. Dr. Clarence Ussher. The neutral position.

Van was one of the most beautiful cities in the Ottoman Empire, surrounded by gardens and vineyards which were well-tended and prosperous. It stood on ground that gently sloped down to the deep blue lake—Lake Van—which is itself surrounded by gaunt and steep mountains. Some miles from the shore lies the island of Akhtamar, covered in greenery, with a serene and beautiful old Armenian church set amongst the trees in the centre, where families, Turks as well as Armenians, would go to picnic in the warm summers.

Just outside the old walled town, in the middle of the Armenian quarter, lay the American Protestant Mission. The buildings, all surrounded by a high stone wall, comprised a Protestant church, several schools, a hospital and dispensary, and residences for the staff. Five minutes' walk away was the German orphanage run by two old ladies. All around were the old Ottoman houses, all in various stages of picturesque dilapidation with their wooden lattice bay windows, sticking out over the street.

The American Mission was led by Doctor Clarence Ussher who was not only in charge of the hospital and the medical supplies, but was also in overall control of the whole Mission. He was helped by his wife, an elder sister, and several Armenian nurses.

Clarence Ussher was the son of a Canadian Episcopalian bishop from a family of devout Christians who had provided Church leaders for generations. He was a large bearded man with a soft round face and gentle eyes, but who had a clear hard inner core the moment he felt certain of his moral position. Like so many in the missionary world, this moral certainty came to him often. He was never at a loss as to what was the right course of action. Doubt never crossed his mind, and this gave him an inner source of conviction, which carried him benignly through circumstances which could have broken many others.

He was a competent general doctor but with fairly good additional surgical skills. An efficient administrator, he was supremely confident and self-controlled. His wife, herself the daughter of a missionary, had been born in Caesaria in Central Anatolia. They both spoke Turkish fluently, and they both had that somewhat narrow dedication of those 'driven' nineteenth century missionaries everywhere. Having over the years failed to convert more than a handful of Turks, they turned their attention to good works and trying to convert one of the oldest Christian communities in the world to their own Protestant beliefs. Not surprisingly, this had not endeared them to Armenian clerics. Furthermore, it had contributed to the loose nationalistic fervour which had been irresponsibly aroused in the vulnerable Armenian peasantry.

Dr. Ussher had been a fairly close friend of the previous Turkish governor—Ahmed Fari Pasha. Fari had been an Ottoman Pasha of the old school, anxious to maintain good relations between all his subjects. Before the secular Young Turks had deprived him of his post at the start of the war, the old Vali, always interested in theological subjects, had delighted in evening dinner parties with the clerics of the various religious sects in the town. On one occasion, the guests were taking their coffee after a meal given by the Vali, at which Clarence Ussher was one of the guests. He was there together with a Nestorian deacon, a Chaldaean Catholic bishop, and a Sufi divine, amongst others. The Vali turned to the Bishop and said, "My Lord Bishop, what then must I do to be sure of getting into Paradise?"

The good Bishop, who had imbibed, not at all wisely but certainly far too well, the excellent wine, which the Vali had thoughtfully included, replied, "I believe your excellency, that for Jesus' sake, the Lord will pardon my sins and allow me into paradise in all circumstances."

The Vali was clearly disappointed at what he considered a facile turn-off. Ussher immediately intervened, and taking the Vali's comment seriously, believing after all that the question was one of the most significant that any man could raise, went into a long debate into the theological differences between Christian and Muslim teaching on this all-important matter. The two of them debated late into the night, much to the boredom of the three clerics in the party.

This old Vali was immediately suspect in the eyes of the Ittihad Committee of Union and Progress, once they had achieved clear power over the old Ottoman system.

The Ittihad leaders knew, without the need for any spies' reports, on whom they would be able to rely, if and when they decided to have a showdown with their minorities. They were aware that to facilitate their xenophobic and almost genocidal intentions, they would also first have to get rid of the old Ottoman ruling class. This was not just because they were fuddy-duddy old-fashioned conservative gentlemen unable to come to terms with the new Westernised Turkey they wished to create, although this, certainly, was the ostensible reason they were dismissed. Rather, it was because the new leaders knew full well that however inefficient and lazy the old Ottoman ruling class may have been, their traditional conservative instincts would not have allowed them to connive at the terrible events which they were planning.

Accordingly, after the take-over by the Committee of Union and Progress, the old Ottoman Governor Ahmed Fari had been dismissed, and the governor of the vilayet of Van became one Djevdet Bey—a brother-in-law of Enver Pasha, a cold and arrogant official of the new nationalist school, neat and always elegantly dressed, with the ubiquitous heavy toothbrush moustache, the well-groomed red fez, swimming in French perfume, and very smart and smooth.

On his return from Enver's disastrous offensive, Djevdet Bey immediately began developing a confrontational policy towards the majority Armenian population. In the second week of April, when disturbances broke out in a suburban area of the town he arranged for four Armenian leaders to go to the area to try to calm down the position. There, he had them murdered by a special police detachment under his direct orders, and he then arrested the Armenian member of Parliament who was in the town, and sent him back under arrest to Constantinople.

At this juncture the remaining Armenian leaders, desperately seeking a compromise offered Djevdet Bey a large ransom to compound the current shortfall of recruits, as if no one had ever heard of the Inca Atahuallpa and his roomful of gold. However, at the same time, they also approached Dr. Ussher asking him to intercede with Djevdet Bey. He agreed to visit the new Governor, whose family he had known in happier days. Djevdet Bey, however, remained obdurate, and professing to be worried about the security of the American Mission stated that he proposed sending eighty soldiers to occupy the American compound.

"Effendi, Djevdet Bey," said Ussher, "I am greatly in debt to you for your suggestion, but I do feel that such a large force appearing in the middle of the Armenian quarter at such a tense moment would be a disaster and likely to lead to bloodshed. Perhaps if your Excellency sent a token force of say five ' 'askaris' (soldiers) this would be more than enough to guarantee the safety of the compound."

"I am sorry, but I intend sending a fully armed detachment to occupy the Mission for your own safety," replied the Vali coldly.

"Your Excellency. I am most anxious that this meeting should not result in our falling out. The American government is a neutral in this war and I will be doing my utmost to make certain that we here remain so. However, I would remind you that by arrangement with the Turkish government over many decades, the Mission here has full diplomatic status, as clear as a consulate. I therefore must insist that I cannot allow the entry of a large body of soldiers into what is technically American territory."

Djevdet Bet, clearly irritated and with rising temper then blurted out, "In that case, Doctor, I demand a written note absolving me of any responsibility for your safety." Ussher nodded, confirmed that he would be happy to provide a note to this effect and left the office.

During the mobilisation that had taken place during the previous winter, the Armenians had been relentlessly plundered under the guise of requisitioning. The rich had been ruined, whilst the poor, though willingly joining the Army when called up, had been deprived of arms and had been forced into doing all the menial tasks for the military. This had resulted in a high degree of tension in the city.

On the day of the outbreak of the so-called 'rebellion'—the excuse which was going to be given for all the later barbarities and for the new alien policy of total ethnic cleansing—some Turkish soldiers tried to seize one of a band of Armenian village women who were on their way to the city. She fled. Two Armenian soldiers came up to investigate, and at that point the Turkish soldiers opened fire and killed them. The Turkish entrenchments which Djevdet Bey had, supposedly secretly, been drawing up round the Armenian quarter during the previous three days, then opened up an intense barrage of fire into the surrounded residential quarter. The guns on Castle Rock also began pouring a murderous fire on the houses below. The siege of Van destined to last for several weeks had begun.

During the whole of the siege Dr. Ussher would allow no armed men to enter the compound. The Armenians, understanding this requirement, gave orders that no wounded soldiers were to be brought to the American hospital. Instead, Dr. Ussher would, usually at least once a day, go down with the nurses to the temporary hospital set up by the Armenians in the church hall. However, only a few days after the siege had begun—and before the arrival of Halil Bey's regulars—Djevdet Bey wrote to Ussher claiming that armed men had been seen entering the American compound and that as a result he would be opening fire at the hospital.

Djevdet Bey and Dr. Ussher corresponded with each other during the siege by sending letters to the Italian consular agent—Italy still being neutral. These were taken through the lines by old women carrying a flag of truce. At least four of these ladies lost their lives acting as postmen during the siege. It was a feature of the siege that a volunteer replacement was always found. Ussher's note stated clearly and explicitly, "Your Excellency, I must make it crystal clear that at no time have I or any of my staff treated any armed, or previously armed man at my hospital. My mission is to preserve the neutrality of our premises by every means in our power. I accept that I have taken in refugees from the villages around, where both regular soldiers and their wild Kurdish allies have been sweeping the countryside—massacring men, women and children and burning their homes. Not one of these villagers had any arms. Our hospital with a normal capacity of 50 now accommodates 187. I remain Your Excellency's faithful servant."

However, the direct bombardment of the American Mission started on the next day.

Despite the protestations of Djevdet Bey that he had given orders protecting the Americans, it was clear to Ussher that in the event of a collapse of the Armenian defenders, the compound would be overrun, and that the chances of survival of the American staff in the bloody massacre that would inevitably follow, would be slight indeed. Despite this, however, and even in the face of the fact that he had a wife and young children present who would inevitably be caught up in any slaughter, he remained absolutely steadfast throughout the siege, both in his neutrality on the one hand, and his insistence on continuing with his humanitarian work on the other. As always he was totally confident of the moral certainty of his stance.

There was never any doubt that Ussher could have left with his wife and three children at any time during the siege. The Turks would have let them through the lines, and the Armenians also often pressed him to escape. But neither Ussher nor his equally staunch wife ever wavered from what they considered to be their moral duty.

It could be made to appear that the terrible killings and massacres, which began soon after these events at Van, were triggered by what Doctors Ussher and Nazim saw from their different viewpoints. However, this cannot stand up as an explanation for the first of the great racist evils perpetrated in the twentieth century. Any question of who started what, and on exactly what day; or who reacted to whom and when; or who provoked who; must be ultimately sterile. Djevdet Bey was unquestionably and simply the wrong man in the wrong place at the wrong time. However, his actions and reactions had in many ways been foreordained by factors which had shaped his formation as an adult, and which, by the coincidence of events, had ended up in this siege.

Clarence Ussher had lived in Van many years before the siege. He had known Djevdet Bay himself as a growing boy, and had been interested in and followed his development into adulthood. He had seen the slow erosion, even in this one individual and in only one area of the Empire, of the old Ottoman values.

First had come the paranoic suspicions and random cruelties of the odious and blood-crazed Abdul Hamid. His incredible hatred towards the people, who had lived amongst the Turks for generations, had deepened suspicions between the two races to breaking point during his thirty year rule. Raised in the closed claustrophobic world of the Harem, it was uncertain whether Abdul Hamid's mother had been a Circassian or an Armenian girl, and this may have aggravated his paranoia. Certainly he himself had had an Armenian look about him as a young man, and sneers to this effect may well have poisoned his mind. Normally the Eunuchs in charge of the Harem were particularly careful to note the times and dates and the pedigrees of any girl who had shared the Padishah's bed. It was accordingly doubly unfortunate that there was an element of doubt in respect of Abdul Hamid's conception.

So deeply suspicious was this horrific little man who had ordered so many tortures and pogroms, that his personal servants were all trained always to move exceptionally slowly in his presence, and not to alarm him by making sudden movements. He was an excellent shot, and always kept at least two loaded pistols about his person, and is known to have shot at least three palace servants who had inadvertently moved suddenly in his presence.

Djevdet had been brought up in this atmosphere of suspicion and hatred, and had, from childhood witnessed the regular pogroms and humiliations visited on his neighbours. The harm Abdul Hamid had done to the minds and attitudes of his subjects, Christian and Muslim alike, was beyond calculation, and that harm had penetrated the mind of the young Djevdet as much as any other.

Ussher reflected that then, following this awful thirty-year reign, had come the 1908 revolution, and the rise of the Ittihad. With this there had arisen a drive towards secularisation, and the erosion now of the older and deeper virtues and values of Islam, for whom 'people of the book' were neighbours, and not racial enemies. Djevdet Bey had been influenced by the impatience of these men with the pashas who had previously run the Empire. These revolutionaries, thought

Ussher, were impatient for reforms and anxious to repudiate the Arab-Islamic element in the Empire and instead promulgate the efficiency of a modern westernised nation-state. Of course some element in these reflections characterised Ussher himself. He had a natural greater sympathy for Muslim gentlemen like the previous Vali, than for those he saw as a godless new generation.

Finally, to put the last touch to Djevdet's character came the domination within the Ittihad of Enver, Talaat and Djemal, all preaching a hard nationalistic creed so alien to the great Padishahs of the past. The Western European style 'nation-state' with all its vicious hatreds and contradictions, had at last arrived in the Islamic world, and Djevdet Bey was the final political product of that movement.

Meanwhile, the siege, started in the second week of April, dragged on day by day without resolution, as Ussher went patiently about his mission dutifully.

Chapter 15

Van. Nevart. An individual view.

Old Nevart was tired. Now a wizened shrunken old lady dressed always in black, she had lived over seventy five years in Van, and apart from trips to the beautiful island of Akhtamar in the Lake, had never left the city. Two husbands had come and gone, and only a widowed daughter now living with her, in her ancient Ottoman style house in the garden city, remained from her family.

Nevart lived in an old cluttered house in the middle of the urban Armenian quarter not far from the American Mission. The leaning and creaking building was made of wood, terraced with others of similar type on either side, all with the ubiquitous latticed windows on the first and second floors. These bay windows stuck out over the street, reducing the view of the sun and sky from below, but giving welcome shade during the day in the hot summers.

Neither Nevart nor her daughter Sona ever really knew what was going on during those April days. They felt the tension in the streets, and they noticed that somehow there was less mixing between Armenians and Turks in the bazaars, hammams and cafés of the centre.

"What is happening Sona? Where have all the young men got to? What is going on?"

"Mother, I'm not sure, but I have heard that our Governor is angry because the town doesn't appear to have produced the full tally of conscripts for the army that it should have."

"On top of all that" grumbled Nevart, not taking much notice of Sona's comment, "the price of fresh vegetables has gone through the roof. There are less and less villagers coming in to town to sell their produce. The open markets are getting more and more bare. I had to traipse around for almost two hours yesterday just to get a few onions, and the price they asked was ridiculous. I got quite angry and was going to refuse, when the woman behind me called out—'come on grandma, I'll take them if you don't want them'. She was a great fat Armenian lady, and I told her to wash her mouth out, but nevertheless I paid up and took the onions after that. I walked back with old Yevret Hanum—you remember her, the wife of Agop's old Turkish friend and partner. She told me that bands of Kurds are roaming the countryside, disrupting the villagers' lives, and even killing as well as robbing, and that is why the villagers are not bringing in their produce."

"Well, mother, I don't know at all. Look, I have to go to work, I haven't the time to think about these things. No doubt it's all just more rumours." Sona grabbed her hat and coat and hurried out of the house.

Nevart sighed and wondered if Sona was going to remarry and give her some grandchildren. Picking up her big straw basket she got ready to spend the whole morning, if necessary, trying to pick up some vegetables and possibly also to replenish her stock of rice. She stepped out into the fresh morning air, hoping that she could make her purchases before the hot midday sun. The whole street seemed to consist only of little old women dressed like her in black, hurrying about, clearly chasing provisions of one kind or another.

She had just walked into the little square where the country folk usually came to spread their wares out on the pavements, when she heard the first shots ring out, which heralded the start of the fighting. This was followed by a frenzy of shooting that opened the siege—a siege the reasons for which she never ever came to understand, and which she had no idea would go on for so long.

Suddenly the great gun on the Castle rock boomed out, and there was an explosion just ahead of her. Screams rang out, and people began running about, all in totally different directions. Nevart stood there quite still without any idea what to do or what was going on. The little old ladies had mostly disappeared—though some were on their knees on the pavement crossing themselves and muttering some pointless prayers. She saw some young men running past shouting unintelligibly to each other. Their eyes looked bright and excited, and she could see that some of them were armed. Another shell burst very close by, and she felt the earth shake—and then a piece of masonry or something flew past her ear grazing her cheek deeply. Blood began to flow.

This suddenly woke her up to the reality of this extraordinary situation that had burst upon her. She began running—not exactly in a panic—but certainly without any idea where she was headed. Within a minute or so she was already out of breath, and found herself outside the Protestant mission. The great doors of the compound were closed, as they usually were except on Sundays. Recollecting that there was an excellent medical clinic inside, she leant against the walls gulping down breaths of fresh air as she rested. She pulled the knob of the door bell, and was immediately let in by the small side door by the Turkish porter, who seeing her bloody face gestured to the little hospital building across the court.

Here she was immediately taken in by a nurse with the name Alicia pinned to her white coat.

"What's happening, mamoushka?" said the nurse, and Nevart recognised the accent of an Armenian from the Russian side of the divide.

"I have no idea, no idea at all" replied Nevart, who by now had recovered both her breath and her senses. "There was a couple of loud explosions—some crashing buildings, and a lot of shooting which went on for ever. A stone or something must have done this. Then there was a lot of young men, who seemed to have disappeared till now, who were running about and shouting to each other."

The nurse who seemed to understand better than Nevart what was going on, continued calmly treating the wound on Nevart's wrinkled cheek and said, "Well, the whole town has been getting more and more tense over the last week or so. It will be some sort of riot I suppose, though I must say I too heard the boom of the castle gun, several times."

"You won't need any stitches, mamoushka, just be very careful and don't wash there for a few days," she went on, as she stuck a plaster on Nevart's cheek. "You better get home now and try not to go out in the streets until whatever is going on, dies down."

Nevart walked out of the little hospital still bewildered, but more her usual self. She could still hear shooting, and the occasional boom of the bigger guns. The great doors of the compound were now flung wide open, and she saw the American Missionary leader standing by the gate, whom she recognised though she did not know his name—a big man with a beard, at least big in comparison with everyone around him. A small stream of women and an occasional old man, all with similar wounds to hers, were just beginning to walk or be carried in to the compound.

As Nevart walked out, she saw the American stop a young man, who had been hopping in on an improvised crutch, and whose leg was clearly badly crushed and incapable of supporting him. He murmured a few words to the boy who nodded, and he then beckoned over one of the Turkish employees of the Mission. The young lad leant on the porter's shoulder and they shuffled away down the street. Clearly he had been denied entrance to the Hospital. Nevart began stumbling home still in a daze as the shooting seemed to intensify, and the old buildings which had appeared so solid only a few moments before crumbled to dust. She was totally disorientated.

Nevart had spent her entire life in the town, mixing in the old Ottoman fashion both as a girl and as a woman with her Turkish and Kurdish neighbours. In the hammams—the baths—she had always joined in the usual rituals in the women's section of the baths. As a naked young girl she had duly scrubbed the backs of the older women, listened to their gossip. She had duly endured and giggled at the age-old sly comments as she had reached and passed puberty. Then as an older woman herself, she too had had her back scrubbed and lathered by other young women in her turn, and she had indulged in the usual banter and gossip about young men who were available as husbands. Both of her own two husbands had been found as a result of discussions between mothers in these same baths.

The point of all this was that there was no difference between a plump naked Turkish woman and an even plumper naked Armenian one—they all gossiped together, although they were well aware of who was who. There were of course always tensions that arose due to outside political clashes—it was not of course sweetness and light all the time—but these racial tensions were dealt with by the women sensibly. When there was trouble in town they just kept apart for a few days, and once the male energy outside had finally spent itself, they drifted back to comfortable tolerance of each other.

As she turned the corner into the street on which her house stood, she saw a little group of women standing both outside and just inside her house, the door of which was open. She knew. She knew instinctively and at once what this was all about. With a cry she ran forward. Two women whom she could no longer recognise ran forward and held her. Sona's broken body lay where she had been reverently placed in the doorway—the victim of the very first shell of the first day of the siege.

Nevart stood and stared, held up by the women. The sobs refused to come. Her last contact with life seemed to have disappeared. She allowed herself to be led into the house. Her neighbours took over the necessary practical details. Nevart, herself, simply drifted into a state of numb indifference.

Once the siege got under way the Armenians in Van were eventually gathered into a district about a mile square, with the American Hospital right in the middle. Protecting themselves against the entrenchments pinning them within this area, several of the old solid stone houses on the edge had been turned into mined and barricaded defences. Dr. Ussher's daughter had recounted to her father that despite the terrible shortage of all the material necessary for warfare, the young fighters, numbering about fourteen hundred men were extraordinarily cheerful, and of a very high morale. They were hopeful of being able to keep the six thousand Turkish soldiers at bay. They were after all fighting for their homes and their very lives.

Some days later, when Nevart had first came out of her stupor of grief, she picked up from the street a notice printed on recycled paper, and which appeared to have been issued to all the young men, which read: "Keep clean. Do not drink. Tell the truth.

Do not curse or denigrate the religion of the enemy."

A manifesto was sent to some Turkish inhabitants of the ancient city, known to their Armenian neighbours. This, somewhat naively, stated that their quarrel was with one man, and not with their neighbours. The manifesto, as reported by Dr. Ussher in a letter to his superiors in America, contained the following sentence, "Valis may come and go, but the two races must after all continue to live together, and we desperately hope that after Djevdet Bey leaves, there may be peaceful and friendly relations between us, as formerly always existed under the previous Vali."

It was of course precisely this necessity, somehow "to live together," that Enver, Talaat and their cronies were now plotting, for the first time in the Twentieth Century, to eradicate.

During those first few hours as Nevart had stared at the body of her daughter, she was comforted and cossetted by those same black-clad women, all well versed in dealing with grief in all its forms. Nevart had now finally lost everything that she had ever previously valued and was simply incapable of dealing with life any more. However, eventually, after a couple of days, a deep atavistic strength emanating from generations of female ancestors learning to cope with tragedy, came to her aid and overcame the apathy which had gripped her. With no one left for her to feed or care for, she locked up her house, which lay close to where all the shooting seemed to be coming from, took her few saved gold piastres, and walked down to the American Mission.

The doors of the compound were now permanently open, and she walked straight in. The formerly neat and tidy court looked totally different from the day she had last visited the place. A large number of people were now sitting untidily about, some under the shade of tattered umbrellas, and some on faded carpets. These were mainly women and old men, although there was a sprinkling of middle-aged men, all of whom were obviously villagers from the surrounding countryside. The women seemed to be coping fairly well chatting and gossiping to each other, but the men were looking apathetic with sad bruised eyes.

Nevart picked her way through to the hospital, where she saw that there were now several women in white coats bustling about. She sought and eventually found Alicia, the nurse who had treated her on that first day.

"Madam Nurse. . ." she began, addressing Alicia, and then went on to explain about the death of Sona, her last remaining relative.

"I would like to help you here. I can cook, I can help in treating wounds, I am prepared to do anything at all."

Alicia looked hard at her, and said, "Mother, are you sure, even if it was a question of risking your life?"

Nevart smiled, looked straight into the young woman's eyes and said firmly, "Yes! Yes! Anything at all, so long as I am not asked to hurt anyone."

"Well, I'll take you to see Dr. Ussher. He needs someone to deliver a letter to an address on the other side of the lines, as the last messenger has, er, not come back, and it can't be a man. Come, he can explain."

And so it was that Nevart became the last of Dr. Ussher's volunteer postal ladies, in his almost daily correspondence with the authorities on the other side of the lines.

Chapter 16

Constantinople. Tea at Tokatlian.

True to her word Olga arrived early at the gates of Nerissa's school that afternoon. No one else was there, and she did not therefore feel at all conspicuous by being without any companion, waiting on the road outside the school.

The longer this meeting with Selim had been anticipated, the more exciting it had become in Olga's mind. She had of course seen and spoken to Selim many times in and around the college since that first time the rendezvous had been arranged, and her original physical arousal had been compounded over the many weeks by an increasing certainty that this was a man of great personal honour and kindness with whom she felt immediately at ease. They had of course never been totally alone together, but his smile whenever he saw her, turned her feelings inside out.

Nerissa came out of the school, ahead of any of her friends, wrapping a silk scarf round her neck, and taking off the rather dowdy round school hat, and putting it into her bag. She too was excited. This was a really major event for her, and she was looking forward to going to the Bedestan—the old antique bazaar—with Olga. She wasn't worried about the rendezvous—she knew she wouldn't be called upon to say much, and she could simply sit back and listen to the little orchestra which always played, and let Olga and the young man, whoever he might be, talk together.

Nerissa suddenly realised that in all the excitement of planning this trip, Olga had never actually told her the name of the young man with whom they were after all just about to have tea together. By this time they were already at the station, and they could see the train approaching down the line. Karekin, although travelling second class himself, always insisted that his wife and daughters went first class when they travelled without him, and Nerissa and Olga duly climbed into their first class carriage and settled down for the fifteen minute ride to the city.

Nerissa snuggled into her window seat, smiling at Olga, ready at last to enjoy this novel experience. Olga was looking so beautiful, she thought, dreamy but clearly so excited that Nerissa found herself catching her breath with a mixture of pleasure and sadness. She was not, nor had ever been, in any way envious of Olga's beauty and social confidence, but she was painfully aware that these were characteristics to which she herself could never aspire.

"Well now Olga, my darling, what is the name of your new friend? You know you've never got round to telling me."

The moment had come at last. Olga had always known in her heart that what she was doing would be unacceptable to her parents, as the mild deception she had been practising clearly showed. But she had not considered the deeper implications which existed due to the whole social structure in which she lived. For her, authority simply meant 'mother and father', and a rebellion against such authority was acceptable, daring and without any real problem, due to the certainty of underlying love. But now for the first time in eight weeks Olga was going to have to face up to the actual disclosure of the relationship to a third party.

"Selim Kemal," Olga replied simply, saying nothing more.

Nerissa stopped smiling. She sat there totally stunned. What could she say? Although only just sixteen, she saw at once and very clearly all the implications contained in those two words. A Turkish boy! In the two minutes of silence that stretched between the two sisters, she analysed all the impossibilities in the situation—impossibilities which in almost two months of thinking about her feelings Olga had not even considered.

However shy and introverted Nerissa was, she remained the most studious, intelligent and reflective of the four girls, and her native wit and the example of her calm and liberal father came to her aid. Nerissa sat thinking, what would her father's reaction be in such a situation? She reflected that so far as she had understood, his principle had always been never to reject anything proposed to you immediately, but always to consider everything calmly from all angles first. However, she considered that he would also have added that once you have made your mind up on the moral position, you must not compromise or fudge the issues, but take your stance fiercely and honestly.

She forced a smile back onto her face. Olga, whose thoughts were entirely on the coming rendezvous, had not even been aware of the two-minute silence, or of the tension in Nerissa's mind.

"So, Olga, he is Turkish," said Nerissa, carefully making sure that she did not look away from her sister's eyes, or appear in any way to be distressed or anxious.

"Yes. He's a lovely boy, you'll like him Nerissa, I feel sure. He's intelligent and thoughtful, and so gentle—not anything like all the other boys. My darling, when he speaks to me I feel so, so, so warm and good and cosy. Oh dear it's so difficult to explain. He has none of that male arrogance which you see so often in the other Turkish students."

Suddenly Olga couldn't stop talking. All her pent-up feelings, all those unaccustomed strong feelings which she had perforce kept to herself all these weeks began pouring out, as she stared back into Nerissa's big brown eyes trying so hard not to appear anxious. But in all her nervous and excited explanations, in all this parade of deep feelings that despite all her social savoir-faire she had never actually experienced before, never once did she allude in any way to the looming problems of such a relationship, neither to Nerissa directly, nor more to the point, to herself.

Nerissa listened, thrilled by being made a party to the feelings of an elder sister, who, in the whirl of her active social life, had until then largely ignored her. At the same time, however, she found herself appalled at what she increasingly saw as a domestic tragedy in the making. She knew—she knew absolutely for certain—that her beloved Olga was going to be badly hurt one way or another, whatever happened.

Nerissa, a keen reader of Shakespeare's plays in the original, found herself thinking of Juliet in her love for Romeo.

"My God," she thought, "Juliet's problem was nothing, compared to what poor Olga has to face. Romeo was the same race as Juliet, he spoke exactly the same language, he had the same cultural background, he belonged to the same religion, for heavens sake they even went to the same father confessor, they were from the same class, and, in fact, but for the silly feud between their fathers—and Shakespeare makes quite clear that it was indeed silly—Romeo would have been a perfect match for Juliet."

But what was Olga up against? Did she realise it even for a moment? Here was a young man, however gentle and pleasant, who nevertheless spoke a different language at home, was of a totally different religion, belonged to a different race, furthermore a race which had been locked in a fierce and seemingly irreconcilable conflict with her own people for over five hundred years since the fall of the old Byzantine Empire.

What was the right thing for her to do? Would Olga take the slightest notice of any warnings she might raise? Clearly she could see that nothing she could say at this particular moment would make any difference at all. Olga, now that the floodgates were opened, chattered on, oblivious to all but her own feelings, feelings that appeared to expand with every utterance, and so Nerissa said not a word as the train slowly pulled into Sirkedji Station—the terminus of the whole European railway system.

As they walked from the station to the covered Bazaar, Nerissa finally got round tentatively to raising the issue foremost in her mind.

"Olga, how far has your friendship with this young man gone? What are your feelings?"

"Nerissa, listen, all I know is that this is a good man—a man of truth and honour whom I believe I will be able to trust all my life if necessary. But, Nerissa, don't go getting romantic ideas over the top! I really don't know how deep my own feelings are, never mind being sure of his."

"But Olga, aren't you aware of the difficulties? What about when it comes to meeting his family."

"Poof! Who cares? For the moment all I want to do is to get to know him better. I don't care a hoot what other people may think. We're two individuals, why should we carry the weight of the past on our shoulders all the time? I am first and foremost a woman, not a representative of my race or religion. What difference would our race make if we were all on a desert island."

"But Olga, my soul, we are not on a desert island, nor in that metaphorical sense could we ever be."

An hour or so later, after a short somewhat distracted visit to the Bedestan, in which for different reasons neither of them were really at all interested any more, they came out and eventually alighted from the tram that ran up from the Galata Bridge and arrived at the front entrance of Tokatlian on the Grande Rue. Here a fairly brisk crowd of fashionable ladies and gentlemen, mixed with a good sprinkling of smartly turned out army officers and cadets were passing in and out of its art nouveau glass doors. Olga and Nerissa moved into the busy vestibule. Here just inside the door was the eager but somewhat anxious figure of Selim, holding nervously in his hand the felt hat he had grabbed from his father's large collection of hats before coming out.

A sudden surge of excitement, coupled with an unusual affection, sprang up in Olga, as she saw and appreciated his nervousness. This came with a surge of confidence in her own ability to manage the occasion. It was as if the nervousness of Selim had aroused in her a calm certainty of her own feelings. Nerissa glanced at her sister and saw there, for the first time ever, a really natural warm smile on her face. This was a smile unlike any of the more superficial and consciously charming smiles that she usually saw on her sister's lovely face. Nerissa's heart lurched and nearly drowned in inward tears as Olga stretched out her hand and said very simply, "Oh hello Selim. This is my young sister Nerissa," to which Selim, taking Olga's hand into his own, and holding it without making any attempt at shaking it, replied, "Hello, Nerissa. Salaam! Shall we go in and get a table?"

It took perhaps no longer than eight seconds before Selim became aware that he was still holding Olga's hand. Olga, herself, however had been aware of every second of his grasp, as had Nerissa. Selim, going deeply crimson, suddenly let go and they moved, somewhat self-consciously into the large tea-room at Tokatlian.

Here in a large and airy room with a glass roof, Nerissa stared at the noisy crowd of men with a surprisingly large number of women also, chatting animatedly at small round tables dotted about the place. The room—or was it a theatre—was liberally sprinkled with potted palms and other plants placed strategically and often shielding the tables from each other. A huge chandelier, magnificent enough she thought to have graced the new Paris Opera House, hung from the ceiling. The setting was grand, though perhaps not very tasteful. No Oriental opulence here, but dark mahogany walls, heavy green foliage, some tall palm trees at the side, small white wrought-iron tables and chairs, and the glittering chandelier hanging over all. A tiny stage at the side of the large hall held a small string orchestra, in front of which was a minuscule polished wooden floor for dancing.

The room was filled with officers of the Turkish army. Nerissa wondered what they were all doing here in the City. Enver Pasha, despite the defeats on the Caucasian front, was clearly still the style of the day. The men were all clean-shaven save for the same brisk hard moustache. They all affected a pose of nonchalant arrogance, with hard eyes and a supercilious regard. Male predators, all of them. As they sat down Nerissa noticed a young man in the uniform of the officer-cadet school—the Harbiye—clearly an Armenian, sitting nearby with a small group of friends and who was looking at her with soft brown eyes, who, as she looked up, smiled at her and then shyly turned away.

Nerissa smiled back and then turned away and tried to concentrate on what Selim and Olga were saying to each other with their lips, though it was quite clear what they were saying with their eyes. The little orchestra began playing a Strauss waltz with that late nineteenth century absurd palm-court sentimental rhythm, and a few couples rose to dance.

To her dying day, and despite the drama of the tragic days that were about to follow, Nerissa would never be able to recall any of the actual unimportant words that passed between all three of them on that hazy afternoon in the old "the dansant" room at Tokatlian, the week before the storm burst over them all. She looked and listened, as Olga and Selim dreamed their dreams, chatted inconsequentially, and touched hands under the table with innocent wonder at the intensity of their own feelings.

Deeply anxious for her sister, but at the same time thrilled by the occasion, Nerissa sat and watched as this last bastion of the old and elegant Europe danced its last waltz away. All these young officers and their ladies dancing away the afternoon, unconscious that their world was about to die on its feet, as a result of the same two fatal shots that had assassinated an Archduke and his lady only nine months earlier.

Chapter 17

Alexandria. Andre and the invasion force.

When the wind blows from the north in Alexandria, blustery and damp, the old trams running along the Corniche clatter and shake about as they proceed. The ill-fitting windows in the houses facing the sea shiver and rattle. All the weekend visitors from Cairo smile at each other and take bracing walks along the seafront, feeling pleased that they had taken the trouble to come. When, however, the winds blow from the south, they seem to bring with them the hot enervating and sultry smells of the whole of the rest of Africa looming oppressively beyond the town—a town which normally turns its back firmly against the continent behind it, trying hard to ignore it entirely. The same weekend visitors from Cairo then wonder why they had bothered to come at all.

Andre Tarkowski and his suddenly acquired Greek girl-friend, Elena Patakis, had managed, as planned, to get to Egypt before the Turkish entry into the war closed the frontiers, and turned the British Empire for the first time into an enemy of the Ottomans. Andre had eventually arrived in Alexandria, where somehow he seemed to have been able to lay his hands on more than sufficient funds. Andre's passport, issued to him by the Embassy in Constantinople following what appeared to be his desertion from the *Goeben*, skirted over his German citizenship by referring to him as Polish. Once arrived, he made a great effort to get work with the British naval administration as an expert in the relatively new field of radio.

By dint of perseverance, and by continually improving his command of English, he finally got a job as a civilian radio operator with Naval Intelligence in their radio transmissions department. His knowledge of four further languages—German, Turkish, Polish and Russian—was the factor which enabled him to be taken on without too many questions. He was never of course cleared for full security on sensitive matters, but managed nevertheless to hear a lot of what was going on in all of which he was much interested.

Andre was getting more and more bored by the unfortunate Elena. Elena, herself, started by having no contacts of any kind with the large Greek community in this city, and had to construct her own entertainment. She really had no reserves of her own. She had had little education, and had acquired few outside interests. Andre was always out at work or wandering round the town, and whilst their sex remained passionate and satisfactory, even the highly sensual Elena began to feel the lack of any common interest, or any common activity beyond the bedroom. The atmosphere between the sexes in Alexandria was however easier than in Constantinople, and fairly soon Elena, ostensibly unmarried, began to attract to herself some of the Greek young men, whom she glimpsed in church, and with whom she began to arrange café meetings. These even led to invitations from the families, though these were not all that frequent. She was always careful to mention these meetings to Andre, but he seemed uninterested, and indeed even encouraged her further.

As April advanced, Alexandria and Cairo began to fill with nationalities from all over the British Empire. In particular there were the bronzed and athletic young Australians, so much bigger and stronger than the somewhat stunted English working-class soldiers. Andre worked in the Navy's special radio telegraph room at the end of the tramline near the seaside Montazah Palace. He would often stand and stare at these glorious men stripped to the waist on the sands by the sea. Andre, whose perverse and brutal bisexuality disconcerted him not a jot, would wonder at the simplicity and beauty of these Greek Gods, each with their own special and entirely Australian 'mate'—a relationship which appeared to have not the slightest homoerotic overtone whatsoever. These 'mates' enlisted together, went into the same regiment together, and in the end went over the top to their deaths together.

Andre could not understand for one moment why these young men were here, and what they were doing voluntarily fighting a war, which in the last resort, despite all the propaganda put out to satisfy the masses, was basically just an old-fashioned European 'balance of power' contest.

"Hello, my name is Andrew, what's your name," he would say, initiating a conversation. "Oh! Hello Jimmy. Tell me Jimmy, what are you doing here? What are you fighting for?" Andrew would continue with his infectious grin, whenever he got the chance.

"Well it's like we're here to play a game of rugby, but with the bloody Turk rather than with each other," answered the New Zealanders, meaning it totally sarcastically, but nevertheless unconsciously putting their finger on their own insouciance and frivolity in joining up in the first place.

The Australians would usually answer more on the following lines, "Well, blow me, I don't know what's going to happen or why, but crumbs it beats sitting at home watching the dust gather on the window-sill. Hey, Geoff, here's this geezer asking why we're here. Well mate, I'm here because he's here" said usually with a great belly-laugh and a clap on Andre's shoulder.

Andre would usually end up also getting details of their regiments.

Andre recalled the joke going round Cairo, where the Australians had acquired a reputation for general irreverent loutishness.

A sentry at one of the camps, hearing footsteps in the dark, calls out, "Halt, who goes there." A voice answers, "Indian Fourth Rifles." "Pass Indian Fourth," sings out the sentry.

A little later again the sentry calls out, "Halt who goes there." A new voice calls out, "Fifth New Zealand Brigade." "Pass New Zealander" says the sentry.

Finally this happens a third time and the sentry again shouts, "Halt who goes there." A loud voice replies, "What the bloody fucking hell has it got to do with you." The sentry calls out, "Pass, Australian friend."

Andre chuckled to himself, but immediately reflected on how his seduction of Elena and the affair that followed had already soured. Sexual contact remained satisfactory for both of them. But once the actual sexual coupling was over, there really was nothing much left to say to each other. Their only common language—the language they had all spoken together in the Patakis household—was of course

Turkish. However, Andre, though a natural linguist, was not all that comfortable in Turkish, and in any case Elena really had nothing much of interest to say anyway in any language.

Andre reflected that Elena was already enjoying the attentions of Greek lads she was meeting at the Church and in the very wide Greek community. He had no feelings of jealousy at all—much to Elena's surprise, and deep down irritation. Their little two-room apartment was at the top of a large nineteenth century building standing opposite the Sports Club grounds, and whilst adequate, was constricting. The building itself housed Greek, Italian, French and even an Egyptian family as well.

This was the middle of April—the landings in Gallipoli were due to take place within a week—and Andre was flabbergasted at the total lack of any security throughout Egypt. No military expedition since the Trojan War had ever been more loudly trumpeted and discussed. First the fleet had bombarded the Dardanelles Forts, and had then pulled back. That pinpointed exactly where a future effort was going to take place. Then, news of the arrival and departure of all the great battleships and the hundreds of transports became common knowledge throughout Alexandria and Port Said, and were reported daily in Cairo. The names and numbers of all the British, French and Anzac divisions were freely referred to in the newspapers throughout Egypt. There were even official references to "the Constantinople Field Force." The word Gallipoli was on everyone's lips. Everyone knew what was coming, as ponies, horses, camels, water lighters, and shipping of all kind were hastily purchased and gathered in the Egyptian ports.

Andre simply could not credit this, in view of his experience of the strict and secretive world of Prussian military security. In the end he came to only one conclusion—they simply did not know what they were doing. From top to bottom they were going into this campaign like a debutante going to her first ball. Excited, but with no clear idea of what it was all about. Above all it seemed to him, that their leaders had made the cardinal error of not having read or understood their history. They were failing to take the Turks seriously, or indeed to take any account of them at all.

The Turks, after all, had a long tradition of military prowess. Whilst, on the one hand they had long lost the brilliance in aggressive offensive warfare of their nomadic ancestors, they had instead acquired that dogged patient stonewalling defensive capacity that had always been the strength of the simple Anatolian peasant, even in the days of Byzantium before there were any Turks there at all. These peasants were mainly illiterate, they were misused and despised, they were badly led by their Pashas and officers from Constantinople, but they were used to hardship, to terrible conditions, and to bad food. They could endure with patience and stubbornness in a way that by 1915 could only be matched by the Russian mouzhik.

The Ottoman Empire, eventually including Greece, the Balkans, most of Hungary, and the whole of the Arab world including the holy cities of Islam, contained an enormous number of different races, creeds, languages and religions. By the eighteenth century it had grown soft and sensual, and the question was increasingly being raised as to what exactly united all these disparate peoples. The Ottoman Empire was the ultimate multi-cultural and multi-racial society, and right up to this very month, despite some notably tragic moments, the Ottoman Empire had in the main treated its many different minorities better than most of the so-called civilised nations to the north.

But as Andre could see, British officers, army and navy, were unable to conceive of soldiers who didn't dress like them or look like them as being of any value at all. Hence their unconsciously racist dismissal of the poor Anatolian peasant reinforced their extraordinarily light-hearted attitude to security. Who cares if the Turks know we are coming, 'our chaps' will still give the rotters a good hiding was the unconscious thought of all of them, from the generals down to the ordinary Tommies.

Finally and to cap it all, Andre knew something that with all the intelligence at their disposal General Hamilton and the planners at Whitehall did not know. Facing them at Gallipoli was not going to be the ridiculous and vainglorious Enver Pasha, who had only managed to emulate his hero Napoleon by retreating from a winter campaign with a tiny proportion of his original force, all suffering from frostbite. The General who had hurriedly been placed in charge, and with a full month to prepare the defences, was Mustapha Kemal. Enver, with his smooth face and delicate feminine hands, hopelessly vain and self-confident, with a remorseless lack of any pity or empathy, was a gambler. Kemal, in contrast, was a cool chess player, who knew his men well, and who, whilst ruthless, never lost his essential humanity.

Andre got home fairly late and had begun resisting Elena's demands to be taken out—not that there was much to do in the evenings in Alexandria apart from socialising.

"Andre, come on please, let's go out. There is going to be a concert of Strauss waltzes, which will include dancing at the Cecil Hotel."

"No, Elena, I'm too busy. I've got things to do. I've got some translating work that the Navy wants completing by tomorrow. But look, there's no reason why you shouldn't go."

"Oh, Andre, I can't go on my own."

"No, but what about that guy. . . What was his name, Gianni or something, you were talking about yesterday. Why not go with him"

"But Andre, I really would rather go with you. Don't you mind my going out with someone else?"

"Not at all, Elena, for heavens sake go and enjoy yourself."

Conversations like this seemed to take place more and more often. Elena became concerned by the indifference shown by Andre and would end up trying to rile him in many different ways in an attempt to get him irritated. She felt that any reaction, even of anger, was better than this total neglect.

The flat was tiny, and sitting under the bed, back against the wall, taking up space which could have been used for something else, was a rather battered locked tin case, which Andre had brought through all their travels all the way from the house in Stamboul, and the inside of which Elena had never seen. Elena's references to it always seemed to irritate Andre unduly, and unfortunately Elena had reached the stage where irritating Andre seemed to be the only way she could get any reaction from him towards her. It would often end in a sort of ritualised violence, when Andre would end up physically hurting Elena in the sexual act, in a way which seemed to satisfy both of them.

It was on that last night, at the start of the third week in April, before all the naval transports left, that Elena returned home unexpectedly early from having visited a Greek family who had invited both her and Andre to supper. Andre had said that he was far too tired to go, but had encouraged her to go without him. On arrival, Elena found that the family were in a domestic crisis in regard to an old Aunt who had just died, and after some moments of giving condolences and exchanging politeness, she duly left. She walked into their little sitting room to see the tin case open on the desk, and Andre tapping at some keys on some machine or other, with what looked like muffs over his ears.

"Whatever is that thing, Andre? It's a funny kind of typewriter," said Elena, as she walked in putting down her hat.

Andre, who hadn't heard her coming in, carefully lifted off the things that were over his ears, and turned to face her—his eyes hard, glittering and full of that violence, which on this occasion suddenly caused her to feel a real stab of unusual fear.

"Just one of my toys, Elena. Come here," he said, as he slowly rose from the desk and came towards her.

Chapter 18

Makrikoy. Breakfast at the Avakians.

Karekin, still in the bedroom, adjusted his tie carefully in the mirror, and indicated to Armineh that she should wait a moment, before she bustled down to see to the family breakfast. He said, "My dear, yesterday Mr. Levonian—do you remember him, a textile merchant dealing mainly with Germany and Vienna—offered me his seat in the tram going up from the bridge. He said he was just about to get off at the next stop. I couldn't refuse obviously, although for heaven's sake he's almost as old as I am. Anyway, he never did get off at the next stop, but after a few general words about the difficult situation in the business world, he began talking about his son George. It seems George has managed to get deferment for one reason or another, and has started working with his father."

"Karekin, for heavens sake, do keep to the point whatever it is you are trying to say. I haven't got all day," said Armineh, tapping her foot impatiently, and with her hand still on the doorknob.

"Ah well, yes, at first I really wasn't clear at all what he was talking about, what with all the usual clanging and clattering of the tram. Ridiculous, I must be getting past it, as I should have realised at once. Anyway—Armineh don't get impatient—suddenly it dawned on me that he was talking about our Sima. I have no idea why it got into his mind at such a critical time, but he seems to be interested in a merger of our two merchant houses. However, he may have a point—sooner or later, Armineh my dear, this war is going to end. Undoubtedly there will be room for expansion into Western Europe, as our cotton crop has not been effected in any way. So, with me fully committed in Great Britain, and he covering Germany, we could do very well in a postwar world. Armineh, I don't suppose life is going to be all that different in 1916 than it is today, if the war ends by then."

"Karekin," said Armineh, whose mind was fairly distracted and who had indeed only been half listening to Karekin's rambling and who, most surprisingly, had not noticed Karekin's reference to Sima, "I've had enough. I can't believe that you are asking me some advice about a purely business matter. You know very well you'll do exactly as you want in that area. Now, unless there is something else that you don't seem to be able to get round to, I am going down. Please hurry yourself, it's getting late."

"Armineh, some patience please my love. The question on which I need your advice is as to whether you think Sima is ready to consider the question of marriage."

Armineh who was just about to leave, stopped and stared, suddenly very much paying attention.

"Of course she is ready to consider marriage—she's already nineteen and most girls of her age are already married and with their first child. She's always been a great help to me, and I'll miss her, particularly as Olga is so useless these days in the house, but it's quite certainly time she was settled. Have we met this young man, George."

"I don't think so, but we are certainly going to meet him tomorrow, as I ended up inviting the family to tea after lunch tomorrow," said Karekin rather sheepishly.

"Karekin, are you mad? You've lost your head! Now he tells me!" expostulated Armineh, glaring at him and stamping her foot in irritation. "I'll simply never manage. You know very well how bad the situation is for entertaining. Really Karekin, how could you, it's going to be quite impossible!" said Armineh, as she stormed out.

"There'll be four of them—the parents, the young man, and a younger sister," called out Karekin to the departing back of his wife. He grinned with satisfaction, being relieved that she had taken it so well. After over 20 years of marriage it was crystal clear to him that Armineh was already working out how she was going to cope. He was also certain that she would somehow—the only thing that he would have dreaded was silence after he had blurted out the deal for the next day.

Armineh herself, irritated as she was by having something like this thrust on her, almost immediately after the love that had passed between them early that morning, nevertheless knew perfectly well that she would manage. Furthermore, she herself had been passing hints to Karekin for some time that he had to start bestirring himself where Sima was concerned. Her mind raced ahead as to how she would plan tomorrow's entertaining. All thoughts of the war, the rumours of a possible Anglo-French attack on Constantinople itself, the awful news from Van, passed right out of her mind—not that it was ever in the forefront of it anyway. What was important was this the first direct approach to be made to her first-born daughter. Oh yes! She would certainly do it right. Mentally rolling up her sleeves, she bustled downstairs for the daily tussle to get her delicate son to eat something before school.

Breakfasts at the Avakians remained noisy and full of life as always—but there was increasingly an undercurrent of tension. Even though Haik had found that many other boys of his own age at the school were also being escorted by elder brothers or servants, he still experienced a slight element of shame. Sima herself was subdued, whilst Olga always appeared to be in a state of febrile excitement, quite incapable of sitting for long at the table. Nerissa remained sensitive to all the tensions and feelings around her, but felt that much of this tension was due to the different personal feelings of each of them as separate individuals. She discounted the subconscious awareness in each of them of the fears and anxieties swirling around them in the city.

Certainly, on the face of it, none of the family, with the exception of Karekin himself, were consciously aware of the possibility of a coming storm. On an intellectual level, the Avakian family, being who they were, chatted on about it all incessantly and with spirit, but only as an academic discussion. Above all, Armineh herself bustled about fulfilling the age-old feminine role of making sure that the everyday practical details of life were sorted out. By competently dealing with this and despite all the problems swirling around her, she thereby gave the five children, and to an extent her husband, a firm anchor from which to contemplate the world's follies.

As Karekin came down to his glass of tea with lemon, Sima rose and said to Haik, "Come along young man, time for school." Haik, having avoided most of the food thrust at him by Armineh, and looking paler and more fragile every day, jumped up, hugged his father cheek to cheek as Karekin sat down, and went out. Karekin looked round at the rest of his children, Olga, Nerissa and little Seta.

"Tomorrow, my dears," he said as he sipped his tea, "some friends of mine will be coming to tea after church. I don't think you've met them—the Levonians—they live in Bebek."

"Gosh! That's quite far out, Baba" said Nerissa, "a long way for them to come."

"Yes, well, there'll be four of them—Johannes and Yvonne Levonian, with their son George, and a younger sister whose name I don't know—nor actually even how old she is."

"Father," said Olga looking at him very directly "and how old then is this son, George?"

"Well, I believe that he's about twenty-four," said Karekin simply. "Anyway I want you all to be well-behaved and careful. They are fairly old-fashioned, and we mustn't shock them in any way—and that applies just as much to you Seta, my girl."

Karekin rose. His breakfast these days were short and sharp. He couldn't wait to get back to the tensions of the city, in order to discover all the rumours and conjectures flying around the coffee houses and the bazaar. He knew for his family's sake that he had to be ready for all possible eventualities. The three girls jumped up and kissed their father, who taking his hat and coat walked out.

"Seta, go and help Marie in the kitchen," said Olga firmly. Seta grumbled, but went out. Then as soon as she had gone, Olga turned to Armineh and Nerissa, and with shining eyes said, "Mother, I know something's going on. Father wouldn't comment about an ordinary tea-party. It's Sima, isn't it. Nerissa, can you believe it, these Levonians are coming to inspect our Sima, and with a view," she giggled, "to matrimony, my dear." Olga laughed out loud.

"Oh no!" wailed Nerissa, "It's disgusting, like a cattle market. Mother, how can Baba even contemplate putting one of his daughters through something like that? I can't bear the thought, poor Sima."

Armineh looking impatient as she sipped her coffee, replied, as Olga looked on with a mischievous grin.

"Nerissa, it's not like that at all. How do you think that Sima or any of you are going to meet pleasant young men if we don't arrange meetings like this? Nerissa, how could you imagine for one moment that your father would be party to a cattle market as you put it? No one, but no one, is ever going to make one of my daughters marry anyone whom in the last resort they do not choose themselves. Look Nerissa, for heavens sake, least of all your father! This is simply an occasion for two young people to meet—neither of them need take the matter a single step further. Nerissa, how could you ever think for a moment of 'imposition' where your father is concerned. You know his principles and his love for you all."

"Oh mama don't get upset," said Nerissa "of course I know that Baba would never force any of us to do anything against our wishes. On the other hand his idea of what is best for us may not be the same as ours. Love is not the issue here, mama. I have no doubts about Baba's love for me, of course. However, that is not necessarily at all the same as trusting his judgement of what is right for me."

"Mother," suddenly Olga intervened, "when did you come to love father. You had only just met him once before when you married him, or so you told us. He was at least fifteen years older than you. You were scarcely much older than Nerissa here."

"Girls, life was very different in those days. Whilst I had brothers and was aware of young men, I never met anyone outside the family. Life at home was constrained. We never contradicted our parents, and frankly had few thoughts that weren't planted there by them. To be honest, I couldn't wait to get away and have my own establishment. I was ready to fall in love with the first young man to whom I was introduced. I was in addition used to doing what my parents wanted, unlike you lot."

"Yes, but when did real love arise?" insisted Olga. "Was it on the very first night."

Nerissa blushed deeply and looked away, although she was just as keenly interested in her mother's answer.

"Olga, my dear, I was only sixteen. Most of my real education came after I got married. I learnt more from your father in our first year together than in years of childhood."

"Yes, Mother, but you haven't answered Olga, what about love?" said Nerissa.

"What about passion?" said Olga.

Armineh sipped her coffee and reflected. She was thirty-six and beginning to get dumpy. Her husband had taught her to read and write. He had been gentle with her always, though he required to have his way in most matters. He relied on her to manage his home and daily life for him, which she did well and efficiently, and he was now fifty-one years old! She realised that she could not even recall very clearly that first night in which Olga was so interested, and for which Nerissa had blushed. She could recall that very morning's act of love, but she knew that that was not what her daughter's wanted to know about.

Her relationship with Karekin, that was what they were after for reasons of their own. 'Contentment', certainly; 'Affection', oh God yes; but 'Love' . . . . Armineh put down her cup and rose as the two girls waited, watching her carefully for the different answer they wanted for themselves.

"Come along girls, you'll both be late." She walked out, slowly and calmly, in no way hurrying, to check on the kitchen, get Seta ready for school, and make plans for tomorrow's tea party.

Chapter 19

Mediterranean. Harry and the invasion force.

Back in London, within a week of submitting his report on the events which had led to the escape of the *Goeben* and the *Breslau* and their arrival in Constantinople, Harry had got his wish and had been posted to an active post on a destroyer, the HMS *Leicester*. As the days drew on towards the end of April, he found himself on this ship making its way at speed to Port Said. The *Leicester* was scheduled to escort the transports of the Royal Naval Division due to participate in the forthcoming landings at Gallipoli.

By the end of 1914, the war in Europe against Germany had already become a Dante's inferno of hundreds of miles of trenches of all kinds, front-line trenches, transverse trenches, supply line trenches, rear-return trenches and others, where men lived and shot at each other, like rats scurrying around in a maze. This was not a war of man against man, but man against the inexorable machine. One man's death, impaled on a bayonet or struck down by a sword, was always an unbearable tragedy, but the death of 25,000 men raked by machine guns in the first twenty minutes of one of the great 'over the top' offensives had become a mere statistic.

Harry had fallen back with a feeling of relief into the easy camaraderie of men at sea. He had never been totally comfortable at the office, and above all he no longer wanted to live at home, where conflicts seemed to occur with his father every day. His fellow-officers on board had a somewhat exaggerated respect for the views of one known to have come straight from the Admiralty. On the very evening before they were due to arrive at Port Said all the officers gathered in the Captain's cabin and began to discuss the question of where they were going and what they were supposed to be doing.

"Harry, you're in the know about what's going on. Tell us what's behind all this, come on man, expound!"

"Yes ok! Ok! Look, this started as an attempt to get round the awful stalemate on the Western front by mounting a flanking manoeuvre with a naval operation as a direct attack on Constantinople. This plan is an attempt to capture Constantinople by some sort of a coup-de-main. It could take the bloody Turks out of the war, give a warm-water supply route to the hard-pressed Russians, and encourage the smaller Balkan states to join our camp. The original idea behind the scheme was that of Winnie—you know, the First Lord. Churchill is an interesting guy with a volatile temperament, but he's inclined to see warfare as a huge historical epic, rather than as a failure in policy. He's charismatic, full of charm and bluster, but blooming impatient and he tends to leave details to others."

"But, Harry, doesn't this mean that we'll have less men available to break through on the western front? Surely, in the long run it's the Germans we have to beat, not the cruddy Turks. What's so important about the Dardanelles?"

At this, one of the other officers, steeped in classical education like so many of them, interrupted, "Hang on there, James, a division or two, more or less, in the trenches isn't going to make that much difference. As for the importance of the Dardanelles, these narrow straits have always been one of the most significant stretches of water in the world. Lots of armies have gone back and forth across these narrows. Xerxes, on his way to take Athens, built his bridge of boats just above the Narrows where the straits are less than a mile across. Alexander the Great crossed going the other way. Arab armies lapped up against the City walls on many occasions. Finally, the Turks themselves crossed and took the City. Honestly, you only have to look at a map to see what an important spot it is."

Harry nodded, as everyone, feeling it was all becoming a little solemn, reached for more drinks, and said, "It was the original intention that this would be a naval battle. We, alone, were going to force a way through the straits, and then appear outside Constantinople."

"But Harry, how the hell could the navy on its own take and above all keep a great city like Constantinople? It doesn't make sense."

"You're right, James, I'm afraid that no one had actually worked anything out. Up to then the navy didn't appear to have done much to justify the huge expense it had eaten up during the previous ten years. Ok, ok, I know, I know what you're all going to say, but that's what Johnny Public thought and the feeling among all the big-wig admirals was that surely for the first time we could now be used as a decisive weapon of war."

"Well, what happened? Why didn't it work? I was always taught at staff college that warships, capable of carrying enormous guns, and offering only moving targets, usually defeated fixed coastal forts," said one of the others.

"To be honest I just don't know. When we finally sailed into the straits, gosh it was only a month ago, we had over two hundred heavy guns, against a mere handful in the Turkish forts. We silenced the forts on the very first day. We heard that the rulers in Constantinople, thought they were finished. Slimy old Talaat is supposed to have had a car ready to take him into the interior at a moment's notice. The Balkan states suddenly thought of getting a bit of the action. The Russians talked of attacking Constantinople from the Black Sea. We even heard that the Greeks thought about using their army.

"Well, come on Harry, what the blazes went wrong?"

"Well, as day after day passed, nothing further happened. Somehow, the clearing of the old fixed forts didn't seem to prevent the hidden mobile guns of the coastal defences from opening up an accurate fire whenever our minesweepers sprang into action during the night, trying to clear the mines to enable the great battleships to move on. At last our admirals decided to make an all-out effort. Seventeen battleships and a host of smaller craft, with a French squadron as well, moved forward. By midday most of the Turkish guns had again fallen silent. God, we were almost there. But then the mines began to take their toll. Three battleships were sunk and several others crippled. Seven hundred sailors died. I know that these losses are tiny compared with what happens in the trenches every day, but it was enough to finish off our admirals.

That evening they telegraphed the Admiralty to say that the plan had failed. They reported that they no longer believed that the Navy could force the straits alone. They confirmed that they would need the Army. My God, what an admission for a British Admiral!"

"Gosh, Harry, how exciting. Nelson would have turned in his grave, wouldn't he? Never mind, we're going to clobber them this time."

It was on the next morning that the HMS *Leicester* finally docked at Port Said. Harry was in a state of tense excitement. He was sure that he had arrived at one of those great heroic moments that might be remembered in history. Even now, still early in 1915, despite the awful experiences on the western front, war was still thought of by all these young men as glorious, exciting, even poetic, the epitome of the male virtues. Each of the European empires believed that 'our chaps' were plucky and gallant, full of honour and duty, ready in a manly way to sacrifice themselves for their particular nation-state, which was also supported, of course, by their particular God.

Harry's friend—the poet Rupert Brooke—had joined the Royal Naval Division, the RND, scheduled to go in with the Anzacs. Brooke had written a letter to another acquaintance, a copy of which had been sent on to Harry, when he had been told that his division was bound for Constantinople. In it he had written, "It's too wonderful for belief. I had not imagined Fate would be so kind. . . Will Hero's Tower crumble under the fifteen-inch guns? Will the sea be polyphloisbic and wine-dark? Shall I loot mosaics from Santa Sophia, and Turkish Delight and carpets? Should we be witnessing a turning point in History? Oh God! I've never been quite so happy in my life, I think . . . I suddenly realise that the ambition of my life has always been since I was two years old to go on a military expedition against Constantinople."

"Oh no!" thought Harry, "Doesn't he realise that people are going to die? That there is going to be blood and moaning, whimpering and involuntarily evacuating yourself."

But even as Harry thought this, he still thrilled to the same passionate desire for male-bonded violent action, never for a moment imagining that he too might become one of the whimperers.

Harry, as an intelligence officer who would be helping in the boarding and disembarkation, went to visit the RND which was camped on the other side of the Canal near Port Fuad.

There he found the tents all in neat rows, and eventually traced that in which Sub-lieutenant Brooke was living. On his arrival Harry saw that clean-cut and handsome face all swollen and puffed up—the lips thick and bloated—a wasted body lying sweating on the meagre camp bed in the dry Egyptian heat.

"Good heavens Rupert, what the blazes has happened to you? What's all this?"

"Hello! It's Harry, Harry Bridgeman, isn't it? It's those blasted mosquito bites, particularly one nasty one I got on the lip."

"Well look. Have you seen the medics? You ought to be in hospital. What are you doing sweating it out here? Rupert, frankly you look bloody awful."

"Harry, for god's sake, do shut up. It's only a mosquito bite. I'm bound to get better soon. Do you think I am going to miss a chance like this? The very first great epic of the Western world where Homer wrote about heroes like Achilles, and Hector, Agamemnon and Priam took place only a mile away from where we are headed overlooking the Dardanelles. Do you think I am not going to be there for this second instalment."

"But, Rupert, you're not going to be seeing much in that awful mess. Look, let me arrange to send some RAMC orderlies round at least to have a look at you."

"Yes, Rupert," said the other young officer who had been standing rather helplessly alongside and who clearly shared the tent. "He's right, these things can get nasty. Please just let someone have a look at it."

"No, Charles. Both of you belt up! Charles, if you want to do something, just go and get some ointment or cream or something and bring it here. There's a good fellow."

He stopped in a fit of coughing and closed his eyes, clearly irritated. Harry felt that he ought not stay much longer. He had a word with the other young officer Charles, said he would look out for both of them on board, clasped the poet's hand for a brief moment, squeezed, and then left.

The very next day the RND packed up their tents and embarked on the little flotilla which was to take them to the Aegean for their kicking off point for the landings in Gallipoli. The harbour and roadsteads at Mudros, the main collection point for the invasion on the island of Lemnos, was by then totally filled with shipping. Harry's flotilla accordingly headed on for the island of Skyros which was to be the alternative rendezvous.

For some days the force—naval and military—remained on this delightful Greek island, all day in brilliant sunshine in a bright blue sky. The whole island seemed to Harry to be made up of great blocks of irregular white marble, piling up on small mountains of up to two or three thousand feet high. This was all covered over with masses of lilac, sage and purple thyme. The shepherds and villagers of the island with their goats and sheep carried on as usual as they always did, ignoring the sudden arrival in their island of the outside world and all these fair-haired, blue-eyed and impossibly young men. Harry had found himself thinking that no doubt they had acted exactly in the same way when Leander had passed by with another invasion force, two millennia previously.

Only two days before the force was due to move out to the invasion, Harry was approached by a Petty Officer who said, "I'm sorry sir, but could you please come to the divisions' lines. I'm afraid that Lieutenant Brooke is dying."

Harry hurried on to the ship's cutter, reached the shore and raced up to where Brooke's tent had been, though it appeared that by then he had been transferred to a hospital ship. Several people were gathered round.

"He died a few hours ago, Harry," said an acquaintance. "After all that romanticising, he never got to witnessing the glory of war, which he so wanted."

"My God, what poetry he would have written if he had had that wonderful experience," said another fresh-faced and incredibly young subaltern.

The poet had died of a mosquito bite on his lip. It was as if Hector had slipped on a banana skin and infected his little finger, or Achilles had died of a bowel infection. They buried him that night under a few olive trees, and Harry helped carry his body slowly and carefully up the hill that evening.

Later in the same night, back on board, writing to his mother, Harry referred to the difficulties in getting the coffin up the narrow mountain path, "Mother, you would wonder at what a beautiful spot it was where we buried poor Rupert. It was at the top of a little stony hill surrounded by weeping olive trees, with that wonderful scented Greek covering of flowering sage, thyme and spring flowers. It was a beautiful moonlit evening. The path up was very narrow, and it was tricky going carrying the coffin. It took us over an hour to go just the one mile. A party of the others had gone ahead to dig the grave. We simply laid him in it, covered it with the marble stones strewn all around, and piled up on top of it all the flowers we could find. We then returned down the same narrow path, by which time it was completely dark as the moon had gone behind clouds."

In the same letter Harry referred to the young subaltern's remark as to the sort of poetry Rupert might have written had he finally got to the war.

"Mother," he wrote, "the lad was right in a way. Rupert did so want to experience the camaraderie and energy of shared action. However, who is to say how it would have affected his poetry. Already you can see how the young poets, who are beginning to actually experience the horrors of trench warfare, are beginning to change their tune and style. Poor Rupert, missing the actual experience, is I think always going to be misunderstood by later generations. Here, mother, is one of his last lines, in case you haven't seen it before:

"These, laid the world away;
Poured out the red sweet wine of youth;
Gave up the years to be of worth and joy,

And that unhoped serene that men call age;
And those who would have been their sons,
Their immortality."

What Harry did not know was that on a piece of cardboard, pinned to the back of the simple little wooden cross that they had stuck at the head of the grave, the division's Greek interpreter had written in Greek, in pencil, the words: "Here lies a servant of God—sub-lieutenant in the English Navy—who died for the deliverance of Constantinople from the Turks."

Two days later the Royal Naval Division embarked to join the Anzacs for the Gallipoli landings.

Chapter 20

Makrikoy. Guests at the Avakians.

There was a clear ritual that Karekin followed in welcoming formal guests in the afternoon to his house in Makrikoy. Finding out the time of the train they would be taking, he would walk down to the Chobancheshme station. There, he would make sure that both Abdul and Mustapha were free with their arabas. He would more often than not take Haik with him, but the girls and Armineh would always remain at home. So it was on the occasion of the visit by the Levonians, arranged the day before.

Hovannes Levonian was a fairly typical Ottoman Armenian business man—corpulent and with a gold chain across a wide expanse of stomach. He wheezed and grunted as he got out of his first class carriage, turning to hand down his wife, Yvonne. Haik, waiting on the platform with his father, with his sharp and curious eyes picked them out at once as being bound to be their guests.

Yvonne Levonian was a thin, somewhat brittle lady, who had the reputation of always bursting into rather poor French at every possible opportunity—one never knew quite why. Following her out of the carriage came a serious-looking young man—beginning already to turn rather plump himself—sporting the usual Enver-style moustache, and certainly looking older than the alleged twenty three or twenty four years old. In his turn he was followed by a pert young girl, with long fair hair and a sharp grin.

"Karekin, my friend, meet my wife Yvonne. My dear this is Karekin Avakian, of whom you have heard so much."

"Enchante, enchante," said Yvonne, extending her hand, as if she expected it to be taken and kissed. Karekin smiled and took it into his own hand, for just the right amount of time, but making no attempt to bend down to it for any old-fashioned ritual kiss.

"My son, George, and my daughter, Tamara," said Hovannes, introducing his two children. Karekin then introduced Haik, who was wearing long trousers for the occasion and who dutifully shook hands with everyone. They all strolled out of the station, and clambered into the two waiting carriages—the three parents in the bigger one, and Haik and his two guests in the other. George and Tamara sat in the comfortable carriage seats facing forward, whilst Haik of course had to sit opposite them in the rather uncomfortable single seat facing backwards. He stared at the pert and pretty Tamara, who stared back at him, swinging her legs under layers of Alice in Wonderland skirts. Although she was physically smaller than Haik, at thirteen or fourteen—Haik couldn't tell—she was a good deal more mature looking. Tamara was plump with full thick lips, while Haik was thin, and his sharp face was all huge brown eyes.

Tea parties in these circumstances in these years in Constantinople tended to follow a fairly standard ritual. First, after the preliminary introductions, the guests would be seated in the main sitting room with all members of both families sitting in a semi-circle round the fireplace. However, this would be without the presence of the girl whom everyone had come to meet—and this was the one part of the ritual always the same. The inference made by the hostess, and graciously acknowledged, would be that she was out preparing the tea—although everyone knew perfectly well that the tea had been prepared by the servants long before.

Talk would be general and would avoid politics or anything contentious. However, matters in this respect were not quite so usual in these days of tension and uncertainty, and the war and the rumours of a direct attack on the City by the Allies were soon the subject of fairly heavy discussion between Hovannes and Karekin. Armineh and Yvonne talked rather desultorily about the cost of vegetables, and also listened dutifully to their husbands. George said nothing. Haik, Tamara and little Seta fidgeted, whilst Nerissa and Olga, knowing that they were not supposed to say anything unless directly addressed, chafed under what seemed to them to be impossible restraint to which they were not accustomed.

"Karekin, my friend, what about the situation in Van? It's time we stood up for our rights. The day of the Ottomans is over. This is a hopeless ramshackle empire, and the best thing would be for either the Germans to take over if they win the war, or for the Anglo-French to do so if they win. Then we can have, as well as an independent Armenia, an independent Kurdistan, an independent Lazistan, an enlarged Greek state, and a Turkish Anatolian state. That's the way we can all become modern and western."

"And what will happen to Constantinople, with all your separate little nation-states? They'll all end up squabbling about it. For, Hovannes, it is this city and the Straits that is important to the world, not what is going on in the mountains of Anatolia or in the valleys of the Caucasus."

"Karekin, for heaven's sake, look what happened under the unspeakable Abdul Hamid. At least if we all had our separate states no one is going to end up being oppressed by their own government."

"Don't you believe it, my friend. Exclusive one-nation states can be just as oppressive as any of the old-fashioned empires—in fact more so very often, as they consider themselves to have a legitimacy that the multi-racial old empires don't possess."

"Come, come, Karekin, let's have done with the decadent and ramshackle old Ottomans once and for all."

So the conversation swung back and forward with the corpulent Hovannes taking a more and more anti-Ottoman line, and Karekin mildly reproving him.

"In the end, Hovannes, this empire however ramshackle has been home to at least twenty different peoples and languages, at least five major religions, a whole raft of cultures, and has kept a tolerable peace between them all for centuries. Do you really believe that the one race, one people nation-states that might follow would be more tolerant of each other?"

The moment would of course then come that the hostess would rise, excuse herself and say she was going to arrange the tea—although again everyone would know that her presence in the kitchen was not necessary, and that all would be ready—but there it is, it was the custom! Armineh dutifully rose and went out. She returned almost at once, and the theory was that she would be followed by a discreet and demure Sima leading in the tea trays, brought in by Marie, herself dressed in her Sunday best.

Sima, however, as an Avakian daughter, was in no way discreet or demure. She came in ahead of the trolley with a plate of cakes, and with none of those downcast eyes called for by the script for these occasions. Seta giggled at Marie, but was immediately quelled by a sharp look from Karekin. Sima, meanwhile, looked long and frankly at George and his two parents and went forward sociably to shake their hands. Karekin smiled to himself, saying nothing, Hovannes was slightly put out, but rallied, Armineh noticed nothing, and Haik looked with pride at his statuesque and dignified elder sister, who had effortlessly taken centre stage without having said a word.

After a notional cup of tea and a cake, the young ones, if there were any, would be excused. So on this occasion Haik, Tamara and Seta got up and left. Nerissa, of course, now sixteen, had to stay with the grown-ups, although she would have preferred to leave. Seta led Haik and Tamara into the large garden at the back but then excused herself as she had to go and help in the kitchen where Marie was alone. Haik was appalled at being left alone with this girl who looked at him appraisingly under thick eyebrows. He had no idea what he was supposed to be saying, and she didn't appear to be listening to anything he was mumbling anyway. He looked at the garden with its dense orchard of apricot and peach trees at the far end, then turned to look at his companion.

Haik saw a young girl, fashionably over-dressed, with several skirts that came down below the knees. He saw long dark hair, strong eyebrows, thick wet lips, and the usual large brown eyes. Tamara for her part saw a boy, who looked younger than the twelve years and over that he was supposed to be, who had pale delicate white features with a sharp pointed nose, unruly long hair, and big bright inquisitive eyes—the whole having a somewhat feminine aspect.

"Come," she said taking him by the hand, "let's explore your orchard."

She led him down to the far end, as if it were her garden, and not his. Haik was somewhat bewildered, but enjoyed the way she had taken over. Amongst the trees, as they wandered, he was aware that they could not be seen from the house. Haik pondered on the fact that they really had nothing much to say to each other, whilst he himself simply didn't have the social graces to make small talk.

Tamara stopped, and began kicking idly at some dead branches on the grass. Haik leaned against an apricot tree and watched, fascinated though uneasy at this first young girl of approximately his own age that he had ever encountered alone. Tamara came up and facing him put her hands on either side of his face on the tree trunk, then she leant forward and touched his lips with her own. Neither of them really knew what they were doing—certainly Haik didn't, though he felt that the moment was important in some way. He was surprised to find that the sensation though surprising was very pleasant. Tamara pulled back and their eyes met. She smiled.

Haik could only stare and wonder. However, the more anxious he became, the more confident she became. Once again she leant forward, and once again her thick lips pressed against his thinner and weaker ones. She held them there for several seconds—no more than the lips touching. Haik felt himself holding his breath and an unaccustomed erection rising, but he kept his arms firmly pressed back against the tree trunk. Unlike during the first touch, their eyes were wide open as they looked at each other. The moment stretched into eternity.

"Haik, Tamara, where are you? Come and join us," a voice called out from the house. Haik shuddered and full of an inchoate guilt said, "We must go," and ran out.

Tamara stood back and walked after him calmly out of the wood. At the far end Sima and George were standing awkwardly, waiting for them to come and join them for a walk in the garden. The walk had been arranged inside, on the clear belief that Haik and Tamara would be there already, able to join them, and it had been a moment of uncertainty for them both when they had walked out of the doors to find the garden empty.

As they came up from the orchard, Sima reflected on the young man standing by her side. She saw a man of about twenty-four though he looked older. He was already turning to plumpness, with smooth well-groomed skin and a round baby-face. On his part George saw a very proud rather stiff and statuesque young woman, with the great Avakian eyes, but rather too talkative and direct for his taste. The irony was that whereas Haik and Tamara had been left free to roam as they wished in the garden, and to get up to any mischief they felt like, Sima and George, both far more mature, had to be strictly chaperoned. Not all the social customs of the time made sense.

Both Tamara and Haik, although only thirteen and twelve respectively, were well aware of what was expected of them. Sima doing most of the talking walked ahead with George, whilst Haik and Tamara, both totally silent walked behind with their own thoughts, as they all slowly paced round the lovely garden.

George and Sima made polite small talk without communicating very much to each other. In an odd way Haik and Tamara were communicating much more to each other without saying a word. Haik, who had already experienced nocturnal emissions, was nevertheless sexually rather innocent. He had become erect immediately Tamara's lips had lingered on the second occasion, and he had felt both excited and guilty. Tamara, on the other hand, had had no problem. She had experienced exactly the sort of thrill that she had expected, and there was no confusion in her mind at all.

And so the four of them walked sedately round the garden, and through the orchard with George and Sima politely appreciating the flowers, with Haik glancing anxiously at Tamara and reddening at the thought of her lips, and with Tamara, well aware of the young boy's confusion, walking demurely alongside.

That night Karekin knocked at the door of his eldest daughter's room, and walked in. "Well Sima, what did you think of the young man?"

"Oh Baba, I don't think I could ever come to feel anything for him. There's no arrangement or proposal, is there?"

"No, no, my darling. The important thing is to be clear right from the start so no one gets any wrong ideas or gets hurt. Don't worry, mother will see that it's all sorted out without any hurt feelings tomorrow."

The next day however was to be the 24th April, the day the government was expecting to have to face an Allied invasion.

Chapter 21

Gallipoli. Harry—the landing

It was completely clear to the authorities both in Constantinople, and for that matter, even in Berlin, that the proud British Navy, having been defeated for the first time in a century, by the Turks of all peoples, a landing by the Allied army was now going to be attempted somewhere along the Dardanelles, and probably in the Gallipoli peninsula. It didn't need any agents planted in Egypt to send messages by the new-fangled radio for the Turkish High Command to be perfectly aware as to approximately where the landing was going to take place. Even the date was fairly obvious, as more and more shipping gathered in and around the islands of the Aegean.

The British plan was that the elite 29th division would land at the tip of the Peninsula in and around Cape Hellas on five separate beaches, flanked by the old Ottoman Castle on the one side, and a modern fort on the other. It was from the start a death trap, unless the Navy could intervene. The small French contingent would make some feint landings on the Asian side. The Anzac, backed by the small Royal Naval Division, to whom Harry's ship was assigned, would land further north at the narrow waist of the peninsula.

The landing was fixed for the 23rd April. The armada grew larger every day, with all sorts and conditions of shipping crowded into the narrow harbours and deep blue bays of Mudros and Skyros and other islands. Then, just as the moment was about to arrive, a fierce but short-lived typical Mediterranean storm blew up, and the landings were postponed to the 25th. The German military agent infiltrated into Alexandria in Egypt could not have reported this decision, as by then the British HQ was no longer there, but on board the *Queen Elizabeth,* already in the Aegean. Nevertheless, the delay simply increased the readiness of the Turks whose dispositions were already in place.

General Hamilton, the British C-in-C was no mere 'donkey commanding lions.' He was a kindly intellectual gentleman of impeccable breeding and manners, a poet manque, with a lyrical turn of phrase, very popular with all the troops, but unfortunately anxious not to hurt anybody's feelings. Whilst capable of commanding a division or even perhaps an army corps, he was simply not ruthless enough to take command of a whole army. From the very start, although he saw clearly the administrative errors and weaknesses of the plan of campaign, he had been unable to stand up against Kitchener and Churchill, two far more forceful characters. Accordingly, he failed to insist on those matters of detail which bored his two superiors, but which he knew were vitally necessary to be dealt with if the botched up operation suddenly entered into—due to the failure of the Navy—had any hope of succeeding. Once again, the wrong man in the wrong place at the wrong time

"Good morning, good morning," the General said
when we met him last week on the line.
Now—the soldiers he smiled at are most of 'em dead,
And we're cursing his staff for incompetent swine,
'He's a cheery old card' grunted Harry to Jack,
As they slogged up the hill with rifle and pack. . .
But he did for them both, by his plan of attack."

The contrast with Mustafa Kemal, the Turkish General in command of the defences of Gallipoli was enormous. Inevitably, as Kemal later became Kemal Ataturk, perhaps one of the most successful dictators of all time—the Turkish Oliver Cromwell—Turkish accounts of the Gallipoli operations have concentrated on the part he played in the defence. But this is, for once, a justified piece of hagiography. General Liman von Sanders, the German military advisor was certainly present, and did a lot to evaluate and distinguish the feints from the genuine landings in the early stages, but in the end it was the dogged defence of the high ground—the spine that ran down the centre of the peninsula—by the patient Anatolian peasants, inspired by the direct and personal leadership of Kemal, that 'did for' Harry and Jack and the entire Allied operation.

He was personally everywhere inspiring his troops with sheer guts and decisiveness, leading them, often on his own, forward to the sound of the guns wherever they might be. On one occasion, riding forward and coming across a body of men fleeing from the enemy he shouted out, "Why are you running away?"

"Sir, the enemy," they replied.

"Where?"

"Over there, over there!" they called out pointing to one of the hills behind them, up to which a British contingent had finally clambered.

"You can't run away from the enemy, men, sooner or later you'll get shot in the back that way," said Kemal.

"Sir, we have no ammunition left," they replied standing about disconsolately, but at least no longer running away.

"Look, you have your bayonets. Fix your bayonets now, and then turn openly and lie down behind this ridge facing the enemy."

Whether this did the trick, or if there was some other reason, the enemy certainly stopped advancing as the Turkish soldiers dropped to the ground and appeared to be taking aim. Kemal himself immediately rode back and ordered up some reinforcements and spare ammunition.

Back on the other side of the lines, the ship on which Harry was stationed lay close in to the shore as the infantry debouched onto the beaches.

"Harry," said the commanding officer, "I want you to go ahead with the second wave of these lads. I believe that the preparations for the wounded have been totally inadequate. The chief RAMC officer here yesterday told me of the ridiculously small number of casualties for whom he had been ordered to make preparations. I blew up, as you can imagine—it seems to me that there is no real provision for taking off the wounded. We could help out a bit, I know that you have had a bit of first aid training. I'll send Seamen Jim Strong, and Jack Jones with you. They're good strong lads. We are not leaving till tomorrow, and we could help out by taking off a few of the wounded if there are any with whom the RAMC can't cope. But look Harry, whatever the situation, I want you back by daybreak as we must leave by 6.00."

So, an hour or two after nightfall Harry landed at Geba Tepe in the dark, and in a miserable sleeting rain. He, with James and Jack, were packed into a lighter all crushed up with the Australians, who while quieter than usual, seemed in fairly good spirits. As they drew nearer to the shore, bullets and shrapnel were splashing into the water, and some thunking into the boats.

"Hey, mate, how far are we from the shore?" said one of the soldiers to Harry.

"Honestly, I'm not at all sure, but it was quite deep here so we were able to come quite far in. I doubt if it's much more than about ten minutes," said Harry carefully, trying to sound as off-hand as possible. He was in a fair state of panic himself inside, much more so than when on board. Somehow the solidity of all that iron on even a small boat seemed so much less dangerous than this feeling of having his soft body so totally exposed.

"I bloody well hope so. I'm getting fucking sea-sick, much worse than when we were at sea. Oh, God! I'm going to throw up!"

"Hey, Jacko, if you're going to be sick come here and stick your face over the side, bullets or not," called out another.

"Don't be daft. I can't bloody well move. Oh God I can't keep it down."

"Look," said Harry, "put your head up and look at the stars, and take deep breaths."

Harry watched as Jacko, or whoever he was, lifted his head, but at the first breath, down came his head again and Harry heard the splash of the sour vomit falling into the scuppers of the boat, as some of the others tried to edge away from the unfortunate man.

"Christ, you fucking old gum sucker! For god's sake belt up and save your breath! You'll be all right lad, just think of how wonderful that hard solid ground is going to feel once we arrive," called out the old Sergeant at the front of the tossing boat.

Harry looked round at all these young men, apart from him and the sergeant none much more than nineteen, excited, deadly frightened, but sickly grinning, carefully hiding their real fears from their companions—not just out of any misplaced male pride, but because they were atavistically aware that a collective show of courage was a help to each other in this sort of situation, millenia of their hunting ancestors coming out in their genes.

Once the boat crunched onto the sand, they jumped out into a scene of indescribable confusion, which had clearly been going on all day. On the narrow strip of sandy and stony beach, at the foot of the hills rising ridge after ridge above them, men were moving about in all directions. Troops jumping out of boats, troops marching west, troops marching east, mules and horses, some stationary with their heads drooping, some carrying stores to god knows where, water barrels dumped haphazardly, and above all stretcher bearers coming down the cliffs with wounded and dying men.

The next day, when he got back to the ship, and as it ploughed its way back to Egypt, Harry sat down and wrote to his mother:

> Before half an hour was over, after I landed, my work began, and after that I never had a moment. It went on till about three in the morning. One wounded and dying man following on after the other. Poor fellows, with wounds of all kinds, all disfigured and caked with blood and dirt. Some of them totally unrecognisable, with their features blown away. But, mother, what's wrong with me—within minutes, in the midst of all this suffering and death, I found that I was ceasing to feel the terror and horror of the situation at all. Sights that ordinarily would have upset me to the point of vomiting, seemed to be passed over by me without any feeling at all. Have I lost my sensitivity for pain and suffering in others? I just don't know. I closed the eyes of one young lad, he couldn't have been much more than eighteen, who had been moaning for his mother for two hours. I did it almost absent mindedly when he died, whilst I was bandaging up someone else.
>
> Mother, dear, it was bitterly cold all night, but one of the desperately few ambulance men around, made and lit a fire. There was still the sound of sniper shots coming from the hills above us, but even this sound died out as the night wore on. At about four in the morning, the noise started all over again. Mother, can you believe it, but we suddenly found ourselves being shelled by the *Goeben*, which had crept up during the night and began lobbing shells at us

> from the other side of the peninsula, anchored as she was safely in the Straits. I thought of the Report I had written, and the dramatic sight of the *Goeben* on that very first day of the war whilst I stood on the bridge of the *Indefatigable*, and saw the great ship slowly slipping away us from in the dusk. Now here she was again, hurling shells at us. At times I had the fancy that she was aiming at me personally.'
>
> The confusion remained incredible. I imagine Dad knows all about this aspect of warfare. Eventually saying goodbye to the ambulance lads, we followed the stretcher bearers still working their way down to the beaches, which were again being raked by rifle fire from the heights above. Jack and I helped to put some final wounded into our pinnace which was waiting, and we set off for the ship. Jimmy was no longer with us. Shrapnel fire from the *Goeben* had done for him, as he had been coming down with the stretcher bearers some minutes before us. Love Harry

Looking over the cliffs onto the other side of the artificial line separating these two such different bodies of men—but ultimately so much the same—there was the same fear, the same adrenaline working, but not quite the same mess or confusion. As the line solidified during the night and the next day, Kemal Pasha set up his headquarters right on the front line, and issued the following order of the day: "Every soldier who fights here with me must realise that he is in honour bound not to retreat one step. Let me remind you all that if you want to have a rest, that this may have the result that there may be no rest for our whole nation throughout the rest of time. I am sure that all our comrades agree on this, and that you will show no signs of fatigue until the enemy is finally hurled into the sea."

This was the authentic voice of the new Turkey Kemal was later to create. It wasn't as lyrical or as articulate as Hamilton's exhortations, but it had a harder more direct edge.

Chapter 22

Olga and Selim.

Several days had passed since that dreamy tea party at Tokatlian at which Olga had sat lost in a haze of romantic vision, staring into the eyes of Selim, not listening in any way to the little orchestra. Selim and Olga had continued during the next few days to speak to each other at least once or twice each school day. All shyness and restraint between them had disappeared. Olga spoke to Selim with a straightforward honesty, that, whilst he found disconcerting, having had no previous experience of such direct outspokenness in any girl, nevertheless thrilled him with the feeling that he was getting into a deep understanding of her mind. For his part, Selim, though not nearly so articulate, gave to Olga an intimately charged warmth that she had never experienced before from any other person outside her family, despite all her sociability and sophistication.

Her father had left home particularly early this morning. Olga herself walked slowly down to the Chobancheshme station, past the open fields of the Vali Effendi racecourse, over the railway lines and into the little station. Although her mind was entirely on the coming meeting with Selim, she was not entirely unconscious of the excited buzz of conversation swirling around her as she waited for the train. Little gatherings of businessmen, mainly Jewish, Greek or Armenian, stood on the platform, huddled into their separate ethnic groups in a way that would not have happened only a few days before. Olga heard but took little notice of snatches of conversation around her.

"Do you know whether they have landed yet or not?"

"I heard the booms of big naval guns last night coming from the Sea of Marmara. The British Navy must have broken through, and I am afraid that we should be expecting a bombardment of the City this afternoon."

"Have you heard that Enver and Talaat have fallen out, and that Talaat has left for Germany together with Liman von Sanders, who has been recalled to Berlin?"

"I have it on absolutely the surest authority that the Greeks have declared war and are marching on the City to join an English force which has landed only fifty miles away in Thrace."

The voices and rumours, most of them well wide of the mark, swirled around her, and the feeling of anxiety and uncertainty was palpable, like a cloud of gas drifting from group to group, and communicating itself to her in a subtle and indirect way. There was a real sense of a whole society on the verge of a collective breakdown, as each group or individual tried to work out for themselves where they stood with regard to a shaky government. These were all family men going to work as a matter of routine and as a means of trying to keep the unfamiliar at bay. They were all clearly worried as to what was going to happen to them and their dependents personally in a desperately fluid situation.

These were also deeply confused men. Despite the clear failures of the Ittihad government, there remained always a residual loyalty to the old Empire, in which they had all lived for generations. There was no historical inevitability that the Empire might end in a maelstrom of ethnic hatred and tensions. It was the actions of men that made it happen, not some historic imperative, and these men were all reacting in their separate individual ways.

Olga, lively, well-educated and politically aware as she was, was only taking in any of this turmoil around her subconsciously. Her thoughts lay totally on the coming day at Robert College, and the delicious knowledge that she would be seeing Selim—and seeing him alone. Selim had made friends with the old caretaker in charge of the boiler room—Olga had no idea how, though she suspected the handing over of baksheesh. Over the past two days the old man had placed a couple of wooden chairs for them by the side of the enormous old boiler that provided heating for the building in the winters.

Twice now, Olga and Selim had sat on these two chairs, whilst the old man bustled about amongst the pipes in the dark depths of the basement room. A wonderful old man with a kindly creased face, a fez always on his head and old-fashioned baggy trousers, he was prepared to provide the chairs, but not to leave them alone. The chairs were placed close enough for them to touch hands for the fifteen minutes or so that they could afford to be together. Somehow it had not crossed their minds to draw the chairs closer together than where old Mustafa had carefully placed them.

How could Olga possibly take any notice of what was going on around her, when she felt sure that as well as having the joy of witnessing his love for her in his eyes, their lips were surely going to touch today for the first time. So she stood and waited for the train and smiled to herself.

However, once she reached the College she simply could not ignore any more the tensions and anxieties amongst her particular friends and all the other girls. Once again snatches of conversation swirled about her.

"My father said that the English and French landed today in the Gallipoli peninsula," said Angelina, her Greek friend. "But he says that it is quite untrue that Greece has declared war and is joining in the attack on the city."

"I heard that the old Sultan has called for a Jihad, but that Enver is opposing the idea, and a good thing too."

"My father's shop, which is just below our flat in Beyoglu was attacked this morning and the windows broken."

This last comment from another Greek girl, was dropped like a stone into the pool of anxious girls, and caused an immediate nervous ripple of silence. Even at seventeen, the girls were well aware of the difference between the ritualised violence of armies manoeuvring hither and thither in remote places, and the immediate unstructured violence of the urban mob.

"I must say, however," said the same girl, after the pregnant silence, "the police were there, for once, within minutes and they got rid of the small crowd immediately."

A discordant voice called out from the back, "You're all disloyal parasites. By God, you're all revelling in the difficulties we're all facing. You'd love to have the bloody Greek army at our gates, wouldn't you! Then you would treat with them, and join them, and betray this country which has nurtured you for centuries."

This comment was then followed by a murmur of nods and agreement by one section of the group of girls, and murmurings of dissent by another group. Racial tensions, dormant and usually well below the surface in this great polyglot city, were clearly rising as a result of the uncertain situation throughout the city, and this was being reflected here in the small world of the College.

Olga looked over to where a much noisier group of boys were shouting and gesticulating at each other. She could not see Selim. There was a fairly significant racial-gender difference at the college. Whereas amongst the boys there was a majority of Turkish students, reflecting the fact that liberal Turkish parents were ready to send their sons to the progressive American college; amongst the girls there were far less ethnic Turks, as that liberal attitude did not extend to their daughters. Accordingly there was a higher proportion of Greeks, Armenians and Jews amongst the girls.

The tension in the college grounds was conspicuous. A group of young men called out, taunting the girls, something unheard of in normal times. Olga was not oblivious to the menace in the air, but although she felt the tension, becoming increasingly nervous and emotional, she related it in her mind to the coming lunchtime rendezvous with Selim in Mustafa's boiler room. Just before going in to the second morning class, she saw a Greek young man, with a bleeding nose and bruised face, being led away by a group of his friends. However, she still didn't register this first touch of violence as anything more than part of the general tension, which in her mind seemed to centre only on her own overflowing emotions and the coming meeting.

The class was already smaller than usual—it was clear that some of the students had gone home or been fetched. Olga could only think of the moment she would be within Selim's touch and presence. The interminable hour did at last pass, and then without looking left or right, she hurried through the corridors into the courtyard and down the stairs leading to the basement room.

Selim himself had, that morning, like everyone else, been caught up in the rumours of a landing by the enemy somewhere or other in or near the Straits. He possessed the ability to compartmentalise his feelings much more than Olga, so that he was able to put his whole mind to the political situation and forget for a moment his emotions where Olga was concerned. Accordingly, he entered wholeheartedly into the debate amongst his classmates. There had always been a much greater racial tension and division amongst the boys at the college than amongst the girls—and accordingly Selim was discussing the events almost entirely with his Turkish friends. Once again the different rumours swirled around, "My father said that the Russians had landed at the Black Sea entrance to the Bosporus."

"The Greek army has entered Adrianople, and there has been a terrible massacre of Muslims. The great mosque has been burned down."

"Did you hear that the French have landed at Bursa?"

Selim smiled at the last one. How did the speaker imagine for a moment that the French had got through the Dardanelles, when the British had failed so signally a few weeks ago? Selim had not forgotten Olga and the coming lunchtime rendezvous, it was just that he could transfer it to a dormant section of his mind, which Olga could not. His excitement at the current situation was in no way insensitive. He was perfectly well aware of the deeper issues and dangers involved. He was simply reacting to the thrill and knowledge of great events happening around him that gripped him, as it gripped most of the other young men.

Before going into the second morning class a fight had broken out between a Turkish student and a Greek. They were separated before any great harm came to either of them, although the Greek boy's face was bloody and he was led away. Selim reflected that these were two young men who disliked each other anyway—there was some rumour about them both paying attention to the same Jewish girl—and the political tension had clearly exacerbated a personal rancour to the extent of them resorting to the blows they had probably wanted to exchange long before.

Despite all the apprehension and excitement, Selim was looking forward to this, his third short meeting with Olga. What, however, neither he nor Olga were aware of, was that their interest in each other had not gone unnoticed by at least some of their fellow-students, although nothing had been said by anyone.

Selim hurried out after class, avoiding all the further discussions, growing uglier by the minute, as the young men began to mirror in the microcosm of the College all the worries and problems of the adult world outside. He raced into the courtyard and down the stairs and called out to Mustapha as he arrived—while handing him the notes he had long since agreed.

Mustapha was a calming influence. He knew that Olga was a 'giavour,' but in a sense this had made it easier for him to accept Selim's tips, as he expected no better from infidel girls. He salved his conscience, which had indeed given him a few moments of guilt, by making sure that he always remained within sight and earshot of the pair. However, when it came to the wider political anxieties in the air, and the possibility of the arrival in the city of an invading foreign army, Mustapha was totally unaware and uncaring. Selim waited.

"Oh Selim, Selim" cried Olga as she ran into the room.

Selim grasped her hand. Even now, despite all the emotional turmoil, their upbringing and training made it impossible for them to relieve their tensions by clasping each other. It was not Mustapha's presence, it was simply a cultural impossibility at that stage. Both of them were aching for physical contact, but it was impossible for them to express it directly. Everything had to pour between them through their interlocked hands and their eyes.

"Selim, my soul, what is happening, what is going on, where are we going, it's all so awful—some of these girls seem to hate me. Oh Selim, it's so wonderful to see you, but what are we to do—Selim, what are we to do?" Olga gasped it all out disjointedly. She was for the first time in their short relationship, afraid and confused.

"Sit down here Olga my love, calm yourself, my loved one. The world is certainly turning upside down, but it shouldn't affect us, Olga. Oh! Olga don't cry, we'll sort something out sooner or later. Please don't cry. Who cares about the other girls or what people say, it will all pass, it will all pass. Today the Germans, tomorrow the British, it will all pass."

Olga felt her heart bursting with an emotion that she had never felt before. She knew that what she was doing and feeling was not just rash but was also positively dangerous. For the first time in eight weeks she felt the cold touch of fear—not fear for herself—but fear for the love that she felt for this man. Selim did not have the same feeling of fear at all. This was partly due to the gender difference between them, but partly also that, not being a member of a minority people, he had never experienced political insecurity. Either way Olga's trembling, where previously she had always been the stronger, merely gave him more strength.

There was a short moment of silence between them as they continued to stand facing each other, but then Olga turned away. She could bear it no longer.

"Selim, we have to part for the moment. I don't know what's going to happen, but oh Selim . . . oh Selim, I love you . . . I love you" she cried out for the first time in their relationship, through tears of joy or fear or whatever.

Selim's mouth went dry as he stepped forward. He grasped Olga for a brief fleeting moment round the waist as she looked up at him. Their lips touched for just a moment, just a touch, then Olga ran up the stairs, as Mustapha coughed loudly in the darkness behind them.

Upstairs in the courtyard, the atmosphere had turned more ugly. Rumours of arrests and worse were running round amongst the students. Something Robert College had not witnessed before was happening, and the student body was fracturing into its racial subdivisions. Already the place was thinning out, but it was the minorities that were hurrying home, whilst the Turkish young men and women were standing about discussing the situation loudly and aggressively. They were all goading each other into more and more unthinking extreme attitudes. It was into this whirlpool of young undirected passions that Olga suddenly emerged from the stairs leading down to Mustapha's basement.

"What were you doing down there, hanum," called out one Leila, whose envious personal feelings about Olga and her relationship with the popular Selim, could at last be given free rein, masked behind a political passion that had suddenly become acceptable.

"Giavour! Why are you still hanging about? Don't you know all your infidel friends have all gone home ready to welcome our enemies?" called out one of the group of boys still milling about in the courtyard and now pressing forward.

"You and your lot are all parasites waiting for the Empire to fall. You can't wait for the enemy to get here, and then you'll spit on us," shrieked Leila, working herself up to answering yells from the other girls, who crowded up to Olga as she tried to walk away.

Olga had no fear of the young men. She knew absolutely and for certain that they might jeer, but under no circumstances would they touch her, not one of them. But the girls were a different matter. For these Turkish girls Olga was a scheming slut of the worst kind, who had contrived to ensnare one of their boys as they now saw it. Little had Olga realised that whereas she had been able to keep her relationship with Selim hidden from her parents, this had not been the case in the closed gossipy world of the college. Furthermore, they all put the worst and most lurid construction on the situation.

Olga was a spirited lively girl, who could stand up for herself in most matters, but the whole emotional atmosphere in which she found herself was threatening to tip her into a state of extreme distress. Her lips quivered as she tried to elbow her way through the girls taunting her and pushing her from side to side. They were not consciously mean these girls. They, too, without realising it, were being affected by the strains and tensions which their parents were feeling, as the war which had seemed so far away, suddenly appeared almost at their doorstep.

No one was really ever going to hurt Olga physically. There were enough level-headed students around to ensure that there would be no real violence, so it was unfortunate that Olga finally gave way to an outpouring of sobs and tears of frustration and anguish at just the moment Selim appeared in the doorway at the head of the stairs. He couldn't see much. All he could take in was the sight of Olga standing sobbing in the middle of a crowd of girls, all of whom were in any case now pulling back, suddenly appalled at their own behaviour.

The sight of the girl in tears of distress had brought most of them back to their senses. But this of course was not clear to Selim.

"Olga, Olga," shouted Selim and began running towards her without thinking. Several young men, good friends of Selim, grabbed him and held him tight.

"*Yok, Yok*," they said gently and without any rancour, but nevertheless holding his struggling form tight to make sure he didn't get himself into any real trouble by going at any of the girls.

Olga looked up at his cry, but through her tears saw only that Selim was struggling and was being restrained by some of the other young men. She looked round at everyone staring at her, and then with a strangled cry, she turned and ran blindly out of the school gates.

Chapter 23

Karekin.

"My Soul," Karekin said, as Armineh bustled about behind him, as they rose in the morning, "You must be careful. The town's in a very excited state. The rumour is that the Allies were supposed to be landing somewhere along the coast yesterday. There have been crowds in the streets, and yesterday I saw that some Greek and Armenian shops had had their windows smashed. However, the police were out in force for once."

"Karekin, what does it all mean? Are we going to have some sort of pogrom or killings in the streets?"

"No, no my love, fortunately the presence of the German and Austrian legations are probably a guarantee that even this ridiculous government is not going to let the mob get out of hand. Nevertheless, in my opinion, individual anti-Christian violence by hoodlums, encouraged by the present atmosphere, is very likely. I do think that you and the girls must be careful. We must all keep a low profile in these circumstances."

"Karekin, my darling, leave me to manage the house and the children—you be careful yourself. Keep away from those politician friends of yours—the deputies—and try to come back early if you must go to work today. Karekin, are we going to be affected in any significant way by the invasion?"

"My soul, if the British break through to Bolis, our whole world will change for ever—of that I have no doubt at all. The opening of the Dardanelles and then the Bosporus to Russian shipping and the ensuing likely collapse of the Committee of Union and Progress will bring us all to a situation, the end of which is totally uncertain. Anything could happen and we must be prepared for all possibilities."

"But Karekin, we've had rumours and crises like this before. Look, why didn't they appear yesterday? They were supposed to be landing on the 23rd weren't they? Perhaps it's all idle chatter like what has happened so often before."

"Armineh, my dear, a British landing of some sort, somewhere within fifty or more miles of Constantinople itself is a certainty. Everyone knows about it—there is no secret. Ever since the British Navy failed to break through to the Marmara, there's been no attempt by them to hide the fact that they have been preparing, in and around the islands of the Aegean, for a major invasion."

Breakfast that morning at the Avakians was as lively as ever, but surprisingly there was little discussion about the war.

"Sima, my dear," said Armineh, "I think it would be a nice gesture if you called on Yvonne Levonian this morning. Take her a bunch of those lovely spring flowers that have just come out in the orchard. Don't worry, George and his father will be out at work, and she has known since yesterday that we have no intention to proceed further in the matter where you are concerned. On the other hand, your father has plans for a possible merger or association with Hovannes' business after the war ends, and it would be a nice way of keeping us well together, quite apart from the fact that it would be a really kind gesture on your part."

"Mama, that's fine. A trip to the city is always welcome. I'll go straight after breakfast, as I really must be back for Haik these days. Honestly, that woman though! It's such a bore having to speak French half the time whenever she gets it into her head to switch. She really is a bit silly! Does anyone want anything by the way, whilst I'm in the town?"

"For heaven's sake, Haik, eat something!" snapped Armineh. "No dear, we're all well stocked. Oh Olga! Are you off? Olga, can't you wait for Sima, and then you can go in together."

"No, I'm sorry Sima, but I really mustn't be late today. We have a test in the morning. Bye everyone, see you all this afternoon." Olga rose, gave Karekin his morning kiss, and rushed out grabbing her bag from the table in the hallway.

"Listen, Mama," said Sima as her mother began to protest, "Olga's right, I have to wait for Haik anyway. Look, I'll go and pick some flowers now. Tell Marie to prepare some nice wrapping paper, and then I'll go on to the station after leaving Haik at school. Nerissa can come with us if she doesn't mind waiting a few minutes."

One by one the family had dispersed. Olga first, then Karekin strode out immaculate as always in his grey suit. Nerissa, with her hated dowdy round school hat and smart leather bag waited for Sima and Haik. Finally came Sima, ready to go, clutching a glorious bunch of flowers, and Haik with his scratched old satchel.

Karekin himself arrived an hour or so later at his office in the city, determined to try to get some business dealt with for once. He felt that he had had enough of political alarms and turmoil, as day after day had passed with excited café talk with his friends and business acquaintances, to the exclusion of almost everything else. The news from Van seemed to have disappeared from the papers, and his friends—the Armenian deputies in the Parliament—had given no hint at all of being aware of any impending trouble. Karekin sighed and considered the good sense of his wife's comments that morning—it was certainly a time for a low profile.

The young men who had been his assistants had departed—one to the army, the other to who knew where. Karekin had had to employ two elderly and somewhat tremulous clerks, one Jewish and the other a Turk, to do some desultory typing and deal with enquiries in the outer office. Karekin was working at his desk, still fairly early in the morning, when there was a knock at his door.

"Effendi," said the old clerk, "There is a policeman at the door asking to see you."

"Well, show him in, show him in," said Karekin rising.

An elderly Turkish gendarme from the local police station, whom Karekin recognised, came diffidently into the office, and bowing respectfully offered Karekin a sealed note.

"Effendi, Karekin bey, I have been instructed to ask you to come down to the station please, to answer some important and necessary questions that have arisen."

"What! Right now?" said Karekin.

"Effendi, yes please. I understand the matter is urgent, and my commander has asked me to impress this upon you. It will only take a few minutes. Perhaps you could accompany me."

Karekin was not completely surprised. These summonses were happening more often, and he did not suspect in any way any deeper motivation. The natural politeness of the old Ottoman policemen was normal. Karekin nodded, and picked up his hat, but left his stick. He gave some minor instructions to his two clerks, and left the office—the elderly policeman politely making way for him at the door.

On the way to the local station, through the busy and crowded streets, the gendarme kept politely a step or two behind Karekin, perhaps out of respect for his privacy, but perhaps also because he didn't want to be questioned. Karekin noticed the restlessness and excitement of the crowds on the pavements. But this was not very different to what had been going on around him for days already. He raised his hat to the occasional business acquaintance. It was all perfectly normal.

On arrival at the station, the elderly gendarme disappeared. Karekin was asked by the clerk at the desk to go in, and he was then conducted by another policeman into a large bare room at the back of the station. This room was like a large white-washed hall with a few tables and chairs scattered about, and with only two or three windows high in the walls, through which one could not see out. Already seated at the tables, or standing about looking puzzled and disconsolate, were a group of about seven other gentlemen, amongst whom he suddenly picked out his old friend Doctor Aram Manuelian.

Karekin felt the first little butterfly feeling of uncertainty, but went forward smiling.

"Aram, my old friend," he said, as he walked forward and the door shut behind him, "Whatever are you doing here—and what the blazes is going on anyway?"

"Karekin, I really have no idea, and neither have any of these others," said Aram gesturing to the others in the room. "All I can say is that we are all Armenians, but there seems to be no rhyme or reason why we should be here at all. We now have here in this room already a doctor, myself, two lawyers, a journalist, and now you, a prominent business man."

At this comment, everyone suddenly started talking together at the same time. This chatter continued unabated for some moments, until the door opened again, and the local commissioner entered with three other people who were ushered into the room.

"Gentlemen I have to inform you that you are all under arrest," said the commissioner, looking at none of them directly. Karekin recognised the man who had called regularly, year after year, at his office during the time of the Bairam festival to extend the compliments of the local police force, and to collect the charitable contribution that would then be offered by Karekin for the local police fund. His bland announcement was met by a babel of comments and objections and questions from the eight people now in the room.

The commissioner raised his hand and called out—again looking no one in the eye, "I can tell you nothing except to inform you that last night Talaat Bey, from the Interior Ministry, ordered the arrest of some Armenian leaders suspected of having extreme nationalist sentiments and of aiding the Allied war effort."

Amidst an ever-increasing tide of objections and cries, he turned and walked out, the gendarmes closing the door behind him, and the prisoners hearing for the first time the ominous turning of the key.

Karekin sank into one of the chairs. Ignoring the noise around him, he began reflecting, though his thoughts did not get him far except to increase the creeping unease in his stomach. As the morning progressed, more and more people were ushered into the room, all as bewildered and annoyed as those already present. There was something particularly odd going on. It wasn't until fairly late in the morning that four of the Armenian Parliamentary deputies were brought in, and by then there were about fifty people in the room, which was becoming crowded. The odd thing was that this was not just a group of people who could be said to be politically motivated in some way or another. There were now scholars, musicians, a heavy group of lawyers, a couple of doctors, and even some clergymen, none of whom by any stretch of the imagination could be said to have any possible connection with the political events surrounding the city at the moment.

This was more than a round-up of what might be termed 'the politicals.' It constituted a microcosm of the prominent men of the whole Armenian community. This was 1915—none of these men had as yet had any experience of the new vicious tyranny that could emanate from governments claiming to act on behalf of a unified tribal people. There had of course been plenty of random cruelties in the old Ottoman system. This, however, was different, and Karekin could feel it in his bones even if the others could not—as yet.

By midday the group had become too large to be accommodated in the hall and they were all led out to the courtyard in the centre of the station. Once in the courtyard—it was a fine fresh morning—yet more people began arriving. One of these, a certain Doctor Allahvertian, was known by Karekin to be a well-known member of the Ittihad party itself. He had raised considerable funds for the CUP, and was supposed to be well in with Enver and Talaat—indeed to be one of their friends.

"Dickran, whatever is going on?" asked Karekin, when he had the chance to get to his side.

"Oh God! I don't know, I don't know," wailed the doctor. "I said to the Commissioner when I arrived that I would be grateful if he could ask the questions to which he wanted the answers as soon as possible; I told him that I had to get back to my office quickly. But he merely smiled and said 'soon, soon' and left me. I just can't understand it."

"But, Dickran, don't you realise that we are under arrest? This is not a matter of answering some questions. That was just an excuse. It's all much more serious."

"Nonsense, Karekin, and I would ask you not to say these things out loud—bad for morale you know. It's all a mistake—someone is carrying out orders that have not been issued as precisely as they should have been. They are acting over-zealously and perhaps too literally. I've asked the Commissioner here to send a message to Talaat."

"Dickran, Dickran! What's the matter with you? Can't you see what is happening?"

"Oh tush, Karekin, leave me alone. You're bats. We are at the start of the twentieth century for god's sake. This is not the days of some crazed medieval Sultan." With that parting shot he walked away, unwilling to continue a conversation he was finding distasteful.

Karekin shrugged, but now began thinking of how he could get a message to Armineh as to what was happening. He could see the signs of something a lot more sinister than Dr. Allahvertian would allow. His friend Aram, though equally at a loss, was also beginning to see a pattern as more and more people were herded into the courtyard. The mood however was still for the moment anxious and troubled rather than frightened and panicky. There were even jokes, as people assured each other that somehow, somewhere, the whole thing was a mistake.

In the age-old Ottoman style, there was the usual inefficiency with people coming and going in and out of the courtyard without too much supervision. Several people brought in had been accompanied by sons or servants who had entered, but who were then required to leave by the guards now permanently stationed round the walls. Names would be ticked off by the clerk now at the door, and those not on his list would be asked to leave after saying goodbye to those they had accompanied.

Karekin sidled up to the doorway set in the wall leading back to the main station, and waited for his opportunity as midday passed. There was by now less movement in and out of the courtyard, and the number of people milling about had already risen to over one hundred and fifty. Suddenly there was a sort of gasp from those standing near the door as, ushered into the courtyard was the familiar figure of Father Komitas—the acclaimed musician and moderniser of the Armenian liturgical Mass, who had given such a commanding performance at the concert before Talaat only three weeks ago. He was looking as bewildered and anxious as everyone else on their first arrival.

Accompanying him was a young man, clearly a student and registered at the Harbiye in his cadets uniform, and also clearly an

Armenian. He was holding the cleric and steadying him as he was obviously distressed and finding it difficult to walk. Karekin recognised that the arrest of this man confirmed his burgeoning suspicions, as in no way could Father Komitas be described as any sort of political risk. This was a man who had studied in Germany, and whose life and passion was ancient music. What was happening was something totally new and very dangerous.

Karekin edged up to the young man, who had now let go of Komitas, as the clerk ticked his name off the list. Father Komitas himself moved into the courtyard to join the other two clerics already there.

"Young man, my name is Karekin Avakian," Karekin said and went on to give the man his address in Makrikoy. "I desperately need to get a message to my wife telling her what has happened. I know it is a lot to ask, but would it be at all possible for you to do this for me?"

Karekin then felt in his pocket and produced a silver Lira and proffered it as delicately as possible. The young man looked at him and glanced quickly at the clerk, who was still checking his list. He shook his head at the proffered coin, smiled and said, "Sir, it's all very tricky in the city at the moment, but I will certainly do my best."

He then went over and kissed the good Father, and turned and walked out, nodding at Karekin as he went past, reiterating with his eyes that he would not forget.

The arrival of Father Komitas, for some reason, raised the spirits of the group. Komitas now radiated optimism, claiming like Allahvertian that the whole thing had to be some sort of administrative error, and would soon be sorted out one way or another. There was after all the approaching Allied intervention on the one side, and there were the foreign ambassadors still in Constantinople on the other. Karekin was not so sure, but wisely he said nothing, as morale was indeed important. Some elderly men were clearly frightened, depressed, and close to tears.

It was in this way that the greater part of Constantinople's prominent Armenian citizens were rounded up during the course of the day. These were not just the politicals, but a whole cross-section of a community, under arrest just for their racial background.

Gathered in three separate police stations they numbered almost three hundred men. Meanwhile, in the middle of it all, an enemy army was approaching scarcely one hundred miles away.

Chapter 24

Sima.

Once Sima had left Haik at the school gates that morning, she walked on down to the little station of Chobancheshme, accompanied by Nerissa, who did not have to be in school for another hour. Nerissa proposed waiting with Sima for the next train in order to keep her company. There was no one waiting on the platform, the station being almost empty. The gates were open as they walked round, crossed the line, and into the little hall to buy a return ticket to town for Sima. The sun was up in a beautifully clear bright blue sky. Sima felt well and pleased by the calm presence of Nerissa, as they sat on the benches waiting for the next train.

"I do know, Nerissa, that Baba and Mama love me, and I know that I love all my family—all of them. However, I'm sort of confused about the way things turned out when I was introduced to that young man who came with his parents recently. I'm sure that I have no particularly warm feelings of any kind for him. None of this matters much I suppose, as Baba has said that we don't have to take the matter any further, but surely, Nerissa, I ought to feel more thrilled by the fact that someone has shown some interest in me as a woman—oughn't I."

"Sima, don't jump about all over the place. Love for your family, but disagreement with your parents, have nothing to do with each other. You're not 'thrilled' as you say, because in truth it was not that sort of interest that was being shown. This was a social occasion only. Neither of you had the slightest chance to explore any possible deeper feelings, and so of course you felt no thrill. It would in a sense be sort of sad if you did."

"Nerissa, my dear, you're really a bit shrewd for your age. Where do you get it from?" said Sima, not thinking for a moment that she was being at all patronising.

"What do you think of this way in which we all get married after social occasions of this sort?"

"I don't know, Sima, my soul. My first reaction is to condemn it entirely. Honestly, how can people think of it as a business transaction? You are, after all, putting yourself into the position of perhaps making a commitment to live with another person for the rest of your natural life. What a decision! It's frighteningly vital that you get it right, isn't it. So how can you leave it to be manipulated by someone else, however much they love you."

"But Nerissa, what other way is there? Would it be likely to be any more successful if we chose ourselves—based on what? It would, I suppose, have to be our purely physical senses towards another human. What would that be founded on? Conversations hurriedly held in school or university corridors, rendezvous in crowded coffee houses, clandestine unsatisfactory meetings, perhaps like we read about in those novels you're forever reading. Would it be any better? Mother and Father's marriage seems to be fine enough, isn't it? And they had only met once before they married."

Nerissa did not answer. She thought of Olga and Selim, and wondered whether Sima unconsciously had some idea of Olga having the sort of relationship to which she was referring. Nerissa thought back to that tea party at Tokatlian.

'Unsatisfactory clandestine meeting'—was that a fair description of that long dreamy afternoon, and that look in the eyes of her sister and the young man as they discreetly held hands under the table and stared at each other? This was certainly not, she supposed, anything that Karekin and Armineh had experienced in their younger days. On the other hand, was it even remotely a reasonable basis for a life-long marriage? She felt confused—she, normally so self-possessed and clear in her opinions.

The whistle of the local train sounded from down the line, and the girls stood up. Not a word had been said about the war and any current tensions, largely because here on this little suburban station in the middle of a glorious spring morning, there appeared to be no tensions at all—an exquisite moment of calm.

Sima kissed Nerissa, who turned to trudge back to her little school, whilst Sima herself settled down in her corner seat, clutching her bunch of flowers. She sat back to enjoy the short journey to the city, the day was really so perfect.

The moment Sima arrived at Sirkedji station, however, the whole atmosphere of the day changed for her. The crowds appeared at first sight to be the same as usual, with a stream of people strolling down from the station to the Galata Bridge. Here the scene also seemed to be the usual one. The trams clattering each way across the bridge, the carriages waiting along the pavements to pick up the passengers from the ferries, the ferries themselves hooting and pushing in and out—getting eventually to the jetties under the bridge, where they dropped off and picked up passengers

There was, however, an undercurrent of nervous tension, which the more sensitive Nerissa would have noticed at once. Clutching her flowers, Sima, less sensitive but nevertheless aware of the excitement around her, threaded her way alongside the trams to the Galata Bridge. She walked down the steps to the quays and eventually stepped on to the right ferry. The ferry duly departed, chugging up the Bosporus, swinging from the European shore to the Asian and back again as usual. The ferry station for Bebek, the home of the Levonians, was not far down the Straits. Soon, Sima stepped out onto the landing stage, and made her way up to the Levonian house. She had been given clear directions how to get there, and on such a lovely morning there was no need for any carriage.

On arrival, Sima was shown into an ornate baroque sitting room with imitation gold-legged Louis Quinze chairs, where Yvonne Levonian sat regally esconsed awaiting her. Yvonne graciously but somewhat casually accepted the simple spring flowers, which suddenly looked a bit bedraggled next to the great blossoms of hothouse concoctions gracing every corner of the room.

"Enchante, ma cherie," said Yvonne. "Assayez-vous, s'il vous plait." The 'tu' originally utilised by the brittle Yvonne in Makrikoy, suddenly becoming 'vous' here in sophisticated Bebek, thought Sima. Having had the thought, Sima then immediately felt guilty, and wondered if she was not being over-sensitive.

After some banal exchanges of compliments in French, Sima, anxious not to spend the entire morning in stilted and indifferent French, changed to Armenian and launched into a description of the unusual atmosphere in the city. Yvonne was not unsympathetic. Even into her shallow mind, centred as it was round her house and her social pretensions, there had come a realisation that some sort of crisis more serious than the previous vague masculine talk of a war far away, was at hand. The decision, taken that morning by Hovannes, that young Tamara was not to go to school, had come to her as a greater surprise than all the newspaper reports read out to her, which had gone in at one ear and out the other.

Once the usual attempts at speaking only in very formal French was avoided, conversation with Yvonne was not too difficult. Sima only needed to sit back and let her prattle on about the many friends and recent social occasions she had attended. These social parties were always referred to with a mild hint of surprise in the voice that Sima herself had not been present at this or that social function.

It was in the middle of all this chatter that the unusual sound of a telephone came through the open door. The Levonians, like several houses in Bebek, possessed a private telephone. There were still none in Makrikoy. Within a few moments, the young Tamara came in, looking prettier and more natural, Sima thought, than when she had come dressed and made up formally to the recent tea party at Makrikoy.

"Mama, that was father. He and George are coming home right away. There's a lot of trouble in town. He says that there's nothing to worry about, but it appears there have been a few arrests, and there is a mob throwing stones and getting excited in the Grande Rue de Pera. Tokatlian's windows have been broken. He says that we must put up the shutters. He'll be back soon."

"Mais c'est affreux—qu'est que se passe?" wailed Yvonne, reverting to her execrable French. "Why the panic? Tokatlian's windows get broken regularly, don't they? I wonder they ever bother to repair them." Sima jumped up, assured Yvonne that she would be quite all right, kissed Tamara on the cheek, and hurried out after suitable goodbyes. She walked briskly down to the Bebek landing stage

Here all seemed to be as it was in the morning. As always, there was hardly a moment needed to wait as the next boat came up and pulled alongside. Out went the board plank, unnecessary really as the deck came right up to the landing jetty without any gap. On pressed everyone who had been waiting. At this stage of the journey, with only a few stops before the Galata terminus, there were no seats left. Sima stood watching as the ferry weaved near the battleships in the harbour, crossed once to Asia and recrossed, and finally began to approach the bridge.

Once here, however, all had changed. Sima looked at the bridge above. This was filled with a large mob of excited and gesticulating men, who were milling about totally blocking the road. The jetties below the bridge were also full of people. There was nowhere for them to go, as such was the crowd on the bridge itself that the passengers coming off the ferries could not get up the stairs leading up and off. Several ferries, unable to dock, were milling about, turning their engines on and off, unable to get in to discharge their own passengers. In all the shouting and excitement Sima could not hear what the mob was yelling.

Suddenly, in the midst of all the noise, there came the unmistakeable, loud foghorn blast of one of the two great battleships in the Straits. Like almost everyone else Sima turned, and saw the *Goeben* and the *Breslau*—oh dear, she thought, what were they now called, *Sultan Selim* or something—belching out great spurts of smoke from their funnels. Even as she looked, the majestic *Goeben* which must have been raising steam for some time, began slowly to move forward turning heavily on its axis, until it had completed a total 180 degree movement. The battleships began steaming south towards the sea of Marmara and the Dardanelles. It was a majestic sight, and Sima was riveted by its metallic grandeur. However, the whole manoeuvre had taken well over half an hour, and meanwhile here she was still stuck on the ferry-boat, admittedly with hundreds of others in the same predicament.

As Sima stood waiting for someone somewhere to do something, she suddenly remembered for the first time that there was going to be no way that she was now going to be able to get back to pick up Haik from school. However, there was nothing at all that she could do about it. Whilst she felt a bit guilty that she had not thought of it before, she dismissed the worry. After all, nothing had happened for days since Karekin had first insisted on Haik being picked up from school, and surely he would make his own way home, once he realised that she was not coming.

By now it had become clear that the demonstration, or whatever it was, involved only a purely Turkish gutter mob—not perhaps the most enlightened group of men. They were yelling the usual stuff about 'giavours,' Greek pigs, Armenian parasites, and Jewish scum. Sima did not feel any personal fear. Quite apart from the fact that the passions were not at this stage directed against individuals, there was a certainty in that old Ottoman world, shortly due to pass away for ever, that a woman, whatever her race or religion, if dressed discreetly and demurely, would not be touched in public. Meanwhile, however, time was getting on, and here she was still stuck on the ferry trying to get onto the bridge.

"Well, Madam, what a mess. I'm afraid we're still going to be stuck here for another hour or so, before we are likely to be able to get off the boat and away."

Sima looked up in surprise to the tall man standing by her side, leaning on the rails. The unusual circumstances in which they both found themselves had obviously given him the courage to speak to her, something which in the normal course of events would have been impossible. Sima saw a rather long angular young man, tall, rangy and rather dour in looks, who stared back at her unabashed by her metaphorically raised eyebrows.

"Hello," he said, "My name is Garen. I'm afraid that you are going to have to be patient for a little while longer." He then smiled at her for the first time. Sima, though taken aback, felt the fellow-feeling of shared discomfort, and knowing now that the young man was an Armenian asked, "What's going on, sir. Do you know?"

"Well I'm not sure, but there are three main rumours. One is that there has been an enemy landing somewhere in the Dardanelles. The second is that Greece has declared war on the Empire, and that the Greek army is at this very moment advancing on the city. The third rumour is that some prominent Armenians are being arrested in the city. I have no idea if any of these rumours are anywhere near the truth. As to what the crowd up there are demonstrating about, again I'm not entirely sure. However, on this last one I can give you a fairly good guess. Some of them are just plain frightened, most of them are just troublemaking unwashed rabble, and some, only a very few actually, genuinely have some sort of a grudge against the Christian millet. My own good mother got worried about my father, who came into town this morning to see the doctor, and I have been deputed to come and bring him home at once, whether he's managed to see him yet or not."

"And where is home?" asked Sima, increasingly at ease with this unusual conversation.

"Buyukdere—right up near the entrance to the Black Sea. I can at least confirm that the rumours about the Russians landing up at the top end of the Bosporus there are groundless, that is if you had any such idea at all," he grinned at her.

"Sir, I had no such thought in my head, though I suppose it might have made sense," said Sima with an answering smile, and then finally introduced herself. They shook hands warmly, exchanging names and addresses.

After some further chat, Garen remarked, "I'm currently at the medical school. I've nearly finished my studies. Normally I would've gone on to a hospital for a further year's training, but now, so long as we're not occupied by the British in the next few days, I think they'll send me to some front or other."

"Which front?" said Sima.

"Well, I don't know, against the British, or perhaps the Greeks, or the Bulgarians, or any of the others anxious to get their hands on our lovely city," said Garen still grinning at her.

It was certainly much less than an hour before the arrival at last of police reinforcements. Then with yells, whistles and a bit of pushing and shoving, the mob eventually began to thin out. All the people still on the wharves were able to climb up the stairs and go on their way, whilst those ferries which had been waiting, were able to move in and discharge their passengers.

Sima said goodbye to Garen, and began to make her way back up to the station. A train was already waiting. She climbed in and sat down thankfully, having been on her feet in the boat now for almost two hours. Her mind turned back to Makrikoy, and she hoped that Haik had already reached home. She determined nevertheless to pass by his school on the way back to make sure.

The train arrived at Chobancheshme station. This was a station where in order to get off the platform on the downside, you had to cross over to the other platform and go out through the little booking hall. Sima, still not hurrying or aware of any problems, crossed over the footbridge, and was just coming out of the ticket hall into the dusty entrance to the station, when she saw a very flustered looking Armineh just alighting from a gharry. Armineh came hurrying up to Sima who was standing, mouth agape, wondering what was going on.

Chapter 25

Vahan.

That morning Vahan was due to go to his weekly singing classes with Father Komitas, which he enjoyed so much, and for which he did not want to be late. Father Komitas gave lessons in singing, not only in the Armenian church liturgy which he had already done so much to modernise, but also, much to the disgust of the traditionalist clergy, in secular classical music. These lessons were a collective affair, usually with about twelve pupils. However, that morning Vahan received a letter from Caesaria from his mother, Mariam, which quite suddenly jolted him from his carefree student life, and which, with the remainder of this day's events, were to change his life for ever.

Like everyone else, he was, of course, perfectly well aware of the tensions in the city, and knew of the rumours of the forthcoming Allied landings due to take place somewhere on the Gallipoli peninsula. However, he had not been following in any way the growing concerns of the Armenian community as to the events in Van, and the imperceptible movement by the Ittihad government towards a 'final solution' in the Armenian highlands. Life was really too good and too exciting for him to allow these external political events to make a difference to his way of life. So it was that he read the letter from his mother with dismay and incomprehension.

> My dear son,
>
> May God bless you, and may you walk with Christ beside you all the days of your life. I kiss your brow and pray for you every day. God be praised, we are now all well. But I must inform you of the shock which we suffered recently.
>
> A week ago a police officer came to our house and told us that he wanted to see your father. Garabed was at home, as it happened, and as we knew the policeman who had come to our house on previous festival occasions collecting for the station, we had no hesitation in summoning your father.

When Garabed came down, the policeman simply said touching his forehead in the usual way, 'Garabed effendi, the Chief Commissioner of Police has asked me to request you to accompany me to the station as he wishes to ask you some questions.'

This was a man, Vahan, my son, who had eaten at our house. Your father, not suspecting anything untoward went with him straightaway.

You may remember that in the year before you were born, we had trouble under the old Hamidian regime, and it was known then that your father's house was a refuge which would have been stoutly defended with firearms if it had been attacked by the mobs. It seems that the authorities had not forgotten this in all these years. For some reason they are now looking for any firearms that the Armenian population might still have.

But Vahan, my boy, there were no firearms left in the house at all. Garabed had handed all of them in at the start of the war, when the order was first given that all firearms were to be brought to the police station. We did have an old Mauser, but your brother Raffi had thrown that away.

I am sorry to have to tell you that your respected father was roughly interrogated, and was beaten several times throughout the day. It seems that they did not believe him when he assured them that there were no more guns in the house. They hit the soles of his feet repeatedly with an iron bar, and kicked his face with their boots. He fainted twice as far as he could remember, but on his revival they kept on at him again and again most of the day. I must say, my son, I had heard of such things being done at the police station to rogues and thieves, but somehow the reality of it had never struck me before, and I never thought it could happen to us.

Your father was returned early in the evening, like a piece of luggage or furniture hanging over the back of a donkey. This was an animal that belonged to a local Turkish carpenter who knew your father and who happened to be passing when father was dumped outside the police station.

My darling boy, I worked for almost a week to restore his ravaged face and to get his swollen feet well enough to walk on. You wouldn't believe the state he was in when he was returned. I had a hard time calming your brother down. But you know your father, he is getting better fast and has become impatient already to get back to work. I suspect he will go back tomorrow regardless of what I say. I have found the time to write to you. Father ordered me very strictly that I was not to worry you about what has happened, so please don't write to him about any of this, but both I and Raffi thought you should know.

I pray to God to keep you safe and in good health, my child.

Your loving mother.

Vahan felt a surge of anger. He knew that this outrage must clearly have been carried out by men who had come to his father's house many times on official business, as his father was a 'mukhtar' of the district. Hospitality had always been offered to them, when they called on official business. But he also recalled that he had been told in an earlier letter that the old Ottoman Commissioner of Police had been replaced by another of those hard-faced nationalistic members of the Ittihad party some months ago. They were in any case no doubt carrying out orders emanating from Constantinople.

He wondered how his emotionally more volatile younger brother Raffi was coping with the clearly deteriorating situation in the interior. For the first time he felt the political situation affecting him personally and directly. However, with the thought that there was nothing he could do about it for the moment, he put on his Harbiye uniform, and after breakfast with the still silent Christine and the now usually subdued Mariam, he went out to walk to the house of Father Komitas where the singing classes were due to take place.

On his arrival at the house, which was in a narrow street behind Taksim, he found a scene of some turmoil and confusion. There was nobody outside, but inside most of the other students had already arrived and were milling about in the small hall at the foot of the stairs. Sitting in an upright seat by the front door, looking a little uncomfortable, was an elderly police officer. Father Komitas himself was standing on the bottom stair expostulating with one of the students, Kegham, an excitable young man with whom Vahan had never particularly got on—and was known amongst them as 'the bruiser'.

"What's going on" said Vahan to one of the other young men.

"Look, this police chap has just arrived and asked the Reverend Father to accompany him to the police station as the Police Commissioner wants to ask him a few questions. You know how jumpy everybody is these days. He says that they'll only need him for about five minutes. But you know the Bruiser, he has got excited and is telling the good Father not to go."

"Hi, Vahan, we need your good sense. Tell Kegham to calm down," called out another of the students.

Vahan suddenly thought of his mother's letter that morning, and felt a surge of fear. To everyone's astonishment he said, "I agree with Kegham. There's no need to go. They can either ask him the questions here, or issue a proper official request for him to attend at the station which everyone can see and check."

This caused yet another uproar. This, however, was dealt with when Father Komitas himself, already dressed in his long black clerical gown, finally raised his hand and said quietly, "My children, I am going with this officer. We don't need any trouble. I am not going to change my habits of a lifetime now. Vahan, my son, if the authorities want to ask me some questions why shouldn't I go and help them. I have nothing to hide."

Kegham, still holding on to the Father's black sleeves said urgently, "Don't go, don't go. At least if you do, let me come with you."

This was met by a chorus of approval.

Father Komitas looked round. The policeman still sat quietly and diffidently on the chair by the front door. The pupils milled about getting more excited, in particular because Vahan, always considered the sensible and calm one amongst them, had so surprisingly backed up the Bruiser's excited objections. Father Komitas knew he had to calm everybody down. It was his own inclination, now clear in his mind, to accompany the policeman to answer whatever questions that might be put to him. However, there was no way he was going to let the emotional Kegham accompany him.

"Very well, if Vahan you don't mind, I would be happy if you would accompany me with this officer," he said, indicating the unhappy police officer who now rose from his seat.

"Gentlemen," he then said turning and smiling at everyone, "although he said only five minutes, we all know how long these formalities can take when dealing with officials, so I am afraid this morning's class must be abandoned. Come Vahan, let's go."

Then, smiling all round at his pupils, and gesticulating at the gendarme to go ahead, he walked out, with Vahan in some confusion trailing alongside. Vahan had called out in support of Kegham instinctively as a result of the thought of his mother's letter, but he had no real anxiety for the good Father. What might happen in provincial Caesaria surely could not happen in sophisticated Constantinople. Furthermore, he also felt a little proud that Father Komitas, whom he admired so much, had chosen him out of all the others.

However, once at the station, everything began to turn into the surreal Kafkaesque nightmare which had already overwhelmed Karekin Avakian. Vahan accompanied Father Komitas, both of them becoming more and more bewildered. Komitas was a man who could not cope with hard or rude words. So when the desk Sergeant brusquely ordered them to go through to the courtyard, without answering any questions and without the usual politeness, the Father's steps faltered. Vahan accordingly linked his arm with the priest to give him support, and they walked through to the courtyard at the back of the station. Here, as they arrived, Vahan gave the Father's name to the clerk at the door.

Vahan heard a sort of gasp from those nearest the door as he and Komitas walked in and people recognised the priest. There appeared to be a crowd of about a hundred or more men—all Armenians, or so it would seem—milling about in the courtyard. Vahan recognised one or two, such as the well-known deputies in the parliament. As it happened by then there were some clergymen there also, and Father Komitas walked across to them and began conversing earnestly. Vahan stood at the door uncertain what to do next. It was then that a tall distinguished-looking gentleman in a grey suit came up to him and introduced himself as Karekin Avakian.

"I know that you don't know me and I'm sorry to have to request a favour from you, but as you can see I can do nothing here myself. I must get a message through to my wife as to what has happened. It is a lot to ask, but could you possibly get the information to her?"

At this point he fumbled in his pockets, and muttering something about expenses, produced a coin. Vahan, still with his eyes on Father Komitas, shook his head declining the tentatively offered coin. However, reflecting that the singing class had been abandoned and that he was free all day, he answered, "Sir, I will of course do my best. I will certainly get a message to your family one way or another. Could you give me your address?"

Karekin was ready and gave him a card showing his private address. Vahan took this and said again that he would do his best. He then strode forward, embraced Komitas warmly, and left the courtyard, smiling and nodding at the grey-suited man indicating again that he would not forget.

Vahan was not insensitive, but Makrikoy was fairly far, and it was not certain that he would have gone personally. If, for instance, one of his many friends had perhaps accosted him at that moment in the street, or if he had found any other matter with which he might have had to deal, he would not have gone himself. Of course he would always have done something, but that might have been simply to send a messenger with a scribbled note. As it was, with nothing much else to do, he wandered down towards the bridge, deciding on the way to go to the station and take the next train himself. The tense atmosphere in the city was getting on his nerves, and the thought of a stroll in the leafy suburbs had its attraction. The collection of over a hundred prominent Armenians in that police station courtyard had still not penetrated into the forefront of his thoughts. He had still not seen any sinister connection, despite his mother's letter.

When he got to the bottom of the Pera hill, he saw that quite a crowd was gathered on both the bridge itself and on either side. This consisted of the usual odiferous riff-raff yelling about 'giavours,' although Vahan was surprised that the emphasis seemed to be particularly against Armenians on this occasion. "Shoot them all!" rang out the cry from the crowd, and although Vahan did not fully realise it at the time, it was clear that news of the arrests was beginning to seep out.

The crowds were not too dense and police reinforcements seemed to have just arrived. Vahan slipped through and walked up to the Sirkedji station. He noticed that many ferries were milling about below the bridge trying to discharge their passengers, but failing to do so as the passengers were only just beginning to trickle off the stairs leading up from the jetties.

Vahan had been to Makrikoy before, to the racecourse, but he had no idea where the address given to him by this Mr. Avakian was. Accordingly, when he got to the little station he felt it essential to get a gharry, and a carriage was in fact waiting in the dusty station courtyard when he arrived. He gave the driver the address, and the old man replied, "Ah, yes, the Avakian house" and named his price for the round trip. Vahan climbed in and they trotted up past the fields bordering the Vali Effendi racecourse.

Vahan breathed in deeply enjoying the green fields and the fresh air, and even the horsey smell of the carriage. They soon passed the fields and almost immediately stopped outside a substantial house, having the usual blank wall with few windows looking onto the street. There were fairly long walls on either side of the entrance, so it was clear that there were large grounds behind. Vahan, not expecting to be more than a few minutes, told the driver to wait and knocked at the door.

Chapter 26

Olga arrives home.

Olga must have caught one of the last trams to get across the Galata Bridge before the crowds gathered. She, of course, noticed nothing through her tears. She stopped running almost immediately after leaving the college—girls did not run through the streets of Constantinople, however distressed. She kept shaking her head, trying to clear the fears and impressions that were running though her imagination. She was oblivious to all the tension in the streets; everything centred round her own feelings. She walked on automatically.

As she sat in the tram, and later on in the train, she became more and more distressed. She had no idea that the young men forcibly restraining Selim were his friends, anxious that he should not get himself into real trouble in his anger by lifting a hand against any of the girls tormenting the unhappy Olga. It seemed to Olga as if he was being attacked because of his friendship with her. Furthermore, although she had been blithely carrying on over the past eight weeks without a thought for the possible consequences, nevertheless, at a subliminal level, she knew that at the very least she had been deceiving her parents. Her supreme self-confidence had for the first time just been shattered, and she now swung to the opposite extreme of despair, and a feeling that she was being punished for the relationship.

The fraught political atmosphere in the city, and the inevitable fears for the future that now lay in the hearts of most residents as a result of the arrival of an enemy invading army, was now totally banished from her thoughts. She could only see everything in terms of Selim and herself, and of their love for each other.

So, on her arrival at the Makrikoy station, seeing that no gharry was currently waiting outside the station, she immediately made the decision to walk home. She knew she would not have the patience to wait for one of the carriages to turn up. She crossed the lines and began hurrying up the hill alongside the racecourse to get home as fast as possible. She was not exactly running, but was walking very fast, and in her distress she found she could not stop crying, although by now, on one level, she was beginning to get impatient with herself.

When in her anxious emotional state, she dropped the distinctive yellow silk scarf she often wore, and she never noticed the loss. If she had turned round at that point, she might have seen the two rough looking louts, who had been trailing behind her all the way from the station, pick up the scarf where it had fallen on the road. She might then have turned back and retrieved it from them—or she might not, as she might just as well have disregarded it. After all, what was a favourite yellow silk scarf compared to the turmoil in her heart. That light kiss, which she knew was going to come, the spitefulness of the girls, the sight of Selim struggling in the grip of some bullies as she thought, and that last heart-rending cry of "Olga" as she ran away—were all churning around in her head, driving everything else from her mind. So it was that a chain of events began with this totally irrelevant incident.

She tried to collect herself when she reached the door of the house. She pulled the bell knob and wondered suddenly and with more rising feelings of panic what she was going to say to her mother. She need not have worried. The door opened, and for the first and probably only time that day everything went right. Instead of Maria at the door or one of the kitchen maids, there stood Armineh. Armineh knew at once, within a second, what this tear-stained girl standing fearfully at the door needed. None of her clever intellectual daughters, nor her strong upright husband would have known what to do or say. Armineh simply and instinctively opened her arms wide in the sort of gesture that mothers have used over the centuries, and with a great heaving sob Olga threw herself into those arms in a way which she hadn't done for years.

"Oh mother, mother," cried Olga as she was quickly drawn into the house and then into the sitting-room. Marie, who had heard the sobs, came out and closed the front door, and the door to the sitting-room, leaving mother and daughter alone. At last Olga began pouring it all out: her love for a young fellow-student at the College, the meeting at Tokatlian's with Nerissa present, the taunts and threats this morning, and finally a somewhat exaggerated version of the young man in question being attacked by the other boys, an incident which she had been continuously building up in her mind out of all proportion the whole morning.

Armineh, continuing to hold Olga tight as they sat together on the sofa, was more and more confused. The name 'Selim' had not as yet been mentioned, and so, seeing little to worry about, she remained fairly calm. In any event, it was clear to her that for the moment she didn't need to say anything, but only continued to stroke Olga's beautiful hair, as she sank down with her head in Armineh's capacious lap. She simply murmured sweet nothings as Olga went on and on pouring out things she had kept bottled up for weeks. Armineh sat quietly, thinking hard, but she had still not cottoned on to the real problem.

As nothing but encouragement seemed to be coming from her mother, Olga began feeling better and better, as her rambling discourse went on. After about fifteen minutes of this, the front door bell rang again. The door was opened and the welcome tones of Nerissa rang out from the hall, "Mama, Mama, I'm home."

The sitting-room door opened, and Nerissa walked in, throwing her dowdy round school hat onto the chair in the Hall.

"Mama, we've been let out early, as there is trouble and demonstrations in the city, and even here. Oh! Olga! What are you doing home?"

"Nerissa, come and sit down," said Armineh, as Olga finally lifted herself and sat up, dabbing at her eyes with the lace handkerchief always kept up her sleeve. In true Olga fashion she had already convinced herself that all was well, and that her problem had somehow miraculously disappeared.

"Oh, Nerissa, come and give me a kiss," she said almost gaily and sitting up,

"I've been telling mother about the tea-party we went to at Tokatlian's, and all about my feelings. She's been so understanding. It's been an enormous relief to get it all off my chest."

Nerissa stood totally amazed. She loved her sister and had great faith in her mother, and it simply did not cross her mind that there might be any misunderstanding between mother and daughter. She rushed forward, hugged the two of them now sitting up next to each other and said, "You mean Mama now knows all about you and Selim? Oh, I'm so glad my darlings."

Armineh's confusion in her mind suddenly and sharply cleared with a snap.

"Selim. Selim. What's this about Selim?"

At exactly the same instant, both Olga and Nerissa realised that Armineh had had no idea that Olga had been talking about a young Turkish boy, and not some Greek or Armenian Romeo. There was a dreadful silence. Then Olga jumped up and ran out of the room upstairs to her bedroom. There were no more tears. The whole emotional merry-go-round had gone on too long. Nerissa was about to follow her, when Armineh, in a voice Nerissa had rarely heard, ordered her to sit down.

"Now, Nerissa, I want no lies or half-truths, no little fibs, no attempts to hide anything. I want the whole story. Who is this young man for whom Olga appears to have lost both her heart and her head?"

"Oh mother, honestly, I don't really know too much, believe me. All I know about him is that he studies at Robert College, and is the son of a doctor, who I think is employed at the German Hospital. I did go to tea with them at Tokatlian's a few days ago—you remember—to be a companion for Olga, and he seemed a nice boy. But oh! Mama, you should have seen them, they are truly in love."

"Love? Tush!" snorted Armineh, as she began to contemplate with some trepidation the awful and tricky explanations with which she was going to have to cope when Karekin got back in the evening.

"What do they know about love, the ninnies? How old is this boy, Nerissa?"

"I think he's about nineteen. Certainly not more than twenty. Oh, mother, what is Baba going to say?"

"Your father is not going to say anything, as he is not going to know about it for the moment. He has enough problems on his mind at the moment without having to worry about his daughter's stupidities. Nerissa, my dear, can't you see the impossibility of the situation. I'm really surprised at you. Haven't you thought for a moment how unhappy this is going to make your sister sooner or later? This whole nonsense would have been out of the question even during normal times, but now with all this tension it's . . . Nerissa really!"

"Oh, Mother! Of course I can see the problem very well, and I always have, even before I met the young man. But, Mama, how could I have put it to Olga. You know she still thinks of me as a little girl. Then, when I first met him, I could say nothing. Mama, you haven't seen them together. I've never seen Olga so sincere and genuinely involved. It's something beautiful, but you wouldn't be able to see it I suppose."

Armineh sighed, and looked sadly at Nerissa, who had the grace to blush deeply and look away ashamed. It suddenly struck Armineh that she had not spoken in any serious and meaningful way to Nerissa for a long time, and that this had been her own fault. However, she mentally braced herself. She was not going to be distracted at this stage with a long heart-to-heart with Nerissa, which she realised she should have dealt with long ago. She now had to face up to a showdown with Olga. It was going to be very uncomfortable, there would be an excess of emotion and tears. However, it was better by far to deal with it here and now before Karekin got home and complicated matters one way or another.

She went to the bottom of the stairs and called up loudly and firmly, trying to keep any anxiety or anger out of her voice, "Olga, my daughter, you must come down, and you must come down now. You know we have to talk."

The door to Olga's room opened, and she came down the stairs, pale and anxious, but with all the evidence of the recent tears washed away, her hair brushed, and with two high spots of colour on her cheeks. Nerissa came out of the sitting-room, unsure whether her mother wanted her to stay or not. Armineh's calm nearly wavered when she saw the stubborn determination on Olga's face. Armineh's emotions themselves were now in turmoil. On the one hand she itched to be able to get angry and lay down the law to her silly daughter, on the other hand she knew she had to remain calm. She said quietly as Olga came to the bottom of the stairs, "Olga, my love, it is vital that there are no lies or any hidden agenda between us now. Please tell me again what you. . ."

At this point there was a knocking at the front door—clearly a stranger who as so often happened hadn't seen the bell-knob. All three glanced at the little window by the door which looked out at the street, and saw outside old Abdul sitting in his gharry, obviously waiting for whoever was knocking.

Nerissa hurried forward to open the door. Standing somewhat anxiously in the door, dressed in the uniform of the Harbiye military college, with his cap in his hand, stood the young man who had smiled at her in Tokatlian's—could it be only a few short days ago? A moment of silence stretched out as the three women stared at the stranger, and he with a shy smile looked back.

Chapter 27

Armineh and Sima.

The moment of silence between the three women on the one hand, and the young man standing at the front door on the other, lasted only a moment, and then the young man said, "I am very sorry to disturb you like this, unannounced. My name is Vahan Asadourian. I have come on behalf of Mister Karekin Avakian—I trust that I am at the house of the Avakians."

Vahan continued to stand at the door. He, of course, had not in any way recognised Nerissa, the eye contact at Tokatlian's had been so fleeting, and it had not for him been such a memorable afternoon as it had been for her. Armineh, whose mind had been entirely on the problem posed by Olga's infatuation, turned sharply at the mention of Karekin's name and came forward.

"What are you thinking about Nerissa, standing there staring like a silly goose. Come in, my boy, come in. Yes, we are indeed the Avakians. This young lady staring is my daughter Nerissa, and my daughter Olga." She waved back vaguely towards Olga still standing on the stairs.

Vahan came into the hall, and wondered where to start. Largely as a result of his mother's letter, which he had received earlier that morning, he was aware, more than many others that day, of the danger in the situation.

"Madame Avakian, I am afraid I have some bad news."

"Oh my God, my God—Karekin—his heart."

"No, no," said Vahan quickly. "He's in good health so far as I could see. However, I am sorry to have to tell you that he has been arrested this morning, and he's currently in the main prison in Beyoglu."

"Arrested!" all three women burst out together.

"Yes. I don't know the circumstances in which he himself was taken. I myself had gone this morning to Father Komitas for one of his group singing lessons. When I arrived, I found that he had been invited to go down to the police station to answer some questions. I went down with him, and when we arrived, we found that there were about a hundred Armenian gentlemen there all in the same predicament, all under arrest without any idea why. Whilst there, I was approached by your husband, Madame, who asked me to do him the favour of coming to tell you what had happened. He gave me this address."

"Oh my God, why? What's it all about? He has always been very particular about paying his taxes, it can't be that. What's going on? Oh Karekin, Karekin! You said there were others there—who were they?" Armineh spoke disjointedly as she tried to grasp what was being reported to her.

Vahan felt distressed that he was unable to give any real comfort or any hard information to these three women. He was the sort of person who was unable to fashion the meaningless purely comforting words that someone else might have attempted.

"I can tell you nothing for sure, Madame, but my opinion is that it's political. I saw two of the deputies there, and the rest also appeared to be men of some importance in the community. There was, unquestionably, an official list, from which names were being ticked off."

"I must go to him, I must go at once," said Armineh, her practical mind already beginning to plan what she was going to do.

"Madame, I must warn you that there is a lot of tension in the City. It isn't entirely clear at the moment whether the British have landed or not, or indeed whether there's been any Greek or Russian involvement as well. The streets are full, and there are the usual mindless mobs milling about and shouting anti-Greek and anti-Armenian slogans."

"Thank you, young man. Olga, I suggest you go up and have a rest, you look all done in. Nerissa, this gentleman—Mr. Asadourian isn't it?—has come all the way from the city to give us this news; the least you can do is to close your mouth—it's been wide open now for at least a whole minute. Please arrange for a coffee and some refreshment to be served to him at once."

Vahan began demurring, but Nerissa had already hurried out to the kitchen. Armineh meanwhile grabbed her coat, stuck a sensible hat on her head, and said to Vahan, "Mr. Asadourian, I wonder if I could call on you for one more favour to the Avakian family. May I take your carriage outside to go now to the station."

"Madame, of course. Indeed I'd have walked up anyway if I had known the way. Please take it. I'll go and tell the driver."

"No need, no need. It's old Abdul, I'll deal with it. Mr. Asadourian, I don't know how to thank you for all the trouble you have taken. I hope we will meet again in happier circumstances, but meanwhile do please sit down, please."

Nerissa came back into the hall and standing at the door asked about how he wanted his coffee—"Shekerli, or mazbout." She called out Vahan's reply to have his coffee sweet to the kitchen. She then came in and stood waiting. Armineh, meanwhile, bustled out of the front door, sticking a pin into her hat, as she clambered into the gharry. Abdul didn't seem to be the slightest bit surprised, and immediately roused the dozing horse and started trotting down to the station.

As they drove down, Armineh began working out more calmly exactly what she was going to do. There was a ritual for this sort of emergency, with which womenfolk had had to deal through the ages, difficult to define, but unmistakeable. She was reacting in the way that women—wives and mothers—acted over the centuries when armies roamed over the land, or when there was civil strife or government oppression. She checked in her bag to make sure that she had the key to Karekin's office safe. The road, as always at midday, was deserted save for two rough looking youths lounging just on the other side of the fence, chewing grass stalks and staring at the carriage as it drove past.

On arrival at the station, she clambered out, handing Abdul some money.

"Madame Avakian hanum," Abdul said waving aside the coins, "I have already been paid by the young gentleman for the round trip."

Armineh nodded, putting the coins back in her bag. This was honesty of the old school to which she was well accustomed, and she made no effort to insult such honesty by pressing him to take the coins. She clambered out of the carriage and was hurrying into the station when she suddenly saw Sima coming out, obviously having just returned from her trip to the Levonians. Armineh had by this time lost all sense of time and she did not register how late Sima was in getting back, nor the connecting thought that she obviously had not had the time to pick up Haik. She made up her own mind immediately and said, "Sima, my darling, well met. Look, we have a crisis. Father has been arrested or something or other. I don't know what exactly, but I will have to go and find him. Can you come with me? Two heads are better than one in these circumstances."

Sima for her part, assuming that by now Haik had already returned home, immediately turned back without a word, and went with her mother to get the train back into the city. On the way, Armineh explained as much as she could of the circumstances, and as she did so, she became ever more fearful. This sort of police tyranny, although rumoured to be prevalent in the provinces, did not take place in Constantinople—particularly against well-known and respectable gentlemen. She could not imagine what was happening, though it must in some way be connected to the supposed invasion. But why should that affect Karekin?

On their arrival in the city, they went first to the office, where the old clerk recently taken on by Karekin was still sitting at his desk, staring into space with bewilderment. Armineh hurried in, as the clerk rose and bowed to the wife of his employer. Armineh didn't mean to be rude, but her mind was now racing ahead of her body. She nodded at him, but immediately hurried into Karekin's back office indicating to Sima to shut the door. Opening the safe, she extracted the little velvet bag of gold coins kept there for emergencies, ignoring everything else. She counted out the coins which amounted to about forty, and popped the bag into her own handbag.

She and Sima then hurried out, nodding to the clerk as they went out, but making sure that they did not enter into any conversation with him, though it was clear that he was bursting to know what was going on. They hurried down to the main Beyoglu police station. Armineh, whose mind was now firmly on what she was about, had not noticed the menacing crowds who were still milling about. The police station itself, however, was totally quiet, and for a moment Armineh wondered if she had come to the wrong place.

"I would like to see my husband—Karekin Avakian—who was detained here earlier this morning," she said to the desk sergeant. The officer rummaged about with some papers on his desk, and then said, "I am sorry Hanum, but I appear to have no record of this name in the list of people currently at this station."

His eye lit on the straight-backed and striking Sima standing behind Armineh and staring at him. He grinned at her somewhat sheepishly, and she smiled back although she was now in a state of nervous exhaustion. The sergeant fidgeted as Armineh also said nothing but stared somewhat belligerently at him, willing him to say more.

"Dear ladies, we have no detainees of any kind at this station. It is however true that more than one hundred men were arrested this morning from this area. About half have been sent to the Yedikule Police station, which has a large gaol, and from where, so I understand, they'll eventually be going to the Sarayburnu boat station to be deported to the interior. The other larger group has gone direct to Haydar Pasha station, where they will be boarding a train this very evening for the interior."

"But why? What's the charge?" said Armineh.

"Madam, I don't know but I suppose wartime espionage may cover it. Either way they are destined for internal exile. Now, ladies, I must ask you to leave. There is no way that I can help further, as I have no record as to who went where."

Armineh and Sima walked out and stood on the pavement uncertain what to do next. Sima, unaccustomed to such emotional crises, found herself unable to think clearly. The effect on Armineh, however, was just the opposite—whilst obviously tense, she was now thinking very clearly.

"Sima, my dear, we have to assume that what the policeman said was accurate. His words are all we have to go on. Those who were sent to the Yedikule local prison are going to spend the night there before going on to Sarayburnu—but those sent directly to Haydar Pasha may be leaving tonight. It's no use trying to find out who was sent where. We must be off to Haydar Pasha now, and see if Karekin is in that group. We can always try Yedikule later if he's not there."

Taking the tram back down to the Galata Bridge, they had no difficulty boarding a ferry taking them across the Bosporus to the landing for Haydar Pasha station. This ferry passes Leander's Tower, and this particular trip gives the best view of the great Constantinople skyline—but neither woman was in the mood to stare and marvel. Sima sat with silent tears running down her cheeks, not just of sorrow, but also compounded of sheer exhaustion, physical and emotional. Armineh with pursed lips just stared ahead trying to work out what she was going to do when they arrived.

On their arrival they saw that the station was brightly lit and was full of soldiers and policemen. The main entrance was blocked off and no civilians were being allowed in without showing valid tickets for trains departing that evening. Armineh thought fast. Trying to get past the surly-looking guards was obviously going to be a waste of time. Even if she could persuade them to go and get an officer, it would waste hours and might still not succeed. It was late afternoon already and now getting darker. She turned on her heel, and went quickly to the ticket booth that was at the side of the station. There was no one waiting there, and she went up and asked for two single tickets to Eskishehir. She cheerfully paid for first class, as she realised that for her and Sima to produce cheaper class tickets on this line would undoubtedly look suspicious.

Back at the front entrance, she and Sima worked their way to the front of the queue. After a careful scrutiny of their papers and tickets, they were let into the main hall. Here, there was no usual hustle and bustle of milling crowds. Instead, there were a large number of soldiers standing about fully armed and all appearing rather nervous. Over in the far corner of the hall, standing outside the station restaurant, was a particularly large group of soldiers preventing any entry. Inside, a group of respectable looking gentlemen could be seen through the pillars standing about or sitting at the tables. Armineh, holding Sima firmly by the arm, manoeuvred herself closer, but she could not spy Karekin through the windows.

Clearly, getting inside the restaurant just by asking was going to be quite impossible. The last scheduled train of the whole day was due to leave in about an hour, and Armineh reckoned that once this train left, the station would be cleared of everyone. She turned and facing away from the guards, she whispered to the white-faced Sima, "My darling, take this bag of coins, and move across a little and stand with me near to that young officer over there. You must be brave, and pretend to faint or feel the heat or something. Just close your eyes, drop down and let me do the talking. If you do manage to get inside, try to see your father, and if you do, give him the bag. Just do your best. If you find out he is there, but you can't get to him, give it to anyone to pass on to him. I can see from here they are all respectable and well-known men."

Sima, whose heart was bursting with anxiety for her father and a deep fear, did as Armineh had directed. They stood for a moment together, then Sima gave a strangled cry, closed her eyes and fainted into her mother's arms. It really required scarcely any acting on her part, as she was exhausted.

It worked. The young officer came forward

"What's the matter Madam?" he said.

"Oh, officer, we are waiting for the next train. There's nowhere to sit, and my daughter here is not well. Can she go in and have a glass of water and sit down just for a few minutes. I'll stay out here," she added as she saw him hesitate.

"Perhaps this soldier can go in with her," she said indicating the young soldier who had come up with the officer. I'm sure he can make certain that all will be well, and he can escort her back here."

Saying this, she produced two notes—both generous, but carefully graded in her mind. The officer had already half made up his mind to let them in, and he took the notes, pocketing the bigger one, and giving the smaller to the young soldier standing alongside. Sima, now recovered, but still looking very white, was permitted to lean on the soldier, and the two of them walked through the glass doors and into the fin-de-siecle old dining room.

Here, milling about amongst the dark mahogany tables, potted plants and dusty chandeliers, the cream of the Armenian community of the city was standing or sitting about in varying attitudes ranging from boredom to near panic. Sima and the soldier went to get a glass of water from the bar, which was doing a roaring trade. Sima's eyes roamed round the room anxiously, as the young soldier sat her at a table near the door—the occupants hastily being waved away. Sima was the only female in the room, and she had no idea what to do next.

As it happened, Doctor Manuelian was wandering about and was the first to spot her. He had the sense not to call out, but immediately went to fetch Karekin, who fortunately was indeed in this group. Sitting in the far corner he had not seen Sima's arrival. Aram warned Karekin that Sima was here, but that she was accompanied by a soldier, and that it was clear that she was here under some sort of false pretences.

Karekin strolled over and then saw her sitting white-faced and with a tearful expression. His heart turned over at the thought of his daughter in such surroundings, and he had to make a real effort not to run across and comfort her, as she was clearly distressed and close to tears.

They sauntered over, planning how they would tackle the situation. Aram came first, making clear with his eyes to Sima that she should not show any sign of recognition. He ordered up two rakis, and offered one to the soldier, with whom, on it being accepted, he began an animated discussion. Karekin moved and stood behind Sima's chair, touching the back of her hair with his chest, but making no other sign. Sima whispered to him, "Oh Baba, we've only got a minute or two. I am dropping this little bag under the chair. It has gold coins in it for you. You are going to need them. Oh baba, baba, what is going to happen?"

"My soul, it's in the lap of the gods—I don't know. Tell everyone that I love them all, and don't weep my love, don't weep."

"Baba, mother is outside. When I leave, go to the window so she can see you; but don't wave, don't make any sign. We are supposed to be travellers on our way to Eskishehir on the next train."

Even in that dire and critical moment, Karekin grinned to himself at the thought of Armineh's deception. Having finished the glass of raki, the young soldier bestirred himself and got up, asking Sima if she was feeling better. Sima, through the tears she could barely restrain, smiled at him and said she was. She then rose and walked out through the glass doors with the young soldier behind, but not before seeing out of the corner of her eye, her father bending down and picking up the little velvet bag.

For twenty minutes Armineh stood beyond the line of soldiers as if waiting for the next train, glancing every few minutes at the figure of Karekin in the window. For his part, Karekin stood there staring at her fixedly without moving. She and Sima clearly had to leave before the last train was called, to avoid any suspicions. Armineh took one last look at the man she had married, knowing that she was unlikely ever to see him again. He raised one arm, and held it palm forward by his ear in salutation, as she and Sima turned to make their way out of the station to return home.

Chapter 28

Raffi, and the arrest of Garabed.

Although he would never have admitted it to anyone, even to himself, Raffi missed Vahan's departure to Constantinople more than he ever imagined he would. Raffi was now sixteen and had already accompanied his father Garabed several times on trips to the highlands of Eastern Anatolia to meet and consult with the families weaving carpets on commission. Raffi was physically the stronger of the two brothers and certainly the more adventurous and the more emotional in his reactions. His elder brother's good sense and unflappability had however helped Raffi in many a scrap. It was Vahan who had often stood between Raffi and the occasional violence which would sometimes explode from their father, who had a hasty and alarming temper.

Raffi and Vahan had slept together in the same room ever since Raffi could remember, and Raffi had in fact absorbed most of his opinions and ideas through Vahan. They had also, however, continually argued and appeared to disagree with each other on almost every subject.

Once war was declared in November 1914, Raffi realised that his own dreams of going to the University at Stamboul himself and studying were unlikely to come to anything, unless the war was soon over. There was accordingly also a slight touch of envy in his reflections, whenever his thoughts turned to Vahan.

Raffi had been deeply shocked at the sight of his father when he had been brought home on the back of the carpenter's donkey from the Police station two weeks before. It was not just the trauma of seeing his father's condition, there was also an odd feeling of shame and fear at the evidence, suddenly forced upon him, that this figure of authority, whom he had looked up to all his life, was as vulnerable as he was himself. When Garabed had not returned immediately from the police station, he had had the presence of mind to find and throw away the old Mauser pistol left over from the 1895 troubles.

However, after his return, Garabed had recovered quickly from the beatings. He had in fact been going back into work for the last few days, despite all the efforts of his wife to dissuade him.

Apart from the extraordinary violence meted out to Garabed, there had so far been no other open attacks on the Armenian minority in the town. By the 24th April the siege of Van had been going on for almost two weeks, together with the slow advance of the Imperial Russian army. Neither of these had as yet resulted in any street violence or demonstrations. Somehow, as the Ottomans had after all been fighting the Russians in the remote mountains of Eastern Anatolia for centuries, the current Ittihad leaders looked on that front with some equanimity. It was the arrival of a Western army within striking distance of their ancient capital, which triggered the paranoia which was to lead to the terrible events of the next few months.

On this morning, bright and sunny everywhere in the Empire, except ironically on the shores bordering the Aegean Sea, Garabed had decided to stay at home and rest. Raffi and his father were sitting together at breakfast, just before Raffi was due to go to school. Once again a policeman came to the house, and being known to the maid, was let into the breakfast room. Raffi's mother, Mariam, hastened in as soon as she heard that a policeman had again arrived.

"Garabed effendi, I have been asked to come and request you to attend at the police station this morning, in order for you to deal with some official business in your capacity as 'mukhtar' of the district."

"Baba, baba, don't go, let them deal with the business with you here," cried out Raffi, whilst his mother remained standing quite still, covering her face with her hands.

Garabed looked at the policeman, who stood diffidently to one side. Raffi, getting more and more excited and emotional shouted again, "Baba, you don't have to go. We'll deal with it together," and he jumped up with clenched fists, tipping over his chair.

It was fairly clear that Garabed was going to comply with the polite request of the policeman, but this outburst from Raffi, and the implication that he might easily knock the policeman down, decided

Garabed. After all, he had little choice. He had no idea of what was happening on this day all over the Empire, and at this stage all he could think of was shielding his family.

He rose from the table, put on his hat and coat, kissed his wife and strode out with the policeman following politely behind. For a short time there was a silence in the breakfast room. Raffi simply could not credit that his father, this strong-willed big man of whom he was both in awe and a little afraid, had meekly gone to the police station, when he had had such a terrible experience only ten or so days before, and knew what might transpire.

"Mother! Mother! Why didn't father object more strongly? Mama what will happen if they beat him again? I can't bear it. We must do something. Why did he go so meekly?"

"My son, my son, calm down. Getting excited like this isn't going to help your father. I think he knows, and I too believe, that there is no question of a repetition of what happened a couple of weeks ago. Several Turkish business acquaintances of your father, old and respected Ottoman families, raised the matter with the Governor. There will be no repetition, believe me. However, as to why he has been asked to report again, I just don't know. Tensions are running high, ever since the Van situation broke out. If I was to have to give you a reason, I suspect that they are going to go for another forced loan from the Christian community."

"If they beat father again I'll. . . I'll kill them!" yelled Raffi, who had scarcely taken in a word of what his mother had said, while jumping up and down, unable to keep still.

"Listen Raffi, for the last time, calm down! The situation here in the town is very difficult. I want you to finish your breakfast, and then go out to the bazaar and see if you can find out anything by listening to the gossip. First, my soul, you must look at me and promise, promise faithfully, that you will avoid speaking to anyone that you don't know and not endanger yourself in any way. Don't go to school today, but come straight back to me."

"I promise, mother," said Raffi, suddenly sobered by his mother's calm but clearly worried tones.

Wolfing down the remainder of his breakfast, Raffi left the house and walked through the narrow streets, eventually coming out into the square in front of the main Armenian Church of St. Gregory. To one side of this was the Kapali Charshi—the covered bazaar—in which most of the merchants were Greek or Armenian. Here, Raffi went in and was immediately met with an uproar of shouting and noise, quite unlike the usual hustle and bustle of the market. He did not have to speak to anyone—the gist of what was happening soon became clear to him. It appeared that that morning there had been arrests of about a hundred of the more prominent Armenians from all over town. He gathered that most arrests took the form of polite requests to come to the station to answer some questions, although it also appeared that some had been more violent.

Raffi went from group to group gleaning all the information that he could, and eventually came across Ismet, his father's Turkish foreman. Ismet looked at him sadly and said, "Ah, Raffi, I'm sorry but I've just found out that Garabed effendi is one of those who have been arrested. He, together with the others, have been taken to the Town Hall, where they're all gathered at the moment in the gardens. I am sorry that I haven't got any more hard or certain information—but, my boy, I believe that they're going to be sent out of the town into exile."

"But Ismet, why? And where to? Where to?"

"My boy, I've no idea, all I know is that bad things are happening, things that I never expected to see in all my days. Please tell your mother Mariam Hanum to be very careful. She can call on my help at any time. I'll surely try to keep the business going until, 'ishallah' (god willing), Garabed effendi returns."

Raffi shook his hand and was about to race home when he recalled his promise to his mother to remain calm. Instead, he sauntered out, hands in pockets, and strolled back.

On his arrival he found the house in an uproar. His old grandmother was roaring at his elder sisters. It appeared that the Turkish wet-nurse, recently taken on to look after his newly-born baby sister, had suddenly, in some fear, given notice that morning, and had fled from the house, not even waiting for the balance of her wages.

Raffi took his mother aside and told her all that he had discovered. Mariam stared at him as despair flooded over her. A beating could always in the last resort be dealt with, but this was something new and sinister, and she had had no previous experience available to deal with it. However, one thing was clear—it was still April, and here on the Anatolian plateau it could get cold again very suddenly. She took Raffi by the hand and led him into her bedroom. There, bending down, she pulled out from under the bed, the heavy old strongbox. Raffi moved to help, but was waved aside.

Taking out a key from her belt, she opened the box. Inside were the deeds of the house and other properties, together with various documents that Raffi could not distinguish, some baptismal and other certificates, and finally in the corner some paper money and a bag of gold coins. Ignoring the paper money, Mariam took the bag of coins and pouring them out on the bed picked out most of them, amounting to about thirty coins, and handed them to Raffi. Then, going to the large wardrobe in the corner of the room, she lifted out the warm sheepskin coat that Garabed used to take with him on his trips into the highlands, and also handed that to Raffi.

"Now Raffi, take these coins—hide them carefully—also take this coat, and give them all to your father, if you can get to see him. Raffi, make sure that he takes them all. He'll make a fuss about the coat, I know him, but say I insist. Once done, hurry home, don't loiter on the way back. I know by experience that the riff-raff will surely be out on the streets, excited by these events and looking for trouble."

She looked at him, and then suddenly put out her hand and said, "My son, give me that cross you're wearing round your neck."

Raffi pulled it over his head and handed it to her without a word. Then taking the coins and the coat he hurried out. Once again, heeding his mother's words, he sauntered through the streets, though he badly wanted to run. He draped the coat over his shoulders, and put the coins in his pockets.

When he reached the square in front of the Town Hall, Raffi saw a large detachment of gendarmes who were guarding the steps up to the entrance of the building. Standing on the steps, there were several Armenian women milling about trying unsuccessfully to get some information from the officer standing behind the guards. Raffi strolled round to the road leading away from the square alongside the gardens of the building. Here, looking through the high iron railings, he saw several well-dressed men walking amongst the trees. Now out of sight of the guards at the front, round the corner, Raffi pressed his face up to the bars and waited. Shortly, three of the men came past, talking animatedly, and Raffi called out, "Gentlemen, please can I talk to you?"

They wandered over and one of them said, "What do you want, my boy? You know you'd better go away, it's not safe here."

"Please sir, do you know my father, Garabed Asadourian, a big man? Do you know if he is here?"

"Asadour effendi, yes, yes, he is here somewhere."

"Could you please, sir, ask him to come here. Tell him his son is waiting."

"Why certainly. You must be his son, Raffi. Look, wait here, but stand away from the railings until he comes. It will be safer for you." The man then turned away and, joining the others, walked towards the Town Hall building, which could just be seen through the trees.

Raffi moved away to the other side of the street, and leaned against the wall. His heart began beating fast. He had not been frightened before, but now that he was about to face his father, childish anxieties began to arise, anxieties which till now had been contained by the sheer rush of adrenaline.

"Raffi, my soul," came a quiet voice.

"Oh Baba, Baba," cried Raffi, racing forward and clasping his father's outstretched hands through the railings.

"My son, my son, calmly, calmly. You must be strong for your mother's and sisters' sakes. No tears now, nothing has happened yet, all may be well."

He smiled at his second son. But Raffi was sixteen, he knew that death was just round the corner, and that his father was trying to comfort him. However, he gulped down the tears that had been threatening to flow, and pushed the coat through the railings.

Garabed said, "Look, for heaven's sake it's hot, I don't need this."

"Baba, mother said I was to insist that you take it. It's still only April, and heaven knows where you'll be at night."

Garabed grinned and said, "Well, we must do as your mother commands."

He took the coat, shook it out, and then draped it over his own shoulders.

Raffi then handed him the thirty gold coins. Garabed took them and looked down thoughtfully at the coins in his hand. He carefully counted out five of them, slipping them into the pocket of the coat now over his shoulders. He then handed back the other twenty-five.

"Raffi, take these back to your mother. You'll all need them more than I will."

The inference was very clear. Garabed knew it, but he did not immediately realise that Raffi, now sixteen, could see the inference just as clearly. Although no one could be sure what was going to happen, nevertheless, one way or another the likelihood was high that within a few days Garabed would be dead. Raffi had no idea what to do or say. All his life he had received comfort from his father. He had no experience of giving it. He knew only two things—firstly that he must follow his mother's wishes and insist on his father taking all the coins, and secondly that he must not under any circumstances give way to any tears now in front of him.

"No, Baba, I can't. Mother said I must make sure you took them all." Raffi hesitated—even in this tense moment he reflected that he had never before had the courage to contradict his father.

Garabed looked at his son, and a short moment passed. Then in a stern hard tone, and exercising all the moral authority of years which he could muster, he said, "Raffi, you will do as I say, and you'll do it now and without any question. Take these coins home and leave straight away, right now. Tell your mother not to despair, and remember, remember that I love you all."

Garabed dropped the coins into Raffi's hand, and without another look at him, without a kiss, without a sign, he turned on his heels and walked away through the trees. He never gave a single backward look but simply walked straight out of sight.

With the departure of his father, probably for ever, Raffi could no longer hold back his emotions. He walked to the other side of the street, leant against the old stone wall, and gave way to floods of tears. Unlike his more contained brother Vahan, Raffi had always got emotional release by letting his tears flow easily—but on this occasion his body was racked with sobs, and the tears gave him no release at all.

Eventually he gathered himself together sufficiently to walk back through the streets, with the twenty-five gold coins guiltily clutched in his sweaty hands thrust deep into his pockets.

Chapter 29

Haik.

Haik's school was not let out early. The age of the boys at this school was significantly lower than the school Nerissa attended further away in the little town. Accordingly, the staff, becoming aware of the tension in the streets and hearing of the demonstrations in the city, were anxious not to let the boys out early. They decided that it was necessary, in order to give plenty of time for those who might be coming to pick them up, to get there.

So, Haik was a little surprised when he got to the school gates and found that Sima was not there waiting for him. He sat with some of his friends on the grass beside the dusty track leading to the school from the road. Eventually, as time passed, the others were either picked up or themselves drifted off to go home. Haik, in the end, found himself alone, throwing stones at the posts of the fence on the other side of the track.

"Hello, Haik, what are you doing still here?" said one of the teachers as he passed out of the school gates on his way home, "Are you all right?"

"Yes, sir, I'm waiting for my sister who is coming to pick me up. I'll go on home if she doesn't come soon."

"Well, don't wait too long. It's a funny day with a lot of excitement and trouble around. She might be delayed in the city, you know," said the teacher and walked on.

The sun was hot, but it was a beautiful fresh clear day as Haik sat throwing stones and thinking of nothing at all. Finally he decided that he had better get on home. If Sima came to find him gone and the school empty, she would know that he had returned on his own. After all, he had been walking home by himself now for well over a year, before his father's recent decision insisting on his being picked up. He hoisted his worn-out old satchel, hitched up his trousers, sauntered along to the road, and began the walk up the hill.

He was about half-way up the slope alongside the racecourse when he first noticed the two rough-looking men—youths really—sprawled out on the ground just on the other side of the fence, chewing long stalks of grass and staring at him as he walked up the deserted road swinging his satchel. One was wearing baggy trousers with a dirty green shirt, the other with an equally dirty old-fashioned red blouse. Turks? Albanians? Gypsies? Haik had no sure idea, and indeed never found out.

The boys at the school had no really clear idea of what was going on. They were certainly conscious of all the tension around them, and both Haik and his friends were aware of their parents' generalised fear. Accordingly, as he had never seen this couple of toughs before, Haik instinctively avoided any eye contact and trudged on—though no longer swinging his satchel with quite the same abandon. All might have been well, if he had not glanced over as he passed and saw one of the louts sniffing at a distinctive delicate yellow silk scarf. Haik stopped, turned, and stared. He immediately recognised it as belonging to Olga; there simply could not be another like it.

"Hey!" he shouted, pointing, "That belongs to my sister. Where did you get hold of it?"

"Does it indeed, squirt!" said one of the youths languidly and with, even to Haik's unpractised ears, an appalling accent, clearly not a city Turk, if a Turk at all. He grinned at Haik and waved the scarf like a red rag to a bull.

Haik, surrounded by a houseful of loving sensitive women, had led a very sheltered life. The only violence he had ever experienced was the rough and tumble of boys of his own age at school. He therefore failed to recognise the menacing danger in the eyes of the two men.

"If it belongs to your dear sister, why don't you come and take it? I'm sure she'll be overjoyed," said the other in an equally strange accent, and with words considerably stronger and dirtier. However, Haik simply did not recognise most of the words used, or again he might have been warned and gone on his way.

Instead, he came over and clambered over the wooden fence and onto the grass verge running alongside the racecourse, where the two youths lay lounging, staring at him. Haik walked up to where the men were sprawled out and held his hand out for the scarf.

"And what are you going to give us in exchange," said greenshirt with a new and even more dangerous glint in his eye, as he stared up at the pale and delicate Haik.

"Look, this scarf belongs to my sister, and I haven't anything to give you anyway. She must've dropped it on her way home. I bet you found it on the road."

"Well, I'll tell you what. . . you give us your nice clean shirt and pants in exchange and we'll give you the scarf. That's a fair exchange," said red-blouse grinning.

Haik stared at them both. He hesitated, not entirely sure what to do—anything might have happened, even now he might have walked away unscathed. What, however, finally took place was that Haik lost his patience. Thin and smooth-featured though he was, nevertheless, Haik had all the Avakian spirit, plus the healthy energy of any twelve-year old boy. What he lacked, however, was any sense of self-preservation or awareness of the need for the avoidance of danger—a danger he did not recognise in any case.

The physical aggressiveness of the two youths was fairly clear to Haik, but what he could not see was their increasingly sexually-charged sadistic impulse, as he had no experience of any kind at all on which to base such awareness. The scarf was now lying on the grass in front of greenshirt. Haik bent down and grabbed the scarf, then straightened and turned to walk away.

Like a flash both youths were up, and to Haik's genuine surprise, he was grabbed by red-blouse from behind and his arms pinioned to his side, whilst greenshirt came in front of him and punched him several times in the face and in his stomach, as he began struggling and yelling out of a mixture of both fear and anger.

"Shut your gob, you little pig," whispered red-blouse with his stinking breath right into Haik's ear. It was unlikely that Haik would have stopped yelling, except that greenshirt then gave him a really vicious punch right across his mouth. Haik's nose now began to bleed, together with his cut lip. Even this might not have stopped Haik's spirited yells, if greenshirt had not produced a long knife from the depths of his filthy baggy trousers and held it firmly to Haik's throat. This, even the simple Haik understood, and two things then happened. Firstly he stopped wriggling or making any noise, and secondly real fear as he had never felt it before gripped his guts, and a trickle of urine involuntarily escaped into his pants.

Tears now began to flow, but without any sobs—tears of fear and frustration. Blood was streaming from his nose and mouth, and his huge eyes for the first time searched the face of his tormentors. What he saw gave him no comfort—greenshirt had a vicious grin on his mouth and a look in his eyes, which Haik was unable to read in any way.

"This is one of those damned 'giavour' kids from the school in that town down below, I'm sure!" said red-blouse still holding Haik tight whilst greenshirt held the knife steadily at Haik's throat.

"Yes, you're bloody right, and you know what? They've all been shouting in the city all 'giavours' are traitors and have to be slaughtered like the pigs they are."

"So, how are we going to make sure that he is a damned 'giavour.'"

"Well, we'll soon be able to tell, won't we," said greenshirt, and with one hand still on the knife, he fumbled at the buttons of Haik's trousers with the other and yanked them down. They both looked down as the pants came down, then both laughed, "There, you see, I knew he was a filthy Christian pig"

"Not a pig, he's a sow. Let's show him."

Even now, even at this late stage, it could have ended with just a scare for Haik—a learning curve—a loss perhaps of shoes, shirt, trousers and dignity. But for the first time Haik realised what they had been doing. He at least recognised now that they had removed his pants to see if he was circumcised or not. This was a known way of checking whether a boy was a Muslim or not, and this was something at last that Haik did know about. The knife, as it happens, had also gone back into greenshirt's baggy pocket, and unfortunately Haik's courage returned.

Haik had no idea what greenshirt had meant by his last remark, even if he had heard, nor did he have the experience or understanding to be aware of the increasingly sexually charged excitement of the two toughs. He simply found the courage, with the disappearance of the knife, to start yelling again and struggling to get out of red-blouse's grip. He was yelling and sobbing at the same time, and it was this that finally tipped the balance of violence from thoughtless brutal aggression to a perverted, lustful and sadistic excitement, which the two louts could no longer control.

The youths had spent the whole morning being part of a mob milling about in the city and hearing adults denigrating and cursing members of the race or religion to which this boy belonged, and referring to them in animalistic terms. That crucial moment had come when those different people had accordingly become totally dehumanised in their eyes. In these situations, sooner or later, the gutter is persuaded to stop thinking of the denigrated minority as humans.

Suddenly, all was action on the verge beside the racecourse. Haik found himself thrown down onto the grass, his face thrust into the earth. His shoes and pants were pulled right off. His shirt was torn from his back. His genitals were pulled and pinched, and he felt one of the youths falling down on top of him. Something was happening to him that was causing a terrible pain. He lifted his head, kicked his feet, which connected violently with the youth on top of him and at least relieved the pain. He let out one enormous cry of 'help', before his face was again thrust down into the earth. He began suffocating, and again greenshirt fell down heavily onto his back. Once again the knife was out, where in complete terror he could feel it against his cheek. He heard the sinister voice of red-blouse whispering unintelligible words into his ear as he almost passed out.

Chapter 30

Van. The last effort.

By this time the rebellion in Van was almost into its third week. Halil Bey and his demoralised six thousand Turkish regular troops and gendarmes were becoming increasingly frustrated at their inability to dislodge the one thousand five hundred or so Armenian irregulars, holding on in their one square mile fortified enclave. Meanwhile, General Yudenich and the Russian army was somewhat ponderously approaching Van from the north. Turkish families in the smarter suburbs were beginning to pack their belongings and drift away out of the town, many in boats crossing the lake to the northern and western shore.

Halil Bey decided that he had to mount one final offensive in an attempt to crush the rising before the arrival of the Russians. The large mob of Kurdish irregulars, originally operating with him, had long since deserted. They clearly preferred to terrorise and loot the defenceless villagers rather than to serve under old Halil with all the constraints of a regular force. He was aware, of the poor morale of his remaining six thousand men, and realised that his only hope of containing the Russian advance was to clear the enclave, so as to turn the town into a proper defensive bastion.

Halil slowly built up an attacking force of about four thousand men behind the entrenchments facing and surrounding the Armenian defensive perimeter. Unlike the smart new Turkish officers of the westernised and nationalist Ittihad party, old Halil Bey did not despise his Anatolian peasant troops, and made sure that there would be adequate medical support for the offensive. Accordingly, Dr. Nazim, and his medical team, were ordered forward into the front lines facing the makeshift barricades and demolished houses round the Armenian perimeter.

The final push, destined to be the last major attempt to crush the little force desperately defending Van's Armenian quarter, opened a day or two before the 24th April. The strength of Turkish military arms had always lain in their capacity for dogged defence, rather than in their offensive ability. Accordingly, like almost all the great offensives of the Great War, this smaller lesser-known one also failed. Like all the other combatants of both sides, the ordinary young men carrying out their orders did not lack courage, but they died in their hundreds against the implacable might of the machines facing them, as thousands did on other fronts.

On the other side of the barricades, similar young men, anxious for their families, fought back tenaciously, unable to retreat anywhere even if they wanted to. The cleared ground around the perimeter became filled with the dead and the dying. By the morning of the 24th April the repeated attempts to break into the enclave had finally been given up, and both sides took a breather.

Within the American Mission compound, Dr. Ussher had been continuing his medical work, careful as he had been from the start not to let any armed men into the main hospital grounds, even though the hospital was still being shelled somewhat inefficiently from the Castle Rock. He prayed ever more fervently with his small group of Protestant converts, and he continued to avoid any political attitude to the conflict going on around him.

However, on this morning of the 24th April, Clarence Ussher went down to the church hall where the Armenians had set up a temporary hospital for their wounded. He saw the piles of dead and dying in the no-man's-land between the barricaded stone houses of the perimeter, and the surrounding Turkish entrenchments. He noted also with some horror the hovering vultures, at which both sides were occasionally shooting, and the moans of the badly wounded unable to crawl forward or back.

Dr. Ussher hurried to his office and composed the following letter to Djevdet Bey, whom he imagined was still in charge of the operations round the enclave:

Your Excellency

Having seen the awful slaughter of many young men on both sides, and the plight of the wounded in no-man's-land between the forces, I would like to take this opportunity respectfully to suggest a twelve-hour ceasefire to enable both sides to bury their dead and tend to the badly wounded. I am sure I can prevail on the Armenian leaders to agree to such a proposal, and to allow your men to remove their dead and wounded. Perhaps you could signify your agreement by giving your answer to these proposals with any alternative suggestions you might have, to this messenger, whom I will instruct to remain at the Italian consulate to receive your reply.

I remain, with the greatest respect, your humble servant."

After signing this note, Dr. Ussher called for the nurse Alicia, and handed her the note.

"Alicia, could you give this note to the good lady who has been carrying letters to the Italian consulate for me? She must stay there until she receives a reply from Djevdet Bey, which she should bring back to me."

Alicia, not one of the small handful of converts to Protestantism from her own traditional Gregorian faith, looked at the doctor, whom she deeply admired. She wondered, however, if the man knew that three of these elderly ladies had already died in this regular exchange of messages that had been passing back and forth throughout the siege. Had he simply chosen to ignore the deaths in the interest of, for him, the greater good of God's work, or was he simply totally unaware about it. She would never know.

"Very well Doctor. I'll deal with it," she said, taking the sealed letter and hurrying to seek out Nevart, who had already delivered four messages since she had first arrived to work at the mission.

"Nevart, mother, I have another letter which Dr. Ussher says is very important for you to deliver as usual to the Italian Consulate. After delivering it you must wait at the consulate, inside if the Signore will allow, for a reply. You see that Dr. Ussher has marked 'Urgent' on the envelope, so you must wait for the runner to return with Djevdet Bey's reply before returning yourself. Be careful, make sure that you hold up high the white flag all the time. You must go now while there is a lull in the fighting."

She kissed old Nevart's creased brow, and handed her the stick with the bedraggled white flag of truce.

Nevart touched the ground and lifted her hand to her brow and crossed herself, took the flag and the letter, and walked out of the compound and along the now quiet cobbled streets to the spot between the demolished stone houses from where she had set out on previous occasions.

This was a sector of the line commanded by one of the revolutionary leaders thrown up by the conflict. This young man was impossibly young, fair-haired and blue-eyed, with that look of fanatical zeal in his smiling eyes that left little room for ordinary human compassion. His name was Aris, and he had already on two previous occasions shown impatience at Nevart's simple, old-fashioned, old woman's blessing.

He stared dumbly at her as she came up to warn him that she was going into no-man's-land with a flag of truce to deliver a message to the other side. His face was set hard, his body dirty and tired after two days unceasing fighting.

"May Our Lord Jesus Christ protect you," said Nevart, tentatively raising her hand to bestow a blessing, and her lips to offer a kiss. Aris stood there staring at her, making it clear that he did not welcome the superstitious gesture, nor did he want a kiss. Nevart, confused and hurt, stumbled away. She lifted the flag high as she had been taught, waited a few seconds so that it could be seen by all sides, and then walked between the rubble of the demolished houses and into the cleared area between the two forces.

Right opposite, and sheltered behind another stone house on the other side, stood Dr. Nazim Kemal, temporarily unoccupied since the offensive had petered out. Exhausted after two days non-stop work, he had spent hour after hour patching up horrific wounds, removing embedded bullets, cutting off shattered limbs, until he was acting almost unconsciously. Nevertheless, he remained sharp and alert. He had, even in these difficult circumstances, already managed to have had a shave that morning, much to the amazement of the men around him.

Nazim was profoundly aware of the badly wounded and dying men still lying about unable to crawl or move at all between the Armenian barricades and the Turkish entrenchments. He contemplated the possibility of going out protected by a Red Crescent banner. However, he then wondered whether it should not after all be a Red Cross banner. His mind went round and round on the point. After all, was this a regular battle? The men on the other side were irregular guerillas, were they not? Would they respect such rules of war? He stood there in a state of uncertainty, wondering what to do, considering all the various options. He simply could not make up his mind, whilst the increasingly demoralised men around him lounged about, smoked, and were clearly losing what little discipline they had ever had.

Nazim was the first to see the white flag waving on the makeshift stick and moving out between the two crumbling houses in front of him. The men beside him stared with tired and lack-lustre eyes, as a small old woman, dressed all in black, but without any veil, shuffled out of the gap between the two buildings and began advancing across the dusty corridor between the two lines. The old lady gingerly stepped round the dead bodies in her path. She had just about reached half-way across, when Nazim saw one of the bodies, with a leg half off and dangling uselessly, and with dried blood all over its face, raise its hand to the old woman and call out in a harsh strangulated cry,

"Mamma! Oh my god, Mamma! Mamma!"

Nazim watched and saw the old lady start and look down. She dropped the flag, bent and took the man's head into her arms, for what purpose Nazim could not see, for just then a shot rang out from the Turkish lines and the old lady staggered forward and dropped to her knees, blood spurting from her side. As she fell she cradled the young soldier's head and then sat up holding his head in her lap. Another shot rang out from the Turkish lines kicking up dust at her feet.

Nazim, forgetting all his cool, all his rational thoughtful consideration before action, all that carefully cultivated overlay of city civilisation, sprang out of his position shouting, "Cease fire! Cease fire you louts!" and raced over the dusty uneven ground. There, alone between the two lines, Nevart was rocking back and forth, blood pouring out of her side, with a trickle now from her mouth. She sat there, cradling the young Turkish soldier's head in her lap, stroking his brow and his black hair, and crooning an old Turkish lullaby.

Nazim, after all the carefully considered thoughts about what type of identification he should show, had come running out without even an armband. As he reached the pair, he was already fumbling for the dressings and antiseptics, which he had instinctively grabbed before running out, when a shot rang out, this time from the Armenian side. Nevart, for the first time, looked up. Nazim and Nevart stared into each other's eyes for a split second—an eternal moment—and then Nazim died, fatally shot through the heart, by the guilt-ridden Aris, who had spurned Nevart's blessing, who had seen everything, and who had inevitably misunderstood everything.

Immediately, the whole sector became a maelstrom of shots as both sides began blazing away at each other. In the middle of it all, Nevart continued to rock back and forth cradling the dying soldier, her own strength slowly ebbing away. Finally, in the midst of a fusillade of shots, Nevart, who somehow had not been touched any further by all these flying bullets, bent down and kissed the lips of the son she had never had, "May your Allah receive you into your heaven, my son," murmured Nevart, as she slumped forward, dead, across the breast of the unknown young Turkish soldier.

"Mother, oh mother," groaned the young man, as with the ghost of a smile on his face, he too finally expired.

The aimless shooting went on in this sector for several more hours, as the message to Djevdet Bey, torn and blood-spattered, fluttered away in the wind.

Chapter 31

Selim and Vahan meet.

Back in the compound of Robert College, shortly after Olga had run out of the school gates, Selim was released by his friends.

"Don't go after her my friend," said Nurhan, "she will have left by now, and consider, at this moment it might be too much for her to have you pounding after her."

Selim, whose body was quivering with repressed emotion, shook himself free. However, he did not run anywhere. The young men, friends and others, stood back, still watching him carefully, some at least with sympathy. The girls looked away and one by one hurried off, many in shame at the pressure they had put on one of their number, but some in exultation. Selim smiled at his particular friend Nurhan, and the others around him.

"Thank you," he said quietly, but without meaning it. "Hopefully I'll see you all tomorrow." He went in, collected his things and walked calmly out of the College gates.

Once outside, he began hurrying down to the Galata Bridge. He knew that Olga would be making for Sirkedji station and the train home to Makrikoy. However, by the time he got to the bridge, it had already filled up with the crowds that were preventing Sima from disembarking from her ferry.

Almost at once, Selim made the mistake of trying to push his way through the crowds. His emotional state and natural exuberance did not allow him at that moment to work matters out with logical thought. Had he waited, even for a moment, he would have seen the impossibility of his attempt to push through, in which case he would have immediately thought of all the other ways he could get across to the Stamboul side. As it was, he plunged impetuously into the milling crowds without thinking.

The shouts of "'giavours' to the gallows!" and "Death to the traitorous pigs," and "Down with the British dogs," and so on—the usual mindless imprecations of the city gutter—passed right over his head as he struggled to get through. But the more he pushed through, the tighter he became wedged. Eventually it got to the point that he could go neither forward nor back. He roared with sheer animal frustration as he remained stuck in the middle of the senseless crowd. No one took the slightest notice of him, because of course they were all enjoying themselves roaring, without much thought of what they were shouting.

Whereas Olga's tram had been one of the last to get through, and climb up on the other side, Selim, who had walked down from the College, got there in the middle of the demonstration. Nevertheless, police reinforcements arrived within several minutes of Selim's frustrated attempt to push through, and slowly, with every minute being agony for Selim, the crowd began dispersing.

Selim, as the crowd thinned, began pushing and shoving his way across the bridge and walked up to the Sirkedji station. No train was in, and he had to wait in increasing frustration and impatience on the platform, by which time many others had joined him waiting for the next train. The group included a statuesque young girl, rare enough in all the male turmoil around, to be noticeable. In any case, Selim himself noticed little, as all he could see in his mind was the sight of Olga standing alone in tears in the middle of the college compound.

When Selim got to the Chobancheshme station, he jumped out. He knew exactly where the Avakian house would be. In all the conversations that he and Olga had had together, particularly the inconsequential chat during the tea party at Tokatlian, she had spoken at length about her house and the daily walk down to the station. As he left the little dusty square beside the station, he saw a dumpy middle-aged lady getting out of a carriage, but he was far too nervous and excited to contemplate sitting in a carriage for ten idle minutes, while it would slowly wind its way up the hill. In any case, the horse looked as if it was on its last legs. Selim accordingly crossed the railway line and began walking rapidly up the road beside the Valli Effendi racecourse.

He was about halfway up, with a field on one side, and the racecourse beyond a low wooden fence on the other, when he heard the piercing scream of what sounded like a young boy, and an enormous shout of "help." Ahead and to the left, there appeared to be a boy, almost naked, being set upon by two rough men, both of whom Selim immediately thought were probably Albanian toughs from the city slums. Selim might perhaps, in other circumstances and at other times, have acted less precipitously, though he would never have ignored it as not being his business. However, in his fraught emotional state, he did not hesitate for a second. Taking the fence at a running jump, he charged up to the little group shouting unintelligibly. The youth who had been on top of the young boy rolled off and began fumbling at his dirty baggy trousers as he stood up. The other lout, who had been kneeling by the boy's face, also jumped up, and Selim saw for the first time a wicked looking knife in his hand.

Selim had had no more direct experience of violence than the delicate Haik, but he was eight or more years older, lived in the city, and was aware of city dangers. Above all, he was in a rage—a generalised inchoate anger at everything, and this gave him a momentary advantage over the two ruffians. Had he stopped to remonstrate with them, as he might have done in other circumstances, he would have been lost immediately. As it was, he roared up fists flailing and knocked down the green-shirted man who was still fumbling with his trouser belt. He then turned to face the man in the red blouse who had an inane and vacuous grin on his face, and who was circling round with his knife held ready to lunge.

The young boy on the floor, clearly traumatised, had lifted his head from the grass, and was trying to sit up, his face a mass of blood, and taking great heaving gulps of air. Selim, still in a rage, jumped for the red-bloused man and they rolled onto the grass. For a moment all seemed well as Selim ended up on top, but then Selim felt the cold steel of the knife bite into his side. He jumped up and felt his bleeding hip, and then he sensed rather than saw the green-shirted tough circling round to his back, as the man with the knife began to get up, ready to strike again.

Meanwhile, back at the Avakian house, after Armineh had left in Vahan's carriage, Vahan had settled in the sitting room, no longer in a hurry to leave this charming house. Olga, though still distraught and red-eyed from weeping, had not gone to her bedroom as had been suggested, but sat on the other couch waiting for Nerissa to return with the coffee. Vahan felt surprisingly at ease, and did not seek any chit-chat with the startlingly beautiful Olga. She, on her part, could only think of that last desperate view of Selim, apparently being man-handled by a group of College bullies. They sat silently, but comfortably, waiting for Nerissa.

Nerissa, who had finally come to her senses, returned very quickly with strong sweet Turkish coffee, and some 'courabides'—oversweet Greek biscuits—which Vahan politely declined.

"Where are you from Mister Asadourian?" said Nerissa as she sat down next to Olga.

"Caesaria, but I have been living in Constantinople now for over eight months," said Vahan with some pride. "I'm studying music and drama at the Stamboul University, although as you can see, I'm also enrolled at the Harbiye military academy. I live on my own as a lodger with a Greek family in a house near the Sirkedji station."

"And what of your family, Mister Asadourian?" said Nerissa, now fully involved and interested in the reply and not just making polite conversation.

"Well. . . er. . . by the way my name, Miss Avakian, is Vahan. . . er, do you think you could call me that?" said Vahan with a glance at Olga, who was not paying much attention, truth to tell.

Nerissa did not blush. She was not that kind of girl. She simply looked at Vahan, and without any hesitation said, "Why, yes Vahan, certainly—and my name is Nerissa."

At this, Vahan rose and came over to where the two girls were sitting together and extended his hand somewhat formally. They shook hands. Vahan, still standing, said, "I have a brother about your age, Nerissa—Raffi—and three elder sisters back in Caesaria."

Who knows how long this ever so delightful and totally unrevealing conversation might have meandered on, if Olga had not at that moment got up to hide some more involuntary tears welling up and said, again extending her hand, "Oh, goodbye, Mister Asadourian. . . I'm sorry, Vahan of course. . . If you'll excuse me, I'm exhausted for various reasons. I'm going up to have a lie-down. Please, however, do feel free to remain and finish your coffee."

It was a decisive moment. It had only been about fifteen minutes or so since Armineh had left. Vahan could see that Olga meant what she said, and that there was no objection to his staying and chatting with Nerissa—an increasingly pleasurable experience for him. Nerissa said nothing and Vahan was tempted. But after shaking hands again with Olga, he finally turned, smiled, and shook hands with Nerissa, indicating that he would be on his way. She accompanied him to the front door. He waved again, turned, and started walking briskly down the hill back to the station.

He had just reached the start of the racecourse when he saw the fight going on down to his right. There appeared to be a couple of rough-looking Turkish or Gypsy youths, a young man standing in a posture of defence but holding his side which was bleeding profusely, and a young boy who was almost naked, with blood running from his mouth and nose, struggling to rise from the grass. The boy was being ignored, whilst the two toughs were circling round the bleeding young man each, as Vahan could now see, with a knife in his hand. The young man was roaring something or other at the top of his voice, the words of which Vahan could not distinguish.

Vahan, too, was not used to violence, but his own experience in provincial Caesaria had taught him to differentiate between poor peasants dressed roughly because they couldn't afford better, and city ruffians. He too did not hesitate, and began racing down the road shouting out at the top of his voice, "Stop, stop, police, stand back, stop. . ." and other words making little sense. He had immediately realised that he would be unable to reach the fight before the knives could do further irreparable damage, hence his instinctive decision to try and advertise his impending arrival.

Everyone looked up at the approaching figure of Vahan hurtling down the road. What gave Vahan the brilliant idea of using the word 'police' in all his shouting and gesticulating he never knew, but it was just enough. The arrival of reinforcements, and the use of the magic word decided the two toughs, and first greenshirt, and then red-blouse took to their heels and ran into the racecourse, across and away.

Selim, still bleeding from his right side, but now pressing his left hand over the wound in an attempt to staunch the flow, sat down heavily on the grass. Haik, who in his earlier terror when pressed face down into the earth had again wet himself a little, knelt up looking first at the bleeding Selim, and then at the panting Vahan, as he climbed over the fence—no careless jumping over for him—and finally arrived at the scene.

"What's going on, what's going on?" panted Vahan as he ran up drawing great gulps of breath.

"Heaven knows, Saviour effendi," said Selim. "All I know is that this young lad was being attacked by those two thugs when I arrived and tried to intervene."

Haik, meanwhile, now for the first time aware and ashamed of his near nakedness, scrabbled about in the grass for his torn pants and shoes, both of which had also been wrenched from him. He still had no idea what might have been about to happen to him, but nevertheless he began to tremble in reaction to the fear which had devastated him. He imagined he could still feel the hard touch of the wicked knife on his cheek. There were no more sobs, the tears had dried up, but he could not control his trembling.

The two young men, however, understood at once what had either happened or was about to happen, and despite Selim's bleeding side, where the knife had clearly penetrated between the ribs, they both instinctively thought first of the young boy's distress. Vahan went to pick up one of the shoes and brought it back to Haik, who was in the act of pulling on his torn pants. Selim, releasing for a moment his grip on his own wound, fitted the other shoe as tenderly as he could on Haik's other foot. Both Selim and Vahan were by now quite aware that Haik, uncircumcised, was a Christian. It made not a whit of difference to either of them. They were careful not to question him, or at this stage even to offer support by touching him. They had no idea how far the assault had gone.

It was as Haik finally struggled up, with a tentative smile at the two young men, that Selim saw and recognised for the first time lying abandoned under where Haik had lain, the yellow scarf. He gasped as all the memories of the day came flooding back. Vahan, who also saw it, did not hesitate. Once he saw Haik's pained and shy smile, he bent down and grabbed the scarf, tearing it down the middle, he tied the two parts together. He then picked up Haik's shirt, still lying torn on the ground and stuffing it over Selim's wound he then bound the scarf very tightly round Selim's waist to hold it in place and to stem the flow of blood.

Selim thanked him with his eyes, but his mind was on the scarf.

"Where did you get this, my boy," he said addressing Haik and indicating the yellow scarf, as Vahan tied it tight.

"It belongs to my sister," said Haik eventually, somewhat hoarsely, speaking for the first time. "These two men were trying to make off with it, when I tried to take it back."

The two young men stared at Haik, wondering at the foolhardiness, and sheer stupidity of this frail boy in risking himself for a mere scarf.

Haik's nose and mouth were still bleeding as he stood there in his torn pants, muddy shoes, and bare chest. Selim was swaying with weakness as blood still seeped through the shirt. Vahan too stood still, stunned, knowing that he ought to be doing something, but also himself now suffering from the reaction of all that adrenaline draining away. It was Haik who broke the moment of silence.

"My parents' home is just up the road. My name is Haik Avakian. Do you think, sir," he said addressing Vahan, "we could go there now? I'm sure that my mother will look after this gentleman."

Neither man had the energy nor the wish at this stage to question what appeared to be an extraordinary coincidence. With both Vahan and now Haik supporting the ever-weaker Selim, they clambered over the fence and shuffled slowly up the road. Eventually they reached and knocked on the Avakian front door, which Vahan had left only a few short minutes previously.

Chapter 32

The Avakians in crisis.

In the Avakian house, after the departure of Vahan, Olga had finally gone up to rest, while Nerissa moped about downstairs. After all the emotion of being involved in Olga's interrupted confession to Armineh, and the devastating news of her father's arrest, she suddenly felt the need to think of calmer things. Her thoughts turned to her younger siblings. So far as the rest of the family were concerned, she had been the one who had always been made responsible for seeing to both Haik and little Seta. Seta, she knew, was being collected from school for her weekly piano lessons with the elderly Madame Chatelle. This would last for the rest of the afternoon, as she always took her tea there as well. However, she was just beginning to wonder what had happened to Haik, when the doorbell rang. This must be him, she thought, as strangers usually missed the dratted doorbell, hidden as it was behind the overgrown ivy.

Nerissa ran to the door, opened it, and met there a scene she would never forget—a sight which more than any other was perhaps the most instrumental in thrusting her during the next few days from a grown child of sixteen, into a young woman of sixteen. Standing there, clearly short of breath and not gabbling away immediately as usual, she saw her young brother with his nose freely bleeding, dressed only in pants and shoes, his chest bare and dirty, and with his mouth covered in dried blood. Partly leaning against him was an incredibly pale Selim, clutching his side with Olga's distinctive yellow scarf round his waist, and with blood seeping between his fingers. Taking almost the whole of Selim's weight on the other side, was the same young man—Vahan—who had left the house only about fifteen minutes ago.

For once Nerissa did not just wait and start reflecting on the situation with an open mouth. She immediately beckoned them in, and yelled out—something she never normally did—for Marie and Olga. She then took Haik's free hand and gently drew him in. At the tender touch of his beloved sister, Haik at last, and for the first time, burst into entirely childish crying, no longer the sobs of anger and fear, but the childish request for comfort, preferably female.

Nerissa saw at once that Selim's physical condition was much worse than that of Haik, but she felt instinctively that Haik's hurt, whatever it was, was ultimately more dangerous. She held him tight as the other two entered behind him. Marie, who had bustled in from the kitchen on hearing Nerissa's shout, took one look at Selim and ran back to collect what was needed. Olga, bleary-eyed, arrived at the top of the stairs, took one look at the melodramatic scene in the hall, and almost fainted there and then, unable to make any sense of what she was seeing. However, when it came to the crunch, Olga had more than enough of Armineh's practical good sense and indomitable will to be able to rise to the occasion. Now fully alert, she ran down the stairs, and like the other women asked no questions, but took the weight of Selim from Vahan, led him to the chaise-longue in the sitting-room, and got him to lie down. Selim himself by now was dizzy and almost on the point of fainting from loss of blood, and was incapable of saying anything or feeling anything other than the pain in his side.

Marie came bustling in with a bowl of steaming hot water, some sort of bottle of bright purple antiseptic, and a roll of linen dressing. Nerissa held on tightly to the now quietly crying Haik who had buried his face in her breasts, while Vahan stood panting and getting his breath back.

"Miss Olga," said Marie when she saw that Olga was not going to relinquish her position by the side of the wounded young man, "You must wash the wound carefully all round. Then you must make sure that this antiseptic goes all over the area, and that some of it goes well into the wound. It will sting and he will shout, but you've got to make sure it goes right in. Don't worry, my dear, he's in no real danger, he'll do fine. The only danger is that the wound gets infected, and that must be prevented above all."

Olga nodded, and delicately undoing and removing the scarf and Haik's shirt now entirely soaked in blood, she began, efficiently and surprisingly calmly, working as Marie had directed. Without any hint of embarrassment or uncertainty, she lifted Selim's shirt and pushed down the top of his trousers to reveal the full extent of the wound—her mind totally on the purely nursing task required.

Meanwhile Haik had finally cried his fill. Some brightness had come back into his previously dulled eyes, and Nerissa decided that it was time he was cleaned up, and whispering in his ear she persuaded him up the stairs to the bathroom. Marie moved to follow, but before she started up, Vahan suddenly bestirred himself and came over signalling her to wait a moment. Marie duly waited looking steadily at the anxious brown eyes of this stranger. Vahan was deeply embarrassed, but he felt it to be absolutely vital that the situation concerning Haik should be made clear. He believed that some attempt must immediately be made, before any major emotional damage had time to sink in, to find out exactly how far events had gone before Selim had turned up.

He outlined the facts as he knew them and which had been quietly confirmed by Selim, making certain that Marie understood that one of the toughs appeared to have been on top of the half-naked Haik when Selim had arrived. Marie nodded—she was well versed in the ways of the world—particularly the Turkish world.

"Madam," said Vahan, who was not quite sure of the position Marie had in the household, "I do believe that you should try to find out the basic facts now, so that you can inform his mother and father when they return, without involving him directly at first. Er . . . Madam . . . I hope that you will be careful, and er . . . also not involve Miss Nerissa at this stage . . . I mean . . ." and Vahan finally dried up at seeing Marie's penetrating stare.

"My dear sir," said Marie haughtily, "I have nursed these children for twenty years. Do you think I don't know my job? Really!" and she marched upstairs. Vahan reddened even more than before, and withdrew, wondering if he had gone too far in interfering.

Marie, meanwhile, arrived in Haik's bedroom with yet another bowl of hot water. He was no longer crying and was sitting up on his bed, shoulders still drooping but his eyes more alive. Nerissa, no doubt cleverer than almost everyone else in the family, was not, after all, so very practical. She was simply sitting on the bed, holding him tight, without doing anything about the still bleeding nose or the cut lips.

"Now then, Miss Nerissa, run along and help your sister downstairs. We need to get this young man tidied up, and my dear, you'll be a little in the way here."

Nerissa nodded, gave Haik a tender kiss, and went out. Haik, at the touch of the kiss, was almost about to start crying again, but was stopped by his old Nurse's stern look.

"Now Haik," said Marie, carefully wiping away the blood from his nose and mouth, "This is not too bad a cut. Go and change into these pyjamas, hold your head right back putting this cotton wool to your nose, and then have a good wash all over and come back here."

Marie knew that Haik had to be left alone to change, the latent shame in his semi-nakedness being fairly clear to her experienced eyes.

Haik returned in about five minutes in his pyjamas, cleaned up, at least to the somewhat half-hearted point natural to a twelve-year old boy. The nose bleed had at last stopped, and the cut lips, now cleaned up, did not look at all bad. Above all the eyes had brightened even further, and there was a new firmness in the previously drooping shoulders.

"Haik, you better get into bed and have a rest."

"But I'm not at all sleepy Marie, and I want to know what the others are doing."

"I know, dear, but it's all been a bit of a shock and you need the rest. Don't bother to try to sleep, you can read until Mummy comes back. Would you like to tell me now what happened."

Haik told Marie about the walk back from school, the two youths lounging on the grass, Olga's yellow scarf, their sudden attack as he tried to take the scarf, the knife, their inspection as to whether he was circumcised or not by taking down his pants, his torn shirt and the assault, all without any embarrassment—after all Marie had bathed and dressed him as long as he could remember for all his life, until the last few years.

Marie listened, then speaking very carefully, said, "Did you feel any bad pain down below when you were thrown to the floor."

"Well, yes, I did feel a sudden pain starting in my bum, Marie, but it was then that I kicked out and yelled at the top of my voice. The pain stopped, and never came back again, as it was just about then that the first gentleman came running up after he heard my shout."

Marie registered these facts carefully ready to be able to pass them on to Armineh when she returned, and otherwise sighed in relief at Haik's words, spoken totally innocently and without any guilty or self-conscious reserve. She knew that it was now just a matter that Karekin was going to have to deal with on his return that night. Indeed, Marie had always felt that Karekin had been neglectful of his son's education in this field, even though she knew it was of course nothing to do with her. She rose, "Call me, my love, if you need anything" she said, and slipped out.

When she got downstairs, she found Selim still lying stretched out on the chaise-longue, with Olga still kneeling alongside putting the final touches to the new clean dressing round his waist and tightly bound over the wound. Nerissa had obviously been helping to tighten the dressing, and was standing behind Olga, waiting with scissors to cut the end of the linen. The bleeding had stopped. Vahan was still standing and dumbly looking on, none of them saying anything. Marie went over to him and said, "It's all right, sir, the other gentleman seems to have caught the situation just in time, thank god. No permanent damage seems to have been done, and I don't think there will be a bad memory problem. Either way it is a matter for his parents now when they get back this evening.

Vahan nodded and smiled at her, probably the first smile that had crossed his face that whole day. With that, Marie left the room, saying that she would be back shortly with some coffee and biscuits.

Selim was already recovering and achieving some colour under Olga's careful ministrations. Olga, herself, having worked almost like a professional ever since Marie had gone upstairs, suddenly became aware of Selim's body—bared to the chest, and with his trousers right down to the hips. She also became conscious that her fingers had worked over this male body. Their eyes met, both of them aware of the swiftly changed mood that had all at once arisen between them all over again.

Olga stood back indicating to Nerissa to finish the work by pulling up Selim's trousers and pushing the shirt back. She felt faint again all of a sudden, and turned away, with different though welcome, emotions flooding over her. It was clear that Selim was not going to be able to move for some time, and so the four young people settled themselves in the sofas and chairs round the chaise-longue, as Marie came in with a tray of coffee and some welcome food.

Chapter 33

A question of identity.

Somehow the drama which in one way or another they had all just been through had removed all constraints between them. The girls aged sixteen and eighteen, and the young men—nineteen and twenty—at last drew a sort of collective breath and settled down to a semblance of normality. Vahan and Selim, already caught up in a male-bonding situation, having shared and overcome danger together, at last introduced themselves and their background to each other. The whole coincidence of events unravelled, even including a guess at the hitherto unexplained failure of Sima to turn up at Haik's school. At the same time the infatuation, or was it love, of Selim and Olga for each other, was openly accepted without any need of any further explanation or comment.

It was clear that Selim could not leave for at least another hour or two while he recovered his strength. It was he, who, now hearing for the first time of the arrest of Olga's father that morning, raised the issue behind all the current problems of the hitherto multi-racial Ottoman Empire. He turned to Vahan as all the explanations finished and commented, "Here I am amongst an Armenian family for the first time in my life, although I have always lived next to Greek or Armenian neighbours. What an experience! Tell me Vahan, do you feel more Armenian, more Christian, or more Ottoman?"

"I feel all three," replied Vahan. "Your identity surely isn't exclusively, or even mainly, one thing or another. Your identity comprises all your many different affiliations, your varied interests, your cultural activities, even the type of food you eat—indeed you're a mixture of many elements, all of which make up your own unique identity."

"But, hang on, Vahan. What about 'deep down inside you', isn't there some deeper inner allegiance that is more 'you' than anything else in your make up?"

"No Selim, I don't really think so. This is the mistake that the much-vaunted new Ittihad party is making here and now. They're trying to suggest that no aspect of identity is more important than that of being a member of a particular national state, one that they are currently trying to create in the place of the multi-national one we have at the moment. It is a narrow exclusive and prejudiced attitude of mind that reduces all the rich varied aspects of a person's identity to one simple and overriding affiliation—your race—often expressed violently and in anger. In the end it is a recipe for massacres and oppression, which I fervently hope the coming twentieth century is going to reject."

"Come, Vahan, my friend, I do agree that of course my identity is unique and is what prevents me after all from being the same as anybody else. However, surely I have one or two overriding allegiances or convictions that are so much more important than some of the others that they might legitimately be called my principle identifying factors. After all, these stupid adolescent freckles I have that stubbornly refuse to go away, are clearly part of my identity, and actually quite important to me at the moment, but they can't compare with my identity as a Muslim or my allegiance of being a Turk. I do believe, for example, that these two allegiances—Muslim and Turk are more significant than my identity as a middle class Ottoman, which is of course one that I would share with you for instance. Basically, what I am saying is that you can rank all these allegiances in a sort of order of importance."

"Well, yes Selim, but think a bit. Your being a Muslim hasn't prevented you as a Turk fighting innumerable wars with the Muslim Persian Empire to your east, nor has your being a Turk prevented you as an honourable Muslim from opposing the previous odious regime of Abdul Hamid's Turkish secret police. Things change. One day your being a Muslim is the most important of your identities, but the next day it might be your education in a liberal American college that becomes the most important factor. Above all Selim, my friend, your identity is likely to change as you grow, and as society itself changes. Yesterday, if asked, you might have answered proudly, 'My identity? Why I am an Ottoman citizen!' Today, or at least very soon, you might say just as certainly and proudly 'I'm a modern Turk'. Tomorrow, if the nation-state wobbles, you might say just as surely say 'I'm a Muslim'. It's all relative to the times, and there is no deeper 'you' at all.

"OK, Vahan, but taking your point to its extremes, aren't you in danger of losing any sense of identity at all? We all need to belong somewhere. I accept that it would be wrong to force millions of anxious people to assert only one side of these multiple identities that you talk about. However, to try and deny that any one of these major affiliations, nationalist, religious, or cultural is no more important than others is to leave bewildered people totally adrift. In the end, Vahan, I have to say that you are speaking like a member of a minority people."

"But Selim, my friend, I am indeed, after all, a member of a minority people. It is part of my identity that this conversation is taking place in Turkish, a language not naturally my mother tongue. It is a language which I and my family probably speak better than millions of Anatolian peasants, but if I had only a narrow version of my own identity—only as an Armenian say—I might resent it. However, I don't. The language I speak reflects only a part of my identity. In the last resort, for me being Armenian does not override everything else."

At this point, Vahan reflected before continuing. He believed that Selim was an honourable man, for whom he could come to have a great affection. However, suddenly he recalled the letter from his mother, and the terrible beating his father had received from men who had always previously respected him, and to whom he had always shown respect. The morning's events also came into his mind and the arrest of the gentle Father Komitas. He gave an involuntary shiver. He wanted to be honest and not avoid answering any of Selim's points, but equally, how far could he express views that might offend Selim or put him into a difficult position?

"Selim, my friend, believe me, you and I understand each other better than you and Nasreddin Hodja ever could—if it was even possible for you to meet him. That, in its way, is another facet of your identity, which your identity as a Turk does not override."

Selim laughed out loud at the thought of actually meeting the legendary old Turkish figure of fun, the Hodja on his peasant donkey. Selim fidgeted a little on the sofa, as he tried to ignore the continuing pain in his side. He was no longer thinking so clearly, though he was certain that he was right. He said, "Vahan, in the end, why do you think that the single-people nation-states in the west have become so much more successful than our own ramshackle Empire? It's not just industrial might, it is because they are one people speaking one language exclusively, and not an amalgam of many. That's what we now need here."

"Selim," Vahan replied, "don't be fooled. The danger of the coming nation-state espoused by the Ittihad party to which you are looking forward so much, is that they will be insisting on a one and only overriding aspect of identity—nationalist and tribal. It has, however, been one of the failures of Western states over many centuries. The Spanish monarchy couldn't abide the different identity of the old Moorish and Jewish elements in their midst, and thus impoverished their society immeasurably by oppressing and eventually deporting them. Louis XIV couldn't tolerate the different identity of the Huguenots, so he threw them out to the great detriment of France in the long run. Even the tolerant British for centuries required a conformity in religion as proof of loyalty to their so-called overriding requirement of national identity."

Nerissa, meanwhile, had been listening to all this in rapt attention, after she had come down. Olga, too, had not said a word, being content to sit on the sofa next to Selim, holding his hand tight, and feeling his body close to her own. At this point, brought up in a household where the girls did not just stay silent and listen to males sounding off, Nerissa interrupted and said, "Good heavens! You're both beginning to lecture each other. In all this question of identity, neither of you have referred to your identity as a male, which after all gives you an affiliation, I think that's the word you used, with half the human race. I have a female identity, which Selim, is surely just as important as my being an Armenian. In the Hammams the most important identity factor between us all gossiping and using the baths is being female. However, I do think that even this isn't 'overriding' as you say. I imagine it's quite a different experience being a woman born in Paris say, to one born here, or even further away to one born in Afghanistan."

"Well, I don't know," said Olga lightly, "I only know that my identity has changed over the last eight weeks."

"Oh Olga," said Nerissa impatiently "Can't you ever think of anything but your own feelings? We are discussing something serious and general here."

Selim looked down at Olga at his side, and winced as he moved slightly closer to her on the sofa. Vahan, looking vacantly on, then said, "Hang on Nerissa, let's hear what Miss Olga has to say."

"Come, come, Vahan, surely 'Olga' by now."

"I'm sorry, 'Olga' of course," replied Vahan with a smile.

"Well, what I suppose I meant was that had you asked me a mere eight weeks ago where my main allegiances—I think that was the word you used—lay, I would have said—I am an Armenian, and a Christian, and above all a member of a closed family unit, and that my principle 'deep down inside' identity was as an Avakian daughter. Now, eight weeks later, I am not so sure any more. My sense of my own identity has suddenly become bound up with the identity of someone else."

Selim squeezed her hand hard, but couldn't squeeze his body any closer, partly in deference to Vahan sitting opposite, and partly due to the fact that his wounded side, already pressed too close, was giving him some pain.

"Oh, please, please don't say 'deep down inside,'" said Vahan going back to his original point. "All the elements of your current loyalties, allegiances, and affiliations are an equal part of your identity to which these new and differing strands are continually being added."

"No, no, my friend," said Selim. "This is surely exactly the nub of where we differ. My own belief is that there is always one major aspect of your identity which you get perhaps from your father and mother and which overrides all others. However I do now accept that this may change with time and as social conditions change."

"No, Selim," said Vahan, "I reiterate that every one of us should be encouraged to accept totally our own diverse forms of identity, and try to avoid raising any one of these affiliations to the status of the most important. Overriding exclusive affiliations so often turn into an instrument of exclusion of others, and perhaps oppression towards those not sharing that exclusivity."

By now they were all four rather flushed and excited. Vahan, because he was enjoying immensely the fascinating argument with a person for whom he was beginning to feel a great affection. Nerissa, because she had never felt so accepted in what she thought of as grown-up conversation. Selim, by the continuing throb of the wound in his side, but more by the whole atmosphere of friendship and affection which boded so well, or so he thought, for his love. Olga, by the simple proximity of the young man by her side whom she imagined she might have lost for ever only a few hours ago.

Time was getting on, and it was clear that Armineh would not be returning for some time. Nerissa suddenly said in some distress, "Oh, Olga, I forgot mother, and probably Sima too, if they met at the station. What can be happening?"

The mention of the dilemma of the arrest, and the departure of Armineh to find her husband, brought all four of them back to practicalities. Nerissa, recalled that Haik had surely now been left upstairs on his own long enough. Olga began worrying about what was to happen to Selim. But it was Vahan who then rose and asked Olga how he could arrange for a carriage to the station, as clearly Selim ought not to walk back. A servant was duly dispatched to go down and come back with one of the gharries.

The doorbell rang again. Nerissa, knowing it must be a member of the family in view of the overgrown ivy, ran to the door.

"Hello everyone—it's me, it's me!" called out a breathless Seta as she ran in not even acknowledging Nerissa, who slipped out and waved a thank-you at Madame Chantelle's maid hurrying away down the hill.

Seta stopped at the sight of the two young men, but she had no shyness and immediately said, "Hello, I'm Seta—who are you?" holding out her hand and not listening to anyone's reply.

"Where's Haik? Did you all hear that great foghorn of the big ship in the harbour this morning? We saw it from the windows, out in the sea. Where's Mummy? Madame Chantelle was all excited today. It must be her birthday or something."

This was not by any means all that she said, but by now the party was breaking up.

Selim and Vahan eventually departed on the carriage when it arrived, with Selim leaning heavily on Vahan. There was no parting physical touch, not even a handshake, between Olga and Selim; only a promise in the eyes that their relationship would not be lost, not ever.

Arriving in the City, Vahan saw Selim into a carriage prior to trudging home himself to his lodgings in the now much quieter streets. Selim trundled home, unaware of the telegram awaiting him from Halil Bey as to his father's death. Vahan too walked home, equally unaware of the letter winging its way to him from his mother as to his own father's arrest and disappearance from home, that very day.

It was the last hours of the 24th April. The City brooded, as the great western armada finally began arriving at the fatal entrance of the Dardanelles.

Chapter 34

Caesaria. Garabed's escape.

The next day, after seeing his father and giving him the coins, Raffi went out again to see if the arrested men herded into the town hall gardens were still there. The place was empty, and after peering through the railings for a time, Raffi turned away. The news of the landings at Gallipoli the previous evening had been filtering through all morning on the telegraph line. The town criers had been calling out what facts were available. Raffi, fearful for his father, walked back through the narrow streets, avoiding any eye contact with other men hurrying along, all of whom appeared tense and anxious. Raffi had not dared to make any enquiries at the town hall as to what may have happened to the arrested men. He returned home to his grieving mother without being able to hold out any hope.

In fact, that very morning, early, before it had even got light, four decrepit old lorries had arrived at the town hall. The whole group, doctors, lawyers, business men, and some district heads had been herded into the back of them, where there was only standing room. There were very few lorries in Caesaria, and certainly no motorcars except that belonging to the Governor. Somehow, this particular group had been considered important enough to warrant the use of these rare vehicles, which appeared to have been provided by the military.

The government had recently released criminals from the prisons, and the whole countryside around Caesaria was to become a killing ground for people about to be deported and made to walk from the town. This was the policy of 'ethnic cleansing', now in the process of being planned in Constantinople by Talaat and the others. But for this group, the first of these deportations, there were lorries! The significant difference from all the later mass deportations was that sitting in the front of each lorry alongside the driver were two or three armed Turkish soldiers. There were several other soldiers also, standing with the arrested men in the back.

There were some petrol cans slung along the sides, but nevertheless, it was fairly clear to Garabed that the lorries were only going to go a short distance, and would then turn back. He soon discovered that the soldiers had received orders to escort the group through the wild countryside, until they reached the borders of the vilayet of Syria, after which the party was to make its own way to Aleppo.

This was an entirely new experience for these men. There was no precedent, no point of reference which they could grasp in order to help them decide how to act. They were perfectly capable of rational discussion, they had after all the experience of cooperating together in managing the affairs of their local communities and churches. They were used to acting in committees or on the boards of their business enterprises. But somehow, the latent violence, the totally new and strange situation, the uncertainty about where they were going or why, had sapped their collective will.

These were strong and successful men—not one of whom would have hesitated to act even with physical violence if one of their children had been threatened. Natural leaders of their community, facing only a few slovenly guards with obsolete rifles, aware that they were in a deeply dangerous situation, yet they took no collective action at all.

The lorries trundled on over rough roads winding up and through the wild mountains and mainly bare countryside. Little was said by the men squeezed together, all standing and swaying as they were jolted about. Garabed reflected that he had perhaps made a mistake in not taking all the gold coins. He had been under the impression that he was not going to survive beyond that night, and that in any case, any coins he might have on him would surely have been quickly stolen. However, surprisingly, none of the deportees had even been searched, and it was clear that many of them had managed to retain their cash.

As they passed through the poor dilapidated villages, those with some money on them purchased bread and other provisions which the villagers offered whenever the lorries stopped. No arrangements for food seemed to have been made by the authorities, and even the guards, with no officer amongst them, appeared to have no provisions and little idea of what was to happen.

Eventually the group came to a halt in a narrow valley, with bare moss-covered hills, rocky, and strewn with boulders on either side. Running down the middle was a little stream—but even here, so far from anywhere, the countryside was ugly, with rubbish and the bones of dead animals alongside the stream. In the middle of the valley there was a small khan—a local wayside inn—a ramshackle building with some rooms for travellers and a large kitchen with trestle tables and rickety chairs. This was a barren desolate spot, and had clearly been chosen to be the first night's stop as it was well away from any inhabited area.

Standing in the dusty area in front of this unprepossessing building were eight or nine high-sided carts. The oxen clearly intended to be pulling these carts were grazing on the sparse grass nearby. Everyone peeled out of the lorries, and some of the prisoners wandered into the khan to purchase food, encouraged by the guards who now produced several bags of unleavened bread which were in the back of the carts. They distributed the loaves. There was little sign at this stage of any racial tension between the prisoners and these local soldiers. This was early days in the horror of the deportations which was about to develop. The prisoners shared their purchased boiled eggs, onions, olives and cheese with each other and with the guards who had accompanied them from Caesaria.

It was still light when the starting handles of the lorries were turned with some effort, and they reversed and drove off back to the town. At almost the same moment a further cart, holding a dozen smartly uniformed soldiers, appeared over the hill behind them and drew up in front of the khan alongside the other carts. The men all piled out of the cart and formed rank. Garabed saw that they were a detachment of gendarmes and were led by a hard-faced officer—an Enver look-alike with the unmistakeable stamp of an Ittihad supporter. The atmosphere changed immediately.

A few bedraggled tents had been in the back of the carts when they had arrived. Some of the prisoners now set about, somewhat inefficiently, putting them up in the grass around the khan. It was not a particularly cold night, although at this altitude anyone without a good coat would have been in real difficulty. Garabed chose to sleep outside, wrapped up in his good sheepskin for which he blessed his wife. Before settling down, he smoked a cigarette with an old acquaintance.

"Garabed, agha, what in heaven's name is really going on? Are we facing some sort of pogrom like twenty years ago?"

"My dear Levon, I've no idea, but I fear the worst. We seem to be a very carefully chosen group, don't you see that? This is not just a round-up of 'giavours' to satisfy the gutter instincts of the mindless mob, but a carefully selected list prepared by some bureaucrat. I believe it presages a campaign of some sort or another in the future against the whole community."

"Nonsense, Garabed, the regime isn't clear-minded or efficient enough."

"Levon, it might not be clear-minded, but it's certainly efficient enough. Think about it, in the old days of Abdul the damned there would have been screaming and shouts and yells; there would have been no lorries or carts laid on; there would have been no food of any kind; there would of course have been bullying and blood-lust and death, but not for god's sake this awful cold Prussian efficiency. I fear that we could be facing executions awaiting us as the next step, somewhere remote on the way, maybe even here. I may of course be quite wrong."

"But look, Garabed. Why would they go to all this trouble, for heaven's sake, when they could simply have had us all shot in the town hall gardens yesterday?"

"Because, Levon, they still have European allies and they daren't risk the adverse publicity. Quite apart from the unrest that would be aroused in the Armenian population if there were open shootings in the town, it is likely that there would be a few influential Turks of the old school who would object and report to Constantinople."

"Well, even if you're right about that, why are they doing it? What's the point of this carefully drawn-up list you're talking about?"

"First, Levon, they get rid of the natural leaders of the community. Most of the young men are gone already, either in the army or in labour battalions. They can then deal with the old men, the women and the children as they want."

"My God, Garabed. Aren't you being over-pessimistic? Nothing like this has ever happened before. Go to sleep, my friend, you'll feel better in the morning."

Once wrapped up and alone, Garabed began considering his position further. On the one hand, although he was not an intimate friend of any of the others, he knew most of them, and they knew him. He felt the warm camaraderie of men sharing the same discomfort and danger. Being part of a group meant the occasional laughter and joke, the occasional breaking into song even in the midst of fear, a fear which was at least easier to bear in being shared.

On the other hand, Garabed was one of the few of the prisoners who had become aware of the changed situation within the empire. This awareness was as a result of the beating that he alone, apparently, had suffered two weeks before at the police station. He recognised a sinister under-current, camouflaged by the basically indifferent attitude of the Anatolian peasant soldiers guarding them, but which was not manifest in the new guards who had just arrived or their officer. In the last few weeks officials had become curt and evasive, answering questions with hooded eyes that did not look at you. Garabed knew that this was not just some war-time emergency measure. Death was present, group or no group.

The choice was clear. Did he stay with the group, sharing all its fate one way or another, or did he try to make it on his own? It was clear to him that if escape was to take place at all, it had to be this very night. It was a pure question of survival. Would survival be more likely if he struck out now on his own into unknown territory in a wild countryside, or if instead he stayed with the group being led like sheep to God knows what fate?

He did not know where he was, he had no food apart from one loaf of bread. Maybe he was abandoning the one chance of survival by leaving this guarded group. He lay awake turning it all over in his mind. In the end it came down to the fact that by slipping away, if he could, he would at least be putting his fate back into his own hands.

Gathering up his coat quietly and wrapping it round the loaf, he began crawling slowly along, avoiding the tent pegs and the sleeping bodies. He had noted the exact position of the two guards on night watch. Both were dozing and he knew that he must get away before they got up to awake the next two for the second watch.

"Good-bye Garabed, good luck, may God be with you," whispered one of the sleeping bodies as he slithered past. An elderly voice, Garabed never knew who it was or what became of him. Slowly and stealthily he drew away from the light of the two fires burning away near the two guards.

Once out of sight and across the stream, Garabed rose, stretched, and began striding away up the hillside northwards. He reckoned that this would be in the opposite direction of that which was going to be taken by the group, which would presumably be going to the south towards the Arab provinces—if it was going to go anywhere at all. He planned to be several miles away, well into the hills, long before the camp rose in the morning.

He stumbled on, heading northwards guided by the stars. As the sun rose the next morning, he found himself in the middle of mossy rocky hills with no sign of cultivation or any life anywhere. Garabed, a leader of the city community, a father of six children, a respected merchant dressed in a dark town suit already crumpled and totally unsuitable for the countryside, found himself in the middle of the Anatolian wilderness, alone, afraid, unable to return to his home, and presumably some sort of outlaw. All this enormous change in his life had happened in just a mere forty-eight hours. For the moment, putting all thoughts of his family and former life out of his mind, he strode on.

Chapter 35

Letters.

Halil Bey to Selim.

In the name of the Almighty, the Compassionate.

My son,

You will already have received the sad news of your father's martyrdom on the field of battle in Van. Although I only knew your father for a short time, since he recently joined our camp, I came to appreciate his excellent qualities, not only as a Doctor, but as an officer. He spoke often about you and your mother, so I feel I know you, and I have therefore an inclination to give you more details about your esteemed father's death.

I was not of course present myself, but I have pieced together the evidence of what took place, which I have gleaned from soldiers who were there. Your father and his medical team moved forward in order to be available for the major offensive I had planned against these traitorous rebels. The Russian army was getting closer day by day, and if we were to have any chance of opposing them, we had to get back into control of Van, so as to have it at our backs as our fortress. This offensive was our last chance, as the Russians are now likely to be here within a week or two.

I am afraid, my boy, that the offensive failed. The Armenian rebels, may Allah smite them, raised no doubt to fanatical extremes by their black crows, the *giavour* priests, fought suicidally, and we were decisively repulsed.

It appears that a messenger, a lady, was sent forward under a flag of truce by the terrorists. For some reason, she stopped in the middle between our forces and appeared to be wounded. Your brave and courageous father ran forward to help her, and was treacherously shot by the enemy. He will undoubtedly be in heaven with Allah. He died for the faith.

After his death, we found in his tent a sealed envelope addressed to you, but which he obviously had not had the time to post. I am sending it on to you now. His other personal effects will follow in the usual way in due course.

Dr. Nazim Kemal to his son—Selim.

My incomparable son,

I am writing to you from my camp bed on the shores of the lovely Lake Van. The nights here are bright and clear and fresh, though still very cold. When the moon is full and high, the lack of any artificial light makes the visibility crystal clear, and you can almost see across the lake to the high mountains on the other side.

I have been moved up to the front with my medical team, as Halil Bey is proposing to mount a full-scale major offensive to clear the town of the rebels, before the projected arrival of the small Russian force currently advancing towards us.

My son, I have had a lot of time on my hands which I have spent thinking about our lives, the Empire, and what it all means. War often consists of days of intense and terrible activity with not a moment in which to catch your breath. This, however, is interspersed with long periods of utter boredom, when there is nothing to do but think about one's loved ones and write letters.

I remain very sad at the way the Armenians here have treacherously risen against the Empire at this moment of crisis in our history, but I am not perhaps quite so incensed as I had been earlier when I first arrived here. The intensity with which they are defending the perimeter of the town does indicate at least a certainty of their moral position, which I had not expected. I have also heard some reports of the weaknesses and cruelties of the Ittihad Governor here, one Djevdet Bey. However, in the end, no rebellion at a critical moment in the history of a state can be excusable.

Their justification, I believe, is the rise amongst them over the last thirty years of 'nationalist' ideas. The belief they have is that a 'people', however you define it, should act together to have a 'state'. It is a feeling which began about thirty years ago with all the literary revivals and studies of history, culture and folk myths by passionate teachers and academics. In the case of the Armenian peasants here, this was accentuated by foreign missionaries as well. It has evolved towards revolution. I am sorry to add that I can sense that it is growing now also, partly as a reaction, amongst the Turks and Kurds of Anatolia. It is precisely what I object to in the current Ittihad government—the urge to create a single exclusive and intolerant nation-state.

But, my son, it is not preordained or unstoppable.

It is possible, my boy, to love one's own religion, one's own language and literature, the ethnic food you have eaten all your life, the dancing and the music and the theatre you have enjoyed, yet still be content to be part of a state that has no particular connection to these things, or which carefully takes no part in trying to regularise or influence them.

I understand that the United Sates of America, across the Atlantic, may be like that. A state which exists without all the narrow tribal requirements of an exclusive nation state. I also believe that the old Ottoman Empire, at its best, was also like this. I fear, however, that a change is being forced upon us by our present leaders, who have an exaggerated respect for the western ideals of nationalism.

My darling boy, I know that you have been brought up with truth, and that your heart is strong, and your convictions firm and honourable. Always consider all sides of any position on which you are obliged to make a stand, but act decisively once your mind is made up. Look after your mother and your younger brother and sisters in case any accident may befall me. You will recall the details of the savings box in my study of which I told you before leaving.

However, I believe that a fully equipped regular regiment with its own medical facilities is moving up to Bitlis shortly, in view of the imminent arrival of the Russians. Should this rumour—it's incredible isn't it how rumours fly around during wartime—be true, I should be due to return to Stamboul soon, as my detachment will no longer be needed.

My respectful embraces to your mother
Your father—Nazim.

Raffi to his brother Vahan

My dear brother,

I know that mother wrote to you a week or so ago about the awful experience our father had to go through at the police station. I was so mad, Vahan, when I saw father slung across the back of that bloody donkey, like a sack of grain, I simply couldn't keep still. Once we had got father inside I left him to our mother's and sisters' capable hands, and went running out into the countryside. I didn't care; if I had been accosted by any bad person, I would have gladly fought with him I was so charged up.

I am afraid, Vahan, that this is not the end. Yesterday something terrible happened and we are all afraid that it is only the beginning. Father was arrested and taken to the town hall. Mother gave me some money to take to him once we got over the initial shock and knew where he was. There were about eighty other Armenians arrested with him. I saw them all milling about in the town hall gardens. Vahan, I was scared stiff—the news of the Allied landings only arrived later, but the general tension in the town was awful. The news of the Van rebellion, and the killings in the East are all over the town and we all move about with a very low profile.

I went again to the town hall this morning, but they had all been taken away somewhere already. Oh, Vahan, father made it clear that he didn't expect to survive. I knew that I ought not to let him see me cry, but I couldn't help it. He held my hand tight and looked hard into my eyes, and then he spoke quite sharply, telling me to go home and look after his wife and daughters. He would not even lean forward to kiss me through the railings—I couldn't bear it.

We keep hearing terrible rumours of what is being prepared for the Armenian community here. My dear brother—if it is at all possible, could you send urgently to our mother your commission in the Harbiye Military academy? I am not certain, but I feel that now that most of the leaders of our community have gone, the authorities are

planning something awful for the women and children left here. I believe it may be very helpful to mother if she can show that her eldest son is an officer in the Ottoman army—even if only a student. Please don't worry if what I ask is impossible—I just don't know. Vahan—look after yourself.
Your loving brother.

Selim Kemal to Olga.

My dearest Olga,
As you know, I only just heard about the arrest of your father yesterday. I believe also that several other prominent members of your community were also arrested. My darling, I am sorry and I feel for you and your family in these difficult times.
However, Olga, I too have terrible news to give you, news which has drained everything else from my soul. My beloved father has died, shot by an Armenian fighter during the current rebellion in Van, whilst he was tending the wounded.
Darling girl, I know that you are not interested in politics, and that you have said more than once that these things ought not to touch us, as our personal feelings and relationship are more important than anything happening around us. I, myself have agreed many times that we are indeed just two human beings with a love and chemistry for each other, who have nothing to do with what other people around us may be doing or thinking. But Olga, how can we ignore who we are? Even if Vahan was right in our recent discussion about identity, the pressures of these differing strands in our make-up are too strong to be ignored.

We are faced with the fact that almost all the more important identity affiliations in our two persons are in direct conflict. Can we go on ignoring it all, as if neither of us had family or friends and relations who are part of our whole being?
My darling, I just don't know, I just don't know.
I love. . . I love you. . . but what can we do. Your very own.
Selim

Unknown correspondent to Boghos Nubar Pasha.

Your Excellency,

You have asked me to describe what happened to the group that was arrested on the 24th April containing amongst its members—Father Komitas. I have been able to ascertain only the barest details from my friend Aram Andonian, who was in the same group.

It would appear that about half the group originally arrested were dispatched in the afternoon to Haydar Pasha station, and left by train for the interior that very evening. The other half containing father Komitas and the other two clerics, remained in the police station courtyard overnight. Slowly the seriousness of the situation began to dawn upon them. Very early the next morning—the day of the actual landings in the Gallipoli peninsula—the group were marched through the empty streets to the little port of Sarayburnu, where they were made to board a small steamship that had been rented by the government for the purpose.

Having become totally like puppets—bewildered and entirely at the mercy of soldiers and policemen, themselves acting like automatons, the group began to break down, as they contemplated their own defencelessness. The ship whistled and set off across the Bosporus to the Asian shore, eventually docking at Haydar Pasha station in the early hours of the morning.

Here, in a repeat, I believe, of the same situation that had happened the previous night to the other group, the railway station had been blocked off for the general public. This second group, numbering I am told about one hundred men, shuffled onto the train specially commissioned by the government—moving forward like sheep, devoid it would seem of will or courage. An extraordinary matter, your Excellency; these were men, leaders in their respective fields, who, faced individually with direct and clear danger, would have risen and fought, but who seemed collectively, in the sheer lack of awareness of what was going on, to be unable to react. I doubt if anything similar could ever happen again.

In any event this group eventually arrived in Ankara station, where they were led out to a line of over thirty carts pulled by an assortment of animals. Each cart included a soldier armed with a rifle and bayonet, but there were some mounted policemen as well. Throughout the next three days, the feelings of fear and uncertainty increased, and Father Komitas in particular, so cool and courageous at the beginning in helping and comforting the others, began to show signs of erratic and irrational behaviour.

They arrived in due course at the remote town of Chankiri at the end of a terrifying journey in which one or two people died each day during the very cold nights out on the bare hills. Here they were led into a dark and forbidding old barracks, where they had nowhere to rest except the dirty wooden floor. Employed against these people was the basic psychological technique of uncertainty. Suddenly, taken from the comfort and security of their city backgrounds, and powerless to affect their own lives, they were in a state of total confusion as to what was to happen to them.

You have asked me, Your Excellency, to explain why Father Komitas in particular was released and returned to Constantinople some days later. It seems clear to me that this was at the instigation of one of the Sultan's relatives—an Ottoman prince. The Ottoman royal family have of course by now lost almost all power, and the government is entirely in the hands of Enver, Talaat and the Ittihad gang. Nevertheless a residual respect for the Sultanate still exists, and when the Prince—I think it was probably Prince Mejid—heard of the arrest and deportation of Father Komitas, whose concert he had attended only a month or two previously, he intervened directly with Talaat himself. Talaat then sent a telegram authorising the release of Komitas and six others.

I will, Your Excellency, try to keep you informed of the position here as best I can. As always my letter will be sent through the Italian embassy so long as they continue to stay neutral.

May God be with you.

Chapter 36

Anatolia. Karekin's escape.

Karekin remained at the window of the restaurant for several minutes staring at the spot where Armineh had been standing, long after she and Sima had already departed. Although few of the group had any idea what all this was about, nevertheless, Karekin rated his chance of survival fairly low. Slowly, after the last scheduled train of the day left, the station emptied until there were not even any railway employees present. In the concourse, groups of soldiers stood about bored and disconsolate, whilst in the restaurant general conversation and even anxiety, had dried up as people waited for something to happen.

In due course, after it had grown dark outside, the special train commanded by the government finally arrived.

There was the usual confused whistling and shouting as the prisoners were shepherded out, counted, and ordered into the coaches. No one had any idea of how all this was to be dealt with, nor was there any order as to how the prisoners sat themselves in the various coaches. Even the officers in charge seemed to have little clear indication of what was supposed to be going on. The world had not previously witnessed the spectacle of trains filled with scared and bewildered humanity being shunted about, and no one, neither guards or victims, were sure how to react.

The coaches themselves were of perfectly good quality, with standard second class seating throughout. The doors from the corridors into the compartments were all open. An order was given out that all the doors must remain open always. Each coach had four or five armed guards allocated, who sat at each end and patrolled up and down the corridor whenever they felt like it. Otherwise, the prisoners were free to sit wherever they wanted, and to talk amongst themselves. Some bread was distributed. Many of the group had bought in the station, cheese, olives and fruit, all of which was shared in each compartment. There were, as always, those among them who were resigned, those who were in a state of denial that there was any real danger, those who were calm, and those who were in a state of complete fear and panic.

Karekin noted that only a couple of officers boarded the train. Both were in the front coach. The rest of the officers with the remaining soldiers lined up on the platform waiting for the train to leave. Eventually, with the usual accompaniment of whistles and yells, the train hissed out steam and began pulling away. The officers left on the platform saluted.

"My, my," muttered Aram to Karekin with a wry smile, "what an honour."

"Morituri te salutant," murmured Karekin, getting his quote totally the wrong way round.

Karekin and Aram had managed to get a compartment to themselves and managed to lie down, sleeping on and off during the night. The train steamed along throughout the night, stopping every so often for no apparent reason in the middle of nowhere, then setting off again. Within two hours of leaving the lights of Haydar Pasha station most of the passengers were sound asleep, exhausted not only by the physical strain under which they had been for well over twelve hours, but also by the mental stress they were all facing.

During the course of the next day the train trundled on, passing through Eskishehir and turning south to take the line which would eventually lead to Eregli, and the as yet unfinished tunnels through the Taurus mountains. Their eventual destination, which they all now supposed, was to be the vilayet of Aleppo in the Arab province of Syria. As a group they had, however, all become too tired, too brain-battered to care.

"Karekin, what is this all about?" said Aram Manuelian.

"My dear Aram, I've no idea, but I suppose it's all tied up somehow with the Allied invasion at the Dardanelles. I can see some logic in why this particular group of people have been picked out. You'll see that they haven't just arrested the 'politicals'—the deputies or the journalists or the active lawyers. It isn't therefore just a round-up of what the government might regard as the troublemakers. It includes all the leading elements of the community, religious, artistic and social, as well as political."

"Well, Karekin, that means, doesn't it, that it is not a simple 'security' issue in the face of an enemy invasion, but is aimed at the whole community."

"I'm afraid that that is exactly what I do think. What we have to face up to here and now in this incredibly slow train is whether they intend to shoot us all somewhere, or whether they genuinely intend to send us to Aleppo."

"My dear Karekin, what the blazes would they do with us all once we got to Aleppo anyway? Are they going to put us in some sort of camp? I doubt it. That would mean having to feed us and provide some sort of shelter. No, no this train has to be emptied soon after Eregli, whatever their present intentions, as the tunnels through the Taurus are not completed yet. So we will have to walk or ride. At that moment, my friend, there will be a story of a break out, or of marauding Kurdish brigands, any old story, and the entire group will disappear—dead—and the authorities will wring their hands and talk about impossible conditions in the interior."

"Well, if that's the case, Aram, why don't we just try to get out of the window somewhere on one of these innumerable stops?"

"Sheer inertia, and the fear of the unknown, Karekin. At the moment we remain somehow in touch, however tenuous, with civilisation and the way of life we've always known. This is a train, it's fairly comfortable, the soldiers belong to our government, and we can't believe in our hearts that it has changed so drastically. Above all, we have the companionship of shared anxiety with over a hundred others around us. Out there, we would be in the middle of practically a desert, on our own, and with no experience at all of how to survive. So, we sit where we are, heading for god knows what, but afraid to make any change."

"Yes, I understand. But we're free agents, we can surely think it out, one way or another," Karekin mused.

Night came again, more dry bread was distributed, and the passengers settled down for a second night as the train trundled on through the desolate Anatolian countryside. Eventually, early in the morning as the sun was rising, the train arrived with much stopping and starting, shunting and hooting, into a goods yard alongside the main station of Konia. Konia, a larger town than Caesaria, was the capital of the vilayet of the same name.

Karekin woke with a jerk. It was about six o'clock in the morning. Checking that there was no guard in the corridor outside the compartment, he opened the window and leaned out, breathing in deeply the cold fresh air with great satisfaction.

"For God's sake, shut the window, it's freezing cold out there!" snapped Aram, turning to find a better place to put his sleepy head, and stretching his legs out.

Karekin grunted and continued to look out. Directly in front of him, on the other side of the railway line, was a platform, clearly not intended for the travelling public, but for some sort of freight handling. Over to his left was a marshalling yard with several lines of goods trucks either waiting for despatch, or just standing waiting to be unloaded. In the middle of the platform were some railway employees, dressed in brown overalls, ready for track maintenance work.

Seeing Karekin leaning out of the window, one of them, a young man scarcely more than a teenager, jumped down from the platform and sauntered over.

"Hello, effendi, this is unusual, to have a passenger train stopping in this goods yard."

Karekin, recognising at once by his accent that he was probably Armenian, switched to Armenian and gave a short account of what seemed to be happening.

"Effendi, there are no guards here on this side of the train. You must get away. We have been hearing all day of arrests and deportation orders all over Eastern Anatolia. It must be that your lives will be in danger if you continue to stay on this train."

Just then there was a whistle and a small engine came in sight pulling several flat trucks loaded with tools and sleepers and rail lines, and some high-sided closed trucks.

"That's our work train," said the young man. "Good luck, effendi, my name is Aram," saying which he saluted and ran across the line in front of the advancing train to join the others on the platform. The train now pulled up with the closed high-sided trucks standing now between the internment train and the platform.

Karekin did not hesitate. Whatever it was that triggered his decision he would never know. Perhaps the bright morning fresh air in contrast to the stuffy atmosphere of the train, perhaps the fact that the railway worker's name happened to be Aram. He never worked it out, he simply acted.

"Wake up Aram, wake up," he whispered, shaking the dozing doctor violently but quietly.

"What is it, what is it?" said Aram, already instinctively whispering.

"Quick, Aram, now's our chance—probably our last one. We've got to get away. Both of us are agile and fairly thin, we can easily get over the window and jump or fall out. There is a train right alongside, we can only be seen from anyone looking out of the windows on this side, unlikely whilst the train is next door. Come on, come on."

Karekin began pulling himself up onto the lowered window, squeezing through and ready to drop out on the other side.

"I don't know, Karekin, I don't know," wailed Aram in a state of shocked indecision, although now fully awake.

"For God's sake, Aram, the worst that could happen at this stage is that we'll get a very painful beating if we're caught. Look, I am going. Are you coming?"

"Yes, Karekin, yes, go, go!" and Aram jumped up, and with a quick look at the still empty corridor, clambered onto the window as Karekin dropped down to the ground between the two stationary steaming trains.

They both stood there, crouching and panting, not so much with exertion, but from the excess rush of adrenaline. Then, running between the trains, crouched almost double to avoid being seen from any window, they sprinted along until they passed the last coach. They both then stood up and acting by instinct they began walking slowly across the rail tracks towards the marshalling yard over on the left. They felt that by walking slowly they might be taken, if seen, for native inhabitants. This was ridiculous if they had thought it out. No one seeing the sight of two middle-aged gentlemen, fully dressed in smart city business suits, even if now soiled and crumpled, would for a moment have taken them for anyone entitled to be there. Fortunately for them, they were not spotted before they reached the first of the waiting goods trains. They ran up and down between the trucks trying out the great metal doors. Most of these were locked, or already wide open, showing empty holds.

Eventually they found one that was closed, but not yet locked. With some effort they managed to pull the door open enough to allow them to squeeze in. Inside there was a cargo of hazelnuts. The space was filled almost to the top, and already the action of pulling open the door had dislodged the cargo and many nuts had trickled down into the grooves of the sliding door. They hauled themselves up and in, and then spent the next five minutes straining and pulling to close the door, as the dislodged nuts split and cracked as the door slid over them. They never managed to close the door completely, as each effort caused yet more nuts to slither down and into the grooves. They then burrowed into the pile of nuts at the far end of the truck—dislodging yet more.

Back at the internment train the open window and the empty compartment had been discovered. When a count of numbers was made the discrepancy was found and a detail of soldiers was deputed to make a search of the station precincts. Like most railway premises in Anatolia, the station area was surrounded by a high wall and barbed wire fencing. There were several gates and entrances, but these were usually manned during the day.

Aram and Karekin heard the soldiers calling out to each other when they finally arrived at the several freight trains waiting in the marshalling yard. With pounding hearts, and unable to say anything, Karekin heard them moving down between the freight carts, trying each door, looking inside those that were unlocked and could be opened. Eventually one of the soldiers arrived at the hazelnut car. Grunting with effort he tried to open up the door, which not being completely shut was clearly not locked. Trying to slide the door open over all the dislodged nuts, he was totally unable to move it at all. Karekin, out of pure nervousness, began chewing a previously cracked nut. The guard continued to strain at the door. He then stopped and called out to his mates, "OK, this one is either locked or rusted, so there can't be anyone in there," and he moved on to the next car.

The search went on all over the station for about another hour, and Aram and Karekin could hear the officers yelling and cursing at their men. As it was, at about 8.00 in the morning, as the sun rose higher, they heard the shriek of the whistle of the train. Then they heard the welcome sound of the pounding of the rails as the internment train pulled out of the station, with the passengers either on their way to safety in Aleppo, or to their doom somewhere before.

The two friends now had to decide what to do. Their quick look at the area had already shown them that the place was surrounded by walls and fences, and that they would not be able to walk out during daylight. Yet, whatever happened, they would have to open the truck door sooner or later. They scrambled out of the midst of the nuts slowly, trying hard not to dislodge too many more. They then began slowly and patiently, using only their pens and their fingers, to prize away the nuts stuck in the grooves. By midday, they were just able to move the door sufficiently to allow them to squeeze out whenever they needed to do so. But they had nowhere to go, with the goods yard buzzing with employees going about their business. As it was, they had to take the risk and slip out into the space between the trains, when the calls of nature made it necessary every so often.

With no food, they munched away at the hazelnuts and waited.

Suddenly in the late afternoon, after boredom had driven them both to distraction, they felt the jolt of an engine being connected to the head of their train. Karekin got ready to jump out, almost in relief, but Aram put his hand on his arm, "Karekin, my soul, don't move. This is one certain way out of the yard. It's only a goods train, it will travel very slowly. We'll jump out once we're free of the station."

Karekin nodded, and they waited tensely.

Karekin kept cracking the nuts and nervously chewing away. Within minutes the coaches shuddered, jolted back and forth, and then began slowly trundling out of the station, through the great gates, and into the outskirts of the town. The hazelnuts were thrown about haphazardly all over the truck and all around. The two friends stood and slithered about as the train jerked and stopped and started again.

Eventually with continual shrieks and whistles, the train began running alongside a beaten dusty path, with houses and sheds on the other side moving very slowly as there were no fences or any other safety devices preventing pedestrians moving across the rails. Karekin stood by the door with Aram behind him, waiting for a moment when nobody would be around, although such a moment was likely to be very short-lived. Suddenly it came.

"Now, Aram! Now!" he cried and jumped out, followed immediately by his friend. They sprinted across the path the moment they landed, and melted away into a narrow street between some houses, not knowing where they were or what they were going to do. They stood panting a moment leaning against a wall, in the middle of a hostile world, where it would appear they were outlaws of some kind. The train moved on and out of sight round a corner. They grinned nervously at each other, catching their breath.

Chapter 37

Constantinople. Mikael and his father.

It was a fine warm day on the 25th April in 1915. Mikael Sarafian stood on the Galata Bridge leaning on the iron railings, staring down at the ferries hooting and tooting and pushing their way up to and away from the quayside. It was already almost six months since the empire had entered so pointlessly into the great European war in the winter of 1914. The war had already changed Mikael's life as drastically as it had changed that of so many others.

Mikael was a tall and thin young man, aged about twenty-four. Sporting the standard black moustache of Ottoman young men of the period, he had flashing black eyes and straight dark hair. He had an uncharacteristically arrogant expression for an Armenian and his looks were therefore a good deal more Turkish. In general he was impatient and did not suffer fools gladly. He had a brusque abrupt manner towards most people with whom he came in contact and had difficulty making relationships with his own age-group.

Gazing over the railings, he was reflecting on the manner in which he had joined the Ottoman army in November, 1914. The revolution of 1908, which he, like most of the minorities, had originally welcomed, had supposedly established the principle of equality before the law. This decreed, among other matters, that the Christians of the Empire should also be entitled to serve in the military, as well as the Muslims. Reciprocally, the Muslims were then supposed to pay the special tax previously levied on the Christian millet in lieu of military service.

Mikael, from a poor family and unable to get any deferment, had been one of the first of the Armenian youths to become a private in a Stambouli army unit training outside the city. He stood recalling the conversation he had had with his father Avedis on the day of his registering at the government office in the suburb of Makrikoy, where the family lived.

"My son," his father had said, "you know my views. I stand totally against all these changes that are being forced on the dynasty. It is simply not the way that the Empire has thrived over the centuries. I and my ancestors were always prepared to pay the exemption tax instead of the right to bear arms. Why change now?"

"But father, it can only be by enforcing absolute equality before the law that the Empire will be able to survive. After all you wouldn't suggest returning to the 'devshirme' system of taking the first born sons from Christian families, just because it worked so well years and years ago."

"Come, come, don't be sarcastic with me, son, I'm not arguing against any change at all. I'm simply pointing out that not everything taken from Western European example is inevitably correct in all circumstances. Above all, I don't believe that the Army will treat Armenian and Greek recruits in the same way as it treats Arabs and Turks. Decrees, my boy, don't change people's basic attitudes that easily."

"Father, you're just plain wrong. The right and duty of all citizens to bear arms is a fundamental part of any nation. That's what being a citizen in a nation is all about ultimately."

"Yes, yes, my boy, that is indeed what we are all being taught by the West. My country right or wrong they exclaim from the roof tops! All that matters to them, son, is their nation's capacity to impose its will on other nations, by force if necessary. All this, for heaven's sake, made more vicious and intolerant by the racial unity of most of those westerners, always preaching at us about our old-fashioned ways. Oh dear, don't mind me, my son, go and fight for the Padishah if you want to."

"Father, it's not just a matter of 'want to'. I have to, in these days of conscription."

Mikael watched as two ferries almost collided as their respective captains tried to nose each other out for the next space on the quayside. He reflected that four months in a Turkish regiment had not encouraged him towards the Ottoman army, and his father had after all been proven right. Mikael himself had experienced no sign of any overt racial prejudice from the other soldiers, most of whom were from Stamboul in any case and used to the rich racial mixture of the city. However, the attitude of the officers, carefully secular though they were now trying to be, was different. The Armenian and Greek soldiers were inevitably given the more menial and less military tasks, and Mikael had in fact been fortunate to escape being sent to the interior in labour battalions to repair roads.

After the many months of training, Mikael's unit was ready to be assigned to a front, and there had been much speculation among all the soldiers as to whether this would be against the British in the Sinai or the Russians in the Caucasus. It was on the 18th April—Mikael would never forget the date—that he had got a message that the duty officer wished to speak to him immediately. He had hurried off to the office of the young lieutenant, currently the duty adjutant. Mikael had saluted and standing at attention waited for the officer to speak.

"Private Sarafian, I must tell you that we have this morning received a note from your mother informing us that your father, Avedis Sarafian, is dangerously ill and not likely to survive for more than a few days. In the circumstances, soldier, I am issuing you with a week's pass to go home. I trust all will be well. May Allah protect you and your family."

With that, Mikael had saluted and turned away. He had packed his very meagre belongings and hurried home. The Sarafians lived in a modest, ramshackle, terraced house in the middle of the small township of Makrikoy. Mikael, in his ill-fitting uniform of a private in the Ottoman army, was entitled to free railway travel, and had no difficulty in getting home, despite the fact that he had hardly a piastre on him. Alighting at the main Makrikoy station in the middle of the little town, he had walked quickly through the quiet dusty streets. At first, Mikael recalled, he had scarcely comprehended the lieutenant's words, and had acted like an automaton. But the closer he had got home the more anxious and upset he had become.

On reaching home, after embracing his mother at the door, Mikael had raced upstairs, his mother having indicated with a nod that his father was in their bedroom. Avedis lay propped up in bed. He was unshaven and looked pale and sickly.

The bedroom, at the back of the small house, was dark and had a faint smell of mothballs, which had never changed since Mikael could remember. There was a large, heavy, dark mahogany wardrobe, which took up the whole of one wall of the room. Mikael recalled that all the linen of the house would emerge from this wardrobe. Always locked, it held all the secrets of the household, the family savings and all the more important possessions.

The small window on the other wall looked out onto the back alley and was always shuttered. On the wall behind the bed hung old sepia photographs, heavily touched up, of the four parents of Mikael's father and mother. Mikael had never known these venerable looking people—his grandparents—except through these old highly-posed photographs. He knew that Avedis' parents were from Caesaria and those of his mother, Vartuhi, were from Erzerum. All four were still alive. Finally, against the fourth wall there was an old French dressing table, probably the only valuable piece in the whole house, which had a cracked and discoloured mirror with two swinging side panels which had always fascinated him as a child.

"Baba, Baba, what's the matter," stuttered Mikael, running forward to his father's side as his mother stood at the door looking on.

"My son, my son, welcome," whispered Avedis as Mikael embraced his father.

Michael, remembering this scene as he continued to stare over the water at the bridge, recalled with a deep sense of guilt that even in that sad and emotional moment, he had recoiled from the musty 'old man' smell of his father, which seemed to be much worse than usual. Mikael, gulping down the wonderful fresh air of this April morning, tried to recollect that peculiar smell—a mixture of bad breath, mint juleps, old man's body odour, and death. He could not do so.

"Father, what's wrong, what's wrong?" he had said, drawing back from that first embrace.

"My son, it's simply a mixture of old age and something going wrong with my breathing."

"But Baba, come, come, you're not even sixty yet. What does the doctor say?" said Mikael, turning to his mother still standing in the door.

Vartuhi had looked hard at him, no sign of any tears or any other emotion in her eyes, but said nothing and turned away.

"My boy, the doctor says it's TB. I just don't know. All I know is that I have difficulty breathing and I cough all night. Come, sit down and let's talk. I've missed our discussions together."

For the week after he returned from the army Mikael had spent his days sitting next to his father by the side of the bed in the dark and enclosed environment of the bedroom, day and night. In the afternoons his young brother and fifteen-year-old sister would return from school and come into the bedroom. Mikael would leave for an hour or two and talk to his mother. Mikael always thought of his mother as an acidic and unsatisfied woman with thin disapproving lips and a sharp unhappy disposition. Avedis, on the other hand, Mikael always knew as an expansive jolly man who had enormous bonhomie and confidence. When guests had come to the house he was always the life and soul of the party. He was clearly well-liked. However, the more he exuded friendliness towards everyone, the more Vartuhi would tighten up. Mikael had never fully understood his parents' relationship with each other.

After an hour or two of desultory conversation with his mother, Mikael would return to his father's bedroom. His sister and young brother would leave, and Mikael would spend the rest of the evening chatting and playing interminable games of backgammon with his father. To his surprise, Vartuhi would not join them. He had been aware that she had made up a bed for herself in the small attic room many years ago, but had been under the impression that she had returned to the parental bedroom. When eventually Mikael had questioned his mother on this, she had told him rather curtly that it was difficult for Avedis to sleep if she was in the same bed. Avedis himself never referred to the matter.

Mikael had scarcely gone out at all during the whole of that week, but on the few occasions that he did, he had become aware of the tensions both in the little town, and also in the city on the one occasion that he had made the trip to the city itself. His father was clearly getting weaker by the day, but was hanging on, and he had remained interested throughout in what was going on in the wider world and it was in fact at the end of that week on the 25th April that he had asked Mikael to go into the city and purchase the latest newspapers, Turkish as well as Armenian.

Thus it was that on that fateful day for the empire, Mikael was in the city picking up all the latest rumours together with some newspapers. The British had landed in the Gallipoli peninsula that morning. There were rumours that the Russians were going to invade from the north, and perhaps even that the Greek army was also approaching. The Greeks in the city were in a state of excited euphoria. The Turks were anxious and angry. The Jews were worried for the long-term future of the Empire, which had sheltered them for so long. The Armenians were in a state of total confusion, caused largely by the arrests of the day before. Mikael had arrived in the city just as the news of the arrest of over four hundred prominent Armenians the day before had become common knowledge. It appeared clear that they had either been deported to the interior, or had been liquidated in some way.

Mikael, who had been staring at the busy shipping and reflecting on the past week for over half an hour, at last sighed and turned away. He hurried across the bridge and turned to go down to the Armenian Patriarchate compound. There, he prayed for a few minutes in the church, and then went round to the office to ask if there was a priest available to accompany him home for a final visit and blessing for his father, who was not expected to survive for more than a few days. He was told that no priest was immediately available, as too many had been called out to minister to and give comfort to families distraught at the loss of their men. However, the staff on duty told him that if he left his address, and the return fare, a priest would follow as soon as possible, the next morning.

When Mikael got home that evening, he reported all the news to Avedis.

"Father, the really devastating news is the arrest of over four hundred of our people. It is clear that they were arrested only because they were Armenians. Even our gentle Father Komitas was among those deported. This is pure racial persecution isn't it? We have to stand up for ourselves. Honestly, it makes me hopping mad."

"I'm sorry, my son, truly sorry," whispered the ever weaker Avedis, but whose eyes remained as bright as ever. "This sounds like state repression of the worst kind. Even that awful idiot Abdul Hamid never acted like this. He would simply arrange to inflame the mob—you know, the scum of the cities—and then withdraw the police for a few days whilst they rampaged. I fear, my son, I really fear for the future of our community."

At this point, the sheer effort of coming out with all that gave rise to a fit of coughing from Avedis, and a hug and a 'hush, hush' from Mikael. There was silence for a time and then Mikael said, "Father, I heard that my army unit has already left for Gallipoli. I will have to go soon. My leave runs out in a day or two."

Avedis had given no reply to this, but had sunk back onto the pillows, already exhausted by the few words he had already spoken.

The next day in the morning a priest arrived. On entering, he blessed the house, and extended the blessing to Vartuhi, who knelt and kissed his hand as he came in. The Sarafians were firm and devout believers. Mikael himself came down, crossed himself at the sight of the priest and also knelt and kissed the priest's ring. He then hurried the priest upstairs to the bedroom. Vartuhi did not follow.

"My name is Father Haroutioun," the priest said to Avedis, who had struggled to sit up a little in his bed. Mikael's sister, who had stayed at home that morning, plumped up the pillows and held her father up as the priest took out his oil, put the sign of the cross on Avedis' forehead, and began reciting prayers in a quiet sing-song voice. Eventually he gave the final blessing to all in the room. Mikael brought forward a chair, and the priest sat down by the bedside and stretched out to hold Avedis' hand.

There was then a long period of silence. Eventually his father had turned his increasingly feverish eyes on the old priest and making an effort said in a whisper, but with his voice clearly audible to all, "Father, my son is a conscript in the army. His unit has been sent to the new Gallipoli front. Armenians are being arrested and deported all over the Empire for no other reason save that they are Armenian."

At this point he began coughing and gasping for air. Everyone in the room urged him to stop talking, but he raised his hand making it clear that what he had to say was important to him.

"You know, Father, I've always been a believer. I've also always supported the Ottoman state. I have never had any patience with the revolutionaries, the Dashnaks or the Hunchaks or any of the other Nationalist parties, whatever they're called. But, Father, where the state has deliberately turned against a part of its own people, do those people still have a moral duty to support that state?"

"Render unto Caesar that which is Caesar's and unto God that which is God's" said Haroutioun a little sadly. "That is the Christian teaching, my son. The Muslims of course say that it's one and the same. The head of their state, the Sultan, is for them the same person as the head of their religion, the Caliph."

The three Sarafians stared at him uncomprehendingly. Haroutioun sighed, belatedly realising and reflecting that here was a family not in the slightest bit interested in the theological difference between the Christian and Muslim attitude to the duty to the state. He therefore paused and thought for a moment before starting to speak again. Everyone in the room at that moment, Father Haroutioun himself included, knew that the new reply he was trying to formulate and was about to give was going to be crucial. Father Haroutioun cleared his throat nervously and said:

"Avedis effendi, a month ago my answer to your question would have been that loyalty to the state that has nurtured you as best it could was all-important. However, the reports that I have been getting from the interior, the deportations that have begun all over the empire and which we have seen even here, the terror that is being turned against our people by the state itself, has, I now feel, unquestionably changed the moral position. Your son must of course act according to his own conscience. However, I do now believe that the moral authority of a state which is openly picking out our young men to be sent to the most dangerous sectors of the fronts, or to labour battalions in the interior like convicts, has been compromised.

I fear that the deportation of whole families, whole villages, to God knows where, Avedis effendi, is the beginning of a great evil the like of which has never been seen before."

There was a long pause—a moment of silence that hung heavy in the air between them all. Then Father Haroutioun stood up, raised his hand high above the bed to make the sign of the cross, and in a loud and firm voice said, "Whatever may befall. . . May the blessing of God almighty, the love of his son Jesus Christ, and the spirit of the Holy Ghost be with you all in this room, now and for evermore and to unending time."

Mikael, whose head had been bowed, looked up and saw the little priest immediately bend down and kiss his father on the forehead. The priest then turned and walked out of the bedroom accompanied by his sister, Nairi.

Mikael remained in the room all day, joined by Nairi once the priest had left. His father clearly began sinking as the afternoon went on and as his breath became more and more laboured. In the evening, Avedis, in a hoarse whisper, spoke his last words to them both, sitting by the bed on either side, whilst Vartuhi stood silently in the doorway, "Mikael, my soul, I have thought hard about what I am going to say. I've thought of all the possible consequences. My advice to you is not to rejoin your unit. Don't go back, Mikael, my son, don't go back. My son. . . my son. . ."

He then looked up at Vartuhi, standing in the doorway. They stared at each other for a moment of eternity. Avedis then closed his eyes and was dead within minutes.

Chapter 38

Constantinople. Mikael's arrest.

On the death of his father that April, Mikael had inevitably been involved in all the details of arranging for the funeral. He was already two or three days overdue from the expiry date of the pass issued by his superior officer. Mikael did not worry too much about this. It was clear to him that he had to fulfil his duty to his family and see to his father being honourably buried before any duty he might have to the state. He knew well that he would be in trouble when he finally did return, but that would be acceptable up to a point. A good Muslim would appreciate the requirement of seeing to a proper burial as a very sound reason for being a few days late in getting back to his unit.

Father Haroutioun had agreed to conduct the service, and Avedis was to be buried in the cemetery at Shishli. Mikael, Nairi and Vartuhi set off early in the morning, Mikael's younger brother, Mardiros, being left with a neighbour at Vartuhi's insistence. Mikael, in an emotional state himself simply could not understand his mother's attitude to the death of her husband. She shed no tears and seemed perpetually distracted.

At the little church in the cemetery the service was duly conducted by Father Haroutioun. There were only about twenty people present —friends of Avedis and several cousins and other relatives whom Mikael scarcely knew. The ancient rituals of the Armenian Orthodox burial service droned on, beautified by the music of Father Komitas. Mikael felt the usual prickle of tears and a welling of emotion as the liquid notes of the "Sourp, Sourp" rose from the voices of the small choir. It was at that moment that there was a slight disturbance as three more people entered at the back of the little chapel. Mikael, intent on his memories of his father did not look back. However, he saw Vartuhi, standing alongside him, glance back. For the first time since he had returned from the army as his father lay dying, he saw that she was distressed. She sat down on the hard pew, as everyone remained standing and as the music soared.

Mikael sat down beside her and took her hand.

"Mama, Mama, cry, cry." He mumbled. She looked at him and then away, pale and trembling. Nairi, on the other side, also then sat and took Vartuhi's other hand, when for the first time some tears appeared, reluctantly, in Vartuhi's eyes.

Father Haroutioun finished a short homily and blessed the coffin. The bearers moved up solemnly and bore it out down the aisle to the graveyard led by the priest. As was the custom, Mikael, walking alone, went immediately after the coffin followed at a short distance by Vartuhi and Nairi behind him. As he got to the door, Mikael heard a short cry and a gasp from the small congregation behind him.

He turned. Vartuhi was standing stock still, her face flushed, staring at a woman, considerably younger than her, standing at the back between two small boys. Mikael, totally unaware of what had happened, stood looking at his mother, who was standing breathing hard. Nairi, looking even more distressed than before, was grasping Vartuhi tightly round her waist. There was a moment of silence. Meanwhile, the coffin bearers and Father Haroutioun ahead of them were walking on through the cemetery, having noticed nothing.

"I am going home," hissed Vartuhi, handing Mikael a brown envelope for delivery to the priest and the small choir. Then, without another word, pulling herself roughly away from Nairi, who desperately tried to hold on to her, she strode past Mikael and down the path out of the cemetery without once looking back. Mikael, in a turmoil of emotion and total confusion could only stand and stare, as Nairi and the rest of the congregation behind him waited for him to move on.

Mikael, not knowing whether to follow his mother or not, hurried after the coffin in a daze, followed by Nairi and the rest of the congregation. They all caught up with the cortege at the open grave, waiting for them. The bearers laid the coffin in the grave, Father Haroutioun gave the final words and the blessing, and the waiting grave-diggers began filling in.

Everyone moved up to shake hands with Mikael and Nairi, and at that point Mikael saw the young woman begin to walk away holding the hand of each boy on either side. Mikael then, at last, and for the first time that day, took a clear decision on his own initiative. Making his excuses to those who had not yet come forward to offer their condolences, he hurried after the trio as they walked towards the gates of the cemetery. He walked briskly past them, and then turned and faced them in such a way that they simply could not walk on. The trio stopped and stared at him.

"Madame," Mikael started, "my name is Mikael Sarafian. I am the eldest son of Avedis Sarafian, whose funeral has just taken place in there. . . May I thank you for attending my father's funeral, and ask you how you and he are related." Mikael had then extended his hand to shake hands.

The woman ignored the proffered hand and said nothing, but continued to gaze down at the ground gripping hard onto the hands of the two boys who were both staring up uncomprehendingly at Mikael.

Mikael was totally thrown by this. He had no idea what to do. There was a long moment of silence as the young woman refused to reply or even look up. Mikael tried to catch the young woman's eyes to no avail. Mikael then squatted on his haunches, bringing himself down to the level of the two boys. He faced the elder of the two, and smiling at him said, "Hello! My name is Mikael. What's your's? How old are you?"

For a moment Mikael thought that it was not going to work, but then the boy piped up, pulling himself away from his mother's grip and said, "My name's Mardik, and I'm seven years old."

Still the woman said nothing, staring at the ground. Mikael turned to the other younger boy, and said, "And you, my lad?"

The other boy, taking courage from the fact that his elder brother had pulled away from his mother, and looking at Mikael with curiosity said, "My name is Ardem, and I'm already five years old. I'll be six soon. What are you doing at my daddy's funeral. Are you his brother?"

Mikael stood staring, saying nothing, upon which the eldest, Mardik, not to be outdone by his brother said, "Well, you must be my uncle then."

The young woman grabbed at the two boys, saying not a word and began dragging them off. But Mikael was having none of it. He stood firmly in their path making it quite clear that he would not allow her to leave. He saw the other mourners walking away from the grave in the distance, and Nairi slowly making her way towards him through the cypress trees.

Mardik, who had clearly had enough of being subdued by his mother, again wriggled free of her grasp, and looking at Mikael, to whom he had obviously taken a liking, said, "Why did that old woman you were with spit at me, sir?"

Mikael was again only able to stare in confusion. Nairi approached, curiosity overcoming all her other conflicting emotions. Mikael had turned again to the woman, "This is my sister Nairi. Could you please, Madam, now give me an answer. You must surely see that neither I nor my sister can leave here without knowing who you are."

"Mikael, my dear brother, what do you. . ."

"Nairi, quiet! Madam, please. . ."

At last the young woman turned and sat down heavily on the grass alongside the stone path just inside the gates. She indicated to her two boys that they could go and play.

"But, Mardik, don't go out of the gates, and always keep an eye out after Ardem. Don't pick any flowers anywhere, and stay in sight."

The boys had run off, glad to be off the leash.

"My name is Katya," said the young woman. Mikael recognised a fairly heavy Russian accent—or could it have been Greek—in the Turkish words."

"There is no way I can say anything to you to make this easier for any of us, except straight out directly. Your father and I have lived together off and on for many years. Those two boys are your half-brothers. Oh my God, my God, we should never have come, we should have kept away, I didn't mean. . ." and she burst into tears.

Mikael, although something close to the truth had been starting to strike him, nevertheless remained stunned and silent. As the weeping continued, Nairi said, "But, how is that possible? I've scarcely ever known my father to be away for any great length of time. At the most he would be away for a day or two every so often when he had to stay in town for work."

"Yes. . . well," mumbled the fair-haired Katya almost under her breath. "We live in Yedikule, in a tiny house near the station. On days when your father stayed in the city, ostensibly working late, he would stay with us. As you know Yedikule is only a few stops away from Makrikoy. My boys knew that their father had to stay away at nights and could only be with us occasionally. Mardik has recently been getting curious, as he sees how other fathers and families live. I've been begging your father to clear up the position one way or another for some time, but you know Avedis, oh my God. . . so charming, easy-going and such fun, but never wanting to make any clear decision or take any responsibility."

At this point Katya again began quietly sobbing, hiding her face from Mikael.

"But, my mother. . ." said Mikael.

"Well, she knew all about us of course," said Katya, wiping away tears. "She came once to my house. She stood at the door, and we stared at each other for what seemed like an eternity, but was probably less than a minute. I knew at once who she was. My boys were much younger, and they came and stood beside me holding my skirts. She stared at the boys and then, without a word said by either of us, she turned and walked away. I never saw her again until this morning. However, Avedis told me that on that very day she had moved her bed, and that they never slept together ever again."

Nairi got up and moved away. She joined the two small boys who had been playing with stones, and squatted beside them, absently picking up stones from the path and dropping them aimlessly. Mikael watched her talking quietly with them, while he sat, absolutely shattered, by the side of the young woman, probably only some two or three years older than himself.

In between the long silences between them, he ascertained that Katya's parents were originally from the Crimea, and that she was in fact half Greek and half Russian. He must have sat there some time before he came to realise that he was suffering from emotional overload and that his mind had completely blanked out. He rose and as they parted, she gave him her address. She and the two boys hurried away as if they were being chased. Almost immediately Mikael begun replaying in his mind all his previous reflections on the state of his parents' relationship.

As he and Nairi took the train back home from Sirkedji station, he found that he was unable to change his feelings towards his mother. During the whole of the previous six or seven years he had condemned his mother in his mind for her bitter and acidic attitude towards his jolly father, for whom he had a great affection. Suddenly the reasons behind his mother's feelings had just been thrust brutally upon him. He was, however, unable to feel any great empathy. He found he was unable to feel in his heart the sense of betrayal that must have been felt by his mother. All he had room for in his mind as he returned home was his father's friendly, open-hearted attitude to life as against what he had always seen as his mother's repressed and disapproving character.

He was simply too young, and whilst he was able to understand on a purely cerebral level something of his mother's feelings, he was unable to feel it, as Nairi clearly could. In the end, he found himself unable to condemn his father wholeheartedly. It was his mother's instinctive realisation of this that then estranged them from each other almost from the moment he and Nairi returned from the cemetery and entered the home.

Neither Vartuhi nor Nairi said anything to Mikael about his continued failure after that day to report back for duty. Day after day passed and Mikael had stayed on in the ramshackle old house. He would take his seven-year-old brother Mardiros to school in the morning, and then take the train up to town to work in the great covered bazaar with a Turkish friend from school, who had purchased deferment, and was currently working for his father at their shop. Mikael received no pay and indeed did not ask for any. In his mind he kept thinking daily that he would make a decision and rejoin his unit, now in Gallipoli.

Twice he went to consult Father Haroutioun at the Patriarchate to talk with him about the discovery of his father's secret life. On the second of these occasions he had referred to his inability to feel for his mother, or wholeheartedly to condemn his father. Haroutioun had replied, "My son, you don't have to condemn your father in order to feel sympathy for your mother. Avedis undoubtedly sinned, but he seems to have tried to keep his original family together as best he could. Your mother could not forgive him, and that was her prerogative, I suppose. However, in repressing her natural instincts for the sake of her three children, she turned bitter and shrivelled up emotionally."

"I don't know what to do Father. I've become a deserter, and I wander about all day without much purpose. I can't get the thought of those two little boys, my half-brothers I suppose, out of my mind. Oh God. . . I'm so mixed up, I'm not even. . . What shall I do?"

"Mikael, you have their address, why don't you go and see them? They're only children, it might do you good. Above all, my son, try to make an effort to understand and comfort your mother."

Fateful words. Mikael felt lighter and more at ease with himself after this conversation. The very next day on his way up to town, he suddenly took it into his head, as the train pulled into the station at Yedikule to alight. He began wandering into the little back streets of the poor working-class area near the old fortress, looking for Katya's house.

He had just turned into the little street he was looking for, when in the road right in front of him he ran into a patrol of three burly policemen. None of them recognised him as a resident of the area, and they immediately demanded to see his papers, surrounding him and making it quite impossible for him to flee. Mikael at first bluffed and said he hadn't got them on him—already an offence. Holding him, however, they took his wallet. Inside was in fact all Mikael's papers, which confirmed his name and his religion. Also with the papers was the military pass which confirmed that he was in the army, and that he had leave of absence only until the 27th April, which was already weeks before.

"*Giavour!*" the burliest of the policemen had spat out, after studying the papers and noting the name. "You're a bloody deserter. You're under arrest."

Then with a mighty blow he struck Mikael across the face, as the other two held him, and then gave him a great punch in the stomach. Mikael was then dragged off to the dreaded Yedikule police station, retching from the blow in the stomach and with a cut lip and bleeding nose.

Chapter 39

Garabed's flight.

Garabed spent that first morning, after he had fled from the group, walking on in an attempt to get as far as possible from the spot where he had left the other deportees and their guards. He kept as high up the hillsides as possible, avoiding the occasional village that he now began passing. The scene was desolate, long hills covered with a green scrubby moss-like grass, dotted with rocks and stones.

This was an area where large flocks of sheep were wandering the bare hills, tended by a shepherd, usually with a boy helping him and a dog. Garabed gave them a wide berth. Whenever he saw a flock ahead, he stopped and watched carefully to see which way they were headed, and then strode in another direction. However, sometimes, after seeing a flock moving straight across his path, he stopped and rested until the way was clear once again.

As the sun came up and it got warmer, Garabed looked about him for a spot to lie down and sleep. He realised that it might be better to sleep during the day, while it was warm, and walk at night during the cold. In this treeless landscape, shelter, if only from prying eyes, was difficult to find. He was now in an area where there were several fairly clear tiny streams running down the hillsides. He could not be sure that they were not polluted further up, but he had no choice and knelt and drank whenever he had the chance.

Eventually, amidst all the rocks lying about, he came across a spot where several were clustered close to each other. Here he found a position where he could lie down between them and not be seen by anyone, unless they came right up close. Garabed, blessing his wife for her foresight yet again, wrapped up in his coat and tried to sleep.

For the first time his thoughts caught up with him. The desolation of the countryside brought forcibly to him the desolation of his thoughts. He was a man who rarely spent any time worrying or analysing his feelings. However, here was a situation the like of which he had never experienced before. What was happening to his family? Were others, like him, wandering lost in this desolation? His stomach rumbled with hunger, and it suddenly struck him that if he was starving, anybody else forced to wander in this area would also starve. He could not resolve anything of course, and eventually drifted into a deep sleep.

He woke just as the dusk was falling, and the chill of the night was beginning. He carefully and slowly chewed at the loaf, eating about half. His clothes, now in a state that would have brought pained tears to the eyes of Mariam, were sufficiently soiled and crumpled to appear somewhat less conspicuous in this remote countryside. However, he knew that he would have to try and get a change of clothes soon. Even with his sheepskin coat he was still far too conspicuous.

Garabed rose, splashed his face in a stream and walked on, guided by the stars in the mercifully clear night. He passed more and more villages as the area became somewhat more cultivated. There were of course no lights or fires in the darkness of any kind, and he was often only alerted to the fact that he was approaching some form of habitation by the barking of dogs. He would at once stop and walk away, attempting to skirt round the farm or hamlet as far as possible in order to keep the dogs quiet.

By now he was getting more and more hungry, but the risk of trying to get into a henhouse and steal some eggs, if there were any, was too great. Every farm and village had dogs all over the place, who started barking the moment he got anywhere near. Garabed felt that the time had come at last when he should attempt to make some contact with someone. His one asset was the precious five gold coins in the pockets of his sheepskin coat. However he could not be sure if, in this deep countryside, a coin of such value would be acceptable. Furthermore, if offered, it would certainly arouse suspicion, and could lead to the authorities being alerted.

Garabed was getting increasingly tired from lack of food as well as the continual walking. He stopped well before dawn was breaking and ate the last of his bread. With no idea at all of where he was, he lay down to sleep just where he was on the bare grass of a hillside.

The sun was already quite high when he next awoke to the sound of a cow's bells. Garabed struggled up, immediately alert. He was on a gentle slope, lying on the coarse grass with rocks sticking out of the ground wherever he looked. At the bottom of the hill were a few rough houses—one could not call it a village. Coming up an uneven path, leading up and past where he had been sleeping, was a young boy, with a small dog running alongside, driving about five meagre cows up the hillside.

Garabed rose, picked up his coat, and draped it round his shoulders. He tried to compose his features into a friendly smile. He realised, however, that with his four days of stubble, and his extraordinary clothes, he must look very alarming to the young lad. Kurd? Turkish? Or even possibly Armenian? He could not tell. The cows came wandering on up the gentle slope, but the boy had stopped on seeing Garabed rise. He called to his dog to come to stand by him. The call was in Turkish, but this of course didn't mean anything.

Garabed moved forward, smiling, and talking in Turkish, the only language after all that he knew well, and said, "Good morning, young man. I've lost my way. Could you tell me where I am?"

"Effendi, our village is called -----" and the boy mumbled something rather quickly, which Garabed did not catch, and which he reflected would have meant nothing to him anyway. At least contact had been made, and whilst the boy remained suspicious and alert, somehow the fact that this apparition had spoken, in a language he understood, had reassured him.

"Do you know the name of the nearest town," said Garabed hopefully.

"I don't know," said the boy, "Do you mean -----," and he came out with another name which sounded like 'kutchuk bagh' and which again meant absolutely nothing to the well-travelled Garabed. Garabed thought to himself that it was in any case probably simply the next village down the valley. Garabed changed his strategy.

"Perhaps you could tell me whether your father is at home, so that I can speak to him and ask him my way."

"Effendi, I'm sorry, but my father is away in the army. He is a corporal," said the boy proudly and straightening up. "My mother told me that he's serving in a group that is defending the big city."

"You mean Istanbul?"

The boy looked at him after this comment, blankly. Garabed again changed tack.

"Young man, could I speak to your mother? Which house is yours? What is your name?"

Garabed knew that here in the countryside, women, Muslim as well as Christian, were unveiled, worked alongside their men, and were ready to speak to a stranger if their husbands were not present. The boy hesitated, but eventually pointed to one of the four houses at the bottom of the hillside, and said, "That's my mother's house. My name is Akhmet. I must go now, effendi."

Saying which, he whistled at his dog and ran off after the cows still plodding up the hillside, waving back at Garabed as he ran. Garabed wished that he had some sweets or a small coin to give the lad, but he had nothing. He nodded at the wave, and began walking down the path to the house the boy had pointed out.

As always, dogs started barking as Garabed approached the hamlet. He walked into the beaten earth courtyard of the dwelling that the boy had indicated. Fortunately this was the first house at the bottom of the path, so he had no need to pass the others. The path ended at the houses, and there was no road or track of any kind between the farms. However, each farm had a rough wooden fence around it, and one of them even had a gate. Garabed saw that after the furthermost building another track started and continued down the valley.

No dogs barked as he approached the faded and rather worn out front door, the top half of which was open. He coughed as loudly as he could, and then knocked at the closed half of the door. He could hear a baby crying inside, but his knocking aroused no further reaction. Somewhat non-plussed, Garabed stood considering. He reflected that these were people who probably had little experience of the 'knock' as a request for entry. They probably just walked in and out of each other's houses, which usually had only one other room.

Garabed called out loudly, "Hanum, I'm sorry to disturb you."

He then stepped well back from the door and out into the yard. A strong-looking and weathered woman appeared at the door with a baby in one arm. A small girl, sucking her thumb, clinging to the woman's long multi-coloured skirts, could just be seen peering at him over the top of the half-door. On seeing Garabed, the woman raised her free arm and put it across her face covering her mouth and the lower half of her face below the eyes. She did not however appear alarmed, much to Garabed's relief.

"Hanum, I must apologise for disturbing you. May Allah protect you and your family. Your son, Akhmet, directed me to your house. I have lost my way. Could you tell me the name of the nearest town?"

"I suppose you mean Malatya," replied the woman. "It's at least a day's walk from here."

Garabed could now see into the house as the woman swung open the bottom half of the door. It was stone built, and as was familiar to Garabed from his travels, it consisted of one large room with a fireplace at one end, with a small fire at present burning in it. There was a door at the other end leading into a small, second room. The floor was the standard cool mud floor, hard and clean. There were iron pots hanging from the walls, together with a couple of faded carpets. There was little furniture save a roughly made table, several solid, wooden chests, and a wooden crib with soft, clearly new, straw, but no linen of any kind. The baby was wearing a long white smock, like a nightgown, but nothing else.

There was a rich variety of smells coming from the dwelling, ranging from the faint smell of a baby's urine and excrement to the musty smell of a rich, bulghur porridge in which there was some spices. Garabed's mouth watered, but he realised that a gold coin here would be quite useless.

"Which is the way to the town, hanum?" asked Garabed.

The woman pointed to the track going down the valley at the other end of the little hamlet, and said, "It's that way. When you get to the end of the track and the stream it follows, you will come to the river, just follow that, as it goes all the way to Malatya."

Garabed considered how best to proceed as his stomach rumbled. Anything was of some value to these people. Slipping off his sheepskin coat, he took off the smart jacket of his dark suit. He offered this to the woman who was still standing at the open door.

"Hanum, please take this jacket. Your husband might like it when he returns from the army."

She stared at him, but did not take the proffered jacket. Garabed continued somewhat desperately, "I am hungry, and I have a whole day's walk ahead of me before I can reach Malatya. Can you give me some food?"

This the woman understood at once. She motioned to Garabed to squat where he was. She then disappeared into the house. Shortly after, she re-appeared, still carrying the baby, and with the little girl still clinging to her skirts. In her free hand she had a bowl of the bulghur porridge, out of which stuck an old, and not too clean, wooden spoon.

Garabed did not rise from his cross-legged position on the ground, and indeed this was clearly what the woman expected. She came forward and handed the bowl to Garabed. He took it in both his hands and raised it to his forehead in thanks. He then began eating it quickly, nodding at the jacket which he had left draped on the swinging half-door.

The woman still did not take it, but left Garabed to eat and went inside again, whilst at long last the little girl left her mother's skirts and stood just inside the door, sucking her thumb avidly, and staring with huge eyes at the strange man greedily wolfing down porridge.

Garabed had just finished when the woman re-appeared. The baby had at last been put down. She had in her hands two large onions and a rough loaf of bread. Garabed now gently rose, leaving the bowl on the floor and salaamed. Silently she handed the food to him, and then for the first time stepped back and picked up the jacket, smelling it. She smiled. Garabed smiled back and said bowing deeply, "May Allah, the all-merciful, protect you and your family and bring your husband back home to you soon, safe and sound."

"Ishallah," replied the woman.

Garabed slipped the food into the capacious pockets of the sheepskin coat, then turned and walked out of the yard. The dogs around immediately began their cacophony, but Garabed ignored them and strode on and away, following the track down the valley, as the woman had indicated. The moment he reached the point where the stream he had been following down the hillside reached the river, he immediately recognised the river as the one he used to follow on his trips to the home of Sarkis, the son of Shahan, whose family made such beautiful carpets.

"Yes!" thought Garabed, almost shouting out the word aloud in glee and triumph. "That's where I'll go. It's obvious. My god, it's a good thing I came in this direction. I'll certainly be safe with them for a while."

Armed with that thought, and with hot food in his belly, and some reserves in his pockets, Garabed began to swing into a euphoric feeling of confidence for the first time since the arrest. He took a long drink at the stream before it reached the river, and strode out with purpose and a renewed hope.

Chapter 40

The Avakians without Karekin.

Even though neither Robert College nor the attached school closed its doors during the whole period from the outbreak of the Great War, there was no way that Olga was going to go back. It was not that she had been intimidated by her experience on that dramatic day of the 24th April. Once Selim had appeared at home and she had seen that nothing had happened to him, she was ready to take on the whole faculty if necessary. It was simply that she felt she had outgrown in that one single day any desire to remain a student at that institution.

This feeling was of course partly induced by the arrest and deportation of her father on that same day. Karekin, had he been present, would undoubtedly have urged Olga to continue her studies. Armineh, however, gave her no such encouragement. Indeed she welcomed Olga's decision not to go back. Everything, in Armineh's opinion, was in favour of Olga staying at home for a bit. Armineh was not in any way devious, but it did cross her mind that a separation from Selim for a time could not also fail to be useful.

On that day, when she and Sima had finally got back home from Haydar Pasha station, Armineh had been totally incapable of taking on board any more problems that may have been thrust upon her. In fact the whole family, emotionally exhausted, had collapsed into bed at the same time as little Seta, much to her surprise.

The next morning, Armineh had to face all the vital matters that had arisen the previous day. First, and probably the most difficult for her to deal with, was the issue of the assault on Haik. Marie was waiting at the bottom of the stairs and accosted Armineh before breakfast, and before the others came down.

"Madam Armineh, I am most sorry to hear the terrible news of the arrest of Karekin effendi. I understood from Miss Sima that you were able to see him and say goodbye. I will pray to the Virgin Mary every night for his safe return. But Madam, something happened yesterday which raises a problem that you will have to deal with immediately."

"Oh Marie - I do know about Olga's unfortunate infatuation with a Turkish lad. Come, it's not all that difficult - she is not a complete fool. We'll sort something out sooner or later."

"No, Madam, I am referring to Haik."

"Haik! Good God woman, what are you talking about? What's happened? He seemed fine to me, fast asleep when I popped in last night when I got back."

Marie explained carefully exactly what had occurred. Haik having to return home on his own - Olga's scarf - the assault - the arrival on the scene of Olga's boy-friend Selim and then of Vahan. Both of them were experienced women and Marie made it clear that she had tried to ascertain what exactly had and what had not actually taken place. Armineh sighed. She knew that she was going to have to cope with everything, the house, the business, the children's education, everything, but this would have been particularly Karekin's task. The chances were that she would only make things worse by talking to the boy.

"Marie, is he all right for the moment?"

"Madam, I believe so. But you know Haik. He is so naive and trusting that he won't realise at the moment what those two young men were threatening. But what about later? I am sure you know, that, even though he is only twelve, he has already started having nocturnal wet dreams. He is at a very sensitive stage, and this is an experience which must be explained and exorcised from his mind."

"Oh Marie, you've been reading too many popular books on this new-fangled psycho-what's-it rubbish coming out of Germany or Vienna or wherever. Typical German tosh! Forget it. He's a healthy boy. Let's just thank God that nothing happened. Too much talk can only do harm, especially if it comes from me."

Armineh knew in one corner of her mind that Karekin would have taken Haik into full confidence and would not have let it go. But already, only twenty-four hours after his departure, perhaps for ever, she was badly in need of her husband. She could and indeed would be ready to cope with everything, but on this one matter she was not going to be able to act. Everything she said and did on this problem was from the very beginning an intellectual argument to herself to convince her that it was right to do nothing.

"Marie, thank you, I think we'll take the whole matter slowly. We'll wait and see. I may try to have another word with him sometime, but he is unlikely to be any more forthcoming with me than he was with you. I believe it will go from his mind soon."

Marie looked hard at Armineh, then nodded and turned back into the kitchen.

Nerissa had been the first down, and Armineh quickly got from her the full details of everything that had happened whilst she and Sima had been gone looking for Karekin. Armineh gently probed, for the last time, but it was clear that Nerissa too had not appreciated the possibility of what might have taken place in the assault on Haik. In the midst of all her other problems Armineh finally put this matter out of her mind. Once out of her own mind it went out of the forefront of everybody's, including Haik's.

Unfortunately—Germanic tosh or not—it began to figure in Haik's dreams, and inexplicably to him, began to coincide with what Marie had coyly referred to as 'nocturnal wet dreams'.

In explaining to her mother everything that had happened, Nerissa showed a new, more unromantic appreciation of Selim as a character, and a more mature reflection on his relationship with Olga. Armineh turned almost thankfully to the problems of her daughters and away from the impossible difficulty of her only son.

"Nerissa, my soul, I accept your valuation of this young man. How can I be indifferent towards a man who might have saved my only son's life. Olga is a silly goose, but honestly I never feared for a moment that she would have fallen for a bad or vicious man. But Nerissa, my dear, we can't live as if we were all alone on an island. My darling, it's not a question of not recognising the existence or the strength of love."

"Oh mother - I've already said I am sorry for saying that to you yesterday. No, I understand the situation perfectly well, and I dare say that Selim too sees the problem clearly. Neither of them are going to act in any way precipitately. I really feel sure that you can rely on that."

Sima had been the next one down. That long hour or two in Haydar Pasha station had brought home to her, more forcibly than to her brother or sisters, the possibility that she would never see her father again. Her eyes were red with weeping all night.

After the others had all come down, they had a somewhat subdued breakfast. Marie then took Seta off to school. Immediately she left, for the first time ever, an Avakian breakfast conclave took place without the all-powerful presence of Karekin. It had been remarkably efficient. It was as if the removal of the patriarch of the family had brought out all the clarities and competence of the women. Some of the decisions taken on this very first morning after his disappearance lasted for the whole of the next year. Armineh was the first to speak.

"With your father away, children, I must go to the office, if not daily, at least once or twice a week to see to his investments and other business interests still proceeding. I think Sima, you must accompany me so that you can pick up the threads. Eventually I'll expect you to deal with most of the routine matters."

"But mother, what about my taking Haik to school and bringing him back", said Sima, who had not yet got over her slight feeling of guilt over her failure the previous day to arrive in time.

"Mama" said Haik, whose bloody lip and nose had already almost completely cleared up overnight. "Yesterday was a one-off. I know I shouldn't have tried to get that scarf of Olga's back. I'm sure Mama that I'll be fine now. You must trust me to be more careful."

There was a deep silence as all the women reflected, then everyone began talking at once. Armineh held up her hand and eventually, reluctantly, there was a silence again. Armineh regarded her son, who was not only eager, but in whose eyes she saw for the first time a sort of anger at what was happening around him.

"Yes, Haik, I agree with you, but we will all have to take more responsibility for each other now. From now on you'll be responsible for taking Seta to school, even though this means that you'll get to school yourself earlier and will have to wait. I'll instruct Seta's teacher that she must be kept at school till you arrive to pick her up in the afternoon. Nerissa will go with you both, until she herself finishes in the summer."

Haik's eyes shone with a sort of pride and Nerissa nodded.

Olga then stated firmly that she was not proposing to go back to the college. Even at that early stage, at that first morning's meeting, she indicated that she would be trying to get work at one or other of the city's hospitals. She went on to say to her somewhat startled family,

"Look, don't stare at me like that. You saw how well I coped yesterday with Selim's wounds. It's work I think I could do well, and would enjoy doing, if people will let me."

"But look Olga - hospital work isn't all tending the wounds of romantic young men. There is filth and excrement to clear up and potties to empty and heavy lifting." said Nerissa pointedly and rather sharply.

"Nerissa - you have never ever considered or allowed in your mind the thought that I might have any common sense. For God's sake - sorry mother I know I'm not putting this well but I have to say it - for once have some confidence in me as a person instead of forever laughing at me."

The blood rushed to Nerissa's head and she went a deep red. This was the second time within twenty-four hours she had been guilty, as she now recognised, of intellectual arrogance.

"Oh my darling Olga, I'm so sorry, I'm so sorry."

Nerissa rose, took a step towards Olga, dropped to her knees by her chair and buried her head in Olga's breast. At this point Olga had suddenly laughed out loud - the first laugh in the house seemingly for days - patted Nerissa on the head, and still giggling shooed her off. Nerissa and Haik then made their way out to school. In the midst of all the drama, and the devastation of their father's arrest, somehow, carrying on everyday routine seemed to be the only way of coping.

Armineh made no comment on Olga's declaration. Neither she nor, despite Nerissa's embarrassment, either of the two girls believed for a moment that Olga would have the resolution to go through with the idea she had just come out with. Although Nerissa was now careful not to say so to anyone, this was surely, she felt, just another bit of Olga whimsy.

As it happened, however, within only a few weeks of that morning Olga had indeed found a job. She deliberately avoided going to the highly prestigious and efficient Armenian Hospital—Sourp Pirgitch—and had instead picked on the Turkish military hospital in Uskudar, even though that entailed a much longer daily journey. Her interview with the administrator who managed the nursing staff, had been a great success. She was already learning how to regulate and temper her outgoing smiles and superficial charm into something a little more sincere and mature. She arranged to do shift work, whereby she could stay in the hospital for three or four days at a time, and then return, for a couple of days off, to Makrikoy.

Of all the children, it was Nerissa, who had the most difficulty in adjusting to the changes wrought by the arrest and disappearance of Karekin. The English High School for Girls had finally closed down for the duration of the war, and without Karekin's guidance and encouragement, Nerissa had no idea what to do when she finished at the local school in that difficult summer. She ended up giving English lessons to the sons and daughters of well-off Makrikoy families, Turkish and Greek as well as Armenian, and this had helped to bring in yet more welcome income to the family. The proximity of an English-speaking army, within a hundred miles, stimulated the wealthier residents of Makrikoy, most of whom already had a smattering of French, to tackle this new language.

So the family struggled on reasonably comfortably. Sima began going regularly into Karekin's office in the city. Whilst there was not much to do, she was able to keep up the correspondence with agents and old customers which trickled in. This at least kept up the feel that the business was still alive. At the same time Olga brought in a small income from her job as a nurse, and eventually even Nerissa too was bringing in some money.

One month after that terrible day of the 25th April, Armineh received an unsigned postcard—postmarked from Konia—with the single word "*GABRIMGOR*" written on it in Latin capital letters. It was this unsigned postcard with its single word, "I am living," on it, which gave the whole family an enormous strength and will to continue.

It arrived at just the right moment. For a month, Armineh had driven the family. She had seen and encouraged Olga in carrying through and making a real effort to complete a project for the first time. She had taken Sima to Karekin's office, dealt with the departure of the old Turkish clerk whom she could not of course afford to pay any more, and instructed Sima in the basic tasks needed. She had dealt with all the rest of the family problems. But at the end of the month, as the little practical matters began falling into place, and she began to have some spare time on her hands for the first time, despair began to eat into her heart. Nothing had been heard from any of the deportees, and several more arrests in the city had aggravated the situation. Rumours went round from one family to another, but there were no real hard facts. Then out of the blue came the postcard. Suddenly it all became worthwhile, and Armineh bounced back redoubling her efforts.

Chapter 41

Anatolia. Garabed's horror.

By the time Garabed finally arrived in Malatya, the town was in a turmoil. There had always been a large Armenian community here. Once again, however, there were no longer any young men in evidence. The usual arrests and exile of the leaders of the community had already taken place, while as always the younger men were away either in the army or in labour battalions. Accordingly the general population again lay helpless and unprotected, facing hatred and cold official policy.

The town of Malatya had been designated by Talaat as one of the main gathering points for the Armenian deportees being driven out from the interior further west. Already people were arriving and assembling in the rocky fields outside the town, where a ramshackle shanty town of tents, broken down old carts, and makeshift shacks was growing.

Garabed eventually managed to exchange one of his gold coins with a local money-changer, and found a cheap khan in which to stay whilst he worked out his best course of action. He was aware that already there was an increasing lawlessness in the countryside outside the main towns. Kurdish tribesmen, encouraged by the clear indications signalled from the central authorities that they would not be punished, were regularly attacking the slow moving lines of the Armenian population being forced out of their homes. Turkish criminals had also been released from the prisons, and they too were roaming the districts around the towns, terrorising the helpless refugees.

Garabed later reflected that it might just be possible to suggest that Talaat and the others may not have realised that, once started, lawlessness to this extent would be impossible to contain. However, reports of the unfolding catastrophe were being sent by the few conscientious Ottoman officials of the old school who were still in place. These were all being further confirmed by the few European consulates that were still operating. All these reports were studiously ignored by the new masters in Istanbul. The scum of town and country, deliberately freed by the government from normal restraint, was beginning to attack and pillage even those who were not yet on the roads.

Garabed stayed in Malatya for a week or more before he decided to make his move to attempt to get to Sarkis' farm, which was some days ride from Malatya in the mountains to the east. He needed to be armed, but it had to be unobtrusive. Pistols would be hard to obtain and dangerous if he was stopped by any soldiers. Furthermore, ammunition would be impossible to find outside the city. In the end, he opted for a long wicked-looking knife. He did not expect to have to use it, but he hoped that the sight of it, coupled to his determination, might deter someone bent on violence. He did not imagine for a moment that it could prevent any gang attack, if he ever had to face that.

He had got rid of the remainder of his clothes, except of course the wonderful sheepskin coat. So now, blending much better into the local colour, he at last set off up the hills. Instead of wearing a fez, associated as it was more with the towns, he had decided to wear a very simple turban wrapped round his head, a headgear still regularly worn in the remoter rural areas. This advertised to the world that here was a pious Muslim walking home. Of course it would not suffice in any way if there was a direct major confrontation, but it might just prevent such a confrontation taking place.

Moving slowly but steadily, avoiding any contact with any other person as much as possible, Garabed took several days travelling continuously uphill to get to the area where Sarkis Shahanian had his farmstead. This was an area with which he was of course familiar as a result of the many trips he had made both alone and latterly with Raffi.

All along the way, Garabed passed burning farms, corpses and some wandering old men, women and children looking lost and helpless—most of them obviously already at the end of their capacity to survive much longer. There were too many sad sights for Garabed to take in and he simply had to steel himself just to keep walking on. It was ironic that, not speaking Armenian, apart from a few phrases, Garabed didn't even understand the few pleading words that were uttered by one or two of these dazed people as he passed.

Garabed pressed on, now becoming anxious, and with his scrap of food beginning to run low. It was now well into June, and whilst the nights were still fairly cool, he had been able to sleep out without getting cold or too much discomfort. On the last day, he pushed on fast in order to get to Sarkis' farm before nightfall. He was relieved to see that he was passing houses and farms that he recognised and which did not appear to have been touched. But he noted that the doors were bolted, and that several of the farmers, who appeared to be Turks, were standing at their gates, with their sons alongside, holding rifles ostentatiously at the ready.

Garabed hurried on as the sun began going down. Everything seemed all quiet as he approached the house of Sarkis. Further down the valley—quite a distance away—Garabed could just make out a group of men, some on foot and some on horseback, who appeared to have surrounded a farmhouse and seemed to be milling about yelling and gesticulating. Garabed could not hear the shouts, but he did suddenly hear the slight popping sound of gun shots. He hurried down the track, once again anxious, and stopped dead.

There in front of him, with the doors and windows smashed and hanging loose but otherwise not too badly damaged, stood Sarkis' neat farmhouse. The outhouses, the stables and the henhouse were all burnt out and were still faintly smouldering, but the stone house itself seemed fairly intact. Garabed ran forward with his heart pounding. What met his eyes as he approached was more horrific than he had ever imagined.

Hanging from the eaves of the roof, just by the space which had been the front door, swaying gently in the breeze, swung the body of Sarkis. Blood, now dried up, had flowed from a deep gash in his side. His face was battered, the eyes were open and staring, and the tongue hung out purple and bloated.

Garabed sank to his knees for just a moment with the shock of the sight. He quickly looked about him but there was no one near. He put his hands on the floor in front of him, and knelt like a dog, with his head drooping, for a few seconds retching, though he was not actually sick. He knelt like this for several seconds, and then for the first time became conscious of a low moaning coming from inside the farmhouse. He arose and went tentatively into the well-remembered main room of the dwelling. At this point, as his eye took in the scene inside, he did become violently sick. His whole stomach heaved and he had to run outside again as his vomit spewed out of him.

Eventually, pale and exhausted, and lifting his rough pullover over his nose, he went back into the room. In front of the fireplace, lying face up on the stone floor, with her clothes torn almost all off, her legs wide apart, lay Adrineh. Blood and semen was seeping from the bruised and battered area between her legs. She was clearly unable to move, and it was from her lips that the low animal noises that Garabed had heard outside were coming.

To one side of her lay the bodies of the two little girls, covered with flies, with their legs and arms hacked off and quite dead. In a state of shock, Garabed next heard a movement from the small bedroom. He staggered over and went in, the door having been torn from its hinges. In the room the sight was even more horrific. Spread-eagled across the bed were the two older girls—Anna and her younger sister. Both appeared to have been violently raped, probably by several people, like their mother outside. Anna's lips were moving but no sound was coming from her. Her younger sister was already dead. In the far corner was the younger of the two boys whose body was covered with sword or knife cuts, also clearly dead. Next to him, whimpering with fear and shock, with huge staring eyes, huddled the eleven-year older boy, his naked body a mass of stripes and weals.

For what seemed like ages, Garabed stood totally still unable to act, his mind refusing to accept entirely what he was seeing. The flies and the stench finally brought him to his senses. He had to act. He first made sure that the younger boy and girl were both dead. He then stepped up to the eleven-year-old lad and took his hand. The boy screamed and shrank back. Garabed stopped and backed off. He turned back, and taking Anna in his arms, he lifted her and took her out into the yard and lay her down near the well.

He then returned, picked up the little bodies of the two girls by Adrineh's side and took them into the bedroom. He tried once more to coax the boy, who again shrank from him in terror. Overcoming any scruples, Garabed, knowing he had to get the boy out of the room, now with four dead bodies, suddenly grabbed him, put one hand over his mouth to stifle the screams, and bore him struggling and kicking out of the room and outside, leaning him against the wall of the house. Finally he went back in to deal with Adrineh.

This was much more difficult, but he had to get her out of the charnel house which the building had become. He could not lift her properly, every movement caused her to cry out in pain. Eventually, he half carried and half dragged her out of the house. He lay her down next to Anna, who was still lying muttering to herself. Garabed could do nothing about the boy, whose name he could not even remember. But he could try to do something for the two women. Fortunately the pail and the pulley above the well in the yard had not been destroyed as almost everything else had been. He drew some water, and came and knelt by Adrineh, murmuring words of comfort, but not sure whether she heard them or not.

He looked at her, and did not know how to start. To use her own clothes, what was left of them, was impossible. He went back into the house, but the place was gutted and there were no clothes or linen anywhere. Swallowing down all his horrified instincts, he took out his knife and went back into the room now holding four dead children. With his eyes almost shut, he cut away the cleanest strips of the children's clothes he could find. He then hurried out, his gorge rising again.

Working carefully and as gently as he could, he dipped the strips of cloth into the water and gently wiped away all the blood and filth in and around Adrineh's genital area, and then turned to do the same for Anna. He kept drawing up more clean water, always giving each of them a sip or two before continuing the cleaning process. The water at last revived Adrineh, who nodded at Garabed in a sign of recognition. Anna, however, remained in trauma and a state of total shock.

All this time the boy stared at Garabed saying nothing, lying, still naked, against the wall. Every time Garabed moved towards him with the pail of clean water, the boy shrieked and drew back in terror. Garabed had no idea how to get round this, so gave up and concentrated on the two women. It was already beginning to get darker, when Adrineh at last lifted herself up at least sufficiently to lean back against the low stone wall of the well. The full realisation of Garabed's presence came upon her suddenly, and to his relief this brought back some sense of modesty, and she wrapped her torn and bedraggled clothes around her legs.

"Garabed agha?" she said, looking directly at his face for the first time.

"Adrineh, hanum, yes it is I."

"Where is Sarkis, sir?"

"Madam Adrineh, you must be prepared for the worst."

"I know, Garabed effendi, my Sarkis must be dead. Oh my God, my two little ones too, my two little ones, oh God my two little ones." She brought her hands up to her face, and at last, to Garabed's relief, she began sobbing deeply.

Garabed had no idea how to proceed. It was clear that she was still not aware of the further deaths. He decided that it would be best if she now started having to deal with the situation directly. He indicated to her Anna, and the boy still huddled up against the wall. Adrineh looked round and stopped sobbing. She staggered upright and shuffled over to Anna, keeping her legs apart in an odd crab-like movement. She fell alongside the girl and took her head in her arms and began rocking back and forward murmuring words Garabed could not follow. Garabed tried to adjust what was left of Anna's clothes, but Adrineh waved him aside. She then looked up and said, "Garabed effendi - could you please fetch some clothes. They will be in the big wooden chest in the back bedroom."

"Adrineh, hanum, there is nothing at all left in the house. No clothes no linen nothing."

There was a long silence in which the only sound was Anna's unintelligible muttering. Then Adrineh said,

"Garabed, effendi, would you please go and ask Nefise Hanum to come. She is the wife of our neighbour Mustapha Mahmud. Their farm is the first house as you go down the hill."

Garabed hesitated, then said,

"But they are Turks. Will they help you? Are there no Armenians nearby."

"Please sir, do as I ask. I know what I would do for her, and what she would do for me."

Garabed looked about at the devastation around him and nodded. He did not however move away immediately. Once he saw that Adrineh was again involved in crooning to Anna, he took out his knife and moved quietly to the front door. He was just able to reach up to the rope from which Sarkis was hanging. At full stretch he sawed away at the rope and held tightly onto Sarkis' body. Eventually the rope gave way, and Garabed gently put the body of Sarkis down, all the time conscious of the young boy's eyes staring at him as he worked. Once completed, he raced off down the hill to deal with Adrineh's request, but with a guilty feeling of momentary relief to be away for a short time.

When he approached the first farm house on the way down the hill, he saw a man standing at his door with an old but serviceable looking rifle held up in his arms. Beside him stood a boy of about twelve years old, himself holding an old hunting rifle. Both looked very grim. Garabed slowed down, made sure that they could see his hands were empty, and walked up to the fence and called out to the two who were staring back at him, "My name, sirs, is Garabed Asadourian. I am a friend of Sarkis, son of Shahan. There has been a terrible tragedy at their farm. Adrineh, his wife, has been, er, er, molested, but she is still alive. She's asked if Nefise Hanum will come to her. There is no more immediate danger, as there is no intruder left."

Garabed gabbled all this out in a breathless rush. Before he had finished, a large well-bosomed lady dressed in several layers of black skirt pushed past the man, and ignoring him, the boy, and Garabed himself, began hurrying up the hillside, taking no notice of the restraining hand which the man had extended as she swept past him. He shrugged and said quickly,

"Burhan, my son, go with your mother and follow any instructions she may give you."

As the boy ran off after his mother, the man turned to Garabed and said, "Yes, I have heard of you from my friend Sarkis. You are the merchant from Kayseri who buys his carpets. My name is Mustapha Mahmud. I must remain here, there are small children inside. But please know that my house is your house. What has happened to the Shahan family?"

Garabed, still catching his breath, told him of the death of Sarkis, and a short description of everything else he had seen. Mustapha, a grizzled weather-beaten man, whose age Garabed could not judge, hung his head during Garabed's recital, then raised his hands palms up to heaven and cried out some words to Allah in a dialect Garabed could not follow. Turning to Garabed he said, "I saw these men passing my house earlier. They were led by an official from the town, and I was relieved that there were even two soldiers with him. However, most of the rest were a drunken mob of those damned Kurds. I am ashamed to say that there were also some Turks—scum from the town. You know, effendi, that a decree has been issued that all Armenians were to leave the area to go to the vilayet of Syria."

Mustapha paused, and Garabed could see that he was clearly now in great distress.

"Oh, my God, my God, I advised my friend Sarkis to stay put for the moment and see what might happen. What have we done, what have we done? I should have realised that the official from the town was one of those atheistic Ittihad devils."

He sank to his knees, but then jumped up immediately as Garabed too turned and saw the boy running back down the hill. Garabed noticed Mustapha hastily arranging his features so as not to alarm his son.

"What is it Burhan, what is it?"

"Oh Baba, it's terrible. My friend Ara won't talk to me. He is lying there naked, and when I went up to him he screamed and turned his face away. Mother says I am to bring some of my clothes for him, and also some of Hikmet's dresses. She also wanted some of that soap you made recently. . . Oh, and something else. . . Oh yes, a cup."

"Quickly then Burhan my boy, bring everything out here, and we'll make a bundle."

Mustapha nodded at Garabed and went into the house, leaving Garabed standing outside. Garabed had deliberately not returned to the stricken farmhouse straight away with the boy, in order to give Adrineh and Nefise some time together to work out what should be done, without any male presence. However, when Burhan came out from the house staggering under an armful of clothes, Garabed took some of the clothes from Burhan, and the soap and a cup from Mustapha, which he wrapped up with the clothes. He then turned to the weather-beaten man and said, "Mustapha, effendi, I salute you. May your Allah reward you for all your kindness, and for the risk I know you are taking in helping your neighbour."

Garabed then bowed and touched the floor at the man's feet, then straightened up and touched his forehead. He did not, however, continue with the sign of the cross across his chest. He then turned and hurried off after Burhan, who had already begun climbing up the path to the Shahanian house.

Chapter 42

Konia. Karekin and Aram.

The first thing that the two friends had done after jumping out of the train, reaching the shelter of the houses and collecting their breath, was to wander down to the clothing bazaar of the town, still open in the late afternoon. The town of Konia was fairly well-known to both of them from previous visits. It was the capital of the vilayet of the same name, and was one of the largest towns in the whole empire. They had no difficulty in finding their way to the bazaar.

There they bought, as hurriedly as possible, thick, rough pullovers, strong, equally rough trousers, and some local shoes. Fortunately Aram had a little small cash on him which they were able to use. At the same time Karekin, wandering round the market, found a money changer and managed to change a couple of the gold coins at his little desk. This was a simple old wooden table covered with many different currencies and scales for weighing gold and silver. The grizzled old man sitting at the desk had looked sharply up at him, but, making a substantial profit, he said nothing. Finally, they also purchased a cheap leather suitcase.

Leaving the bazaar as quickly as possible, as their city clothes, however creased and shabby, were already attracting some attention, they found a sheltered spot between high blank walls down a side alley. Whilst Karekin mounted guard, Aram changed into the shabby, ill-fitting, newly purchased clothes. Aram then took up the look-out position at the end of the alley, whilst Karekin changed. They then stuffed their city clothes into the case. Feeling much less conspicuous, they walked out of the alley and wandered down to the old square of the food vendors. With night falling and hour by hour feeling more confident and anonymous, they sat on the rickety bench of a kebabji and ate a couple of the surprisingly tasty shish-kebabs.

"My God, Aram," said Karekin, with meat juice running down his face, "What an enormous difference some decent hot food makes to the way we face the world."

Aram edged along the bench towards the little charcoal grill on which the kebabs were cooking, and warming his hands, said, You're right Karekin, but I'll tell you what, I'm beginning to get a bit of a reaction. Look, I'm shivering and feeling cold. It's all been too exciting, and we're not out of the woods yet. It's going to get cold tonight and where the hell are we going to stay?"

As it happened, both of them knew that there was a small Armenian community in the town, most of whom lived together in one of the suburbs, which had even become known locally as Ermeni-mahallesi or Armenian quarter.

"We certainly won't be able to find anything tonight," said Karekin, "but I suggest we walk out of town in the direction of the Armenian quarter, and see what we can find tomorrow."

The two men were replete with bread and kebab. They were enjoying the feeling of comfort which came from the normality of the meal they had just eaten in the friendly noisy atmosphere of the dimly-lit eating areas in the square. They were still euphoric from the sheer adrenaline flow of their escape from the train, as they walked through the suburbs and into the farming area outside the town. Here they eventually came across an old ruined barn not too far from the road, in which they had fallen fast asleep on the mud floor, exhausted by the emotional energy they had spent.

The following morning, now once again much more nervous, they walked over into the small Armenian quarter. Sitting in a miniature coffee-house, smoking a narghileh, and speaking as little as possible, trying to slur over their distinctive Stambouli accents, they sipped their coffees and began enquiring as to possible lodgings. They were at last told of some lodgings with a young Armenian couple who owned a modest house nearby. On going round they discovered a friendly woman, who was just about to go to work, and who on payment of a good deposit agreed to take them on immediately. She explained that she and her husband ran a little sweet shop in the centre of the town. They had no children, and she said that she worked with her husband, and indeed that they were fortunate that it so happened that on this day she had decided to stay at home to complete some domestic tasks.

For several days, Karekin and Aram hardly stirred from the house, surprisingly feeling more nervous, now that they were more settled than they had when they were on the run. Eventually, however, they had to begin thinking of the future, and how best to survive the situation. In any case, they soon became bored of their interminable games of tavloo in which millions were won and lost each day.

The situation in Konia was somewhat unusual at this time. The then Governor of Konia, Djelal Bey, was still the old Ottoman appointee. He had little sympathy for Talaat and the Ittihad gang in Istanbul. He was in no way a liberal and not even particularly sympathetic to the Armenians, who were in any case only a very small minority here, being far less numerous than the Greeks in the town. Nevertheless, he had ignored, and continued to ignore the spate of vicious decrees and widespread deportation orders emanating from Talaat's ministry, requiring all people of Armenian origin to leave Anatolia and move to one of the Arab vilayets.

Karekin very quickly became aware, even at that early stage in the unfolding catastrophe, that the severity of the enforcement of these deportation orders was varying from vilayet to vilayet according to the character of the governors. The general pattern was that the further east in Anatolia, the more severe were the effects of the decrees. In the furthest eastern vilayets, bordering on or close to the Russian frontier, where the Armenian rural population was at its densest, long lines of women, children and old men had trudged through the countryside in the general direction of Aleppo. Set upon by released criminals, Kurdish tribesmen, and Turkish riff-raff, including even soldiers, large numbers of them were dying on the roads. The women were being raped and the children abused. Those that were managing to struggle through, out of Anatolia, were then dying in their thousands of starvation in the Syrian deserts.

During these early days and weeks, whilst Karekin was coming to terms with his situation and planning his survival, he had plenty of time to watch, listen and reflect on what was happening in the

Empire. It became clear to him that the whole terrible catastrophe had been carefully stage-managed. It was not in any way unfolding as a spontaneous massacre taking place due to chaotic conditions in the countryside. It had begun all over the Empire with that carefully considered list of the leaders or potential leaders of the community, who were usually quite politely arrested and removed, as had indeed been his own experience. The young men were already mostly in the army or in the carefully controlled labour battalions. With the leaders arrested or killed, and the young men disarmed and out of the way, the stage was thus deliberately being set for the removal of the whole general population, with the absolutely clear knowledge that in the prevailing conditions most would perish on the way.

Karekin and Aram survived those months entirely due to the invaluable gold coins that Armineh and Sima had brought to Haydar Pasha station at such risk to themselves. Once settled in their lodgings, and ready at last to venture out, Karekin began looking about town for some opening. Eventually his natural entrepreneurial instincts led him to use a good part of the coins to buy up the stock and shop of a dealer in that thin diaphanous material from which the better-class yashmaks were made.

Once he had purchased the shop, Karekin threw himself wholeheartedly into improving the lay-out, and using his natural talents to make the decoration and atmosphere of the shop really welcoming. Aram, although having only ever been a doctor all his life, found himself working enthusiastically in this new trade, and eventually getting considerable personal satisfaction, despite the occasional panics when police or others questioned too closely. With Aram helping in the shop, and with their unfailing courtesy to all, they had not only kept going, but were indeed doing quite well. In the course of time, with a bit of bribery and using some connections they had made, they both got false papers, though they retained their identity as Armenians.

Despite the underlying danger of their situation, they soon fell into a steady routine. The friends would leave early in the morning. On the way into town, they would pass the local villagers bringing their produce into town to sell in the open food markets.; The shop itself was opened early in the morning, and would remain open all day until the bazaar closed in the early evening. Lunch would be provided by the itinerant vendors who went round all the stalls and shops, and would be eaten at the back of the shop. The two friends would then walk home at night to their lodgings, where their evening meal would be taken with the young couple, whose sweet shop closed earlier.

So those first few months had passed. Karekin, fearful of giving himself away, or endangering his family, nevertheless contrived to send an unsigned postcard to Armineh—the postcard which had given such comfort at home, and which had been so instrumental in helping to keep up their spirits in their own survival efforts.

Most mornings, towards the end of this period, they began passing each day on their way into town a bright young lad pushing an enormous wheelbarrow filled with fruit of one kind or another. They even began buying fruit from him for their lunch, as it was so obvious that his fruit was fresh and carefully chosen. Karekin reckoned that despite the rough Turkish clothes the man was Armenian, but the youth, when asked, said his name was Soliman. Karekin and Aram began arguing about it, and as always with them it ended up in a bet.

"You wait and see," said Karekin, "If we see him again tomorrow, I'll prove he's Armenian."

"All right. I currently owe you five million seven hundred thousand. Double or quits, but you only get one chance."

"Done!"

The next day, as it happens the last day of tranquillity in Konia, they again accosted the young Soliman. They stopped him and Aram chose a couple of peaches and some grapes. Karekin waved the lad on after the transaction was completed. After a couple of seconds he shouted out at him in great alarm, "*Deghas, deghas, shood, shood vazeh!*"

There was no hesitation or any sign of any kind from Soliman who clearly hadn't understood a word and who plodded doggedly on. Aram burst out laughing, saying, "My boy, my boy, for heavens sake, run away fast. Oh Karekin! You're priceless. Anyway my good fellow that makes us even."

Still roaring with laughter Aram, followed by a sulky Karekin, overtook the boy, clapping him on the back and asking him where in town he usually set up his wares, in case they wanted more fruit.

However, as the summer was just beginning to fade, the even tenor of their fugitive life began to disintegrate.

As the weeks had passed, the Armenian population in Konia had been continuing to hang on, keeping a low profile, unharmed for as long as Djelal Bey remained at his post. But Konia was not Constantinople or Smyrna. Sooner or later Talaat and his cronies were bound to step in and enforce their policy. It was only in Smyrna or Bolis itself that the old Ottoman ruling class, backed by the presence of foreign ambassadors, was strong enough to object successfully to Ittihad pressure. As the summer of 1915 began to turn to autumn, the moment finally came when orders arrived from Istanbul to the effect that Djelal Bey was to be dismissed. His replacement was to be an Ittihad appointee, yet another 'one language, one folk, one culture' fanatic. It was clear that shortly coming to take over in Konia would be a man impatient to have done away with Ottoman diversity.

That evening, as the posters announcing the deportation orders went back up on the public notice boards, the mood in the town began to change. Karekin and Aram, all bets forgotten, began the long discussions as to what exactly they were now going to do.

Chapter 43

Caesaria. Raffi faces life and death.

It was still early in May in Caesaria and the days were getting perceptibly warmer. Almost two weeks had passed since the arrest and deportation of Garabed, together with most of the other leaders of the local Armenian community.

Cries of "*Giavour asiliyor, giavour asiliyor!* (an infidel is to be hanged!)" rang out in the meat market, as Raffi, Garabed's younger son, Vahan's brother, stood waiting to be served in the butcher's shop.

Since that terrible moment when his father returned the coins into his reluctant hand, and then turned and left without a further word, Raffi and the whole family had had to come to terms with the knowledge that they would very probably never see him ever again. Raffi increasingly had had to take on the role of his father, and be a support to his mother and all the other women in the household. Thus it was that on this particular morning, he had come out to the market to buy some fresh meat—a task formerly regularly carried out by Garabed as he returned from work in the evenings.

"An infidel is to be hanged. . . Quick, quick, let's go."

Raffi found himself pulled along helplessly as everyone in the shop, and indeed almost everyone in the whole market, began running excitedly to the nearby main square in front of the town hall. There, pressed in by the crowd all around him, unable to get away, Raffi watched as he saw his gym teacher from school being frog-marched down the road between two policemen. He was swinging his arms vigorously in the characteristic manner that he had, and which the boys used to imitate in happier times in a somewhat cruel way.

Raffi's immediate neighbour in the crowd, who was to his surprise a fairly well-dressed man, laughed and dug Raffi in the ribs saying, "See, the giavour pig, swinging his arms like a soldier. Doesn't he know that he is going to be hanged? They won't be swinging like that when he himself is swinging from the gibbet—the bastard!"

Raffi had already grown years in the weeks since his father's disappearance, and he had no difficulty in stifling any tears that might previously have arisen unhidden to his eyes.

"Yes, yes, amazing. . ." he muttered.

A great roar arose as the man's body was raised, kicking and swinging, and with the noose tight round his rather scraggy neck. The gym teacher was still swinging and jerking there, when only a minute or two later Raffi saw coming down the road, in the same way, the headmaster of his school, also accompanied by two policemen. Raffi had always been particularly fond of this man, whose name, like his brother's, was Vahan. The headmaster was young for the seniority of his post. He was a teacher who had an inspiring way of rousing enthusiasm in his boys.

Raffi found he could not help a trembling that took over his body. He looked down and to the side. Raffi was not in any case tall, and he had no difficulty in shrinking himself down below the level of all the men in front of him in the crowd. He knew that he had to hide his feelings, but he could not prevent his trembling, and he felt dizzy in all the heat and mindless anger of the crowd. No one fortunately seemed to notice his distress. He simply had to stand there, unable to move to either side, mumbling pointless noises about 'giavours' and 'Christian dogs' whenever his neighbours said anything to him.

Eventually, as the crowd continued to roar out its mindless hate, the edges began to drift away and the crush eased. Raffi was free to start moving. He looked up for the first time since his first sight of Vahan the headmaster being led down the road. At that moment, he almost fainted away, for there, swaying in the breeze, with swollen tongues purple and hanging out of their mouths, eyes staring and bloodshot, were the six principal teachers from his school. For a moment he almost vomited, and could not move. He then turned and hurried home forgetting all about the meat.

On reaching home, at the sight of his mother when she opened the front door, he burst into paroxysms of tears. There was of course no more school for anyone.

Very shortly after this incident, the deportation orders emanating from Talaat's ministry in Istanbul were posted all over town, and reinforced by the town criers calling out in all districts. All Armenians were to leave the town within a week. There was to be no selling of any goods, no drawing of any money, everyone simply had to leave and make their way to the Arab vilayets. Supposedly there were to be guards posted along the way.

The only exceptions at this stage were to be families of officers serving in the Turkish army, and those few who could show that they were Catholic or Protestant, rather than Orthodox Armenians. However, even this latter exception lasted only a week, as it became clear to the Ittihad leaders in Stamboul that their Austrian and German allies were not after all going to raise anything more than a formal protest at the expulsion of Catholic and Protestant Armenians as well.

Raffi had written many weeks before to Vahan, asking for evidence as to his officer status. Vahan had immediately contacted his superior officer at the Harbiye military academy. An upright old Ottoman official, he had promptly furnished a stamped and signed copy of Vahan's commission. Vahan, sensing the possible importance of this document for his family back in Caesaria, had written to Raffi immediately, confirming that he had passed on the document to a trustworthy Turkish merchant, who had known and done business with Garabed, and who was travelling to Caesaria within days.

Raffi in fact received the document within a day or two after he had been forced to watch all his teachers swinging in the breeze in the town square.

The emptying of the Armenian quarters now began. Raffi, himself, had already purchased a large tent and a couple of donkeys ready for the journey. The streets of the Armenian quarters were filled with Turks looking for a bargain, knocking at doors and asking people if they had anything to sell, despite the formal government ban. People were parting with valuable heirlooms and all their furniture for a pittance.

Raffi was in a state of panicky indecision. Everything happening around him seemed to him to be so utterly arbitrary, so completely tyrannical and lawless, that he did not know what would happen when the local commissioner finally arrived at their house. After all, in the last resort, Vahan's commission was only a piece of paper. There was nothing whatsoever he could do if it was not accepted at the moment it was presented. Meanwhile, he would have lost his chance to sell some of the contents of the house. Suddenly, those twenty-five gold coins which Garabed had returned into Raffi's care became vital to the chances of survival of the family.

Eventually the day came when their little street was ready to be emptied. Accompanied by some local policemen who knew the district, the local commissioner came down their little cul-de-sac. Almost everyone was ready and began moving out. Raffi watched from the door as he saw his neighbours leaving. He, like all his neighbours, knew the dangers; he was well aware of the rumours of all the killing in the countryside outside the towns. Nevertheless, neither he nor his neighbours were of course aware that not one Armenian from this street would survive the killing fields which went on all the way to the Syrian deserts, where almost all of those who made it that far, then died of starvation.

Raffi knew everyone in the street. In one of the first houses, Raffi watched as the elderly father of a family with many children remonstrated in vain with the commissioner, having established that he had two children who were serving with labour battalions of the army.

In the last house before that, of the Asadourians, the family was ready, as they all were, but they asked to be exempted at least for some time. It appeared that their old grandmother could not walk at all—indeed could not be moved from her bed. They had no cart or anything. Raffi watched as the old man explained all this to the commissioner. It was to no avail. In the end they were forced out, and the whole family trudged away, leaving their sick grandmother in bed in the house. They left some food and water by her bedside, and left the main door open. Raffi watched as they walked away, eyes downcast, saying nothing to anyone. In his own state of anxiety, he forgot almost immediately the plight of the old woman left in the house.

At last, the police group came to the Asadourian house at the end of the street. Raffi had prepared the tent and all the other items on the backs of the two donkeys, which were still inside the courtyard standing patiently fully loaded by the side of the old well. He now stood, trembling with anticipation at the door, with his mother a step or two behind him, as the commissioner approached.

"Come, come, you must leave now Everyone in the house must be gone today," said the official, who had repeated these words all day to a series of desperate and confused people.

"Commissioner bey, my brother is an officer in the Ottoman army," said Raffi as confidently as he could manage. He then handed over the Harbiye Commission. The official turned to the local policeman standing beside him and said, "Whose house is this?"

"It belonged, effendi, to one Garabed Asadourian, who has already been deported."

"Well, did he have an elder son or not?" and the Commissioner looked at the document in his hand, "called Vahan?"

"Yes, your Honour," said the policeman.

There was a long moment of silence as everyone waited for the commissioner's verdict. Law was breaking down completely as the war continued. Anything could have happened at that moment, and Raffi was well aware of that. Raffi, even at that moment of stomach-churning panic, reflected in a corner of his mind that this was the true definition of tyranny, the totally arbitrary nature of a society where a decision of life or death could depend on the whim of a single unaccountable person.

The moment stretched out, as Raffi waited tensely. Then the official took a piece of chalk and wrote in large letters on the front door: 'Zabit ailesi'— 'officer's house.'

Without a further word he turned, and he and the other policemen walked out of the now totally empty street.

Raffi, whose nerves were stretched to the limit, almost fainted, as his mother came forward and held him tight.

Three days later, a Turkish old lady who lived on the next street, and who knew Mariam and her daughters, came knocking on the door, and asked to speak to her.

"Mariam hanum, I have just heard some weak shouting and crying coming from the last house in this street. I went in, the door was open, and lying there was the old lady. . . you know, the grandmother, I don't know her name. . . I think. . . er, where was I? Oh yes. . . crying, there she was, abandoned and unable to move. What shall we do?"

Mariam said nothing but immediately called out to Raffi, who was listening in the corridor behind her, as the old lady walked away muttering to herself.

"Raffi, listen, did you hear that? I had no idea. You must go right away and bring her here."

"Mother, my soul, mother, listen! We have grandma already in bed here. We have sisters and a baby. Also, your old bedridden aunt will come when she hears that we've been exempted. How can we look after anyone else?"

"Raffi, please, we must! You know well that knowing what we do, neither of us is going to be able to sleep if we don't act."

Raffi felt guilty that he himself had forgotten the plight of this old woman in all the worry, and he immediately left. Taking one of the donkeys he went into town. Here, he eventually traced Hassan the local garbage collector, who had his own donkey. He persuaded him to come back with him to the little street, and they both went into the empty house and found the old lady.

The woman was lying on her bed, covered with her own dirt and urine, abandoned, weeping softly, and unable to move. Working together they lifted her, carried her to the street, and put her on the back of Raffi's donkey. They brought her back to the house, where, again working together, they lifted her into the bathroom, under Mariam's direction. Hassan left, refusing any baksheesh, but instead giving a deep bow to Mariam. Raffi, without any embarrassment, then helped his mother carefully wash the old woman all over, and with difficulty they then took her to a bed.

The house now held seven women, including two helpless old ladies, who had to be fed, bathed and changed. In the midst of it all, half boy half man, the hapless sixteen-year-old Raffi, who had to do all the lifting and carrying to the bathroom, found himself fortunately too busy to think too much. Meanwhile, the whole of the rest of the little street now stood completely forlorn and empty.

Chapter 44

Constantinople. Mikael meets Loris and Olga.

The police station in Yedikule was at the southern edge of Stamboul, right up against the great Theodosian walls of the city. Mikael, held firmly between two burly policemen, was dragged rather than walked into the station, still retching and with his lips and nose bleeding.

"Name?" rapped out the sergeant at the desk.

Mikael did not reply, but looked up at the officer with that dark, somewhat arrogant look that was his unfortunate trademark.

"His name, sergeant, is Mikael Sarafian, and he's a fucking giavour deserter," said the policeman putting the papers down on the desk, and indicating the out-of-date pass.

"Put the bastard in the cells," said the sergeant dismissively.

"One of the large public. . ."

"No," interrupted the sergeant, looking meaningfully at the three policemen, "in one of the single ones down below."

Mikael was taken down to the basement. He was thrust into a dismal old dungeon, stone-walled and without any window, with a single, dim electric light swinging from the damp roof. There, almost absent-mindedly, he was punched, thrown to the floor, and kicked as a matter of formality rather than viciously. He lay there, spitting blood and thinking, 'well I suppose it could have been worse. I'm in for it when I get back to the army.' He lay there imagining the more formal punishment that would be awaiting him when he was returned to his unit.

However, that night, the desk sergeant accompanied by a couple of guards, had come into the cell, where Mikael was sitting on the stone bench set into the wall—the only item of furniture. Then, without a word being said, Mikael was systematically beaten for almost half an hour. Dragged up from the bench he was punched in the face and stomach until he collapsed on the floor. There, he was struck repeatedly with the sergeant's thick cane, whilst the two guards kicked him as he lay curled up on the floor over and over again. The men said not a word, and the only sound was Mikael's screams. However, the screams soon became moans. Mikael did not have a very solid body and he mercifully passed out in the middle of the beating. He did not recover consciousness until long after the three men had left the cell.

Mikael was left bleeding and alone in the dimly-lit cell for over twenty-four hours, without food or water, lying in his own urine. In the early morning following that, three soldiers accompanied by a young lieutenant, came down to the cell to take him back to the unit headquarters.

"Good God! What the blazes has happened to him?" said the officer to the guard who had opened the cell door.

"I believe that he tried to escape and had to be restrained," replied the guard.

"For heaven's sake! Some restraint!" said the young lieutenant. "What do you say soldier?" he said, addressing Mikael.

"Water, water please," Mikael managed to croak through cracked and bloody lips, his body a mass of pain.

"Bloody hell! Take him out, wash him down, and give him some water, and let's get going from this place. Is there a shower or a hose or something here?" said the young man addressing the guard.

Mikael was carried out into the courtyard where he was undressed, hosed down, and after lying on the floor naked for a few minutes, was given a blanket to wrap round himself. He was totally incapable of standing on his two feet, so he was carried out of the police station and put into the army carriage which was waiting outside.

Mikael himself, forced into temporary consciousness by the cold water and the movement, kept going in and out of awareness. He barely realised what happened to him during the next forty-eight hours, and was only able to piece together the events much later when reflecting back on what must have occurred.

Driven back to the city headquarters of his unit through the streets of Stamboul and out through the gates, he was eventually seen by an army doctor. It was immediately clear to the doctor that the soldier was in fact much closer to death than had appeared at first sight. After careful examination, the doctor diagnosed that apart from the terrible bruises and outward damage, Mikael had a ruptured liver, and his kidneys did not seem to be functioning properly. Either way, the army could not possibly have him back on active duty as he was.

The administrative officer of the regiment—the unit itself and Mikael's direct commanding officer being already stationed in the Gallipoli peninsula—decided that he should be sent off immediately to the military hospital at Scutari. What happened to him if he did not die there could be considered later. Thus it was here, in one of the huge and rather shabby wards, that some days later Mikael eventually first regained consciousness and opened his eyes.

Bending over him, looking anxious, was his old boyhood friend, Loris, dressed in a white, or rather a once-white, coat, obviously a hospital orderly of some sort or another.

"Loris, oh my friend Loris, did you get the apricots," murmured Mikael with a smile of recognition, and then drifted off into complete oblivion again.

Mikael only slowly recovered as the weeks went by. His friend Loris visited him every day and made sure that he got all the attention and medication that the harassed doctors prescribed. Without that personal attention, Mikael would undoubtedly have been neglected, like so many of the others, and would have most probably died.

Mikael discovered that on being called up, Loris had claimed to be a qualified vet. He had hoped thereby to be put in charge of the army's horses and mules, and it was true that he did know something about animals, as his father kept a small herd of cows in their ramshackle old house on the outskirts of Makrikoy. Loris, when he was not at school, often went with his father delivering milk to both the terraced houses in the town, and the grander houses up the hills above the Valli Effendi racecourse.

However, in true army style, recognisable in all armies all over the world, this claim had resulted in him being posted not as a vet, but as a hospital orderly attached to a certain Doctor Turhan, who practised at the military hospital in Uskudar. Here, Loris had, with great good fortune and the support of Doctor Turhan, eventually been allocated a tiny room of his own at the back of the enormous barracks/hospital.

As Mikael's health slowly and painfully progressed and he began to be able to shuffle about, he also began to spend more and more time in Loris' tiny den. He knew that he would never fully recover and that he would never be as active physically as before, and this threw him back into trying to improve his hitherto rather cursory education. He began reading voraciously any book he could lay his hands on.

As there were not, after all, that many Armenians working at the Barracks hospital in Uskudar, it was inevitable that Loris would eventually come across Olga Avakian. Olga used to stay in the nurses' dormitory at least two or three days every week. She returned to Makrikoy for her days off, but even when on duty, there were many moments when the staff could interact. Loris had indeed seen Olga several times, but they had done nothing more than nod at each other.

There was a considerable shortage of female nurses. Normally these would have been provided by the minorities—the Greeks, Armenians and Jews. Turks of the old school did not encourage their daughters to indulge in this sort of work, and this feeling had not changed much even for the modernisers. However, the news filtering in throughout the summer of the killing fields in Anatolia had left the Armenian community fearful and in a mood to keep a very low profile, and so there were few Armenian nurses left. This meant that all the girls were overworked, and that Olga had only Greeks and Jews as colleagues.

It was Dr. Turhan who on one occasion drew Loris' particular attention once again to Olga, "Loris, my boy, did you know that one of our most conscientious nurses here is an Armenian girl? She's really very good. Every time she works with me, she seems to have improved on the last time. I understand that she often stays at the hospital in the female staff dormitory. You should make an effort and meet her."

"Certainly, sir, thank you, I'll make a point of it," answered Loris, without any intention of following it up. All his attention was given to the frail Mikael, whose condition remained critical on a long-term basis, even though he had now begun to shuffle about.

Loris and Mikael had been close boyhood friends in the little Armenian school in Makrikoy. They had clambered over the walls of the wealthier houses in the Osman Agha area of the town above the racecourse, and stolen apricots and peaches from the ample orchards there. They had kept watch for each other. They had wrestled together in their early teens, combats which would inevitably be won by the bigger and heavier Loris, who would end up sitting astride the frailer Mikael, demanding an abject surrender which would never be given.

Loris had spent Mikael's first month at the hospital feeding him, bathing him, caring for his body on a daily, almost hourly, basis. There was not a spare moment which he did not spend with Mikael, at first by his bedside, and then as Mikael began to shuffle about the corridors, alongside each other on the bed in the little room. Here they would reminisce about their past, and make rather impractical plans for the future. Whenever Loris finished work, he would often come back to his room to find that Mikael had been there most of the day reading.

Soldiers from the Gallipoli campaign kept pouring in every day, all with the horrendous wounds which were so much part of the experience of all the combatants of the Great War. Everyone was overworked and overtired, and thus it was that on one occasion in the afternoon Dr. Turhan and Olga found that they had been working together since the early morning on the emergency cases that had been coming in all that day. All were stretched to their limit. Both Olga and the doctor had been on duty without a break, with nothing to eat for ten hours since six o'clock in the morning. The doctor's hand slipped for the second time as he and Olga began stitching up a wound. There was a gasp from Olga and the other nurse as the doctor hastily corrected himself and finished the task.

"Yes, yes. All right, Nurse Avakian. We're both exhausted. Neither of us can do any more good here. Nurse Stefanides, please clear up here and make sure this soldier is given a bed in my ward. I'll get Doctor Fadil to take over. He should have been on duty by now anyway. Nurse Avakian, I believe you know the room belonging to Loris Sarafian. I think you'll find him there as he should be going on duty in an hour or so. Please go and tell him to report to Doctor Fadil immediately as he will be needing some assistance. Then you must go and get some sleep yourself. That's an order."

Olga washed up, took off her white apron, dressed and went off rather reluctantly to find Loris' room. Contrary to what the good doctor thought, having as he believed introduced them to each other, she had never been invited there, and was not too sure exactly where it was. She had never spoken to Loris in any way except for some cursory professional comments. She was aware that he was not in the slightest bit interested in her in any way, and furthermore, she thought that he would in any case already be on duty in view of the emergency atmosphere in the hospital. She did not therefore hurry, but nevertheless trudged up the stairs and knocked on the door. Somewhat to her surprise there was a call from inside.

"Yes. Come in, the door's open."

Olga walked in. She saw a youngish man with a thin frail body dressed in the regulation pyjamas and a threadbare dressing gown lying on the bed, reading a slim book. He had dark and feverish-looking black eyes, with a hard arrogant look in them. However, this was belied by the drawn and haggard feel about his face. Mikael, still on the bed, put down his book, and stared up at a tired looking girl with reddened eyes but still with a remarkable sparkle in them. A girl, whose commonplace even dowdy dress seemed to hang on her effortlessly with elegance and style.

Mikael struggled to stand up off the bed, and at that point his whole life changed yet again. Olga's face softened, and she gave him a warm and devastating smile, putting forward a firm restraining hand saying,

"Please don't, sir. Lie still. Can I see what you're reading?"

She leant forward and took the book from his fingers as he sank back on the bed.

"Ah. Namik Kemal, the early poetry. You admire his work? Are you a friend of Mr. Sarafian or a patient? My name is Olga, Olga Avakian." And she held out her hand to the supine Mikael.

Mikael had none of the shyness with girls usual in the young men of the Ottoman world. He sat up on the bed, shook Olga's hand, and moved his feet off the bed, inviting Olga to sit on the bed next to him.

Olga, without any embarrassment, sat.

Working since the early morning, Olga was tired. For his part, Mikael, though healing slowly, was always in residual pain, particularly towards the end of the day. Nevertheless, they talked together in Armenian for three hours. Only once did Olga get up and go and fetch some water, but she hurried back immediately. They soon discovered that they both lived in Makrikoy. They had even attended the same early primary school, though of course at different times, he in the boys' section and she in the girls. As Olga described her house and her life, Mikael thought to himself that she probably lived in one of the grand houses that he and Loris had raided for illicit fruit when they were young.

This inconsequential chat, which they were both so enjoying, could have gone on all evening without any thought of time. However, the moment came when Loris finally walked in, himself exhausted. Mikael began making an effort to rise with an odd feeling of guilt, the reason for which he could not place.

"Hello, what's going on?" said Loris, as he took in the sight of Mikael shuffling to get up, and Olga sitting on the bed, smiling and with her eyes alight.

"Oh, hello Loris," said Mikael. "I've been reading in your room. Er. . . I suppose you know Miss Avakian. . . er. . . my friend Loris Sarafian. . . er. . . you must know each other, surely."

Olga remained seated on the bed between them as Mikael finally managed to stand up facing Loris.

"Are you well, Mikael? You look tired. Can I help you back to the ward," said Loris, ignoring Olga.

Olga scarcely had room to stand, but she did so at this stage, and facing Loris, still in the door, she said, "Oh, Mr. Sarafian, Dr. Turhan sent me up here to ask you to go on duty early, but you were already on duty when I got here.

I've been chatting with your friend. We've discovered we are from the same town, isn't that a coincidence? Anyway, I must go now. Goodbye."

She flashed Loris a somewhat artificial smile and went out.

Loris looked at Mikael. He too saw a frail vulnerable thin body with the far too large black eyes and the look almost of contempt. He too saw the shabby regulation pyjamas and the meagre gown and the fact that this man was still ill. But Loris was seeing something more, again. He sighed, clasped Mikael round the shoulders, and said, "I'll walk you back, Mikael. You look really tired. I hope that girl didn't exhaust you. Please be careful of her, she has a bad reputation, and I believe she's a hopeless nurse. One of those rich spoilt girls playing at nursing. I'll see she doesn't worry you."

They shuffled back to the crowded ward.

Chapter 45

Caesaria. Raffi escapes.

As the weeks passed, two further old women, unable to walk and so left behind as the population was forced out of their homes, had ended up being brought round to the Asadourian house on the back of Raffi's donkeys. In effect, within a few weeks of the day that the little street had been emptied, there were eight women living in the house. These were Mariam herself, Raffi's two elder sisters who were probably widowed by now, the two bedridden grandmothers, the baby sister, and the two newcomers.

The whole of the Armenian quarter around them had become a ghost town. The streets were quiet and empty, and the atmosphere was eerie and oppressive. One or two displaced Turkish families from the areas currently occupied by the Russians had moved into a couple of the empty houses, but the majority lay quiet and abandoned. Indeed, the whole town was subdued. Most of the remaining Turks found to their own great surprise, that the forced departure of the politically hated Armenian minority was not, after all, as welcome to them as the idea had seemed to them before it actually happened.

The government was now calling up the seventeen-year-olds for military service. It had therefore become dangerous for Raffi to wander the streets. Whilst there were still a few Armenian families still left in the town, none of these included any young able-bodied males.

Raffi would undoubtedly have become depressed and likely to have started taking risks, if he had not found himself having to do all the heavy work of taking care of the three bedridden old ladies. Mariam and his sisters did of course do most of the pure nursing work. However, it was Raffi who had to carry them to the toilet, and turn them over in their beds, and help with all the heavy work. Accordingly, he rarely went out. Mariam had paid heavily, by using two more of those gold coins Garabed had returned, to get some false papers for Raffi, which gave his name as Soliman, his religion as Muslim, and his age as sixteen.

It was Raffi's own grandmother, his father's mother, out of the three women, who was sinking the fastest. Her condition had been deteriorating from the moment her son Garabed had been arrested, and it was fairly clear that she was going to die soon. She was a particularly pious old lady, who had been with her husband on a pilgrimage to Jerusalem many years before. Raffi was aware that while there, she had purchased a specially blessed and holy burial shroud. This garment was a beautiful white linen cloth, embroidered with angels and crosses, replendent with the whole paraphernalia of Christian iconography. Raffi had often seen her take it out of the wooden chest, hang it up, and contemplate it with great satisfaction.

The day eventually came when Mariam and Raffi sat by her bedside as she slowly slipped away.

"I will be buried in my shroud, won't I?" she whispered to Mariam.

"Yes, yes, I promise, mother. Don't be anxious," replied Mariam.

Raffi said nothing, but continued to hold his grandmother's withered old hand, as with a sigh the old lady finally expired.

There was of course no priest left in the town so far as Mariam knew, and the Armenian churches were all closed and boarded up. Mariam and Raffi sat together whilst the others in the house came, kissed the old lady, and left. Eventually Mariam rose, called her daughters, and as Raffi looked on, they bathed the body and brought out the burial shroud and began putting her in it.

"Mother, for heaven's sake it's far too dangerous," said Raffi urgently. "How can we take her down to the cemetery in this climate, with that garment calling out our race and religion to all the world. You know how it is in the town at the moment."

"My son, my son, it was her last wish. I promised, I promised. I'll suffer years of guilt if I don't fulfil it now."

"But mother, it's just superstition. What does it matter what she's buried in?"

"Please, son. I'll find a blanket to wrap round her whilst you take her down, but you must remove it before you bury her. Raffi, don't shake your head like that. I know it's not a religious duty, but I couldn't live with the thought that we didn't do our best. It was such a source of pride for her."

Racing through Raffi's mind was the thought, 'for god's sake, she's dead, nothing can affect her now,' but what he actually said was, "Very well mama, get her ready. I'll do it this evening."

Raffi was impatient of what he thought of as religious nonsense. He had always been much influenced by Vahan's totally secular attitude to life. Raffi agreed with him that religion was 'women's business.' However, it would simply never have crossed his mind for a moment to consider converting to Islam, as some others had done to save themselves from the deportation decrees and the death that almost inevitably followed. Raffi never analysed this in himself. It never crossed his mind for a moment, that, as he basically believed that both religions were a 'load of old superstitious rubbish,' it could make no difference at all if he paid lip service to one rather than the other. Vahan would have thought it out and tried to analyse it, but Raffi just took his feelings for granted.

So, that afternoon, Raffi went on one of his rare trips into town to seek the help of old Hassan, the local rubbish collector who had always been a friend of the family. There were after all no Armenian males left in the town to whom Raffi could turn for help, at least as far as he knew. Hassan blinked and hesitated when Raffi explained the task that was required, but he did not refuse. Hiding their spades in bags, they carried the old lady's body, wrapped in the blanket, laid her across the donkey, and set off.

The gates of the Armenian cemetery were open, but Hassan drew the line at going inside. He and Raffi began digging a grave just outside in the grass by the gates. They had not gone far when an army officer came by on a horse. Leaning down, he said to Hassan, whom he recognised, "Giavour or Islam?"

Hassan was tongue-tied and said nothing, but Raffi quickly answered in his place, "We don't know, sir, as we found her already dead in one of the empty Armenian houses."

"Well, take her down to the Muslim cemetery just in case," said the officer. He then lit a cigarette and trotted off. Hassan stared at Raffi, and there was a long moment of silence between them.

"Hassan," Raffi eventually said, "I can't do it. I simply can't."

"Oh for God's sake Raffi, what does it matter where she's buried. Her own God will no doubt claim her. Come on, that man is a fellow who could easily come back to check on what has happened."

"I can't do it, I can't. Mother will collapse with the shock."

"Look, I have every respect, as you know, for Mariam hanum, but just don't tell her. I can't take the risk. If he comes back and takes a look under the blanket and sees the shroud, we're in for it—you're dead, and I'll be badly beaten."

Raffi was momentarily lost, with no idea of what to do. But he was growing up fast. He grabbed one of the spades and said, "Hassan, my good friend, start walking the donkey and the old lady away towards the Muslim cemetery as you are supposed to do. Go in a circle. I'll finish the grave here. When you get back, it'll only take a moment to tip her in and bury her here quickly."

It was of course a totally unnecessary risk. Neither of them could have explained why they persevered. However, when Hassan did do as suggested and then returned, it did indeed take only a moment to bury the old lady. Raffi pulled away the blanket, as the first clods of earth were hastily piled back onto the resplendent shroud.

When in due course he recounted these events to Mariam, Raffi somewhat mischievously paused at the point that they had been ordered to bury the body in the Muslim cemetery. Mariam paled and almost fainted. Raffi knew then that he had been right to have taken the risk, when he saw his mother's face clear, as he hastily proceeded with his narrative.

It was not long after this incident that the police arrived at the house. One of the new neighbours, a displaced Turkish family who had moved in from Russian-occupied Erzurum, had seen Raffi on the roof and denounced him to the police.

Quite by chance, that same morning, a Turkish family, the wife, sisters and elder daughter of a certain Major Suleyman—an old acquaintance of Garabed—had come visiting Mariam and her two daughters, whom they knew well. They were all sitting in the reception room of Raffi's sisters taking coffee, when there was a knock at the front door.

Raffi himself of course never answered the door, but would make himself scarce whenever there was a strange knock. The policemen explained to Mariam, who had hastily covered her face with a yashmak, that they had been informed that there was a young man in the house. Mariam, speaking loudly to make sure that Raffi could hear, said, "Yes, it is true. My second son was here recently. However, he demanded money from me, and when I told him that I didn't have any, he hit me here and ran away. I haven't seen him since."

"Madam, we intend to search the house. Please stand aside."

Raffi had long since slipped through into the private women's area of the large house. He walked into his sister's room. The Turkish ladies all began hastily drawing down their veils, looking at Raffi curiously. Raffi himself immediately faced the wall so as not to look at them. He quietly told his sister, Sira, with his back to the room, what was happening. She bundled Raffi into a cupboard as the Turkish women looked on in excitement. Shortly after this the police appeared outside the door to the area which would normally be 'haram'—forbidden—for any honest Muslim.

"Madam," said the senior policeman to Mariam, who was still with them, "we have to search the whole house."

"But officer, we have the family of Major Suleyman here visiting my daughter. They are inside, unveiled."

"Madame. Certainly, of course we cannot go in while they are unveiled. However, please ask them to perform 'namekram,' and then come through to the other part of the house where we have already looked.

Mariam knocked at the door, not knowing that Raffi was inside, and told Sira what was to happen. The ladies hastily donned their veils, while Sira went to the cupboard and pulled Raffi out. She then brought a feradjeh, and ladies shoes, and dressed Raffi in the loose gown and veil, whilst again the ladies of the Major's household, now fully veiled, looked on in both wonder and a frisson of excitement.

Sira then opened the door, and she and the ladies walked out—each lady carefully looking down at the floor as they passed. However, the policemen also avoided looking at the ladies as they passed, trained as they were by years of culture and custom. They were already uncomfortable enough being in that part of the house which would normally be 'haram' for any strange males. Raffi, in a state of terror and scarcely able to walk, shuffled past the policemen with downcast eyes as Sira waited behind to show the policemen round.

The lovely ladies of Major Suleyman's family said not a word, neither then nor later when they left the house. When it was the policemen's turn to leave they said to Mariam, "We know full well that your second son is somewhere around. We'll be calling again, we can assure you."

That night Raffi packed a small bag and took out his false papers. He kissed his mother passionately and said his farewells to everyone. Mariam's men were finally now to be all gone. She took out the gold coins, now down to fifteen, and wrapping them up in a cloth gave them to him with her blessing. Raffi, with a deep pride in his heart mixed with the pain and excitement of parting, carefully counted out five, as his father had done, and returned the rest to her.

Raffi left early in the morning whilst it was still dark. He spent the whole morning in the dusty square, where the carriages and lorries set off for other towns, watching out all the time for police presence, and waiting for his chance to board.

Chapter 46

Anatolia. Garabed drives on.

When Garabed arrived back up the hill at the ruined farmstead of the dead Sarkis, accompanied by Burhan the young twelve-year-old son of Mustapha, the situation had not greatly changed. Adrineh herself was now looking somewhat less dishevelled. Both she and Nefise Hanum were gathered round the still recumbent figure of Anna. Neither woman appeared to have made any attempt as yet to comfort or deal with the problem of the naked Ara, who was still crouched up against the old wall of the farmhouse.

Burhan handed over the women's clothes to his mother. Garabed carefully looked away after nodding at the two women and moved over to stand near the boy, wondering whether he could try once again to make some contact and get through to him. Dusk was falling and Garabed felt that the first priority, if he couldn't do anything about the boy, was to start a fire somewhere. It was clear to him that no one was going to go back into the slaughter house that the farmhouse had become, and so, with Burhan's help in bringing twigs and then wood, he prepared and lit up a fire in the yard.

The flames immediately began to add a touch of warmth to the scene as the dark began cutting out the sight of the devastation around. Continuing to ignore the two women still fussing around Anna, Garabed motioned to Burhan to fetch the pottery cup. Garabed filled it from the well and then went over to Ara, who had been watching all the activity around him, but clearly without much recognition of what it was all about. He crouched beside the boy and tried to hold the cup up to his lips. But Ara, though now no longer screaming, turned his head away and squeezed up in a foetal position against the wall.

Garabed, in some irritation and impatience backed away. At this point, Burhan, who had been watching this latest attempt to get through to Ara, came and took the cup, before Garabed in frustration was about to pour the water away. Burhan walked over and for the first time a tiny flicker of recognition came into the dulled eyes of the young boy.

Burhan held forward the cup, not pushing it demandingly towards the lips as Garabed had done, but offering it to be taken by the hand, and said, "Ara, my friend Ara, please drink some water."

For the first time Ara did not shrink back, but took the cup from Burhan's hand and began drinking. Once started, clearly needing water as Garabed could see, he began asking for the cup to be refilled and drank and drank, as Burhan ran happily back and forth to the well.

Garabed did not take in the emotional reaction of the young Turkish boy, whose face was suffused with a grin of pure delight at what he had achieved where an adult had totally failed. Garabed was not after all that sensitive to this sort of feeling. Burhan watched with satisfaction his friend's increasing awareness of his surroundings, and indeed within a few further moments Ara took up the clothes Burhan indicated that had been left by his side. He began to dress himself.

It was fortunately a warm evening, and Garabed now asked Burhan to go down to his father and bring back a spade. Nothing had been left intact in the Shahanian farm, and there were certainly no tools anywhere. Whilst Burhan was away, Garabed now carried out the bodies of the four children, and lay them down side by side on the grass outside the courtyard. During this time, whereas Nefise looked across every so often in sorrow and sympathy, Adrineh carefully looked away continuing to concentrate on Anna—she could cry no more.

When Burhan returned, he helped Garabed drag the body of Sarkis across the courtyard to be laid alongside the children, and Garabed started digging. The bodies were buried in two shallow graves, Sarkis in one and the children together in the other. Anna had by now been washed and dressed by the two women, and Nefise persuaded Adrineh to come and stand by the mounds, as with arms outstretched and palms up to heaven in the fashion both of the Muslims and the Christians of the area, Garabed mumbled some words which at least sounded like prayers. To everyone's relief, Adrineh began crying again, but now softly and copiously, whilst Nefise hugged her all the time.

Nefise gathered together the remaining clothes, squeezed the hand of the still weeping Adrineh, and bowed to Garabed saying, "May Allah preserve you, sir."

Garabed raised his hand to his forehead and bowed in his turn without saying another word. Burhan and Nefise returned home, taking the remaining clothes and the spade but leaving the cup. Garabed tried to wrap his sheepskin coat round Ara, but the boy flinched away from his touch, clearly he could not accept the presence or touch of another adult male. Adrineh and Anna huddled together and fell asleep by the fire.

Garabed though completely exhausted could not sleep. He stared at the flickering flames, rising every so often to throw on some more wood. What was he going to do now, where was he going to go? Suddenly, from being an active strong middle-aged man on the run with good survival prospects, he had become saddled with a whole family: A woman who had just been raped, and who had lost her husband and four of her children; a girl in a state of total and traumatic shock; a young boy, fearful, unable to face reality and who looked on him with suspicion. Whilst there were many possible courses of action, one was quite impossible—there was no way he could now abandon them and carry on on his own.

Garabed looked round, and there wide-awake and staring at him with an almost mad intensity, he caught the eye of Ara, lying nearby. Garabed shuddered a little, but then turned and eventually dropped off into a troubled sleep in the early hours of the morning.

The next morning, with no food available and just some water, Garabed had to start making some decisions. Adrineh clearly looked to him, as she would have done to her husband. It was impossible to stay. Sooner or later authorities from the village below would catch up with them. Questions would be asked as to why Sarkis, or whoever was at the farm, had not left with the other deported Armenians. On the other hand, where were they to go, and how?

Garabed decided. He strode down to Mustapha's farm in the hope of catching him before he started work in the fields.

"Mustapha, effendi, I will have to leave today, and I must take Sarkis' remaining family with me."

"You are right, Garabed bey. It is not safe for you to remain here. I have spoken with my wife, and we are prepared to take in the boy Ara. We don't require him to take up Islam, but we will want to have him circumcised, both for his and our own protection. It has already been decreed that anyone harbouring Armenians will be punished."

"I will put it to Adrineh hanum. I thank you, but I don't believe that she will want to separate the family. May I propose that Adrineh formally gives you all her husband's farm. If you have some paper, any paper will do, I will write a formal gift and get her to put her mark. Perhaps in return you might be in a position to let us have two of your donkeys."

Garabed knew it was not a fair exchange. After all, once they had left, Mustapha could have walked up and simply taken over the land in any case. However, it might be of help to Mustapha in the future to have some evidence of formal ownership, and he agreed. Garabed then produced one of the invaluable gold coins, deciding to keep the already changed notes. He handed the coin to Mustapha saying, "Mustapha effendi, I would request you to load one of the donkeys with any spare rice or provisions you can manage. Perhaps your son, may Allah be with him always, could walk them up the hill. We will be leaving as soon as possible, but will be going on the hills and away from the valley."

Mustapha took the gold and nodded. The two men looked at each other for a long moment, and then without a further word Garabed turned and walked back up the hill.

When Burhan arrived later that morning, the still silent and distracted Anna was sat astride one of the donkeys. The other donkey was laden with a bag of rice, a couple of pans, a bag of onions and two squawking hens tied by their legs.

Burhan tried to embrace Ara, but stopped as soon as he sensed Ara flinching away. He salaamed Garabed and stood watching as the little party began trudging away. Garabed led the laden donkey in front, followed by Ara firmly walking alongside his sister, making sure that she did not fall, and with Adrineh trudging along behind.

Garabed had decided to make for Diyarbekir and Mardin which were on the way to Aleppo, but to keep away from the recognised roads and tracks. On the first night, he discovered hidden at the bottom of the bag of onions an old but usable pistol, with some ammunition. Not much use against a band of determined men, but maybe just enough to ward off the individual robber.

Day after day passed as the little party trudged on, avoiding any towns or villages, and indeed any human habitation at all as far as possible. Garabed moved in a sort of tense daze, but he knew the country and managed, almost absent-mindedly, to avoid the bands of Kurds and lawless men roaming the countryside looking for 'giavours' to rob and murder. They had been travelling for about two weeks when Garabed became aware that they were now coming out of the bare mountainous terrain, and that there were more and more villages to be avoided. He began to see the occasional camel, and the days were getting warmer.

One night, Garabed awoke in the early hours of the morning and lay staring at the stars above him. He became aware of a very soft weeping. He turned quietly onto his side and looked at the form of Adrineh lying beside him. Garabed pushed off his sheepskin coat. There was no analysis, no thought process, he moved over and wrapped his arms round the silently weeping woman. Adrineh herself responded immediately, though her weeping continued. Her arms came up to envelop him. Garabed moved gently across her and their lips sought each others with intensity, but without a sound.

Garabed fumbled with his trousers, whilst Adrineh did the same with her rough and tattered skirts. Silently, and scarcely moving at all, Garabed and Adrineh made love, not mechanically but nevertheless with a desperation that had little of affection in it.

However, as they continued during the day to move down from the Anatolian plateau towards the Syrian desert, their nightly encounters became more and more passionate, and less just a physical need to be assuaged. They were still in a regular state of tension as they travelled, with their eyes peeled for strangers and possible robbers, yet they scarcely said a word to each other during the day, and certainly there was no acknowledgement or analytical communication between them as to what was happening. They simply fell automatically into the physical comfort they gave each other in the middle of the nights.

It was probably about five days later that the whole daily trudging and nightly comforts came to an abrupt end. Garabed, increasingly eager to relieve his tensions and knowing that Adrineh now wanted him as much as he wanted her, mounted her with greater confidence. The coupling had become stronger, more passionate and less silent. So it was that on this occasion, in the midst of his passion, Garabed felt a sudden presence, a warning, a sixth sense of danger. He stopped and looked up. Staring at him with mad inflamed eyes stood Ara. Held in his hand was the long knife originally bought by Garabed in Malatya. Adrineh was still wriggling below him, but she quickly sensed that Garabed had become suddenly still, and although she had no idea what was happening, she opened her eyes and looked up at Garabed, who was staring up at something behind her.

This tableau—this threesome—with Ara glaring at Garabed in a tremor of rage, with Garabed breaking away gently from Adrineh but keeping his eyes warily on Ara, and with Adrineh just staring up at Garabed, held for a long impossible moment. Then with an almost insane scream, Ara lifted the knife and shouting incoherently, "turk, kurd, beast, murderer!" he struck down at Garabed with all his sparse boyish force.

Garabed had had sufficient time not to be taken totally off guard. His arms were still around Adrineh. With all his considerable strength he rolled the two of them away as the knife came down, but he felt it slice through his arm. With all passion spent, and now free of Adrineh, he jumped up, blood pouring from his arm.

Ara screamed again, dropped the knife, turned and ran off into the night. Anna, who had woken and seen all, was gibbering and muttering, but for the first time there was some reaction in her eyes. Even in that dramatic moment, as Garabed sat heavily down on the ground holding his bleeding arm, the thought came to him that Anna had either gone completely over the top and had become insane, or she had been jolted out of the dazed trauma of the last few weeks.

"Garabed, Garabed!" said Adrineh, addressing him familiarly for the very first time in their relationship, "What happened? What happened? Your arm is bleeding, come let me see it. What happened? Was that Ara? Oh my God what happened, where's he gone?"

"Adrineh, my love," said Garabed, himself responding with affection to her first words of warmth, "Ara must have awaken and been watching us. You must know how far your son is aware of the facts of life, but even if he was, what he saw must have brought his mind back to. . . Well you know. . . and how could he tell the difference?"

Garbed stopped and then called out, "Ouch! That hurt!" as Adrineh poured some precious cold water over the wound and tied a rag tight above the wound to stop the flow of blood.

It was of course pitch black, and there was no question of anyone going to look for Ara before morning. Anna, still muttering, moved over to cling fiercely to Adrineh. This was the first positive reaction that Garabed and Adrineh had seen from Anna since that terrible day. Adrineh held her tight, and they all sat quietly together as they waited for the sun to rise from the east. Garabed felt that he had more affection from and communication with Adrineh during these few hours sitting together waiting for the sun to rise, than in all the passion of the previous nights' couplings.

At first light, early next morning, Garabed rose, splashed his face, took up his knife, and taking one of the donkeys set off to look for Ara. They were in a fairly populated area where he had seen men around, and before leaving, he carefully took out the old pistol, loaded it, and handed it to Adrineh.

"My darling," he said to his own surprise, "You know how to use this, I'm sure. If anyone approaches point it and first fire away as soon as possible if they look like molesting you. Ara looked as if he would run for ever and only stop when he became completely exhausted, so it might be some time before I get back. But don't worry, I'll find him. I'll find him, I promise you."

This was a countryside of scrub and low hills, interspersed with cultivated fields surrounded by small boundary stones. There were no woods beyond the occasional single tree and no bushes at all.

Accordingly there was no cover at all. Garabed at first walked round the campsite in ever increasing circles until he was fairly sure which way the boy had run. He then set off in that direction picking up the occasional sign.

Surprised and worried at how far the boy appeared to have gone, it was two hours or more before he finally saw the huddled form of the young boy, fast asleep, lying up against a solitary rock. Garabed stopped, left the donkey, moved up, and considered how to approach the problem without arousing another alarmed reaction. He slowly shook the boy by the shoulder and said as he saw him awakening, "Ara, my son, Ara, my soul, my son Ara."

The boy still half asleep stretched up his hands as Garabed, straining with the effort, picked the boy up in his arms.

"Father, father," said Ara and clung on tightly to Garabed nestling his head into his shoulder.

Garabed began slowly walking back to the two women, followed docilely by the donkey. He held Ara tightly in his arms without the slightest intention of putting him onto the back of the donkey, brought along specifically for the purpose. The boy was heavy, the wound in his arm began bleeding again. Garabed, however, short of food and exhausted, never faltered, never once contemplated removing the boy from his position, but weaved his way back in a state of triumph that he had not felt for weeks.

Chapter 47

Damascus. Selim and the Arab dimension.

After the funeral service for his father and after writing his letter to Olga, Selim decided, without much hesitation, that he could not return to Robert College to resume his studies.

Although he had never been very close to his father, his death had inevitably come as a shock, and he felt that he needed to make some sort of a clean break with his past. He had known his father, Nazim, as an educated, honourable and dignified man, always correct in his dealings with everyone. However, Nazim had always kept him, and indeed the rest of his family also, at arm's length. Nevertheless, Selim felt both a grief and an anger which surprised him. Unlike his mother, Selim felt no bitterness towards the men who had caused his father's death, but they had inevitably become the enemy, and this in turn coloured his thoughts of Olga. Finally, like all the young men in these years, Selim felt the need to be part of the unfolding historical drama surrounding him. He could no longer remain a student.

As he contemplated his future, the old arguments with his father about the CUP and the Young Turk movement came flooding back into his memory. Who exactly had his father Nazim died for? The new modern Turkey which Selim hoped that the triumvirate of Enver, Talaat and Djemal were perhaps creating, or the old multinational Ottoman Empire? Selim did not know, nor did he suspect for a moment, that Nazim had in fact probably died for neither, but simply for humanity as a whole.

Either way, Selim, despite his mother's appeals, soon went round to the local Army Board. He handed back his deferment papers, and asked to be taken into the army immediately on active service. Selim had of course, like Vahan, been seconded to the Harbiye officers' training establishment. He had been attending regularly there, and the army took the line that he was to all intents and purposes fully trained. Selim expected to be sent to the Gallipoli front. He was therefore surprised and excited to hear that he was to be posted to Damascus, where he was to join one of the three Arab divisions stationed in Syria.

Before leaving, Selim wrote another short letter to Olga. She had answered his earlier letter very shortly, telling him that she was not going back to College. The death of Nazim at the hands of Armenian revolutionaries, and the arrest and deportation of Karekin at the hands of the state, had left them both anxious not to upset their respective mothers in any way at this time. By a sort of mutual agreement, without actually communicating with each other directly, they had taken the decision not to meet again for some time. So, apart from simply telling Olga that he had been posted to Damascus, Selim made no further attempt at contact, and left from Haydar Pasha station in a state of excitement and anticipation.

The railway tunnels through the Taurus Mountains were still not completed, so Selim alighted at Belemlik, like everyone else, and travelled on, across the mountain passes to the end of the line on the other side, and then on by troop train again to Damascus.

The triumvirate who ran the CUP or the Ittihad party consisted of Talaat, the sinister Minister of the Interior, Enver Pasha, the flamboyant Minister of War, and Djemal Pasha, once military governor of Istanbul, but now in charge of the whole Arab front. Just as Enver fancied himself as a great general, so Djemal Pasha also thought that he knew how to command armies. Enver's absolutely disastrous campaign against the Russians at the start of the war, was mirrored in the south when Djemal took command of the Ottoman Fourth Army and made a wild stab at crossing the Sinai desert trying to take the Suez Canal. He had been decisively defeated by the British in Egypt. Since that defeat, Djemal had settled in Damascus and had ruled, as Governor of Greater Syria, the whole of the Arab vilayets of the Ottoman Empire, almost as a private fiefdom.

Selim, once arrived in Damascus, reported first, as ordered, directly to Djemal Pasha. Djemal was a large jolly man, the son of a respected army officer who was not particularly high up in the old Ottoman circles. Due to his large corpulent frame he was known—to his great secret pleasure—as 'Buyuk Djemal'. He was a clever and ruthless man in his forties, and had been an early adherent to the Ittihad and a member of the CUP. Djemal, however, had been partly educated in Paris, and of all the Ittihad leaders he was the one most committed to the continuation if possible of the multi-cultural aspect of the Ottoman Empire.

Within a few days of Selim's arrival and his first interview with Djemal, he had been appointed to one of the three Arab divisions stationed in Damascus. His official position, for which he had the acting rank of Captain, was as a liaison officer between the division and the headquarters of Djemal himself. His job was to represent his commanding officer in the headquarters, and to transmit any orders from Djemal back to the division.

There was a tension in the city of which Selim soon became aware. The attempts by a cabal of young English officers in Cairo to arouse the Arabic-speaking population of the Empire against the Ottomans was well known to the astute Djemal and his staff. Secret societies, all with innumerable different proposals as to the political future for the Arabs, abounded in the town. Djemal was aware of all of them and periodically engineered a crack-down whenever they appeared to be getting out of hand.

Slowly, officer by officer and without any great publicity, Arab officers in the Fourth Army together with many ordinary Arab soldiers were being transferred to the killing grounds of the Gallipoli campaign. They were being replaced in Syria by Turkish officers. Selim himself had been a replacement for an Arab officer who went to Gallipoli and who, as Selim later discovered, duly died in the trenches like so many others.

The official motivation for this slow and steady draining of the Arabs from the army facing the British in the Levant was based on the clear and reasonable belief that in Gallipoli, less than a hundred miles from Constantinople, the Ottoman Empire was fighting for its life. Here in Syria the battle was far less decisive, and so it was a valid military requirement that troops should be transferred to the more important area. However, Selim also saw that it was helpful to

Djemal that most of the officers so removed were often those active in the secret societies milling about amongst the Syrian elite.

Selim soon settled down in the town and started work with his unit and the HQ staff. A quick learner, he soon mastered vernacular Arabic and came to enjoy the café life of the town and the continual restless talk of the future. The day came when Djemal asked to see him in his office. Saluting, and standing to attention, he was asked to sit.

"Selim, my boy, how do you like Damascus?" said Djemal jovially

"Sir, I find it fascinating."

"And your work here?"

"Equally so, sir," replied Selim rather stiffly.

"Well now Selim. I want you to know that I have today arranged for your commanding officer, Colonel Al-Hussein, to take over a post under General Mustapha Kemal in Gallipoli. He will be leaving shortly. Your new Commander will be arriving within a week, and as he is from Istanbul you will have that in common. I want you to help him to settle in quickly on his arrival."

"Certainly sir," replied Selim.

"Selim, my lad, I knew your father quite well in the days when I was military governor of the city. I was very sorry to hear of his death at Van. I remember him as a great supporter of the Ottoman imperial idea. I'm sure you discussed these matters together. Where do you stand in our great debate? Please do speak frankly, we are all soldiers here, not politicians."

"Well, sir, my father and I did disagree at times on these matters. He was, as you say, a believer in Ottomanism, and I understand that in his younger days as a student, he was a member of that group who called themselves the Young Ottomans, you know, in Abdul Hamid's time. I, myself, however, have always believed that our nation should base itself on its Turkish national identity, rather than on any spurious imperial mission."

"And what about here, the Arabs? What about Islam and the Holy Places which we have guarded for so long? What about the Caliphate?" replied Djemal, leaning forward, watching for Selim's reaction carefully.

"I don't know, sir, I really don't know. After only a few weeks here I do see that they can't govern themselves, We are a necessary governing force, I do see that. But, sir, for us, all this Caliph business is nonsense, isn't it sir?"

"Hmm, maybe," said Djemal, fiddling with a pencil on his desk. "Leaving aside the Arabs then, what about all the various Christian sects living amongst us for centuries? The Orthodox, the Jacobites, the Armenians, what's to happen to all of them?"

Selim, losing his stiffness in his involvement in the interest of the discussion and in the keen intellect of his superior, contemplated. He realised that all these problems, all these questions which he had discussed so often with his father, had slipped from his mind as a result of the events of those last few days in April. Now here was a man he looked up to and respected forcing him to start thinking.

"Yes, sir," he said, "the problem does go much deeper than perhaps I first thought."

"Good, well said my son. What about my friend Enver's special bee in his bonnet, Pan-Turanism or whatever they call it, you know, a union of all Turkic people all over from Central Asia to here?"

"Oh no sir, I don't care for any of that at all. It's a total fantasy, isn't it."

"Ah, my lad, there I agree with you totally. Now listen, Selim. I believe you attended for some years at Robert College. You must have met many races there, and you must have met Armenians. I believe that your father, who put on that great concert last April, wasn't it? Or was it March? Anyway, he had many Armenian friends."

Selim's interest quickened, but he remained silent waiting for what was coming, probably the real reason for his presence here.

"Look, the reason I have said all this is to ask you whether the death of your father at Van means that you can't deal with Armenians any more. I want you to undertake for me a somewhat delicate task, which will involve contact with them. But I wouldn't want you to do it if it would be objectionable to you in any way."

"No sir, although I do now think of them as 'enemy', I have no prejudice against them at all, on the contrary," replied Selim.

"Right. Here in town, I have been approached by the Dashnaks—you may have heard of them, they're an Armenian political society, which I might add, I do believe to have terrorist connections."

"Yes, sir, I'm well aware of them."

"Well, I've agreed to meet them and see what they want, and I want you to arrange it. I'll give you an address, and I want you to meet their representatives and bring them to see me here in this office as discreetly as possible. Can you do this for me? It's got to remain a tight secret of course."

"Certainly, sir."

"You have, I suppose, heard of the deportations and killings going on amongst the Armenian population in Eastern Anatolia. Many are being driven towards us in Aleppo, and I believe people are dying in their thousands."

"Only very vaguely, sir," replied Selim. "Nothing like this seems to be happening in Istanbul."

"No, well. . . well yes. . . it's all very difficult. Thank you Lieutenant, you may go now. I'll be in touch with you later."

Over the next few weeks after this conversation, Selim collected two well-dressed and middle-aged Armenian business men from a non-descript address in the bazaar, clearly used only as a meeting place. He then escorted them through the sentries and directly to the inner office of Djemal pasha. Selim never discovered exactly what was discussed between Djemal and these representatives of the Armenian Revolutionary Federation, a legitimate Armenian political party for some, but a treasonable terrorist organisation for others. Either way, Selim understood perfectly well that Djemal was sticking his head out one way or another. However, he never discovered what it was all about.

Selim came to have considerable respect for Djemal as a man of great intelligence. Selim recognised that Djemal, like Selim's own father, was an Ottomanist at heart. Despite having been a member of the CUP right from the start of the Ittihad revolution, he feared the growth of the idea of an exclusive nation-state. Selim, in his many further conversations, could see that Djemal looked at all the wonderful diversity of the peoples of the Empire, and didn't want to lose it. It was the old argument going on, round and round, as to the future for the region.

As the meetings grew longer, Djemal became less open with Selim, who felt that he was now being kept at arm's length by his superior. Eventually, after a few more weeks, Selim heard that he had been promoted to full Captain on the recommendation of Djemal, and been posted to the garrison at Baghdad, facing the advancing British Indian army slowly moving up the Tigris from their outpost in Basra.

Selim left for his new posting, travelling with many other soldiers on the newly completed line to Baghdad—the end run of the Berlin to Baghdad railway that had caused so much conflict between the British and German Empires before the war.

Within days of his arrival at Baghdad, Selim was sent to the unit to which he had been posted several miles down the Tigris. This was part of the Turkish forces facing a British force taken from the Indian army, commanded by General Townshend, which was advancing very slowly up the river heading for Baghdad. General Townshend had arrived at Basra, and had started this advance in that same ill-fated month of April which had also seen the landings at Gallipoli.

The Ottomans had been unable to do anything about the initial British landing. They had only a few weak Arab units there, and they were operating at the end of a long and tortuous supply line. However, as Townshend advanced, until eventually he was only some fifty miles south of Baghdad, it was his supply lines which became longer and equally tortuous, whilst the Turkish supply became easier and correspondingly shorter.

Selim joined an Arab unit, officered of course by Turks, and found himself continuing the slow retreat as the British were drawn further and further away from Basra. Selim was in a countryside of swamps and deserts, where there were no roads of any kind at all. Everything, men and materials, arms and even basic food, had to move up and down the meandering and shallow river Tigris. The conditions were terrible. There were maddening and sickening swarms of flies and mosquitoes. Pestilence and fever was in the air, and the climate was hot, sticky and lethal, for the Turks were used to the more equable north. The Arab soldiers were immune, but on the other side the British were losing more men to disease than to any military action.

So it was that the day came when Selim received a bad wound in the lower part of his arm whilst he was in the front line commanding a company holding back a British patrol advancing ahead of the main army. After the skirmish died down, he retired and had the wound roughly patched up when he got back to the main camp. There were of course no sedatives of any kind, and after drinking a half bottle of raki, he went to his tent to rest.

The next morning Selim awoke in his tent with his face swollen and unable to open his eyes, and with a raging fever. Delirious and often unconscious, death in these circumstances tended to follow within days. His arm was infected and would have to be dealt with. As the British were advancing, though slower and slower each day, Selim had to be evacuated back to Baghdad immediately. There, in the incredibly primitive conditions of the makeshift military hospital, Selim, who had still not regained proper consciousness, was operated on. His increasingly gangrenous arm was cut off just below the elbow.

More dead than alive, it was decided that as, surprisingly, he was still alive and fighting to remain so, that he should be sent back to Constantinople. Once there, if he survived the journey, he could be treated at the military hospital at Uskudar.

Chapter 48

Cairo. Harry, Andre, and the Arab Bureau.

The ship on which Harry had been serving had had several further journeys to and from the Gallipoli staging areas, escorting supply vessels going out to the peninsula and then hospital ships returning loaded and crowded with the wounded. The innumerable dead however, the numbers piling up in that dreadful campaign, remained on the peninsula, often unburied.

Eventually, it was almost inevitable that Harry, a bright and knowledgeable regular officer who had already worked for several months in the Admiralty, would be transferred back to an Intelligence job. Despite his request to be left on active service, he found himself working at the administrative naval headquarters in Alexandria, a building situated near the Montazeh Palace at the far end of the corniche tramline.

Harry had only been stationed there for a few weeks, when he first met a young Polish deserter from the German navy, who was being employed by the Navy as a general translator. They met in the staff canteen, where the young man had approached Harry, who had been sitting alone, and asked to share his table. He introduced himself as Andre Tarkowski. Harry, looking up, saw a strikingly handsome young man with rather hard glittering eyes, but with a warm and charming smile, and, as it later turned out, a wealth of lively and interesting conversation.

Harry smiled, and indicating the empty seat said, "Harry Bridgeman—Intelligence."

Then as he picked up his knife and fork to continue eating, a memory stirred, and he looked up and said, "Hang on, weren't you a radio officer on the *Goeben*?"

Andre looked very startled and glanced away for a moment. He dropped his fork with something of a clatter and bent down taking a rather long time fumbling to pick it up. When he rose, his smile was firmly back in place.

"Why yes, certainly, I was indeed on the *Goeben* at the beginning of the war. I suppose you have seen my file. As a Polish patriot, I found myself in a bit of a difficult moral dilemma. I felt unable to support the German Empire. I left the ship, well... look... not to put any gloss on it, I deserted whilst I was on leave in Constantinople. I eventually made my way here, where I offered my services to the Allies. So, here I am."

He flashed yet another warm and friendly smile. Harry reflected for a moment on the opinion that had been given by the military attaché in the British embassy in Constantinople who had interviewed this man. He recalled how the attaché's report had given a completely different slant on the reasons for Andre's desertion. However, he made no reference to this, saying simply, "Well! Well! What a coincidence! I was on the *Indefatigable*, you know, on that moment the day before war began between England and Germany, when we passed the *Goeben* and the *Breslau* going in the opposite direction."

"I can't believe it," said Andre, "Good heavens, I remember it so well. What a dramatic moment! But how did you know that I was the radio officer on board that ship?"

This time it was Harry's turn to hesitate and consider for a moment before replying. He realised that he could not after all refer to the report he had seen, "Well, old man, as you just said, I have indeed been looking through the files of our employees here, and I noticed yours. Well, you know, because of the fact that you had been on the *Goeben*."

As the days passed, both of them being single and of the same age and without many connections, they became good if not particularly intimate friends. Harry had always been rather shy and diffident in his relationships with others. He was basically lazy when it came to personal contact, and his friends tended to be those who were prepared to make the effort and the running in involving him. Andre appeared to be such a person, an extrovert ready to make all the necessary effort to sustain the relationship on his own. He had a fund of interesting stories, and Harry was fascinated by the confident cosmopolitan atmosphere which always seemed to surround Andre. There was always an exciting almost sexual tension whenever Andre was present. However, he never forgot the comments about Andre's character in the report. He therefore kept a distance between them, which Andre always worked to reduce. This was a reserve, which was both natural to Harry's character in any event, but which he felt to be necessary in the relationship.

Harry made no effort to try to find out more about Andre, but in due course Andre himself told him how there had recently been a personal tragedy in his life. He explained that while hiding in Constantinople and waiting for the embassy to issue travel documents for him, he had fallen deeply in love with a Greek girl. Harry, who remembered well all the details of the report said nothing. However, he was relieved when Andre openly and without any guile talked about this aspect of his life, as it cleared up the slight query as to what had happened.

"I and Elena—oh sorry, yes, that was her name—got the necessary travel documents, and as this was just before war broke out between the British and the Ottoman Empires, we managed to make it here to Egypt. Ah! Harry, what a wonderful period for me that turned out to be. Here we were in the middle of this terrible war, living just for each other. An idyllic moment in the midst of terrible events."

"Gosh!" said Harry, all his rather boyish naive romanticism aflame. "What an experience! And what happened?"

"Terrible, Harry, terrible. I'd been working late at the navy office, and I came back soon after midnight to our little flat. When I got in, Elena was fast asleep, or so I thought. However, I sensed that something was wrong, and when I came to try and wake her, I found, oh my God, Harry, that she appeared to be dead or at least totally unconscious."

Harry stared at him.

"I immediately contacted a doctor I knew who lived close by—a Swiss, Doctor Gurstein. The doctor did rush round as I was so distraught. He said that she had had a massive heart attack. At least she hadn't suffered, as it must have happened in her sleep. God, Harry, you can imagine how much I was devastated. Thousands are dying daily in this awful war, but one death, like this, inevitably affects you more than a thousand others."

Andre buried his head in his hands, as Harry somewhat clumsily tried to comfort him by patting him on the back. But there was something—something about this event—which troubled Harry. He could not put his finger on it as to why. In due course he made a point of looking up and seeing the death certificate. He then felt ashamed, blaming his suspicions on the wartime atmosphere, as it all seemed quite clear. The certificate referred clearly to a coronary attack, and was duly signed by a registered practitioner—a Doctor Gurstein—who appeared to have lived in Alexandria for some years.

Harry watched and wondered as the horrific death toll of the Gallipoli campaign got worse and worse. Nothing that was tried ever seemed to go right. Harry recalled all those eager young Australians on that landing craft with him on that April day earlier in the year. He wondered how many of them were still alive. Even then, however, despite his sensitivity, it still never crossed his mind to question the morality of the war.

It was well into the winter of the year that the Gallipoli campaign was eventually wound up by a brilliant evacuation during which almost a quarter of a million Allied soldiers were evacuated in the very face of the enemy and hardly a single life was lost. It was the only moment of glory in the whole mishandled campaign. Harry had of course long since lost any illusions of the glory of war. Nevertheless, he was thrilled by the sheer military brilliance of the event.

A group of young Englishmen, imbued with romantic ideas about Arab sheiks riding through the desert in flowing robes, were organised in what was known as the 'Arab Bureau' in Cairo. They were obsessed with trying to engineer an Arab revolt against the Ottomans. Their chosen method was to act through Sheriff Hussein of the Hejaz, the Ottoman nominee ruler of that province, which included the two Muslim holy cities of Mecca and Medina.

The Ottoman governor who would be most involved if such an outbreak could be engineered, would be Djemal Pasha—the governor of Greater Syria, and of all the Arab provinces of the Empire. As it would after all be the Navy's task to give whatever logistical support would be necessary, if an Arab revolt could be instigated, Harry began a concentrated research into the character of this man, known to be one of the three principle leaders of the Ittihad. Harry also began a consideration, on behalf of the Navy, of the whole Arab situation within the empire.

Harry had had the same basic educational background as these young officers of the Arab Bureau. They were all products of the English upper-middle class educational system—Oxbridge and ex-public school boys, all with a strictly classical education. However, Harry was different. It was not just that he had become disillusioned by his experiences at Gallipoli. The adolescent conflict with his father and his mild rebellion against the attempt to push him into the army, already separated him somewhat from his class peers. The fact that he had studied science, rather than the classics, also gave him a further fresher outlook than his contemporaries.

Harry found himself questioning the romantic visions of the young men of the Arab Bureau. As he researched the position more thoroughly, he saw clearly that what real strength there was amongst the Arabs, lay in the great Arab towns of the fertile crescent—not with any flamboyant idea of hard-riding Bedouin tribes of Arabia. He could also see that when it came to the crunch, a thinking Arab from these great cities would always in the last resort tolerate a foreign Muslim Imperial ruler, however moribund, above a foreign Christian one.

It was in the middle of all this ferment of ideas and proposals passing between the young Oxbridge officers of the Arab Bureau in Cairo and the more careful Naval Intelligence Services in Alexandria that Harry was informed that a representative in Cairo of the Armenian Revolutionary Federation—the Dashnak party—had contacted the High Commission with an extraordinary proposal supposedly emanating directly from Djemal Pasha himself.

By this time, it was known that Harry had become the Navy's expert on the person of Djemal Pasha and the Arab dimension in the Ottoman Empire. He was accordingly invited to go to Cairo to be at the meeting with the Armenians—together with Army Intelligence, officers from the Arab Bureau, and other experts on the question of the future of the Ottoman Empire.

On the day of the meeting Harry took the tram along the corniche to the railway station. He left for the three hour train journey through the lush Egyptian delta to Cairo. He stared out of the windows, which were always kept spotlessly clean, despite the soot and smoke of the engine. The train passed by the ancient panorama of the fellahin working in the fields, unchanged for centuries, with the patient camels and donkeys slowly plodding round and round the picturesque water-wheels, tended by a small boy with a stick. A few looked up as the train passed. 'What great War?' they might have asked.

A most extraordinary meeting then took place in a room at the British High Commission. There were several young English officers there, all ready to carve up the Ottoman Empire in their own image. Present also was Lord Kitchener's current favourite and representative, Sir Mark Sykes. There was in addition a young official representing the Foreign Office, two young officers—classical scholars from the Arab Bureau, an Army officer and Harry himself.

Harry knew that on his return he would have to give a clear report to his superiors. He was never very articulate and clear thinking when he had to speak directly on any matter. Like so many Englishmen in his time and class he was often more articulate on paper than in direct speech. Accordingly, it was his usual practice to jot down in his notebooks like a diary entry, his entirely personal impressions of what had occurred in any event on which he had to report. He duly followed this system, and wrote down his impressions as he returned to Alexandria later in the day on the evening train.

> "I went straight from the station, with its usual bustle and pandemonium to the High Commission building. It was surprisingly not particularly heavily guarded, and I was directed without much questioning to a large boardroom where the meeting was to take place. This looked out on the gardens of the compound and was cool and shaded by blinds. It had electric fans in the ceiling, which I had never seen before, and a wonderful mahogany table in the middle of the room.

There were several people in the room already when I arrived. I remember in particular the three young men from the Arab Bureau—an Oxford Archaeologist, Philip Graves a journalist from the Times, and another young officer, Thomas Lawrence. However the most important person there was Sir Mark Sykes—a Tory MP—who was probably the oldest person there, but who was not much more than thirty-five. He is a great expert on Ottoman affairs, and is a protege of Lord Kitchener. I believe that, whilst he is a good and amusing talker—he has an easy and fluent turn of phrase that I envy—he tends to hold very strong opinions and is impatient of any opposing point of view. He is a committed Roman Catholic, a convert, and I believe that that factor is an important part of his make-up.

After introductions and some general discussions between us, two Armenians were brought into the room and given seats at the end of the table. One was another young man—a scowling, aggressive, dark-haired individual who introduced himself as Aris from the city of Van. He looked as if he was about to explode throughout the whole proceedings. The other, the only man present over forty years old, was a tired looking grey-haired merchant who introduced himself as Sarkis Papazian. It was he who opened the discussion when he informed us all that party members in Damascus had informed him, in great secrecy, that Djemal Pasha had indicated to them that he was prepared to act to overthrow the current Ottoman government, if he could be supported by the Allies.

"How did you get this information" asked one of the officers.

It was the young Aris who replied, speaking rather brusquely.

"I, myself was present at one of the last discussions between my party's leader in Damascus, and Djemal himself. We were regularly taken to see him in his private office by a member of his staff. I brought the letters from our party members addressed to my friend Baron Sarkis here, which set out Djemal's proposals, and which authorise him on behalf of the party to approach the Allied authorities."

"It appears," then continued Sarkis, "that Djemal wishes to distance himself from the terrible massacres and deportations of Armenians currently taking place in Anatolia. He is prepared to act to save those surviving Armenians still in the area, if he can get allied support."

One of the Arab bureau's young men present then shook his head, and looking directly at Sarkis said, "So, why should we be that interested in saving Armenians? Djemal's got it all wrong if he thinks that that is any sort of priority in Allied thinking. In fact, it is providing amazingly good propaganda for us against the Central Powers."

I have to say that I do tend to agree with what the young man said, but it wasn't very tactful in the circumstances, and could have been put more gently. I felt rather uncomfortable. As it was, after this comment, the scowling Aris jumped up and was about to say something when Sarkis sharply pulled him down and muttered something to him in Armenian. I've learnt a few words of Armenian while in Alex, and all he said simply was, "my boy, sit down and keep calm."

The old man then continued with a tired sigh.

"Look, I believe that the same suggestions proposed by Djemal have been passed on to the Russian foreign ministry, and Sazonov has already indicated that the Russian government are interested. Djemal has proposed, with allied help to march on Constantinople, depose the Sultan and the current government, and set up a new alternative regime."

The young foreign office official, who to my mind had been looking more and more ill at ease, at this point nodded his head and said:

"Yes I can confirm that we have indeed heard something on these lines from the Russians. The proposal seems to be to create a new Empire, including a Turkish Anatolia, a greater Syria, an autonomous Christian Armenia, and a Kurdistan, all under a new Imperial dynasty - I suspect probably Djemal himself."

At this point Sykes, making sure that he had everyone's attention by rapping on the table, started speaking for the first time.

"Our political masters would not agree. Our friends the French will insist on taking most of Syria, and frankly we have our own eyes on Mesopotamia at the very least. Forget Djemal's proposals, we can finish off the Ottomans without his help."

Sykes then stood up and surveyed us all as if he was going to give a speech in the House of Commons. He totally ignored the two Armenians, sitting somewhat disconsolately at the end of the table, and said, as indeed I'm sure he will report later in writing to Kitchener, and as I have carefully noted, word for word:

"Never mind the natives, Armenians, Jacobites, Maronites, whatever. This ramshackle middle-eastern Empire must cease to be. Smyrna can become Greek; Adalia, Italian; Cilicia and Syria, French; Filistine and Mesopotamia, British, and everything else can go to the Russians, yes, even including Constantinople itself. Gentlemen, I shall sing a *Te Deum* in Constantinople in the Santa Sophia, and a *Nunc Dimittis* in Jerusalem in the mosque of Omar. We'll even be prepared to sing it in Polish or Armenian or Welsh, in honour of those gallant little nations, bless their bleeding hearts."

I have to say that I was frankly surprised. It was not the lack of empathy or the hard-edged rudeness that struck me. It was the fact that it was so unnecessary. Surely, simple silence would have sufficed. However, perhaps I'm wrong, and it might indeed be kinder to be clear about our own priorities right from the start. In any event, I looked around and it didn't seem to have worried any of the others round the table, who smiled, but did have the grace not to look at the two strangers at the end of the table.

Aris stood up, fists clenched and eyes smouldering, but once again Sarkis was too fast for him. He too stood, and holding Aris by the arm tightly, in order to make sure that he said nothing, turned and said to everyone in the room:

"Gentlemen, we have carried out our task. No doubt you will have your own ways of communicating with Djemal Pasha if you want to. For us, of course, what was important was the possibility of finding some means of bringing to an end the terrible murders and deaths affecting the whole of our population in central and eastern Anatolia. I see and accept, though sadly, that your priorities are naturally different, But gentlemen, bear in mind that you have not as yet conquered the lands you are blithely dividing up amongst yourselves. You may well, in all your internal intrigues, and your conspiracies with the French, be storing up great problems for the future in this vital area. Beware, gentlemen, beware of the quagmire you may be creating for future generations."

I expected the young Aris to come out with some more remarks, but the two Armenians then left without another word. I returned on the 7.00 pm train."

Harry did not record that after the Armenians left, Sykes and the young men of the Arab Bureau then spent the next hour discussing and finally dismissing the Djemal proposals. This was then followed by a further happy hour which they all spent drawing lines across the map of the Ottoman Empire, as their young fancies and romantic ideals led them. For all of them, and in a sense, despite his greater awareness, this included Harry, this land was a mere blank playground for their romantic and heroic impulses, not a place where people had lived and died for generations.

Harry returned to Alexandria on the evening train, bringing with him these notes of the meeting. This was written in Harry's own rather cryptic shorthand, which would not mean much to most people. Nevertheless, Harry knew they should be kept carefully, and he put them in a small file in the bottom drawer of his desk, after preparing and submitting his much more official fair copy to his superiors.

It was about a week later that he came into his office to find Andre waiting to see him, as he often did these days. Andre had been sitting at his desk in his chair as Harry walked in. Andre rose immediately with a ready grin and started his usual friendly chat. That afternoon, when looking through the Djemal papers, he imagined that they were no longer in the order that he had left them. This worried him, but then he realised that it must be his own memory at fault. In any event, to be on the safe side, he arranged to have them burnt.

Chapter 49

Constantinople. Karekin and Aram return.

Seated at a coffee table in a shabby run-down part of the city, close by the Kapali Charshi—the Grand Bazaar—was a tall, middle-aged, and bald-headed gentleman. He was dressed in good clothes which had however seen much better days. The fez worn on his head was faded and rather shapeless. A careful look at his hands would have shown any curious onlooker that this was a man unused to any kind of hard physical labour.

Karekin Avakian sat, eking out his one tiny cup of coffee to make it last, and waiting for the return of his friend Doctor Aram Manuelian, who had left him only an hour ago. He sat pondering on the events of the last year since he and Aram had jumped out of the train in Konia. It had been a time consisting of short moments of high tension interspersed with long periods of intense loneliness and boredom. He fiddled with his teaspoon as he thought of those last few weeks before they finally had had to leave Konia.

Fiddling with his coffee-cup and pretending to sip the cold dregs, Karekin was now beginning to get anxious as to Aram's continual failure to turn up as promised. Karekin thought again of that first year in Konia, and how news had soon begun filtering in of the raping and killing going on in the eastern vilayets. Sivas, it seemed, had been emptied of Armenians. Erzurum had become a ghost town. Everywhere the news had been of the dead and dying on the roads going south and east.

Karekin knew that the Russians had finally blundered their way into Van, relieving the encircled Armenians. However, within the year they were in retreat once again, and here too the remaining ordinary Armenian civil population had died in their tens of thousands, whilst the professional national revolutionaries had slipped away, as they always do in such situations.

Thinking back to Konia, Karekin recalled the worry that had crept in, as the police had started making their rounds, arresting one or two, and marking those houses owned by Armenians.

In fact, as soon as Djelal Bey had been dismissed, and the new governor was on the point of arrival, Karekin had immediately realised that their refuge was on the point of disappearing and that they would have to think again. In the interminable discussions Aram had thought that the best place to go was Smyrna with its large untouched Greek and Armenian population. It was Karekin who had made the startling suggestion that they should return to Constantinople, under their new assumed names. Karekin, still sitting at the coffee table, recalled the final critical conversation,

"Look, Aram, neither of us have ever been to Smyrna. We have no connections there, we don't know our way around, and being such a sophisticated city we won't find it as easy to melt into the local populace as we've found here. Let's slip back to Bolis. We can't of course go to our old haunts, but so long as we're not arrested and our true names come out, we're safer there than anywhere else. It's a big city, we know how to avoid the police and where to go, and above all, there are no deportation orders there."

"You're totally crazy, Karekin. If we're recognised in the streets by any policeman, or even by one of our own Turkish acquaintances, it could be immediate imprisonment or even worse."

"But Aram, of course we wouldn't be going to Makrikoy. In the city we wouldn't be strolling into Tokatlian's for lunch, or going to places where we would meet business friends. Above all, we would know exactly where to hide out in the poorer quarters of the town."

Karekin reflected that it had not, after all, taken too much argument to persuade Aram to a course of action which was so much to his heart. He reflected that everyone from Constantinople—the Bolsetsi—always retained an inner love of the city whatever the circumstances of their departure.

Karekin also thought of the anxious attempt they had made to persuade the young couple with whom they had been lodging to come with them.

"Forget your sweet shop, your little house, your friends, everything you hold dear—your actual lives are now in danger," was their continual refrain. The young couple, however, could still not accept that they might suddenly have to leave the place that had been their home all their life, and in which they had grown up next door to each other. Karekin reminded them of all the news coming from the east. They merely shook their heads in disbelief, commenting that this was not the Ottoman way, that their parents had lived in Konia all their lives, that they had friends, Turk as well as Armenian in the town. In the end Karekin sighed, made over the shop and all the remaining goods to them, and wishing them luck, he and Aram had left.

With a sizeable amount of cash, reconverted into gold coins, and with the battered old suitcase still holding their old, but now cleaned, city suits, Aram and Karekin had got seats in a carriage going to Bursa, from where they had then travelled on to Yalova and got a boat to Bolis. Karekin recalled that he had spent enormous energy persuading Aram not to go in the train which ran directly to Constantinople, which would have been much quicker and a good deal more comfortable. Trains, he had pointed out, were always patrolled and controlled by efficient police guards, whilst the gendarmerie on the roads were lax and always open to a bit of financial persuasion. Karekin had also made sure that they travelled in a carriage with mainly Turks on board, not that there were that many Armenians left in the area anyway.

"Well, well, Karekin, now that we are here," said a voice, "what are we going to do in the long run? Our cash isn't going to last for ever, and one thing is obvious—there is no way that you are going to be able to open up any little business."

Karekin looked up from contemplating his coffee grounds with relief, as Aram, already talking, sat down at the table. The waiter, with his dirty white cloth over his arm, hurried up thankful to get a further order from this table at last.

"Effendim?"

Karekin ordered two coffees, one sweet and one without sugar.

"First things first, Aram. Did you get to see your partner, at your old surgery?"

"No, Karekin. It's boarded up and there is a note on the door saying that the surgery is closed, but that it will be re-opening again soon with new doctors. The note looks fairly new, so I suppose Avedis couldn't manage on his own and has recently sold up. I went off to the library to take a look at a list of current medical practitioners—that's why I'm late by the way—but Avedis is not listed anywhere. I'm supposing that he has either retired or perhaps even died. He wasn't too young. He certainly isn't living any more in the flat above the practice, as that too is empty."

Karekin nodded and said, "You know I do agree with you that we're not going to be able to attempt here in Bolis the sort of thing we managed in Konia. I will be recognised sooner or later wherever we open a shop or anything like that."

"Yes, but look here, Karekin, what about your family and the business. If I know Armineh she might well still be managing to keep your business going. Now that we are settled in, what about contacting her discreetly."

"Aram, whilst the present situation continues, I simply can't take the chance of putting my family at risk by appearing at home. If they are discovered harbouring a man officially arrested and deported, they too will all be thrown out, imprisoned or worse. No, for the moment that's out. Armineh knows I'm alive and somewhere in or near Konia—that's enough. I must pick carefully the moment I make myself known to them, if I ever do at the moment. I'll do that only when I know there'll be no danger to them."

"All right, I do see your point, Karekin. However, honestly, whilst it seems increasingly clear that the days of our poor old Empire are numbered, the war could still last another year or more, and meanwhile how are we going to manage. Living here in Bolis is a good deal more expensive than it was in Konia, and sooner or later our cash is going to run out."

"What about your flat in Makrikoy, Aram. Surely no one will have taken that over. Do you still have your key?"

"Yes, as it happens, but Karekin isn't that a ridiculous risk? We can't possibly live in Makrikoy."

"No, probably not, but you must have some valuables of one kind or another in the flat, things we might be able to sell. Your spare cash might still be there."

"I doubt it. I had a Greek maid. She was a nice girl, but if the caretaker has let her in with his master key, after cleaning up, believing that I was gone for good, she would probably have taken whatever she could find."

"Yes, perhaps, but we have to find out. We've been here a week now, it's time we began looking about and considering the future. I've grown a moustache and my wispy beard is coming along nicely—I doubt if anyone in Makrikoy would recognise me. Actually, you know, I never had more than a few acquaintances there, not in the same way as business circles in the city."

"Karekin the position is different for me. I might well be seen by one of my several old patients in the town, and they would certainly recognise me, even if I grew a beard. Being arrested a second time would almost certainly mean death for either of us. Think about it—escaped deportee, false papers—there would be no hope at all. Good heavens, the caretaker alone will be enough to ruin us."

Karekin considered for a moment,

"All right, here's the plan. First we buy some flowers from one of those smart shops on the Grande Rue de Pera which do personal deliveries. We get them sent to one of the ladies in your block—you must surely remember the name of one or other of them. Pick one who might not be too curious as to why she has received flowers from an anonymous donor. Fine. When ordering the flowers we ask to speak to the boy who is going to make the delivery on the excuse that the building is difficult to find and we need to give him directions—it's often done. Then, here's the tricky bit, we ask him to find out the name of the caretaker who lives in the basement, and to give us a description if he sees him. We tell him that he'll get a good tip, and that we'll call the next day."

"Where does that get us?"

"Right, first it tells us whether the same caretaker is still there. You know how often they change. If it's the same man, it will have to be a risky night job. But if it's a new man, we can bluff our way in during the day. We might even be able to use the flat again if we play our cards right."

"Karekin, you know you've got a criminal mind. I think it's terribly chancy, but then almost everything we've been at has been risky throughout. All right, let's do it. I do in fact have some money hidden under a loose floorboard which might well still be there. Look, I know that I'll start worrying and thinking of everything that can go wrong if this drags on, so let's start right now this very afternoon, before I start getting cold feet. I know absolutely the right flower shop, and the lively Jewish widow on the floor below mine will adore getting the flowers. She thinks that every male who sees her is immediately heavily smitten and she'll not be the least surprised or raise any objections getting some nice flowers delivered. Come on. Pay up, let's go!"

Chapter 50

Uskudar. Olga and Mikael.

Olga could not get the frail and rather prickly Mikael out of her mind. As the days passed she often encountered Loris in the long dreary and increasingly dirty wards of the old hospital. Any cleaning that was being attempted was not very effective, and the hospital probably looked little different from the days of the Crimean War.

Olga sensed very quickly that Loris did not approve of her. She began to try on all that rather artificial flirtatious charm which had been her stock-in-trade prior to the change that had come into her life with her first contact with Selim. To her surprise and irritation, no amount of the stunning smiles, the sympathetic eye contact, nor any of her other weapons, made any difference. Loris remained indifferent, indeed even hostile, towards her. He never volunteered any information about Mikael, and made a point of telling her that Mikael remained very ill and needed to be left alone.

Nevertheless, Olga took the trouble of regularly going to the enormous ward in which Mikael languished. She would sit by the side of his bed and chat to him whenever she had the time. When she was with Mikael she felt no need to exercise any artificial charm but chatted freely and with spirit, enjoying the straight pleasure of mutual discovery. Slowly Mikael began to recover his strength, although Dr. Turhan said that his kidneys had been permanently damaged. Whenever he felt stronger, and if Olga had any free time, they would walk together, shuffling along the hospital corridors, she in her ugly, regulation uniform, he in a shabby threadbare dressing gown.

A rather unlikely affection began to grow between this aggressive but insecure, lower-class Armenian young man, and the confident, sophisticated, upper-middle-class Olga. Class distinctions in the Ottoman world were never anything like those in the highly class-conscious West. The Turks never had any entrenched, hereditary, ruling elite. Indeed, until the eighteenth century, most of the Turkish Viziers and ruling Pashas were technically 'slaves' of the Sultan, and rose and fell independent of family background.

However, there was always a considerable difference in terms of education and sophistication between the wealthy professional and merchant classes of the cities on the one hand, and the porters, workers and small shopkeepers on the other. On top of that, at the same time, neither side of that divide within the cities took into any sort of account the vast hard-working Anatolian peasants of the countryside of whichever race.

Day by day, regardless of any of these differences, Mikael and Olga became more and more friendly and intimate with each other. They now began walking hand-in-hand when outside the hospital in the grounds. Olga, lonely at work, and with the rest of the family at home more and more involved in their own affairs, found a great source of strength in the growing relationship.

It was well into the winter when Loris told Mikael that he would be going to stay for a few days at the house of Dr. Turhan in Stamboul. It appeared that the doctor was due to attend a conference of army medical officers at the War Ministry. He had been asked to bring with him a secretary to take notes of what was discussed and any decisions that might be made. He had asked for Loris to take on that task.

Mikael had been continuing to use Loris' little room as he grew stronger, although he was beginning to try to be careful to use it only when Loris was on duty, so as to leave it free for him when he got in from work. On this particular occasion Loris came in early, insisted on Mikael remaining, and confirmed that he would be away for about a week as from next morning. When Mikael rose from the bed on which they were both sitting, Loris also rose to say goodbye. Loris held and embraced him fiercely, cheek pressed to cheek. As Mikael eventually drew away, in order to leave, Loris' lips appeared quite accidentally to pass fleetingly across Mikael's lips. Mikael turned away, slightly taken aback and embarrassed, and opened the door. He looked back, smiled and said, "Well Loris, goodbye till next Sunday.

Do you realise that we've seen each other almost every single day, at least once during the day, for several months? It'll be nice for you to have a change from my incessant company."

"I don't want a change," replied Loris rather sharply, his eyes smouldering with some emotion that Mikael could not place.

"Come, come. Good God, Loris, you must surely be totally fed up with this bloody building. Just crossing the straits is going to be great for you. Look, visit our old haunts, have a good time. Right, well then, till you get back." Mikael smiled, walked out, and shuffled back to his ward.

It was two days later that Olga, off duty for a few hours at last, came to Mikael's ward early in the afternoon for their usual stroll and found him already dressed and sitting on his bed.

"Well, well, Mikael. How are you feeling? No dressing gown today. You're dressed. You need new trousers, you know. They're pretty scruffy. Actually Mikael, my dear, forget what I just said, you look better than I've seen you for some time. Your cheeks are all, er, coloured, and your eyes seem brighter. What's the doctor said?"

"Hey, Olga hanum, come and sit on my bed for a change!" called out the soldier in the bed opposite, who had only one arm and one leg.

Olga flashed him her wonderful, but meaningless, smile and turned to Mikael.

"Well, let's go, or do you want to sit here?"

"No, no," said Mikael. "I've got a surprise for you. Let's go and have a chat in Loris' room."

"No thanks," replied Olga with a flash of anger. "You know perfectly well that for some reason he can't stand me, and for my part I don't want to go up there and have to face up to his snooty disapproval when he arrives."

"No, look Olga, Loris has gone away for a week. . . we won't be disturbed, we can have the room all to ourselves."

Olga, startled, looked at him long and hard. Mikael stared back at her—eye to eye—with that slightly contemptuous arrogant stare of Turkish young men everywhere in the Empire. This was the look which Olga had found so refreshingly absent in Selim. There was a long moment of silence between them, though all the noise and hubbub of the cavernous ward continued as before all around them. Olga thought back to her actual words to Nerissa when she had said of Selim, describing him to her, that he had none of that hard arrogance of most educated Ottoman young men.

Olga would be eighteen soon. She knew perfectly well that Mikael was not seeking privacy just 'to have a chat' as he put it. Olga saw a tall and thin man, slightly stooped due to the long period of pain from his ruptured insides. His moustache—Enver style—was not now so cock-a-hoop, and his black eyes looked sadder, and had deep lines at the sides. However they still flashed with pride and latent violence. Olga felt aroused.

"Very well, Mikael; but look, I can't be away too long. I have to be back on duty again soon," she said, lying without any qualms at all.

Mikael was in a sense cursed with this arrogant expression that somewhat belied his real character, which was a good deal more insecure than appeared on the surface. He tried to stride out as they walked through the long corridors, but he soon had to give up. When they arrived, Mikael shut the door behind him as they walked in. Olga turned and found herself clasped urgently and fiercely round the waist. With the one sigh, "Oh Olga," she felt Mikael's thin lips pressed with rough passion against her own full ones.

This was Olga's first real kiss. It was totally different to that wonderful moment when her lips and those of Selim touched and quivered for a second in the basement boiler room at the College. This was passion—she knew it—her body flowed with it, and she wanted Mikael to continue, to force her, to press harder, anything.

This was not Mikael's first kiss, nor his first sexual experience—but the emotion accompanying the moment was new for him. His body urgently stirred and he felt he would burst with desire. He had experienced these feelings before, and recognised them—nevertheless over and above this, he felt a tenderness and affection which had not accompanied any previous experience.

They sank onto the bed—there was no place to stand in any case. Olga shifted and Mikael naturally came across her. Olga was fully dressed in her Nurse's uniform, and Mikael was wearing a shirt and his own shabby trousers for the first time since coming to the hospital.

The kiss continued, as Mikael got more and more excited, and as Olga squirmed and felt his pressure. But as Mikael's hands strayed, and as he began fumbling both at his dress and hers, Olga came to her senses. A part of her was desperate for Mikael to go on, to loosen her clothing, to impose on her. Another part of her, however, knew it was impossible. She had to hold back, urgently and at once. Already she had allowed matters to go far beyond any possible reasonable level. A kiss was indeed in these days becoming more and more permissible, though even now, not of course in the circles in which Olga lived. But more than that was out of the question.

Olga moved her free hand, and held the busy hand of Mikael hard and tight. Mikael responded at once to her unspoken command. They remained clasped together. They continued to kiss and explore each other's lips—but it was not going to go any further. Olga sensed in herself both relief and frustration, both at the same time and rather difficult to deal with.

Eventually they lay side by side on the bed, and talked about the war, about nursing, about Olga's family, and about Makrikoy. Mikael's feelings got deeper and more and more centred on Olga herself, and less on his own desire. They remained together far longer than Olga had envisaged. She seemed to have forgotten having said that she would have to go on duty again.

Meetings in Loris' room at the top of the hospital began to take place daily, often only for as short as half an hour. Mikael now came looking for Olga, whereas Olga began trying imperceptibly to cool down the relationship.

After several days of increasing contact between them, Loris returned. The meetings ceased abruptly. For many days there was no question of any meeting between them—even the previous walks together stopped. But Mikael became more and more obsessed with his desire to speak to Olga and touch her—if only just to hold her hand. At last, one day, he caught her in the corridor outside his ward.

"Olga, you've been avoiding me."

"Not at all, Mikael, my dearest. But look, Loris is back and you know he hates me for some reason. You've been seeing him and I am not welcome, you know that."

"Olga, my love, my soul. I think of you all the time. I want you—you must know that I love you. I'm getting better day by day. I'll be able to walk out of here soon. Heaven knows what is happening around us, or where we're all going to be when this bloody war ends. But look, sooner or later it will—sooner or later we'll be picking up our lives again. Will you wait for me Olga? Will you marry me when I am in a position to marry? I love you, my darling, I love you. It's not just desire. I want to live with you always. Say something Olga, for heaven's sake say something!"

Olga looked at this man. She thought of her family and her parents' reactions. She reflected on her own feelings, on the good qualities of this man six years older than her, of those moments of thoughtless anger and violence of which she was well aware he was capable. She then suddenly remembered that no thought of her parents or her situation had ever entered her head once during the relationship with Selim.

"Mikael, I don't know what to say. My dearest, we're living in such uncertain times, and in such uncertain circumstances. Is it right to enter into such long-term promises? You know we can't marry or even think of anything like that until this war is over and you yourself get back some health. All I can say to you is that I have no feelings for anybody else other than you."

Olga leant forward and gave Mikael a warm kiss on his lips. She then turned and walked away without another word.

That night, as she lay awake in the nurses' dormitory, she reflected that even at that moment, when a young man had bared his soul to her, and begged for a word from her, she had still failed to come out with those vital three words—'I love you.' Why not? Wasn't that what she had felt during that first passionate kiss? Olga mentally shrugged and turned and fell into an untroubled sleep.

It was on the very next day that Olga's situation complicated itself once again. On that day she was on duty doing the rounds of the officers' wards with the duty doctor, Dr. Fadil. The officers' wards were both smaller and cleaner than the great dirty white-tiled wards of the ordinary soldiers. They moved slowly from bed to bed, as the doctor inspected and the nurse, in this case Olga, took notes or administered the doctor's recommendations.

Olga suddenly stopped as they approached the next man. She found herself staring at an officer with one festering and badly bandaged half arm, and whose whole body was shaking with what appeared to be malarial fever. It was Selim Kemal.

Chapter 51

Anatolia. Raffi hangs on.

When Raffi left his home early in the morning after that terrifying moment when he had passed in front of the police dressed as a woman, he had no clear idea of where he was going to go. He knew by then that the areas west of Caesaria had not been as badly affected by the deportation and killings as the lands to the east up to the Russian frontier. Furthermore, at the back of his mind there was always the thought of his brother Vahan, seemingly still completely safe in Istanbul. So his first thought was to go westwards to Konia, which also had the advantage of being on the railway line to the capital.

As so often happens a minor and purely accidental incident changed this plan. Raffi had always been 'streetwise' and sensitive to the customs and habits of the town. In particular, he knew how to avoid the unwelcome attentions of policemen and officials of any kind. Accordingly, when he got to the dusty square where the carriages and lorries set off for other towns, he knew how to keep a low profile as he milled about amongst the crowd.

Even at this early hour the square was filled with horse dung. There were almost as many animals as there were humans—chickens trussed together, donkeys carrying heavy loads, lambs and goats—some of which were actually about to be loaded on the older carriages accompanying villagers returning home. There were also old, badly maintained, petrol lorries carrying passengers and yet more animals to destinations further afield. Everything and everybody were all mixed up together in an atmosphere of complete confusion, as well as noisy and friendly bustle.

Raffi had already pinpointed exactly where the four or five policemen on duty were standing. He also thankfully noted that he did not recognise any of them. They were ignoring most of the villagers with their chickens and other produce. However, Raffi could see that they were looking at the papers of anyone dressed at all smartly, or any young men who might appear to be of military age.

Raffi drifted, checking on the destinations and passengers of the lorries and coaches going westwards. It was while he was at this task that his eye caught another young man ahead of him who appeared familiar in some way. As Raffi came closer, he saw a thin and very frail-looking young man, scarcely more than a boy, with a pale almost consumptive look in his face. The lad was clearly nervous, and sooner or later, thought Raffi to himself, he would catch the eye of one of the policemen.

Raffi was just about to turn away when he saw and heard the young man ask the price of a 'simit', the round hard bagel which was a speciality of the town. At that same moment he also suddenly recognised that this was a boy, whose name he did not know, who had attended at the same school as he. This lad was if anything older than he was, but had always looked younger. As he walked forward, he saw the boy's eyes go up under his upper eyelids, and he began to sway, clearly about to faint. Raffi did not hesitate—he was almost alongside by then anyway—and grabbed him as he fell, holding him up and calling out so that at least all those in the immediate neighbourhood could hear, "Abdul, Abdul, stand up! Are you all right? Allah be praised, he's only ill. He just needs a little air."

The simit vendor, who thought he had been just about to make a sale of one of his products, was anxious to help. Holding him on the other side, they carried him and sat him down on a rickety chair at one of the decrepit old cafés dotted around the edges of the square. Raffi, checking carefully that the commotion had passed unnoticed, paid for a couple of simits, and handed one of them to the young man who was just recovering.

"I am sorry, effendi, to be such a nuisance. I do thank you. I will be all right now and on my way," said the boy rising to go.

Raffi not only could now recognise the lad but, once noticed, the tell-tale features of an Armenian became increasingly obvious. The lighter hair, curly rather than straight and black, the large round eyes, and the long face, all gave it away. There was in this case also a haunted expression. Before he could run off, Raffi leant forward.

"*Hay yem* (I am Armenian)," he whispered, whereupon the lad collapsed back onto the old cane chair and covered his face with his hands.

Raffi called out for a large coffee and passed both the simits to the young man, who began eating them eagerly. In a surprisingly short time, Raffi learnt that the lad was already sixteen, though he looked, fortunately for him, much younger. His name was Dikran. He had left the town with the one or two that remained of his family many weeks ago at the time of the first deportation orders. The guards allocated to this particular group had melted away after the first few days, and the wretched column had been continuously attacked, hunted down, robbed, and killed as it made its way slowly through the desolate countryside. At one particularly vicious encounter, Dikran had lost the last of his family and had decided to escape from the column almost entirely consisting of women, children and old men—and which was diminishing day by day.

On running off, Dikran had realised that they had not after all got very far from the town although they had been walking for days. He had decided to make his way back to the town. He had been sleeping in cellars and the empty houses of the old abandoned Armenian quarter. However, he had no money, and he had been slowly starving, living off what scraps and rubbish he could find. He had not dared to try and get any work as he had no papers at all.

It turned out that Dikran had been told that well to the south of Caesaria, where the main railway line to the Arab vilayets passed through the Taurus mountains, the big German company, still finishing the Berlin to Baghdad railway, were taking on workers without asking any questions. If he could get there, he had been told, he would be safe for some time, as the Turkish government was very anxious to have the railway line completed. Only the tunnels through the Taurus needed to be completed for the connection finally to be made between the great Arab cities of the Levant and Constantinople.

Raffi had also heard this, and he added the information that the government was even allowing army deserters to work there unmolested, so important was the project to the war effort. From Raffi's point of view it was completely in the wrong direction. However, the two boys—for after all, despite the way that they had had to grow up so quickly, that's all they were—talked and made plans together, and so Raffi became more enthusiastic.

Raffi felt excited and was stimulated and ready for danger in a way that he had not felt during all those difficult days at home. Whilst not a great thinker like his brother Vahan, he had been sensitive to the needs of all the women in the house, and this had had the effect of making him depressed and nervous. Now, for the first time, he had a male friend of his own age. They found themselves bouncing ideas off each other in a more childish, but a more relaxed, manner.

The first task was to get to the railhead. Raffi changed the first of his precious gold coins, and the boys paid a lorry driver who was carrying passengers to Ulukishlar railway station. Buying some bread and kebabs for the journey, Raffi and Dikran stood the whole way in the back of the lorry as it bounced and swayed its way along the terrible roads to the railway line. Without thinking about it, they found themselves chatting together without a break, laughing and giggling, as they exorcised the terror and difficulties they had just lived through.

When they arrived outside the station, they clambered down from the lorry with most of the other passengers. Raffi had not lost his innate caution, and he looked carefully around, but there were no more than a couple of policemen, leaning against a low stone wall separating the railway line from the road, smoking and chatting and taking no notice of anyone. The boys were in fact now in an area where there had never been any significant Christian minorities, and the atmosphere appeared much lighter generally. Nevertheless, there was clearly going to be a problem as to how they were going to get onto a train going to the strategically important Taurus tunnels.

It was Dikran who came up with the bright idea of getting one of the many troop trains regularly coming from the capital on their way to the Palestine and Mesopotamian fronts. They would get on by posing as 'simit' sellers going to the next station.

"Look Raffi, we go over to that bakery over there, and buy up all the simit they have. We get a pole of some sort, you know the way they do it, drop the bloody things round and down the pole in the same way, get on the train, and walk up and down the corridors, selling like all the other kids do."

"It's all very well for you Dikran, you could pass for thirteen or fourteen, and even that's a bit old for running up and down a train selling things. But look at me. I already need a bit of a shave, and I shaved last night before leaving."

"Right, as a safety measure, you get two tickets if you can anyway. Then what we do is that I go round piping up and doing the selling. You come along as my big brother, saying nothing, but ostentatiously taking the money."

After they had stocked up with the bagels, putting them down two poles, they waited on the platform for the train due from the capital. It was as if the poles of simit were a passport—they were not challenged. When the troop train arrived, all the wagons were full of soldiers. All the seats were taken, and young, shabbily uniformed soldiers were leaning out of the windows laughing and joking. There were military police all around, who got off the train and stood about on the platform by the doors of the carriages as the train came to a hissing stop.

Very few 'civilian' passengers were getting on the train, and those that were were having their papers carefully checked. Raffi had his papers in the name of Soliman ready, and his heart was pounding with excitement as he and Dikran approached one of the carriage doors. But Dikran, frail and consumptive though he might be, was a natural actor. He grinned cheekily at the two military police at the carriage door, made a breezily ribald remark, offered them each a simit, which they declined, and walked boldly onto the train calling out "Simit! Simit!"

Raffi scrambled up after him in a state compounded of anxious fear and triumphant excitement in equal parts. While the train stood, hissing and steaming in the hot and dusty station, whilst guards and police of one kind or another paced up and down on the platform, whistles blew, and people in all sorts of uniform shouted, Raffi stood in a sweat of fearful expectation. Meanwhile, Dikran sang out his goods, exchanged rude and sexually explicit suggestions with the soldiers around, and made a play of having to hand over the bits of cash to his older and surlier companion. Then at last, with a great jerk, the train hooted and set off. It was only then that Raffi relaxed, as the presence of the boys now rather desultorily selling pastry was taken for granted for the rest of the journey.

On arrival at Belemedik—the end of the line where the tunnels were being constructed—the boys tumbled out with all the soldiers, who cheerfully wished them well as they paraded ready to march off.

Raffi soon got work with the German engineers building the railway line, which had caused such tensions between the German and British Empires before the war. From the start, it became clear that Dikran was not going to manage to get any sort of employment. Here, Raffi's sturdy masculine frame was what was in demand, whereas Dikran's frailty and his youthful looks made it very difficult for him, quite apart from the fact that he had no papers at all. Furthermore, he was already beginning to look sickly again.

Raffi, with his false papers, found work as a brakeman for the construction gang trains going through to the tunnels. This was a hard and difficult, back-breaking job, which really needed a man's strength and physique. Fortunately for Raffi, one of the German engineers, noting his education, asked him if he could read and write in the Turkish Arabic script. When Raffi confirmed that he could, he was removed from that first job and taken on to work for the engineer's family. The engineer had a very young Syrian wife who was only seventeen, and who had relatives in Istanbul with whom she wished to correspond.

Raffi very soon established a position of trust in the family, which lived in a small house below the hill into which the first of the tunnels had already been completed. He dealt with the correspondence of the engineer, read the letters from Constantinople to the young wife, and wrote her dictated replies. He very soon got hold of some tools, boards, and nails from the main depot, and got permission to construct a small cabin for himself and Dikran near the house. Dikran helped to build it as he had more time, and they moved in together when it had been completed. Until then Dikran had had to remain in the makeshift shanty town for the construction gangs in the valley, having to use up the second gold coin.

But Dikran had changed. All those high spirits, that flash of inspired adventurousness had gone. A high bright feverish red colour had come into his pale cheeks. He ate badly, and indeed, there was always a shortage of food in Belemedik, particularly of fresh fruit or vegetables. Dikran became querulous and fought with Raffi at every opportunity. He stopped going out to buy the food, his only task, and began staying in bed all day. At night, Raffi would be woken with sighs and whispers as Dikran went through nightmares of some kind, nightmares which he could never recall the next morning.

It soon became clear to them both that Dikran was badly sick of something and could be dying. Neither of them had had any experience of medical matters, but as Raffi began asking around he soon discovered that Dikran was suffering from cholera or a severe form of dysentery. Raffi was at his wit's end. There were no doctors or medical services anywhere. He went down to the town one day and sought out an old woman to whom he was recommended by one of the maids at the house. She came up one evening, muttered some imprecations over the dirty and sweating Dikran. She then boiled up some foul-smelling herbs and roots and made Dikran drink it. Dikran vomited it all up almost immediately after she left. He had not eaten for days by then. At least Raffi had had experience of looking after and cleaning up wasted bodies, and he fell back into this routine. But here it was all so much more difficult—for a start, there was just never enough water to keep Dikran clean.

Dikran simply wasted away, and the day eventually came when Raffi returning wearily from the house came into the cabin to find that he had died. Even though he knew it was going to happen, it was still a shock when he had to face it, alone. Raffi sat up the whole night and reflected that they had never talked much about Dikran's family. He had chatted on, time and again, about all his own life, his big brother in Bolis, his mother and father, his trips to the farms in the highlands, but thinking about it, he realised that he had not enquired of Dikran's experience of life. Guiltily, he realised that he was not even sure of his friend's surname. Dikran had become simply one of the awful statistics of these events. He held the boy's lifeless hand, and eventually in the early morning, thankfully, the tears came and flowed until he slept kneeling on the floor, still holding Dikran's hand, with his head on his unmoving chest.

The next morning, Raffi went down and collected a spade from the house. He dug a deep grave by the side of the cabin and buried the body. He did not mark it in any way. He made no attempt to repeat prayers that he did not believe in. By this time his tears had also all dried up.

All the joy that Raffi had got in Dikran's cheeky behaviour during the trip from Caesaria and for some time after they arrived had evaporated. Raffi, though now relatively safe and able to wait until the end of the war, became restless. He missed his new-found and new-lost friend, and this in turn resulted in him missing his family. It was largely a matter of isolation and loneliness. Living alone was not natural to his character.

He continued to fulfil his duties towards his boss, who sometimes had to stay away for more than a day when he was needed at the far tunnel. He also regularly attended on Mme. Leyla, the young wife, writing her letters for her and reading back the replies. But the death of Dikran began preying on his mind. The cabin seemed cheerless, and the grave of the boy so close by began to upset him, even though he was not particularly imaginative.

This was, of course, a German household, and there was no question of a separate man's section and a woman's section in the engineer's home. Raffi found himself getting more and more uncomfortable in the presence of Leyla. He found that he could not be relaxed when sitting in the same room with the unveiled, Syrian young girl. Furthermore, he found that she had started to come and lean over him as he wrote at her dictation at the desk. She seemed to have less and less covering, and Raffi did not know where to look.

Raffi had no experience at all—rather like his brother Vahan—and he became confused and nervous, particularly as he found himself becoming aroused against his will. He could not interpret the young Leyla's smiles and provocations. He had no idea that she was deriving great pleasure from arousing this young male, knowing that it could go nowhere.

On the day that Leyla leant forward as he sat at the desk and touched her breasts to the back of his neck as if by mistake, Raffi decided that he would leave. He left that very night, leaving a careful note to his master who was absent again for a second night working at the far tunnel, explaining that he had had to return quickly as his mother was very ill.

This time he was determined to revert to his original plan of heading back towards Constantinople. Already there were few Armenians now left east of Caesaria, except individuals surviving alone in tense circumstances. Travel was getting easier and less fraught with the danger of being recognised and killed as an escaped deportee. The danger was now more that of the anomalous matter of whether he was liable to military service or not. Either way, if his true identity was known as an Armenian deportee, death would inevitably follow. But Raffi was now fully experienced in the art of survival in these dying days of the Ottoman empire. He decided that arriving in the capital suddenly was too risky. Instead, he would go to Konia, where it was known that the current Ottoman governor had not applied the Ittihad deportation orders stringently.

Nevertheless, when, after the usual difficulties and adventures, he finally arrived in Konia, Raffi decided to retain his identity of Soliman, as set out in his papers. Only two of the precious gold coins were left, and Raffi, having failed to find any risk-free work, took the decision, perhaps inherent in his character, to go into business for himself. He found lodgings with a respectable, old Turkish family on the outskirts of town. He invested in a large wheelbarrow, and getting up very early in the mornings, he would go round to the local farmers who lived closest to the town. There, he would buy their fresh vegetables at a good price, as they knew that it would save them a long trek into town, and a wait for a sale. He was a good judge of fruit and vegetables and was rarely cheated.

Raffi would then trundle his wheelbarrow to the central market, where he hired a small wooden platform to lay out his wares like those around him. He was usually sold out well before the end of the day, as his fruit was always fresh and well-chosen. This would allow him to go home in the afternoon with a small but perceptible profit on which he could live.

He avoided going to the public baths, where his uncircumcised state would be noticed, and was always very careful to maintain a strictly Turkish appearance. Soon after he arrived, the old Ottoman governor was unfortunately replaced by another fanatic Ittihad appointee, and once again the remaining Armenians had to leave. Raffi found that he had done well not to change his habit of never admitting his origin to anyone whatever the circumstances, particularly if people became suspicious or challenged him in any way. There were Armenians who still remained, but it was clear to Raffi that they were there only on sufferance, and he continued never to betray any knowledge of the language.

Raffi was lonely, that was his main problem. He could afford to have few friends, and had to keep himself to himself. As the Armenians even here in Konia began to disappear, he knew that the only way to survive was to wait patiently for the war finally to come to an end. He survived, but that was the highest he could put it at, as the months went by. He survived.

Chapter 52

Uskudar. Olga and Selim.

Olga stood transfixed and stared at the young man lying apathetically in the bed. Doctor Fadil was already beginning to start gently taking off the dirty bandage inexpertly tied round the stump of the arm. Turning to Olga, he said loudly and impatiently as she just stood there, "Nurse Avakian, what's the matter with you for heaven's sake? There's a job needing to be done here. Stop dreaming. This bandaging is terrible. He'll need a complete change at the least, though I suspect the arm is again infected."

Selim himself was still suffering from the effects of the awful seven-day journey by coach and train all the way from Baghdad. He had been lying feverish and dizzy for days, and was only just conscious. The words 'Nurse Avakian' shouted rather than spoken by the irritable doctor penetrated his hazy consciousness, and he opened and focused his eyes for the first time for many days. There he saw, standing behind the doctor who was fussing over his arm, the girl who had never left his dreams for a year. Olga was tired and already somewhat bedraggled from all the work of the rounds. Nevertheless, she carried her ugly regulation hospital coat, as always, with style and a natural elegance. Giving him a quick, harassed smile of recognition, she hurried round to help the doctor.

Selim had, since he was first wounded, lived only a sort of half-life until this moment. Suddenly he forgot everything—his father's death, the war, his pain and the lost arm, and all the old problems. He simply gazed at Olga as she came round to his left side to deal with the festering dirty bandaging. He then gave her a great beaming heart-warming smile, the warmth of which flooded his own whole body right down to his toes. Nothing else mattered to him any more. Out of the blue, life had suddenly become worth living again.

As he became more and more aware of himself and his surroundings, questions raced through his mind, but then he cried out in pain as the doctor finally tore away the bandage from the stump of the arm, cut off at the elbow.

"Good God, this is already getting infected and gangrenous all over again. Nurse! A sedative for this officer right away. Young man, listen, I see you are fully awake. I'm going to have to cut away some more of the re-infected area and clean up your original surgery properly. It's best done right away. It will be painful and Nurse Avakian here will give you a heavy sedative which will send you off to sleep."

"Doctor, I won't need it. I'm sorry I cried out. Please just get on with it."

"Son, you may not need it, but I do. I can't do the job properly whilst you are in obvious pain, whether you cry out or not. Just relax. Now nurse, get on with it and join me at the next bed when you're done. We have the rest of the ward to deal with, before we can return to finish this one once he's asleep. Get on with it girl. What's the matter with you?"

The fussy little doctor moved on to the next bed, while Olga took the ether bottle and a fresh gauze mask from her trolley and moved alongside Selim.

"Olga, Olga my love, what are you doing here in this soldiers' hospital? Oh, my God, how wonderful to see you. I haven't been so happy for months. Oh God, let me touch you," gabbled Selim hysterically.

"Hush Selim, my soul, hush. Your arm is really bad, even I can see that. We've caught it only just in time. Don't move my darling."

Olga gently put the gauze mask over Selim's nose, holding his arm tight. Even in these somewhat melodramatic and coincidental circumstances she still felt a quiver as she held his bare arm. Looking carefully at what she was doing, she began to drip the ether bottle onto the mask. She was aware all the time that his eyes were burning and staring at her, trying to make that vital eye contact, which she carefully avoided.

"Nurse, nurse! What is the matter with you today? Haven't you finished yet? For heaven's sake, it's only a simple anaesthetic. I've finished here already," said the troubled and overworked doctor as he came back to the bedside. Olga finished and closed the bottle.

"Come, my boy. Look at me, let me see your eyes, good. Now start counting, yes, yes, just counting."

"One, two, threeee, frr........," and Selim was gone.

When Selim woke again several hours later, his arm was throbbing with pain, but he had been washed all over and had clean white bandages over his stump. Above all the fever, that awful feeling of perpetual illness seemed to have passed, though he remained very weak. He knew that he would not be able to stand up on his own two feet. He had not, however, forgotten a single moment from the instant that he first recognised Olga to the point that he had lost consciousness. He waited in ever-increasing impatience for Olga to come and visit him.

For her part, Olga got through the rest of her working day mechanically and in the full knowledge that she was not giving her best. Everything that had occurred a year ago came back to her vividly as if it had happened yesterday—the tea party at Tokatlian, that moment in the basement of the College, the subsequent meeting in Makrikoy on that fateful 24th April. It was not just the memory that returned. That smile, that look in his eyes, as suddenly Selim saw her for that first moment, made her heart leap with a joy that she had not felt for a year.

She was due to return home that evening after work as she had a full day off the next day. There was of course no way that she was going to follow that routine. On this night she would again sleep in her bed in the nurses' dormitory. The evening would be for Selim, when he awoke.

The moment that Olga arrived and sat down on the bed beside Selim on his better right-hand side, he grabbed her arm with an intensity that almost hurt her. Olga smiled, leant forward, and kissed him on his cheek.

"Oh Olga! Oh Olga, my loved one. What joy, what joy, just to see you. Allah is merciful. I can't believe it. Oh God! Tell me, my love, tell me what you are doing here," gabbled Selim in a hoarse whisper, aware of all the other beds and patients around him.

Several hours passed as they sat like that with Selim holding tightly on to Olga's arm the whole time. Olga talked quietly and told him of all that had happened to her since their parting. Food came and went, nurses on duty moved around, conversation hummed amongst the other patients around them, there were even some visitors, whilst the two talked on and on.

Selim soon began to feel sick. The usual effects of a dose of ether. What with that, together with what almost amounted to a re-amputation, though it was only a fraction further up the arm, he kept coming out in a sweat. However, he would not let go of Olga's arm, and she did not want him to anyway. Olga took a cloth by the side of the bed and kept mopping his brow, and she occasionally touched her cheek to his.

It was whilst this intimacy, deeply private even though they were in the middle of a large ward, was happening, that Olga felt that someone was staring at her. She looked up and saw at the door the figure of Loris staring at her with a look she could not immediately place. She did not worry in any case. It was not till later that she recognised it as a mixture of hatred and triumph. When he saw her look up, he walked away. Olga really did not care, but it suddenly reminded her that she had promised to call upon Mikael before going home that evening. Selim, meanwhile, was still talking urgently and rather disjointedly. His fever seemed to have returned, and Olga realised that she would have to calm down the emotional mood, as the excitement was not doing him any good.

"Enough, my darling, enough. I'll have to go now. Tell me, does your mother and sister know that you're here? Honestly, the army's organisation in this kind of matter is hopeless. I've known patients here whose parents lived almost next-door, but who were never told that they were here."

"Oh, Olga, yes of course. In all my joy I forgot about my poor mother. She may not even have heard about my having been wounded in Mesopotamia, never mind that I am now here. My darling, could you possibly let her know? Heavens, they could even visit me here. That would be wonderful, wonderful."

"Of course, Selim, of course. Look, it's my day off tomorrow. I'll go into Bolis, and go and visit your mother."

"Olga, that would be really kind. But listen, do you know where she lives?"

"Come, Selim, of course I do. I passed it every day in those days before the British arrived in Gallipoli. I would look up and think of you inside, I really would. It's that big, modern block almost opposite the Galata Tower, isn't it?"

"Olga, you're a marvel. Remember, it's on the fourth floor, rather a climb, my sweetheart, flat eight."

"Selim, my soul, sleep now, sleep. I'll come and visit you again tomorrow as soon as I get back from seeing your mother. I'm sure she'll make an effort to come and visit you herself very soon."

Olga then made the necessary effort to withdraw her hand from Selim's. She leant forward and gave him a light kiss on the lips. Already the war had changed everything. Only a year had passed since that previous moment when their lips had touched ever so lightly in that basement cellar, but now, even in the midst of a ward full of other men, neither Olga nor Selim thought twice of a light kiss, unimaginable only a year previously.

The next day, and still in a state of wonder and excitement, Olga took the ferry and crossed over to the Galata bridge on the European shore. She was dressed simply as always, but she knew she was looking her best. Mounting the stairs in Selim's building, she knocked on the door of flat eight. The door was opened by a young girl with wavy black hair, who looked about twelve years old. She was wearing the uniform of the German Gymnasium, and she looked at Olga questioningly.

"Hello, I am Olga Avakian. I am a nurse at the Uskudar barracks Hospital. Is you mother in? I've some news for her."

"Mama," called out the girl, and opened the door further to let Olga into the compact hallway.

A woman dressed in black but with style and with one beautiful, Ottoman diamond brooch on her left shoulder came out of a door.

She did not offer to shake hands in the modern style, but bowed her head and nodded, saying, "I am Halideh. Can I help you?"

"Yes, I am sorry to disturb you. I am a nurse at the Uskudar military hospital. I have brought news of your son, Selim."

The excessive and somewhat strained politeness and formality vanished from the woman's demeanour. She took Olga's hand and led her into a small, but neat and tidy, sitting room. This had potted plants, two exquisite Turkish carpets, some low coffee tables, two pouffes, a sofa and a settee. She called out "coffee" to the maid, who was hovering at what Olga assumed must be the entrance to the kitchen. "Shekerli or mazbout," she asked Olga.

"No thank you, I have to return soon," said Olga, warming to the sign of anxious love clear from Halideh's eyes. They sat side by side on the settee.

"I've come at Selim's request to tell you that he is here at the Hospital and. . ."

"What's happened, what's happened? Is he all right?" interrupted Halideh.

"Yes, yes. He's improving. He has been wounded, but his life is in no danger. However I . . ."

"Allah be praised, Allah be praised. Now, my dear, tell me more. I won't interrupt again I promise you," and Halideh laughed out loud in relief and touched Olga's hand.

Olga now quietly told her all that she had heard from Selim about his experiences in Damascus and along the Tigris facing the British Army. Halideh winced and looked down as Olga came to the wounded and amputated left arm, but she continued to listen carefully to all the news.

"When can we see him, Nurse, when can I go to him?" said the mother as soon as Olga had finished.

"Well, you can visit officially during the afternoons, but many relations bring food to the men at other times as well, so it is all rather informal."

"Thank you, thank you. May Allah preserve you for ever," said Halideh. "What is your name, my dear? I did not catch it when you first came in."

"Olga Avakian."

There was a long moment of deep silence. Olga felt the woman draw back and freeze. Olga realised then that knowing this to be a Turkish Hospital, Halideh, not having heard her name, which she had given to the young girl, had assumed that she was Turkish or at most Greek or Jewish.

Halideh stood up from the settee clearly in an emotional turmoil. Still not a word was said. Olga sat with her hands clasped together on her lap. Now, for the first time since she had first seen Selim again, all the old problems which had driven them apart earlier came back to her. She suddenly recalled the circumstances in which Selim's father, Dr. Nazim Kemal, this woman's husband, had died at the siege of Van. It suddenly came to her that this was why the lady was dressed in black. Nazim Kemal, for whom this woman was still in mourning, had died at the hands of Armenian rebels, and Halideh Hanum, wife of Nazim effendi, was clearly still bitter.

The silence was broken by the voice of the young twelve-year-old girl who had been listening intently throughout in the corner.

"Mama, Mama, Selim is here, Selim is here. Let's go and see him now, right away," and she jumped up eyes aglow.

Halideh, tears appearing in her eyes, but with a hard glint in them, turned away, as Olga rose in some confusion. Carefully avoiding looking at Olga, she walked to the window, and looked out and down into the street below, with her back to the room, whilst the young girl looked on in some puzzlement.

"Yasmin, please show Nurse Avakian to the door."

"But, Mama, what. . ."

"Yasmin! Do as I say. Tell her as she goes that whilst we are grateful for the trouble she has taken in coming here to give us this news, she will not be welcome here in this house again. Now Yasmin. Do as I say. Now!"

Yasmin took Olga's hand, totally innocent that there was any problem, though she was aware at one level that her beloved mother had acted in an unusually rude manner to this bringer of good—and bad—news. Olga herself now became prey, for the first time since she had seen Selim again only the previous evening, to all the doubts that she had had a year ago. She squeezed Yasmin's hand and walked out into the hall and out of the front door without saying another word.

Olga was less prone to tears than she had been before entering the hospital, but the humiliation to which she had been subjected now struck her, and she felt the tears trickling down her cheeks. All that unallayed pure joy that she had felt with the return of Selim evaporated completely. Selim himself appeared to have resolved his own doubts, and that had given her enormous satisfaction. She now saw, however, that the problems of a love between her and Selim had not gone away. In many ways they had become even more intractable. Fitted into the equation were now two mothers—Halideh and Armineh—both of whom had lost a husband in circumstances which made it impossible for them to be able to face up to any relationship Olga and Selim might have for each other.

Olga was the last person to board the ferry just before it left the quay, but she could not sit, although several men offered her their seats. On her arrival back at the Hospital, she recalled her promise to Selim to go to him immediately. This was still her day off. She had no idea what to say.

"Olga, my love, tell me, tell me. How was it?" said Selim, as she came along the ward and sat by his side on the bed.

"Selim, yes, I saw your sister, Yasmin. What a lovely girl she is, isn't she? She was really happy to hear that you were here, and they are going to try and come to see you very soon."

Olga held the hand that Selim stretched out to her, but said nothing more. Selim looked questioningly at her.

"Yes, yes, Olga, yes?"

Olga knew that he was disappointed at her failure to say more—to speak more warmly about his mother, his home. However, the days when Olga could cheerfully make up stories and charm her way with lies out of tricky situations were over. Olga felt that silence about that morning's events was better than giving some false impression, though she saw and felt his hurt.

Olga chatted on about all that she had seen at his home, and all that she had told Halideh about Selim. But she kept silent as to how Halideh had reacted. She saw that Selim seemed to sense that she was holding something back. To her deep sorrow she also saw that Selim believed that it was she who had not taken a liking to his mother. A year ago Olga would not have accepted that double humiliation, but would have blurted out the truth, however much it would have hurt him. Today, she was prepared to take the consequences of appearing in a bad light, in order to save this young man a greater pain.

She felt her tears coming, so she leant forward, kissed Selim on the lips, smiled, and got up to go. Selim grabbed her arm, but she moved free.

I'll see you again soon, Selim, but first you must be ready to welcome your mother and sister. I'm sure that they'll come this afternoon."

Olga walked out of the ward, for the first time not acknowledging with her usual smile the friendly, affectionate, and slightly ribald remarks directed at her by the other officers in the ward. She suddenly felt enormously tired and made her way up to the nurses' dormitory. As she arrived in the corridor leading to it, there, waiting for her, squatting back against the wall, was Mikael, fully dressed and with a cheap cloth bag by his side.

Chapter 53

Vahan escapes and survives.

It was one of those wonderful fresh spring mornings, with a crystal clear blue sky and a rather weak sun shining on the clear dark waters of the Bosporus, the kind of day so beloved by the people of Constantinople, the Bolsetsi.

Vahan sat at his desk in the offices of the main electricity company of the town. This was a Belgian company now being run by German directors. His job required him to go through all the electricity consumption accounts for most of the city, working out the totals, and typing up the ensuing invoices on an old decrepit typewriter. There were no envelopes to be prepared, as all the accounts went out and were delivered by the Company's messengers—mostly young boys, but including a sprinkling of elderly men, semi-retired former employees. These messengers milled about the offices all day giving a continual bustle and animation to the surroundings.

The offices situated on the Pera side were modern and airy. Vahan was able to walk from the Patakis house down to the Galata bridge, across and up the hill on the other side every day without any difficulty. Vahan found the work easy, and in a way quite satisfying. It gave him a sense of steady, rather automatic, routine, which soothed him and prevented him from worrying too much about his current circumstances. However, he had a sharp brain, and he tended to finish his assigned tasks quickly, and he was then left staring out of the window with its dusty slatted wooden shades into the gardens of the courtyard. This in turn would bring him back to his besetting problem which was over-analysis of everyone and everything around him.

That extraordinarily packed day of the 24th April a year ago had of course changed the whole course of Vahan's life. The arrest of Father Komitas, the arrest and deportation of Karekin Avakian, the assault on the boy Haik and his meeting with the Avakians, had all affected him profoundly. However, it was not until he received the letter from his mother telling him of the arrest and deportation on that same day of his own father, Garabed, that the situation had struck him with an emotional force far stronger than any he had experienced till then. He reflected that it was one thing to read the newspapers, listen to gossip and rumour, or watch terrible events unfolding around you, but quite another when someone with whom you are intimately connected is the person directly involved.

The news filtering through from the interior, and the reports of the appalling events taking place in the eastern vilayets, made it almost a certainty that his father was now dead. Furthermore, despite the occasional postcard, it was not clear how long the rest of his family back in Caesaria could continue to survive. Vahan was particularly worried as to how his volatile and emotional younger brother—Raffi—could keep out of trouble.

Vahan finished his current task and sat back musing about the past year, and about his future prospects. After that significant day, he had continued drilling at the Harbiye Military Academy and learning the business of being an officer in the reserve.

Like everyone else in the dying days of the Ottoman world, Vahan found himself politically confused—though from a different viewpoint than his Turkish colleagues. On the one hand, the success of the old Empire in holding at bay the arrogant self-confident Westerners at the Dardanelles was a source of great pride to the Ottoman youth from whichever racial divide they came from. Suddenly, their despised country, the butt of so many jokes by the Western newspapers, read regularly in the city prior to the war, was fighting back against people who looked down on them, whatever their cultural identity might be.

On the other hand, the minority peoples of Bolis were bit by bit hearing of the horrors that were being inflicted upon the Armenian peasantry of the interior. It might be that rumour exaggerated those horrors—truth may well be the first casualty of war—but the Armenian community had the example of what had occurred on a small scale to their own leaders here in Bolis, and that showed that there was likely to be a great deal of truth in what was filtering out, not only from Turkish civil servants, but also from reports from the European embassies in the city. How, then, could an Armenian Ottoman citizen continue to retain any loyalty or duty towards a state which had clearly turned violently against others of his race and culture, and indeed even against members of his own family?

Vahan recalled, as he twiddled with his pencils and stared out through the slatted shades of the blinds, that sheer inertia meant that he had continued his training and his military service, as that spring turned into summer. However, it had become obvious that he would soon have to make some sort of decision. The ordinary soldiers in the army facing the British in the Gallipoli peninsula were becoming less and less ethnically Turkish. Large numbers of Arab soldiers were taking over the terrible gaps in the ranks of the original divisions which had been plugged into the lines with such distinction by General Mustapha Kemal. Mixed in with all this Arab cannon-fodder were Armenian young men who were fed into the front lines and who duly died in their thousands like everyone else. It was ironic that when the young men on the other side of the lines, from England or Australia, shouted jocularly from the trenches, "Hey, Johnny Turk!" the chances were high that the lads they were addressing were actually Arabs or some other race and not Turks at all.

The Harbiye military barracks was quite far from the Patakis house, and Vahan recalled that he would spend many nights, illicitly, in the little sick room at the barracks to save the long journey home and back again each day. As it happened, just across the fields at the back of the barracks was the house of his violin teacher—a certain Madame Tombak—a widow, of French extraction, of a former Ottoman Turkish army officer, who had died many years before. Vahan would keep his violin in his locker at the barracks and several times crept out in the evening to call upon the old lady. She, for her part, delighted in feeding the young man who always seemed to be perpetually hungry with titbits and pastries. They would discuss politics in a rather desultory fashion and play duets together in her cluttered dark and velvety sitting-room, before he clambered back across the wall into the barracks.

Madame Tombak, now a somewhat dried-up old lady, wrinkled like a walnut, loved Stamboul and was deeply immersed in Ottoman culture. Vahan had come not just to admire her, but to love her. She provided an emotional anchor which was of inestimable benefit to him. Vahan broke into a smile as he thought of her.

On a daily basis, like a regular bombardment, the good lady had pressed him to leave the Harbiye and to hide out until the war was over. Vahan smiled to himself as he recalled the almost daily arguments, "My boy, this government has exiled, if not murdered, your father. They are carrying out some awful deliberate policy against your unprotected people in the east. Your family are barely surviving, living in terror with all their neighbours, mostly already dead. Why, oh why, are you proposing to go and fight for them?"

"Well, because for better or worse, it is the state in which I live and. . ."

"But, Vahan, that state has turned against you. You haven't turned against it, nor have most of your people. It's they who have decided to liquidate you. Think, boy, think! For heaven's sake, I'm not a pacifist or anything like that. I married an officer after all. But this is different. Words like 'duty', or 'obligation', or whatever, don't apply."

"Yes, all right Madame, but what you are suggesting is 'desertion' however you dress it up, and deserting is an immediate hanging offence."

"And so, Vahan? Are you scared? Is that it? Come, have another cake my lad."

Vahan recalled that the day had come when he had again stayed one night illicitly in a bed in the sick bay. He had shaved that morning, had given a fond, quick kiss to the night duty nurse who had let him in, and who grinned at him and pushed him away. Vahan had run down to have some breakfast in the canteen prior to joining the morning's first drill in the parade ground. He recalled that moment when the fearsome drill sergeant, with his ferocious, huge moustaches, had come up to him and barked out, "So, trainee, lieutenant Asadourian, you so love the army you stay with us all night do you? The Captain wants to see you now, you horrible little man, now, at the double!"

Vahan, still sitting at his desk, recalled with even now a sick feeling the terror he had felt at that moment. He remembered the deep sinking feeling in his stomach, but looking back he could not understand why he had reacted so extremely. He clearly was not under arrest. The Sergeant had shouted and swore at him, but he had walked away. His punishment might have been severe, but it was not a life or death matter or anything like that.

Thinking back, Vahan realised that he had not actually made a very conscious decision. All the confusions of those past weeks, the terrible news and rumours coming from the countryside, the continual worrying words of Madame Tombak, the probable death of his father seemed to have frozen in his mind all at once. He had pushed aside his meagre breakfast and stood up as the sergeant moved away. Without saying a word to any of the others around him, he had gone straight to his locker. There he had taken his rifle, as if he was going out on parade. However he also took down his precious violin and his few personal belongings. He left all his books. He had then, with beating heart, gone down to the armoury, handed in his gun with some murmured comments about returning in the afternoon, and had then walked, not run, through the fields at the back of the barracks, and clambered over to Madame Tombak's house on the other side of the road.

As he mused, Vahan marvelled at what he had done. Without any real thought he had cut himself off from all the comfortable conformity around him, and put himself into the utmost danger—all without any plan or foresight.

Madame Tombak, sixty years old, frail and brittle as she was, had not hesitated for a second when she had opened the door to him at that early hour in the morning. She had known at once what was behind his sudden arrival at her door. She waved away the Greek maid who looked after the house, and took Vahan into the kitchen. At this point Vahan, who had been acting almost mechanically, had begun to react and had started trembling. Madame Tombak went upstairs and sorted out some of her husband's old clothes, while

Vahan had sat at the kitchen table, actually shivering now in a mixture of excitement and fear.

"Take off that uniform, Vahan," the old lady had commanded, handing the clothes she had picked out. As Vahan had undressed in that old-fashioned kitchen, she had picked up the ill-fitting uniform and had pushed them, item by item, into the kitchen range. Vahan recalled that the burning cloth made a terrible smell, as he had dressed in the equally ill-fitting clothes which had once belonged to the long-dead Major Tombak.

"Have you finished with the first lot of invoices," piped up one of the messenger boys standing at his desk with a cheeky grin and his hands outstretched. Vahan came to the present with a start. He had in fact already completed the whole lot of his assignment for the day, but he carefully picked out about half of them and handed them to the boy who sauntered off. He carefully left the other half of them on his desk as if he still had to deal with them and called out to one of the other office boys, "Sourj, Osman, sourj. Shekerli please"

Vahan sipped his sweet black coffee as he pondered on the whole of the past year. The false papers which he had obtained in order to keep that one step ahead of the police were still with him, still stating his age as under eighteen. It was however all getting more difficult as the war dragged on and on. Vahan sighed and turned his attention back to his work. In the evening, he walked home, down to the Galata bridge where he stopped as always for a few minutes and watched the ever-fascinating traffic of boats up and down the Horn and onto the quays under the bridge. Then, looking up at the Stamboul hill, to the sun setting behind that incomparable skyline of domes and minarets, he walked on home.

On the next day, Vahan walked out of the Patakis house after breakfast into the little street, which was a cul-de-sac. He saw immediately that it was cordoned off at the far end, and that the police were examining everyone's papers at the exit. Another group of policemen were moving down the street searching the houses. Vahan turned to go back into the house, but then reflected that there really was nowhere to hide there and he did not want to get Christina in trouble. He could see that the police were searching pretty thoroughly, and that this was not just a question of a single policeman who could be bribed.

Vahan walked boldly to the end of the street and handed his papers to the policeman at the gap who studied them closely.

"Effendi's name is Sami, and you are Ermeni and not yet eighteen."

"Yes officer."

"Join that small group of men over there," said the policeman.

Vahan moved over and joined a group of young men, some boys and a couple of perhaps older men who were standing about guarded by yet another policeman. They were a totally nondescript and disparate set, with no particular identifying characteristics, save that they were all youngish males.

Eventually the whole group were herded off to the local police station. Here, Vahan found himself locked into a small room with all the others. There was nowhere to sit, and there was a smelly open bucket in the far corner for urinating. No one spoke to each other, and it was unclear why they were all there. The door was regularly opened and one by one they were led out and away. About half had gone when it was Vahan's turn.

It was fairly clear to him that they had not believed his papers, nor that he was under eighteen. However, he had no idea what was going to happen. With his heart pounding, and in a sweat of anticipation, he stumbled after the policeman who had picked him out and found himself in another white-washed room which was much cleaner, and in which there was standing a doctor and a male assistant. Here, he was told to take off his upper clothes. The doctor carefully examined him, and in particular studied his mouth and teeth. Then he turned away and said, "This man is probably twenty, but is certainly over nineteen at least." He then marked something on the card given him by the policeman and called out, "Next!"

Vahan said nothing, though he was surprised by the accuracy of the doctor's comments. He was then taken out and made to sit in the lobby of the police station, which was a fairly small station not far from the Patakis house. Vahan was now at last caught up in the official coils. The desk sergeant laboriously wrote out the details of the arrest, and indicated to the numbed Vahan that he would have to go to court the next day. It was at that low point that he heard a cheery voice call out, "Hello Vahan, what's going on?"

It was Mariam Patakis. If the sergeant noted that Mariam, who was now nearly seventeen, was a cheerful addition to the atmosphere of the station, he said nothing. He also seemed not to have noted that Mariam had said 'Vahan' and not 'Sami.' Either way he smiled at the young girl who smiled back. It appeared that Mariam had seen the arrest of Vahan from her window. Having persuaded Christina, her mother, to let her have some money, she had hurried down to the station and waited.

"Sergeant, this young man lives with us at this address nearby," and she handed over her own papers, which the sergeant carefully perused.

"He won't run away. Can we please bail him in the usual way?"

The sergeant considered, then said, "Very well, mamzelle. He must report here tomorrow morning early to go to the court in Beyoglu. The bail will be set at two hundred piastres. You better make sure he comes."

Mariam who had just enough, handed over the money and they all waited whilst the sergeant laboriously wrote out bail papers, the copy of which he gave to Mariam. Vahan and Mariam then walked home. Christina, who had never really recovered from Elena's sudden departure said nothing.

Vahan now wrote out a letter of resignation to the electricity company, explaining that due to a complication in his affairs he was going to have to resign. He then arranged for a messenger to deliver it. He then spent the rest of the day in a state of fear and anxiety as he kept trying to imagine what could happen to him when he went before the court the next day. Vahan failed to sleep the whole of that night.

The following day, Vahan took the copy of bail documents and arrived at the police station early. Here he waited for almost two hours, sitting on a stool by the reception desk, a prey to a host of fearful presentiments. Eventually the moment came when a new desk sergeant called over a bored policeman, handed him the documents of the arrest, the doctor's report, and the original bail papers, and ordered him to escort Vahan to the district court in Beyoglu.

There was no question of any handcuffs or other restraint. The bail papers guaranteed by Mariam Patakis were still in the hands of the policeman, and there was no way Vahan could do any sort of disappearing act. Once again Vahan walked across the Galata bridge by the side of the policeman, looking at the scene with a weary eye, and with a shuddering feeling of butterflies in his empty stomach. How different the vivid scene seemed to him this morning. He had no wish to linger. He just wanted to get it all over.

He had forgotten that the court was on the same street, just a little further along, as the electricity company offices. They walked into the large and once-imposing marble hall of the court. It was now looking a bit shabby and dirty, but it had certainly previously been a handsome building. Vahan stood well back as the policeman walked up to the busy reception and handed over the bundle of complaint documents, Vahan's papers, and the bail papers. Vahan was standing back, still contemplating his likely future.

He watched as the policeman took out his duty book and got a signature from the man at the desk for the papers. Then to his surprise and increasing delight he saw that the policeman, having completed his duty, and his task being over, did not say another word but left the papers on the reception counter, turned and walked out. The clerk was still writing out something on his desk and dealing with another person. It suddenly came to Vahan with a clap of possibility that the clerk had no idea that Vahan had arrived under arrest. Vahan joined the queue and eventually said to the clerk when he reached the front, "Ah, effendi, I believe that these papers apply to me. Can you tell me where I should go and to whom I should report?"

The clerk motioned that he was busy and was dealing with several matters. He then gave a quick look at the headings of the papers on the desk and said, "Look, take these papers and report to Chavik Bey. He will see to the matter. He's on the first floor, along the corridor to the right as you go up the stairs. The last office at the end."

Unbelievingly, Vahan, his heart now pounding with the biggest torture of all—hope—took the papers and turned to walk up the grand but dusty marble stairs. Once at the top he saw a long corridor with office doors on each side, and many clerks and messengers wandering up and down, smoking and chatting. No one was taking the slightest notice of him. Vahan stood, taking deep breaths surreptitiously to calm himself down. He looked over the balustrade down into the entrance hall, which had become increasingly busy as the time for the morning petitions and hearings drew closer.

Vahan waited, and then at a moment when the reception clerk was busiest, he walked back down the stairs and straight out of the building. No one challenged him, and with the bail papers and his own documents firmly in his hand, he walked along the street. He knew there was no other documentation evidencing his arrest with the possible exception of a note in the station records, and he walked along taking great gulps of the wonderful Bolsetsi air, and turned into the electricity company offices.

His boss still had his letter of resignation on his desk when Vahan walked in. Vahan explained that his affairs had all been satisfactorily arranged and he would therefore like to withdraw his resignation if that was possible. Vahan's boss, who was Jewish, sighed with relief—getting sufficiently educated young men was becoming increasingly difficult. He told Vahan that he had not as yet taken any steps on the resignation letter, and that Vahan could simply go to his room and carry on working without any change, the previous day to be treated as an illness.

Vahan sank onto his chair, called for a coffee, and then spent a good half hour controlling a trembling, which, now that he felt safe, had broken out in his body. He then threw himself enthusiastically into the mechanical but curiously satisfying work of preparing invoices in order to catch up on the previous day's missed workload. It was nearly lunchtime when one of the old porters came up to him and said, "Sami effendi, there is a soldier outside who has given us your description and who is looking for you."

Vahan, who had thought himself safe suddenly felt almost sick with apprehension. He did not think, he simply assumed that he had been caught out. There was, however, nothing to be done. His colleagues were looking at him curiously as sweat broke out on his brow. The porter waited courteously.

"Ahmed, can't he come up to see me here?"

"No, effendi, he insists you come down, and truth to say I can see that he can't come up. He has someone with him."

Vahan could not make head or tail of any of this, but nevertheless he arranged his desk—most of the work had been finished—took some personal items out of the drawer and followed Ahmed down to the front door. Through the door, out in the street, waiting on the other side of the narrow road, he saw an elderly-looking unshaven, shabby, and badly turned out soldier, whose arm was in a sling, standing with a young country boy alongside him.

Vahan walked across, now no longer quite so concerned that this had anything to do with the morning's events, and approached the soldier. Still not quite yet on the pavement, and ignoring the passing vehicles, Vahan stopped and stared, "Oh my God! Father, Father, my loved one—Baba, Baba. . ." Stepping forward he clasped the malodorous Garabed in his arms and began, there and then, at last to cry softly.

Chapter 54

Constantinople. Garabed finally arrives.

Vahan rarely ever wept openly. But this day had finally been too much for him. From moments of deep fear and anxiety when he believed that even death was a possibility, to moments of euphoria when everything suddenly changed again, he had been on a roller-coaster of emotion all day. The sudden appearance of his father, whom he believed to be dead, finally broke his self-control. There and then, standing on the pavement, with all the bustle of the city crowd weaving its way beside and around them as they stood clasped together, Vahan wept and wept.

It was Garabed who first pulled away and gave Vahan a warm and final kiss on his cheeks, as Vahan himself swallowed and composed himself. Almost immediately, they both started talking at once, and stopped and started again together, and then finally stopped again, laughing as the tension snapped.

"My son, we came to try and find you the moment we arrived in the city. We've only been here a few hours."

"Father, look, we can't talk here on the street. Wait a moment. I'll be back in a minute. Are you all right, baba? Is your arm badly wounded or something?"

"No, son, don't worry, it's just a disguise. Off you go, we'll wait here."

Vahan ran back across the street, back into the building. He hurried to obtain leave to take the rest of the day off, assuring his boss that he had already completed most of the day's quota of invoices. He then rushed back out again, marvelling to himself at all the changes that had occurred during the day. Garabed was still standing outside, and still with a young boy standing alongside him rather tightly holding on to Garabed's free hand. Vahan had no idea who this young boy might be, but it was clear to him that this was not the moment for explanations. Whilst there was no shortage of wounded soldiers now to be seen in the streets of the city, this particular soldier in an extraordinarily ill-fitting uniform, far too small for him, and more than usually dirty and dishevelled, stood out rather more than most.

Vahan had spent a lifetime looking up to his father and following his lead and decisions in almost everything. Suddenly it was now clear that everything was up to him. This was his city, it was he who would have to make the decisions, it was he who would have to guide his father. He did not hesitate, he only had the one small matter to clear up as he motioned to his father to follow him down the street. Looking at the young boy, equally dirty and wearing worn-out country clothes, he said, "Well, baba, who is this young man?"

"His name is Ara," said Garabed simply. "Ara, say 'hello' to my eldest son, Vahan."

"Parev baron—hello sir," said Ara, speaking Armenian, the first time that language was being used. Vahan was startled, knowing as he did that his father could not speak Armenian. However, he held out his hand, then seeing that Ara did not know what to do with it, he took the boy's free hand and shook it.

"Welcome Ara, welcome to Bolis. Come, father, the first thing we are going to do is to get you both cleaned up."

Vahan put his arm round his father, noting that Ara on the other side did not once let go of his tight grip on Garabed's other hand. Strangely connected like this they walked rather awkwardly down the street. Vahan went straight to the local small hammam, where it was the day for the men. He ordered and paid for a private room.

This was one of the more opulent of the city's baths. Having picked up their thick warm white towels, and with their white dressing gowns in hand, they walked through into the marble courtyard inside. This had a large, green-leaved tree growing in the middle. All round the court were small but comfortable rooms, each with a rattan table and chairs, with lockable doors and a small window looking into the courtyard. There was a small, inner staircase, which led up to a first floor which had a balcony running all round the court, with regular, thin pillars holding up the tiled covering. Coming off this wide corridor there was a further line of rooms. These were higher-priced as they had small windows to the outside. Several of the occupants, clad only in their white towelling and dressing gowns, had taken their table and chairs out of their rooms and put them out in front, on the balcony looking down into the courtyard. Having just come from the baths, they were sitting chatting, drinking gazoz or raki, smoking narghilehs and eating snacks brought to them by white-coated waiters.

Ara, eyes wide with wonder, stared and stared, and clung on tightly to Garabed. Vahan got to their room, tipped the attendant generously and ordered kebabs and bread.

"Come, baba, get out of those awful clothes, and take off that sling. Father, I've forgotten, what's your chest and leg size? Oh. . . yes, thank you. Look, you and Ara go into the baths. Have a really good scrub down. Take your time, baba, go into the steam rooms, and when you are in the hot water rooms, make sure that they use one of those really harsh loofahs on you. You too Ara, come on, get undressed, don't be shy. Have you never been to a hammam before?"

"No, Vahan," said Garabed rather gruffly, "He's lived in the country all his life. Leave him to me please."

"Fine, fine, baboushka. Now look, I'm going to go and get some clothes for you both. They'll be pretty rough, baba, but they'll be better than what you've got on at the moment. We're going to burn this lot. They're not only filthy but they stink. Frankly I'm amazed that you got this far in Pera without being stopped by the police."

Vahan was all hustle and bustle. Suddenly he felt in total control and it felt good. He watched for a few moments as Garabed gently disengaged Ara's hand. Vahan felt a surge of warmth for his father, though he also noted that Garabed had been far gentler with the boy than he would ever have been with his own two sons. Had Vahan or Raffi hesitated to do as he ordered Garabed would have used hard patriarchal authority to command obedience at once. Here, however, to Vahan's surprise, Garabed gently urged Ara to get undressed and to put on his dressing gown and follow him into the baths. Vahan himself hurried out into the streets and began searching for the cheaper clothes shops of which there were several in the back streets.

With Garabed washed and shaved, and Ara too scrubbed, and both as pink as babies, they dressed in the clothes Vahan had purchased. They all walked back across the Galata bridge and to the Patakis house. There was no sign of any police, and in any case all the trauma of the day had passed out of Vahan's mind in the joy and activity of seeing his father and dealing with the basic practical details. Christina was at home when they arrived. After a slightly sticky start, Garabed turned on all the charm he could muster. This was a side of his father that Vahan had never seen. Indeed, Garabed was usually reserved and tightly controlled in front of his children. Here, however, he needed something, and he was accordingly very gallant towards Christina who lapped it up.

The arrangements were soon made. Garabed was to take the old attic room which Andre had used, and which had never been re-let after his disappearance with Elena. Ara was to sleep with Vahan, whose room opposite was a little bigger and could take an extra bed.

After an early supper eaten mainly in silence once Mariam got back from school, Vahan gave a brief account of what had happened to him at court, and gave the bail papers back to Christina. He did not elaborate of course on how he had got them back into his possession. Garabed took Ara, who was exhausted, and to Vahan's astonishment sat with him until the boy fell asleep. Vahan meanwhile sat on the bed in Andre's old room. Garabed eventually walked in and sat on the only chair in the room, as Vahan lay back on the bed.

It was still fairly early, and it had only just got dark when Garabed finally began recounting everything that had happened from the moment that he had been arrested at home. He passed fairly quickly over the things he had seen and done at the farm of Sarkis, and then went on to the difficult and tiring days when he and Ara, and Ara's sister Anna, and his mother Adrineh had plodded with their two donkeys through the desolate countryside after leaving the farm. Garabed finally came to that last night when he had been attacked by Ara. Vahan noticed that at this point Garabed, who had been pouring out all his feelings as he relived those moments, hesitated, and clearly was not telling everything.

"Well, my son, on this particular night, perhaps I was more relaxed as we were clearly getting closer to the vilayet of Syria, and I could feel that the evenings were getting warmer. Anyway, my soul, in a nutshell I awoke to find that Ara had got my knife and was. . . er. . . looking around wildly. I thought he must have seen or heard something, so I too sat up and looked around. It then so happened. . . er, in all the confusion in the darkness, quite by accident. . . in all the rush, Ara accidentally almost hit his mother with the knife, and wounded me in the arm."

"Good heavens! How extraordinary and what was it?" said Vahan a little puzzled.

"Yes, well anyway, realising his mistake and feeling upset. . . you must remember Vahan he is only twelve, and think of what he had seen and lived through, and what he had been having nightmares about. Anyway, as I say, realising, he dropped the knife and ran away into the dark. Well, Vahan, you know how pitch black it can be on moonless nights in the country, and so we sat down. I built up the fire, so he could see it if he wanted to come back, and we settled down to wait for first light."

"I don't know, Vahan, whether it was the light of the fire, or whether it was fate or what, which caused the events that followed but. . . Anyway, at the crack of dawn, I left the old pistol that Mustapha had slipped into the bag of onions—fully loaded—with Adrineh. You remember Adrineh, Sarkis' wife?"

"No father, I don't remember. You never took me, you only took Raffi. Have you forgotten?"

"All right, all right. Anyway, I told her that if anyone approached, she should stand and tell them to keep away and fire a warning shot to show she meant business if they ignored her. Vahan, I never for a moment. . . Oh God, Vahan, I had so many things to think about all the time. It just seemed to me that the needs of the boy, out alone in that wilderness, frightened, guilty or whatever, were more important at that moment than the two women."

"What two women baba? Oh yes, of course, there was the traumatised sister as well, wasn't there."

"I should have thought more. I could have packed everything up and taken them with me when I went out looking. But I thought, in the pitch dark, the boy couldn't have gone far. Oh, Vahan. How do these things happen? Anyway, after about three hours I eventually found the lad curled up fast asleep against some rocks. He was bruised and dazed, he must have wandered for hours. I picked him up and we started back to where I had left his mother and sister. I don't believe that I was even two kilometres away, when I heard in that still morning air the distant sound of shots. Oh Vahan, my son Vahan, I knew that the worst had happened. I tried to put Ara down and told him to follow me, but he clung onto my neck so hard I couldn't shake him off. I began running as best as I could, but it must have taken me almost half an hour before I came in sight of the dying fire. Oh my God, my God."

At this point Garabed buried his head in his hands. Vahan rose from the bed, stepped over and went onto his knees and hugged his father. Even then, with Garabed in extremis, it was not a position that could last for more than a moment. For better or worse, Garabed was not able to draw sympathy or comfort in this way from his son. He thought of it as a weakness on his part, and there was a level on which Vahan, himself, also felt awkward in trying to give such comfort to this strong authoritative figure. He rose, stepped away, and flopped back down on the bed.

"Continue, baba, what had happened?"

"Well, my soul, I will never know for sure of course. Lying dead by the side of the remains of the fire was the girl Anna. Her clothes were intact and she looked fairly tranquil. She had been shot at fairly close range by one shot in the heart. Away from her there was more blood on the ground and signs of a lot of scuffling. The donkeys, our provisions, and Adrineh herself were all gone. I believe that what must have happened is that a party of men—who knows, Turks or Kurds or whatever—maybe only three or four, looking, as they all are, for wandering deportees to rob and rape, came upon these two. Anna was already hovering on the brink of madness. I think that after Adrineh fired off her warning shot to no avail, she then shot Anna before they could get to her, and then probably tried to shoot herself before they grabbed her. Vahan, I saw no body anywhere. She's gone—gone for good. Who knows where, or what'll become of her?"

"And what about Ara in all this, in view of what you told me about his reaction to the awful events in the farmhouse?" asked Vahan.

"Well, I don't know, my boy, I just don't understand these things. It needs that man from Vienna we were all reading about before the war, I've forgotten his name, to tell us why. Whatever the reason may be, Ara was fantastic. It was almost as if this last horror kicked him back to reality, whereas until then he had been in a sort of denial of what had happened. Vahan, I had no spade, nothing. We had nothing left, only two gold coins left in my pockets, and the knife which thank god I had picked up quite by chance before setting off to find Ara. Yet we had to bury her somehow. Vahan, my love, it took us the whole of the rest of that day—and even then it was more of a mound than a grave—but we did it. It was a very bare hillside, but we just managed to keep the fire going. That night, Ara crept up after I had gone to sleep, and curled up into my arms. He's still a child Vahan."

"That was still the summer. What happened over the winter?"

"My son I could go on for ever. The details will have to remain for another time. In a nutshell, I decided that we had to press on into Syria. There was no point in turning back now that we had come that far. I'll tell you something Vahan, poverty and deprivation in the city is pretty awful, degrading and squalid. The conditions are dirty, you sleep in abandoned smelly corners. You never seem to be able to get clean. But, my soul, poverty in the country is worse, desperate. It may be cleaner, but you will starve very quickly. In most towns, however poor you may be, somewhere you will find a tap dripping to get some sort of water. You will usually find some scraps somewhere. Above all, there are people around. But that bloody, sparse, barren, rocky wilderness of a countryside, sometimes with not a soul for miles, and those that you do meet you usually have to avoid anyway. . .

Ara may be a naive country boy—did you see the wonder in his eyes when we went into the baths?—but he was good at scavenging and finding things possible to eat. You wouldn't believe the things we got round to eating. We were hungry all the time. Well, we got to Aleppo eventually, and there at least things began to improve. Here I came into my own, and whilst currency is collapsing in value all around us, the gold pieces were doing well—and I had two left. This was just enough to get us started, and I found a hovel in which we could hang out. You know I'm pretty strong and I was able to get a job humping cotton bales and other goods in a shop in the bazaar. Knowing the trade well, as you know, I was able to give the shopkeeper who was an Arab, a lot of help. Eventually he agreed to take on Ara as well, for just the day's food of course—to run around getting coffee and tea, which he would bring along on a brass tray for the customers.

My lad, this was just pure survival during the winter. I saw many Armenians—almost all poor peasants—in the town, and many of them simply collapsed and died in the streets. But the richer merchants and professional people who made it this far moved on to Lebanon or Damascus. We heard that most of the population had either died on the way, or when they made it to Syria, had died in the desert.

Vahan, my boy, this was no life, and when the summer came, I decided I would try to make my way to Bolis where you were, and where I knew that most of the Armenian population has not been touched. Caesaria was out of the question of course. We spent months slowly collecting everything we needed—a soldiers' uniform, some false papers, that bloody sling, and most difficult of all, a medical pass for a broken arm. Once ready, we travelled by a combination of train and walking and more trains. But, my boy, my soul, we made it. We made it! Then to cap it all you tell me that Mariam, my sweetheart, and my darling daughters are all alive, and that you heard from them quite recently. The Lord Christ be praised, Vahan, we're through. We're here. Who knows, if what you say is true, then Raffi might also still be alive somewhere."

Father, calma, calma. This war is not going to end just like that. We've got a bit to get through yet. But yes, baba, yes. I think we've a good chance now. Ara is young, and now that he's here, he'll be in no more danger. You too. I myself will just have to be more careful. Oh father, father, how good it is to have you here by my side. We're going to make it. My God, we're going to make it!

Chapter 55

Constantinople. Karekin and Aram part company.

The plan had worked perfectly. Karekin and Aram had waylaid the flower delivery boy on his return to the shop, having already promised him a large tip. The lad had given them the name of the caretaker at the block. As Karekin had thought likely, the previous young concierge was no longer there. It was probable that he had been called up. There was instead a new elderly man, who, if the boy could be believed, was so old as to be almost senile.

Karekin had already grown a fairly respectable beard by the time that they plucked up their courage to make the train ride which had been Karekin's daily trip in the happier days before the war. This time, both of them travelled third class without argument. Aram, who had had a local practice in Makrikoy as well as his city office, muffled himself up in a thick greatcoat even though the weather was fairly warm. Karekin laughed at him, and took nothing but an old scarf.

It was only a few minutes before the train was due to steam into the Chobancheshme station that Karekin suddenly thought of a problem, "Oh, my God, Aram, I've forgotten old Abdul and Mustapha, the gharry drivers at the station. They'll recognise me for sure whatever I do. I've used them almost every day for years."

Aram replied a little smugly, "Ah ha, Karekin my dear fellow, so you're thinking about it only now. For once I'm way ahead of you. I've thought of that already. As it happens they might recognise me too, though I rarely took a carriage except in bad weather. Anyway, when I bought the tickets at Sirkedji, I got tickets for the main Makrikoy station in the middle of the town. It's only a short distance further to my flat from that station than from Chobancheshme."

"Well done, Aram, good thinking. You owe me two million or thereabouts so far. I'll let you off a straight million for quick thinking. I'll soon get it back anyway."

Karekin sat back in his seat as the train stopped at the familiar station. They had chosen the middle of the day for their trip, so there weren't many people in the train or on the platforms. He said nothing, making no attempt to relieve the tensions and emotions which swirled within him as the train moved on and trundled past the level crossing and into the town. Neither man made any attempt to release their feelings by making the usual dry or ironic comment which would have been their normal reaction. Three minutes later the train stopped in the main Makrikoy station.

Karekin was not given to indulging in much introspection. He tended to get on with life as it arose, enjoying without guilt its many pleasures, and facing up without complaint to its many difficulties. But now, he found himself contemplating the little town as the train was pulling into the station, with a warm emotional attachment which he had not consciously ever felt before. This was the town in which he had lived and brought up his family for so long—the town which, during the past year, he had feared he might never see again.

Both Karekin and Aram were nervous as they made their way through the main street back towards the first station. They walked past the shiny new shop-fronts, and alongside them the old-fashioned, tiny shops where people were still making the goods at the back of the shop, which they then sold at the front. Nobody took the slightest notice of them, and they eventually ended up outside the modern block of flats, just behind the main street where Aram used to live.

It was an awkward and decisive moment for them. To get into the block, the caretaker had to open the main door after dark, but the door was usually left open during the day, as it was on this occasion.

"Karekin, I think we should get this out of the way right from the start. We'll contact the fellow now, whilst it is broad daylight and in less suspicious circumstances than if he accosts us coming out," said Aram, knocking at the door of the concierge's little room looking into the courtyard just past the main door. The door opened.

"Effendim?" said the man who came to the door, nothing like as old as the flower delivery boy had made out.

"Porter bey," said Aram, "I am Doctor Aram Manuelian. I live in flat seven on the third floor. I don't think we've met before, I believe you are fairly new. I've been away at the front and have only just been released. Here is my 'nufus' paper. And your name is?"

Aram handed the old man his original internal passport papers, which he had been careful to bring with him.

"Ah yes. Er. . . my name is Murad, Doctor effendi. I've been here three months already, and this is indeed the first time we've met, though I do have your name on my list of owners," said the caretaker looking at the 'nufus' paper and handing it back to Aram, whose confidence and middle-class arrogance was increasing with each word.

"Well Murad, my good fellow, I'm a doctor and in these difficult wartime conditions I have to spend a lot of time at the hospital. I've been back a couple of times in the last two months, but haven't seen you before. This is my good friend, Mahmud Acimoglu, who will be staying at the flat for a few weeks whilst I am away."

At this point, Aram handed the old man the false papers of Karekin, which they had obtained in Konia. Confidence was what mattered, and Aram found himself oozing assurance. In many ways he was talking to Murad with a superior haughtiness, which he would never have shown before when he was not a fugitive. He then clinched the situation by showing the man his keys, "I have my keys with me, Murad effendi, so I can go straight up as always. Has my cleaning girl been coming?"

"Oh no, effendi, she hasn't been here at all as far as I know."

"Ah well, never mind," said Aram, holding his hand out for the papers, "I'll find someone else. Meanwhile, Murad effendi, this is for all your trouble, and I hope you will be helpful to my friend if he needs anything." Aram gave the man, whose face creased up into a great grin, a large tip—but not too large. He and Karekin then walked up the stairs in a mixture of triumph and excitement.

The keys still fit. There had clearly been no official entry.

Karekin and Aram walked into the empty flat. It was almost a year since anyone had lived there, and although the flat was clean, there was a musty, rather damp odour about the place. Aram went straight to the main bedroom. Here the bed had been left unmade, the blankets and new sheets folded at the end of the bed. Aram pushed the bed to one side, whilst Karekin stood at the door watching hopefully. Aram knelt down, feeling the boards, and called out to Karekin, "Karekin, my soul, go and get me a knife from the kitchen."

When this arrived, Aram began working away at one of the wooden tiles forming part of the modern parquet floor, digging the knife in between the cracks. Eventually he prised it up, and felt down with his hand, and very gingerly brought out a vicious looking mousetrap which sprang shut as he put it down. He then felt down further, lying flat on the floor.

"Karekin, my friend, Karekin! It's still here, still here."

He carefully pulled out a largish cloth bag. He upended this on the floor and out poured some coins, mostly gold, and some wrapped-up large denomination notes.

"Hey! Well done Aram. My God! What a lot you've managed to save. I didn't know that you doctors did so well."

"No, no Karekin. This is money left by my father for my mother, which she passed on to me just before she died. Good God, I couldn't have saved anything like this on my fees."

Both men were flushed and excited. Aram admitted that deep down he was fairly sure that the cache would still be there untouched particularly if there had been no official entry. He said that he had been anxious not to say so, in case they were disappointed.

The two men had discussed for hours exactly what they would do in the event of being able to get into the flat openly and finding the money intact. It was clearly far too risky for Aram to be seen in Makrikoy. Quite apart from the other residents in the block, who would be certain to recognise him, he had many personal patients in the town, so it would even be risky for him to be on the streets too much. However, the case of Karekin was different. Almost all his friends and business acquaintances were in Bolis and not in this district. Whilst he had indeed lived in the Osman Agha area for years, he had rarely come into the little town. He never did any shopping here. There was never any question of his accompanying the children to any of the local schools, and he never used the main station, always going from and alighting at the Chobancheshme halt.

It was agreed that Karekin would stay in Aram's flat, whilst Aram himself, taking most of the money, would go back to the city to find and settle down in a lodging where he could have his meals prepared for him, and where, alone, he would be safer and less likely to attract police attention than if they were together. Neither of them were even remotely eligible for military service, and it was unlikely that they would ever be stopped, or even if they were, that it would be discovered that they were deportees who should have been shot or exiled a year ago.

The friends agreed that they would meet regularly twice a week on Mondays and Thursdays at a particular café in the Stamboul side of the city. This rendezvous was sometimes changed by them at a previous meeting, but usually it was an old dilapidated spot beside the old Moslem cemetery above Eyup. This was a quiet spot well away from the traffic and most policemen, right at the end of the Golden Horn inlet. Certainly there could be no suggestion of Karekin wandering about anywhere in the Pera side of the city.

Karekin's moustache and beard had grown to a respectable size. He was irritated by the fact that the hair growing was grey, not exactly white, but certainly not the black of his original head of hair.

Karekin fell into a hazy dream-like existence as the winter ended and spring arrived. There was far too little for him to occupy his mind, and he was aware at all times that he was within a few miles of his family and all that he loved in the world. Twice a week he would take the train into town, and he and Aram would meet at the café agreed the time before. They would play innumerable games of tavloo, and slowly Aram's debt mounted into many millions of gold or sovereigns or whatever—they never specified what currency it was. Aram would always be waiting for him at the same rickety table outside the old coffee house above Eyup.

Karekin, bored to tears, began taking risks that he had promised Aram he would avoid. Anxious to have a glimpse of at least some of his family, he began to make a point of hanging about outside the little primary school for girls that Seta attended. On the first occasion, pressed back against the wall of one of the houses across the square from the school, he saw Haik walking along, hand in hand with Seta. His heart lurched as he saw his only son, laughing and restraining Seta, who as always was skipping rather than walking, and never once appeared to stop talking. Karekin wondered why it was Haik who was bringing Seta to school and not Marie or one of the maids. After seeing Seta into the school gates, Haik would turn and sprint away, and Karekin realised that he wouldn't have much time to get back to his own school on the outskirts.

Karekin began making a point of wandering past Seta's school in the afternoon to watch Haik come running back to pick her up. Karekin could see that Haik was very careful to take Seta by the hand, and he noted that they immediately went off together to walk up the hill past the racecourse without saying a word to anyone. He ached to press them to his chest, and envelop them both in his arms. However, they appeared cheerful, and he knew well that suddenly appearing before them would be difficult for them and dangerous in the long run.

It was April, almost exactly a year since he had been arrested, that the two events occurred that once again was going to totally change Karekin's life. Already several weeks had gone by since he had moved into Aram's flat and they had separated, though continuing to meet and exchange news twice a week, as well as to play their innumerable games of tavloo across the little wooden tables by the side of the path up to the cemetery from the mosque at Eyup.

That morning Karekin took the late morning train into the city and stepped out at Sirkedji station. There were always police about at the station, stopping people at random and asking to see papers as they showed their tickets at the exits off the platform. Karekin had been stopped before, his tall bearing tending to stand out. However, it was clear that he was well beyond military age, and his new grey beard made him look even older. Their inspection of his papers was accordingly fairly cursory. On this occasion he was again stopped, and their inspection was a little more thorough, although they soon waved him on.

Karekin felt an atmosphere of suspicion in the city, and for some reason there were certainly more policemen about. These days of added tension happened about once a month, and were usually associated with some sort of news from the front, or scare-stories about spies, or riots of one kind or another in the city. He took the tram that went to the suburb of Eyup. On arriving he walked past the remains of the old Blachernae Palace of the Byzantine Emperors, through the little streets surrounding the Eyup mosque, and up the tiny cobbled street—looking like a country lane—leading up along the old Muslim cemetery. He passed by the old tombstones slewing to one side or the other in crazy angles, and walked round the corner which brought him in view of the simple old round wooden tables with rickety chairs, set outside the café, where Aram would sit in the sun and wait for him to arrive.

The moment he turned the corner, Karekin immediately saw four policemen, all with their backs to him. One had a gun in his hand, and another was waving some papers and shouting. Standing, staring straight at him as he appeared, was Aram with blood coming from the side of his mouth, or his nose, Karekin could not tell. Aram's face must have shown the light of recognition or something, as two of the policemen then began turning to see exactly what Aram was looking at.

It all happened in a flash—scarcely more than a few seconds—but it was as if time slowed down as each action and reaction took place. Aram, seeing the two policemen beginning to turn toward the corner of the lane behind them, suddenly yelled at the top of his voice into the air, "Pakheh—get away," and struck one of the policemen who was turning—a heavy push really rather than a strike. He then turned and began in a rather clumsy way to run away in the opposite direction. He could not of course get far in view of all the tables and chairs around him.

Karekin stared for one second, then turned and strode back round the corner, after which he started running. Despite the panic and the rush of adrenaline, there was little doubt in his mind that he heard the sound of a single shot that rang out behind him. He stopped and there was a long moment of silence. For another second he hesitated and then began walking down the lane and into the busy bubbling streets of Eyup.

He began walking back to the station. His legs felt weak, and the moment came when he had to stop. He wandered into a rough and rather dirty eating house, ordered he knew not what, and sat staring into space piecing together in his mind what appeared to have just happened. He let the scene run back in his mind moment by moment. He had no idea what the police may have been looking for, but the blood on Aram's face showed that he had been arrested and struck. It slowly became apparent, as he faced up to the incident, that his old friend had deliberately shoved the policeman away in order to distract them from his arrival on the scene.

A wave of guilt swept over Karekin and tears came into his eyes as he thought of Aram and all that they had meant to each other over the years. Karekin never wept in front of his family, but here in the midst of a huddle of dirty, uncaring strangers, he silently sobbed and sobbed, impatiently wiping away his tears as they came out of his eyes.

Once again, and without Karekin being consciously aware of it, there were riots erupting in corners and alleys all over the city. Once again the mindless cries of 'giavours this' and 'giavours that' were being yelled by crowds milling about, whose real problem was not the damned infidels in their midst, but the lack of reasonably priced food and other deprivations caused by the interminable war.

But this was not Eastern Anatolia. The government was aware of the presence of their Allies' embassies in the city and knew that the Empire could not afford to be seen to be involved in any racial or religious killings. Hence the police were out in force with direct and clear orders not just to stand by as they usually did, but to control the mobs. The churches, Greek and Armenian, and the synagogues were well protected and the centre of the city saw no deaths or looting.

Karekin was unaware how long he sat at the little corner table in the shadows. Eventually, however, he rose, having eaten or drunk nothing, left a payment and, walking all the way, made his way to

Sirkedji station. Feeling guilty and still in distress, he got on his train in a daze.

Sitting in a corner seat, he stared out of the windows as the sea walls passed, and the train went through the gap driven through the great walls of the city. Still not entirely conscious of his surroundings, he got out automatically at the Chobancheshme station, instead of continuing into the town. He was lucky—neither of the carriage drivers were present. However, the mistake suddenly brought him with a snap out of his reverie and back to the dangerous present, as he began walking on into the town.

It was then that he first noticed that there was a mob of gesticulating and yelling rough-looking men running past him up the road. Turks, Albanians, riff-raff of one kind or another—where they all came from he could not tell. They were certainly not local Turkish townsmen. He walked on paying little attention, but then he heard what they were shouting.

"Allah be praised! Allah be praised! The bastards are burning. The filthy giavour school has been set on fire. They're going to rot in hell. Come on, come on."

Chapter 56

Uskudar. Olga decides.

Mikael scrambled up from the floor where he had been squatting as Olga approached down the corridor.

"Olga, hello, I'm leaving the hospital today. I've been given a medical discharge, and I won't have to go back into the army. That's the positive side, Olga. The negative side is that Dr. Turhan has told me that my kidneys will never recover. He says that sooner or later it will affect my life expectancy."

Olga, still in some anguish at the outcome of her last brush with Selim, said nothing but just considered this man, clearly wanting more from her than she could give. At one level the problem with Selim was a racial and historical one, whilst with Mikael it was background and educational. At another level, however, it was simply a matter of chemistry. She simply could not feel the same towards the man Mikael as she felt for the man Selim.

"I expect, Olga," continued Mikael, "that you knew this when you told me to forget our feelings. But Olga the doctor said that I could have years of fairly healthy life, and that in all other respects I am cured. Olga, I intend to go far, I know it. Say at least that we'll meet again. For God's sake, Olga, you always chat away so passionately, but whenever I approach deeper feelings, you clam up."

"Oh Mikael go home, my dear. Of course we'll meet again, we live in the same small town for heaven's sake. It is in any case unworthy of you to imagine for one moment that I would reject any idea of marriage because of some story about your state of health. Really Mikael!"

Mikael's face reddened.

"I'm sorry Olga, my soul. However, I'm not in fact going to go back to Makrikoy. I was setting out to visit my half-brothers and their mother, my father's. . . er. . . mistress, I suppose one could say, at the moment that I was arrested. No, I'm going to go back to Yedikule to finish that visit, and then I am going to look for something in the city."

Olga leant forward and gave him a gentle kiss, by way of an attempt to say goodbye. But Mikael was having none of it.

"No, Olga, we can't part like this. I love you. You know I love you. It has only been your presence here that has kept me going. You are going to be mine. We are going to live together once this war is over. Just say it, just say it!"

Olga looked at him, hesitated for a moment, but then looked down at the floor and in a mumble and without any smile said, "Go carefully, Mikael my soul. We will surely meet again whether you are in Makrikoy or Yedikule. I know it."

Mikael lifted his hand and touched Olga's cheek, shook his head, and turned and walked away.

Olga soon heard that Selim's mother and sister had indeed turned up and had sat with Selim several hours that afternoon. It was clear that Selim would soon be discharged, once the stump of his left arm had fully healed. The final defeat and departure of the British and Australian forces from Gallipoli some months previously had slowly eased the pressure on the military hospital and Olga found more and more time to spend with Selim.

Shortly after Mikael left, Selim had been getting up and about, and it was the turn now of Selim and Olga to walk up and down the corridors and into the fresh air of the grounds. Once again it was Olga who took the trouble to reduce the emotional atmosphere of their meetings as much as possible. Under her careful and balanced nursing attention Selim began once again to take up his natural interest in the difficult and confused politics of these clearly dying days of the Ottoman Empire. Most people were aware that even though the Empire had done remarkably well against the Western Allies, and even if Germany won the war eventually, the Empire as it was currently constituted was doomed.

Now, however, for Selim, for the first time, an Arab dimension had been added. During his few months in Damascus Selim had become aware of a latent Arab intellectual ferment amongst the intelligentsia and middle classes, such as there were. This awareness had been broadened as a result of his experiences on the Tigris south of Baghdad, where he had found himself in command of ordinary Arab peasant conscripts, whom he had come to like and respect. Enthusiastically he poured out his ideas to Olga. For her part, Olga, whilst still an Avakian daughter ready to question everything, nevertheless had during the past year learnt how to listen sympathetically.

"Olga, you wait and see. Although the Empire in its present form is finished, we do have a great future. Djemal has some great ideas, and he's going to be very influential once this war ends, as it will, my love, as it will sooner or later. It was a revelation to me how loyal and reasonable my men in the Baghdad vilayet were. The British can intrigue as much as they want, but at the end of the day the main Arab population of the Empire would still prefer a Muslim Turkish power to a Christian Western one."

"But Selim, my love, you must have heard that a revolt has been declared in the last few weeks by that man who was put in charge of the Hejaz, what was his name?"

"Yes, yes, Hussein. He is a Qureshi of course, of the tribe of the prophet, but he was and remains a mere nominee appointed by Constantinople. Look, it's quite clear to me that he has only revolted now because Djemal was about to depose him and appoint one of his rivals as Sherif of Hejaz. In any case all we are talking about is some miserable bedu tribesmen. Olga, what matters amongst the Arabs, my darling, is opinion in the great Arab cities, in Cairo, Damascus and Baghdad. There is no Arab revolt. It's all a myth—a great soap bubble invented by some enthusiastic young British officers in Cairo for the benefit of their own Empire. You just wait and see. When it comes to the crunch, when the choice finally has to be made, you will see that not a single Arab soldier from our regular army will desert. Furthermore, the vast majority of the Arabs will fight to the bitter end for the Ottomans."

"Selim, Selim, my love, calm down. Let's sit here for a while. Are you saying that there is no real Arab national movement at all?"

"Oh yes, of course there is, Olga, of a sort. I'm afraid that what is happening is that the more our leaders, particularly Enver and Talaat, want to Turkify everything, the more there is a reaction by the other peoples of the empire. Suddenly, an Arab is being forced to see the Caliph not just as a Muslim leader, but also as a Turk. Oh dear, Olga, I think that my poor old dad might have had some point to his Ottomanist arguments after all."

"Come on," said Olga rising, "Let's continue walking. The doctor said that exercise was good for you. What about my people, Selim, what about all the Armenians in the empire?"

"Well, Olga love, here I think Djemal Pasha might have the answer, an Empire of federated peoples—Kurds, Shiites, Sunnis, Christians, Assyrians, whatever—all living under a traditional dynasty."

"Selim, my sweetheart, I recall that long discussion we had over a year ago after you rescued my little brother from those thugs. At the time I thought that chap Vahan—do you remember him?—was rather confused about how he thought the Ottoman world ought to develop, whilst you on the other hand had seemed very clear. But now aren't you getting confused yourself? I know nothing about the Arabs, but surely you can't have a Turkish national state on the one hand, and the old Empire in whatever new form you want at the same time on the other."

"I know, Olga, I know," burst out Selim. "If only Baba was still alive. He was always so very clear. He was certain that the Ittihad were wrong, and that 'nation-states' are not the answer for the Asian lands of the Ottoman Empire. What I suppose I would like is an all-Turkish modern state in the core lands, and some sort of federal empire for the rest."

"And Constantinople, Selim? Is that going to be part of the core? And if it is, is your brave new nation-state going to tolerate all the different minorities, religions, and cultures, all the wonderful diversity, like the Ottomans always did."

"Oh God, Olga, I don't know, I just don't know. However, going back to what I said earlier, of one thing I am sure. There is no national Arab revolt. I've been there. I've fought with them against the British on the Tigris. I've spoken with the Damascus intellectuals and so-called revolutionaries. It's all a put-up front, dreamed up by those English in Cairo and latched onto by Hussein and his sons to save their own skins. It's all got much more to do with British relations with the French and the Russians. It's all part of the carve-up going on, and they haven't even beaten us yet. They don't care two hoots about the Arabs. All they bloody care about is their precious route to India."

Olga put her arm on Selim's shoulder to urge him not get too excited.

"Oh Olga, I do love talking to you. You've changed, you know. I wouldn't have gone on like this a year ago. I suppose we've both changed. Olga, forget the politics, we do have a future together don't we, despite my lost arm?"

"Selim," said Olga, speaking very carefully, "Unfortunately we can't forget the politics. Your father was shot by an Armenian revolutionary in Van and. . ."

"Yes, but. . ."

"Let me finish, Selim my love. A year ago, you wrote me a letter warning me of the insuperable difficulty we face in developing any lasting relationship. I had to agree, and I tried putting you out of my mind. I have to tell you that I never succeeded and. . ."

"Olga, darling, I. . ."

But Selim, listen. It isn't only you who've lost a father—your mother has lost a husband. We, both of us, live in a society where family ties are vitally important. Have you ever considered what your mother might think of an Armenian daughter-in-law?"

Olga was careful not to say a word about the meeting with Halideh, even though Selim belittled the problem. Then he too made the same comment that Mikael had made many days before.

"It's my loss of an arm, isn't it? You think I won't be able to look after you properly, but Olga I'll. . ."

Somehow, Selim's comment upset Olga much more than Mikael's had done. She felt the tears coming to her eyes and burst out in a flash of real anger, "Selim, how could you! How could you! Oh Selim, you know I'm not like that. I won't carry on this conversation any longer," and she walked off in a real temper.

"Olga, I'm sorry, I'm sorry," called out Selim. Nevertheless, in a part of his mind he really did think that his new disability was affecting their relationship.

It was soon time for Selim to leave and return home. Meanwhile, Halideh and Yasmin were now making regular visits to the hospital, and walking out with him into the grounds.

On the day before he was due to leave, Selim had had to have some further minor surgery to his stump, which was otherwise healing well. He accordingly had to stay in bed when Halideh and Yasmin appeared with a set of clothes he could wear when he came out the next day. It so happened that on that day Olga had occasion to pass through the officer's ward whilst on duty. Selim saw Olga passing and called out, "Nurse, hello. You remember my mother and sister?"

Olga stopped and came over.

"Hello, it's Olga isn't it? See I remembered your name. What a wonderful job you do. I'm going to be a nurse when I grow up," gabbled Yasmin, smiling up as Olga approached.

"Hello, Yasmin," said Olga, then turned to smile at Halideh. Halideh nodded, but very clearly turned away. Olga blushed, then turned to Yasmin, "Would you like to come along with me for a few minutes whilst I do some more of my rounds? You must promise just to watch and not say anything."

"Oh yes please, yes please. Can I?" she turned, not to Halideh who was about to say something, but to Selim. Selim, who had not noticed anything of Halideh's quiet rejection of Olga's advance, beamed with pleasure, "Yes, of course, off you go Yasmin. Be good now."

Olga took hold of Yasmin's hand and they walked off out of the clean and neat officers' ward. They went through to one of the soldiers' wards, where Olga usually worked. Here the atmosphere, and the smells were quite different. There were scarcely ever any visitors, most of these men being from the Anatolian interior. Olga inevitably was an attraction for these men, all of whom were nevertheless brought up to extend a deep respect towards her, one of the positive sides of the 'haram' system of the separation of the genders in the home.

The presence of Yasmin, a friendly pretty twelve-year old, brightened the whole ward. She walked solemnly behind Olga as she went on her rounds with the midday medications. Her natural bouncy spirit soon broke through her promise to Olga, and she began chatting inconsequentially with everyone.

On their return, Halideh was standing.

"Where have you been, Yasmin? We're very late. You should have been back ages ago."

"But mother I. . ."

"Not another word, my girl," and Halideh grabbed Yasmin by the hand. Turning to Selim she said, "The military are sending a car—yes, a motor-car—for you tomorrow to meet you off the ferry at the Galata bridge Selim. We'll see you at home. Good-bye till tomorrow."

Halideh then walked out without another word, and without even a glance at Olga, who stood and gave a sad little wave to Yasmin, as she turned and looked back at her as she went out. Selim, sitting up in bed looked at the back of his retreating mother, then looked at Olga, who looked back at him for a second then turned and walked away. She saw that Selim was totally puzzled, with no idea at all of what had happened. However, she knew, and she knew that Halideh also knew perfectly well, what was behind all the bad temper.

That night, before she went to the dormitory, she came and sat for a few minutes by Selim's bed. He had been lightly drugged in order to give him a good night's sleep before leaving the hospital the next day. Accordingly, he was only half awake when Olga came, sat by the side of his bed and held his good hand tightly for several minutes. He murmured at Olga and then fell back into a sleep.

"You were right, my darling, you were right after all. We're going to have to part again, at least until the politics sorts itself out. Your mother has to be given more time to complete the grieving process. It's all too soon for her. I love you, Selim. Oh God how I love you, but there is really no hope for us. Oh, Selim!"

Olga leant forward and gave a long lingering kiss to Selim's forehead, and then rose and left as Selim stirred, murmured something, and then turned over to his other side.

The next day, Selim dressed and then waited and waited for Olga to come and see him off. No one knew where she might be, and eventually Selim left to go home. That same day Olga applied for and was given a week's leave to return home to her family in Makrikoy.

Chapter 57

Makrikoy. The Avakians from all angles.

Haik had for months now been taking Seta to school every morning and picking her up in the afternoons. He was now thirteen and the memory of the assault on the 24th April the previous year had faded in the welter of all the other dramatic events which had been taking place around him. Whilst in many respects he remained innocent and naive, he had certainly become more street wise. He was at last ready to accept that not everyone who ever met him would necessarily automatically like him. Surrounded as he was by loving and caring females, he was, however, not old enough to take on the role of the only male in the family. Armineh's decision to make him responsible for the safety of his little sister had been brilliant, but he remained vulnerable and immature.

Thus it was that on this afternoon early in April, about a year since that day which had changed so many people's lives for ever, that Haik, coming from school earlier than usual, realised that there was a lot more tension in the little town than normal. His teacher had let them out early as there were rumours that there had been riots in the city. The rumour was that the crowds were rioting about the price of food. There were no anti-war feelings as such, but the continuing death toll was nevertheless also a factor in the tensions.

In the Ottoman Empire during these more decadent days, whatever the trigger, riots almost inevitably turned into attacks on the Jewish and Christian minorities, and this often affected the outer suburbs as well. Haik was now much more attuned to these matters, and he was therefore alert and ready for all eventualities as he trudged into the town to pick up Seta. He was aware of the running crowds and the shouting around him as he approached.

Meanwhile, this was also the same day that Karekin returned from his last fateful rendezvous with Aram at the old café in Eyup. As

Karekin heard what the crowds were actually shouting, he began joining them and running as fast as he could into the town. There was only one 'giavour' school inside the town, and this was Seta's. As he ran, he now saw for the first time smoke rising up ahead of him over the roofs, and he imagined that he could smell the fire ahead of him.

Panting, he arrived in the little square—the Nusretiya—which was fairly close to the centre. Here, in the middle of the square, was a dusty area of bedraggled trees and some thin, scrubby bushes, growing out of a sparse grass which was fighting a losing battle against the dust and the dryness. On one side of the square was the buildings of the Armenian primary school and on the other three sides small modest houses. Smoke and flames were billowing out of the centre of the school building.

There was a large crowd standing around the sides of the square. The police were out in some force, and the crowds were being pressed back away from the fire. Karekin was in a state of complete emotional despair. His only thought was, 'first my best friend and now my youngest daughter.' Completely oblivious to what was happening around him, he now edged forward, avoiding the police, and arrived at the end of the grassy area directly in front of the entrance to the burning building across the narrow street. The large main gates leading into the courtyard within were wide open.

Haik, meanwhile, had himself arrived some minutes earlier. He had no idea what to do. There was, as always, an enormous amount of shouting and yelling, and he too saw that there were many policemen about. He remained calm, and immediately noticed that many of the teachers were already outside, with their young pupils gathered around them on the side of the street. They were counting their charges over and over again, and handing over the children to distraught parents who were running up to grab their own with a fierce intensity. As Haik wriggled forward through the crowd, he saw and recognised Seta's teacher, and pushed his way through towards her.

A strange change of roles was taking place between father and son without them even being aware of each other. Haik, with all his new-found responsibility and care, was calm and considered what he was doing. Karekin, on the other hand, usually so cautious and thoughtful was in a state of enormous emotional conflict as a result of what he believed had happened that morning in Eyup. He stared in a dazed manner at the burning school, as the flames licked round the sides and began to burn the high wooden fencing which came up to the main gates.

Then, at the far end of the courtyard, to the right, by the side of the main school building, out of sight of everyone who was not standing directly in front of the gates, he thought he saw a little girl who had clearly just come out of the outdoor toilet building, confused and too terrified to move. Karekin's cup boiled over. He raced forward across the street, and standing still for a moment with his back to the crowds, he pushed aside a policeman trying to hold him back.

At that moment he heard a voice, a little girl's voice, cry out, "Baba, baba!" To his disturbed mind it seemed to come from the terrified little girl that only he appeared to have seen so far inside the building. With another cry, covering his eyes, he ran through the wooden gates, now themselves beginning to catch alight, and into the courtyard, into which burning beams and other debris were beginning to fall.

Meanwhile, Haik had finally made his way to the group standing around Seta's teacher. She had stopped her frantic counting, as all her class was accounted for and grouped around her. Seta was there and ran round on seeing Haik and grabbed his hand.

"Oh, Haik, I'm so glad you came early and you're here. Isn't it exciting? There's no danger, we're all out, or so our teacher says. There was a shout of 'fire, fire' in the school and we all ran out here. I wasn't frightened, Haik, I really wasn't, whilst we were inside. I didn't really see anything until I got out. But when we did get out and I looked back and saw all the flames, well, that did get me a little scared all inside."

Haik squeezed her hand and they sidled forward to the front of the little group, getting smaller and smaller as more and more parents came running to pick up their little girls. It was then that Haik saw a tall man with a grey beard and moustache run forward towards the gates. Seta did not see the man from the front. She looked up only as he stopped for a moment with his back to her and pushed aside the policeman at the gate.

Seta, only nine, was herself in an excited state. In almost any other circumstances, she would never have made the connection. However, only seeing Karekin from the back, not aware of the grey beard, she thought she recognised her father. She screamed out, "Baba, baba!" and saw the man then run into the flames.

Nerissa too that morning was in Makrikoy giving one of her English lessons to a Greek lady in the town. They did not hear any of the shouts or noises in the street, but looking up, Nerissa saw the smoke coming up above the roofs a couple of streets away. On pointing this out to her elderly pupil, she became alarmed when the old lady said as she walked up to the window, "My, my, that's coming from the Nusretiya Square."

"Oh Madame," said Nerissa, reverting in her anxiety from the English in which they had both been conversing to Turkish, "That's where my little sister's school is. I must go to make sure she's all right."

Nerissa hurried out as soon as the old woman nodded. When she arrived at the Square, the old and rather decrepit town fire engines had arrived and a start was being made in controlling the fire, starting from the gates at the front of the school. To her relief, she immediately saw the remaining knot of pupils by the side of the square, with Haik and Seta, hand in hand, staring at the front gates. At the front gates, she saw that the flames had taken hold of the wooden posts, and the gates themselves were beginning to smoulder. A group of three or four policemen were standing close and staring into the courtyard into which burning wood was now falling.

Nerissa began working her way round the square to Haik and Seta, and had almost reached them when suddenly there was a shout from the policemen at the gate. The firemen began training their leaky old water-pump hoses onto the gates, and Nerissa saw a young policeman run into the courtyard between the flames. Nerissa then made out through the smoke a middle-aged man with a singed grey beard and with bloodshot and rather crazy-looking eyes, who was staggering out from the flames, and handing over a weeping child to the young policeman.

To her utter amazement, she then saw little Seta, now just ahead of her, pull her hand away from Haik and run forward to the gate. The man, clearly badly burnt but not now in any immediate danger, had sunk to the ground outside the gates, as the school's headmaster came running forward to take the girl from the policeman's arms. Nerissa instinctively moved forward to try to grab and restrain Seta, when she heard Haik, behind her, call out, "Nerissa, leave her, leave her! I don't know, I really don't know, but if she's wrong she has to find out herself."

Nerissa stopped and turned, "Whatever are you talking about, Haik?"

"Oh, Nerissa, my little sister, Nerissa. Just wait a moment, please just wait a moment."

All this happened and was said in a flash—in a moment—all within the time it had taken for Seta to reach the man, who was now sitting, legs outstretched, and with his head buried in his hands. Nerissa saw Seta go down on her knees alongside the man, and put her arms fiercely around him, and press her cheek to his. At that point Nerissa suddenly saw. She saw. She saw that it was her father. Neither she nor Haik moved, as Karekin, wincing from the pain that Seta was causing him by clasping him hard and pressing her cheek against his own burning skin, turned and himself hugged Seta equally fiercely to him.

The next moments were chaotic, noisy, basically undisciplined and inefficient, but warm, as was only possible in the Ottoman world. The little girl was reunited with someone, it must have been a grandmother. Karekin, suddenly coming out of his daze, managed to pick up Seta in his arms, and seeing Nertissa and Haik standing at the side and staring at him, staggered over, put Seta down, and said urgently, "Come, my lovely ones, come. Let's go before anybody starts asking any questions."

He took Seta's hand and began walking away as an elderly woman came up to him and started talking to him. He turned and said to her,

"No, no Madam, that young policeman over there. Yes, he was the man who saved. . .Yes, Madam, do, do. . ."

Karekin hurried out of the square and away down the streets through which some people were still running towards the spot, followed by Haik and Nerissa, both in a state of complete confusion, unlike Seta, who was quite clear and without any questions, simply holding on tightly to her suddenly reappeared father.

Once they were out of the town and on the road going up past the Valli Effendi racecourse, the questions, the love, the urgency, began pouring out of all of them. Being Avakians of course they all talked at once and wanted to touch and hold each other all the time. It was a very inefficient way of walking up the hill. Every so often Seta kept demanding to be carried by Karekin, and he tried—but it was the inevitable grasp on exposed and inflamed skin that kept defeating him. In the end Haik squatted down and Seta was hoisted onto his spare but willing shoulders. However, she still insisted on holding on to her father's hand, and thus, in an awkward group, they moved up the hill.

Karekin was feeling spasms of pain from the burns, whilst Haik, with Seta on his shoulders, could only walk slowly. Nerissa in her usual anxious way began worrying how Armineh would cope with this sudden arrival. Karekin for his part knew well that the dangers, which had kept him away from his family for these past few months had not in any way passed. However, for the moment he was so full of joy, so completely overwhelmed by the sudden falling away of all the loneliness of the past year, that nothing else mattered. They struggled up the hill, all continuing to talk at once.

The noisy party walked straight into the hall of the Avakian house, Nerissa having a key to the front door. Haik dumped Seta somewhat unceremoniously onto the sofa, from where she immediately jumped up and ran to fetch Armineh shouting, "Baba's back, baba's back!"

Armineh came running in. If Nerissa had expected her to faint or something equally dramatic, she was to be disappointed. Armineh stood stock still, drying her hands on a hastily swept up tea towel. She stared at Karekin, and he stared back, both suddenly oblivious of the noise around them, of Seta's chatter, or of Marie's and Sima's arrival into the hall.

Slowly the noise and the chatter died away as the family stood for just a moment, each with their own thoughts, frozen in their turn by the immobility of Armineh. A rare moment of silence suddenly washed over the Avakians.

It was uncertain how long it lasted—no one ever thought about it—but it was broken as Armineh walked forward and took Karekin by his hand, noting him wince as she touched his skin. Without another word, without waiting for any explanations of what may or may not have occurred, or why her lost husband was suddenly there again after a year away, she led him up the stairs. Half way up she turned and said, "Salve, and the burns ointment, Marie please, from the medicine chest. Haik and Seta get a move on. Start laying the table for tea. Nerissa, my soul, for heaven's sake close your mouth. Come Karekin, my husband, come, let me see to these awful burns."

She lay her hand gently on his cheek for a moment, smiled for just a moment at the children all staring up at them both, and then turned and walked up the stairs.

END

ABOUT THE AUTHOR

Haig Tahta was born in Manchester of Armenian parents who came to England in the twenties from Constantinople. The connection with Stamboul continued throughout his formative years when long holidays were taken with grandparents and a large extended family in that City.

Haig read Modern History at Worcester College, Oxford, where there were at the time some very stimulating history tutors. Inevitably he specialised in "the Eastern Question" and the fall of the Ottoman Empire, his tutor being Alan Bullock.

On leaving Oxford, after a short spell working for the airline BOAC in India, he became a lawyer and remained in the profession for forty years. Haig married Sonia, an Armenian girl from Alexandria, and they have had three children. During his working life as a lawyer, Haig has taken an interest in Armenian diaspora affairs, and has acted for the Church in several matters, and particularly in respect of the legal position of the Church in Bombay.

GAROD BOOKS

PUBLISHERS AND DISTRIBUTORS OF BOOKS
ON MODERN ARMENIAN AND NEAR EASTERN HISTORY

Editorial and Head Offices
42 Blythe Rd.
London W14 0HA
England

www.garodbooks.com
info@garodbooks.com

Designated distributors for Gomidas Institute Books,
Taderon Press, Sterndale Classics and Parvana